Configure

Load Pull-downs...
Edit Pull-downs...
Password...

Preferences...
Startup Programs...
Button Bar...
Confirmation...
Clock...
Video/Mouse...

Editor...
Screen Saver...
Network...
Printer...
Compression...
Desktop Link...

Save Configuration

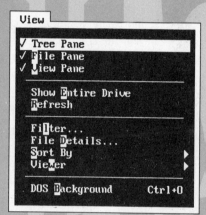

View

√ Tree Pane
√ File Pane
√ View Pane

Show Entire Drive
Refresh

Filter...
File Details...
Sort By ▶
Viewer ▶

DOS Background   Ctrl+O

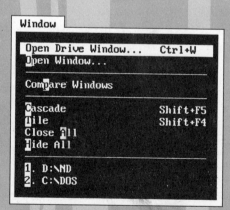

Tools

Menu   F2
Edit Menu...
Calculator
Calendar
(network message...)
DOS Session   Ctrl+D

UnErase
Speed Disk
Norton Disk Doctor
Norton Backup
Norton AntiVirus
Mail

System Information
Scheduler

Window

Open Drive Window...   Ctrl+W
Open Window...

Compare Windows

Cascade   Shift+F5
Tile   Shift+F4
Close All
Hide All

1. D:\ND
2. C:\DOS

Help

Advise

Index
Keyboard
Commands
Procedures
Using Help

Guided Tour...
About...

Computer users are not all alike.
Neither are SYBEX books.

We know our customers have a variety of needs. They've told us so. And because we've listened, we've developed several distinct types of books to meet the needs of each of our customers. What are you looking for in computer help?

If you're looking for the basics, try the **ABC's** series. You'll find short, unintimidating tutorials and helpful illustrations. For a more visual approach, select **Teach Yourself,** featuring full-color screen-by-screen illustrations of how to use the latest software.

Learn Fast! books are really two books in one: a tutorial, to get you off to a fast start, followed by a command reference, to answer more advanced questions.

Mastering and **Understanding** titles offer you a step-by-step introduction, plus an in-depth examination of intermediate-level features, to use as you progress.

Our **Up & Running** series is designed for computer-literate consumers who want a no-nonsense overview of new programs. Just 20 basic lessons, and you're on your way.

We also publish two types of reference books. Our **Instant References** provide quick access to each of a program's commands and functions. SYBEX **Encyclopedias**, **Desktop References** and **A to Z** books provide a *comprehensive reference* and explanation of all of the commands, features, and functions of the subject software.

Sometimes a subject requires a special treatment that our standard series don't provide. So you'll find we have titles like **Advanced Techniques, Handbooks, Tips & Tricks,** and others that are specifically tailored to satisfy a unique need.

We carefully select our authors for their in-depth understanding of the software they're writing about, as well as their ability to write clearly and communicate effectively. Each manuscript is thoroughly reviewed by our technical staff to ensure its complete accuracy. Our production department makes sure it's easy to use. All of this adds up to the highest quality books available, consistently appearing on best-seller charts worldwide.

You'll find SYBEX publishes a variety of books on every popular software package. Looking for computer help? Help Yourself to SYBEX.

For a complete catalog of our publications:

SYBEX Inc.
2021 Challenger Drive, Alameda, CA 94501
Tel: (510) 523-8233/(800) 227-2346 Telex: 336311
Fax: (510) 523-2373

SYBEX is committed to using natural resources wisely to preserve and improve our environment. As a leader in the computer book publishing industry, we are aware that over 40% of America's solid waste is paper. This is why we have been printing the text of books like this one on recycled paper since 1982.

This year our use of recycled paper will result in the saving of more than 15,300 trees. We will lower air pollution effluents by 54,000 pounds, save 6,300,000 gallons of water, and reduce landfill by 2,700 cubic yards.

In choosing a SYBEX book you are not only making a choice for the best in skills and information, you are also choosing to enhance the quality of life for all of us.

Understanding Norton Desktop for DOS

ACQUISITIONS EDITOR: *Dianne King*
DEVELOPMENTAL EDITOR: *Gary Masters*
EDITOR: *Kathleen Lattinville*
TECHNICAL EDITOR: *Sheldon M. Dunn*
WORD PROCESSORS: *Ann Dunn, Susan Trybull, Chris Meredith*
CHAPTER ART AND PASTE-UP: *Claudia Smelser*
SCREEN GRAPHICS AND TECHNICAL ART: *Cuong Le*
TYPESETTER: *Thomas Goudie*
PROOFREADERS/PRODUCTION ASSISTANTS: *Arno Z. Harris And Janet K. Boone*
INDEXER: *Ted Laux*
COVER DESIGNER: *Ingalls + Associates*
COVER PHOTOGRAPHER: *Mark Johann*
BOOK DESIGN BASED ON A DESIGN BY AMPARO DEL RIO.

Screen reproductions produced with Collage Plus.

Collage Plus is a trademark of Inner Media Inc.

SYBEX is a registered trademark of SYBEX Inc.

TRADEMARKS: SYBEX has attempted throughout this book to distinguish proprietary trademarks from descriptive terms by following the capitalization style used by the manufacturer.

SYBEX is not affiliated with any manufacturer.

Every effort has been made to supply complete and accurate information. However, SYBEX assumes no responsibility for its use, nor for any infringement of the intellectual property rights of third parties which would result from such use.

Library of Congress Card Number: 92-61129

ISBN: 0-7821-1137-8

Manufactured in the United States of America

10 9 8 7 6 5 4 3 2 1

UNDERSTANDING NORTON DESKTOP™ FOR DOS®

Peter Dyson

SYBEX ®

San Francisco • Paris • Düsseldorf • Soest

For Carol and Russell, thanks for all the times in the
tree house at the beach.

Acknowledgments

s always, I have enjoyed my part in writing this book, and as always, many other people have also provided support, advice, and technical information to help complete it.

At SYBEX, thanks as always to Dianne King, Acquisitions Manager, for her good humor in adversity and her practical, sound advice. Thanks to Gary Masters, Developmental Editor, for playing such a large part in making this book happen, and of course for all those bad jokes. Thanks also to Kathleen Lattinville, Editor; Mac Dunn, Technical Editor; Ann Dunn, Susan Trybull, and Chris Meredith, Word Processors; Claudia Smelser, Artist; Cuong Le, Screen Graphics Artist; Thomas Goudie, Typesetter; Arno Harris and Janet Boone, Proofreaders; and Ted Laux, Indexer.

At Symantec/Peter Norton Group, thanks to Kraig Lane, Product Manager for the Norton Desktop for DOS, for all his advice and assistance over the years, and thanks also to Nancy Stevenson, Manager of Third-Party Support for Symantec.

Thanks to Stephen Wilson for lending me his computer when mine broke.

And as always, thanks to Nancy for everything else; I really will paint the bathroom when this one is done.

CONTENTS AT A GLANCE

TABLE OF CONTENTS

Chapter 4
HOW TO GET HELP 37

PART TWO

THE NORTON DESKTOP

Chapter 5
MANAGING YOUR DISKS, DIRECTORIES, AND FILES 51

Chapter 6
VIEWING AND PRINTING FILES **89**

Chapter 7
USING THE NORTON DESKTOP EDITOR **105**

Chapter 8

LAUNCHING PROGRAMS **119**

PART THREE

PERSONALIZING THE DESKTOP

Chapter 9

CUSTOMIZING YOUR DESKTOP **131**

Chapter 10
CREATING YOUR OWN MENUS 173

PART FOUR

PROTECTING YOUR DISKS AND FILES

PART FIVE

USING THE DESKTOP UTILITIES

Chapter 16

Chapter 17

Chapter 18

WORKING WITH THE SYSTEM TOOLS **389**

Chapter 19

THE REFERENCE GUIDE TO THE NORTON DESKTOP 451

Appendix
AN INTRODUCTION TO DISK AND DIRECTORY STRUCTURE

Introduction

This book describes the programs in Version 1 of the Norton Desktop for DOS, released in the early summer of 1992, and is designed to help you get the most out of the Norton Desktop in the shortest possible time. It is written with both the new and the experienced PC user in mind and assumes only a modest familiarity with DOS. On the rare occasions when you will have to use the DOS command line, all the steps will be described in detail.

WHO SHOULD READ THIS BOOK

Understanding Norton Desktop for DOS is intended to meet the needs of a wide variety or readers. You don't have to be a computer expert to understand and use this book. Every attempt has been made to minimize jargon and to present the material in a clear and logical form. This book will serve as your guide and tutor as you learn the fundamentals of the Desktop. You will find that all the examples are short and concise so you won't waste time figuring out a long, complex example.

You don't have to read this book from front to back in strict sequence, although you certainly can if you wish. The five parts each stand alone as discussions of individual components of the Norton Desktop for DOS.

If you are new to a graphical user interface, you should pay special attention to Part I—including the description of the installation and how to get the most out of the user interface—before moving on to the more advanced material presented in later sections. If you are familiar with this type of user interface, you can probably move straight on to the sections describing specific problems and solutions.

HOW THIS BOOK IS ORGANIZED

This book is divided into five parts, containing a total of nineteen chapters and one appendix. Every chapter provides clear examples of how to get the best out of your system using the Norton Desktop.

Part One, "The Basics of Norton Desktop for DOS," presents essential information about the Desktop and your computer. It builds the strong foundation necessary for any user. You will learn how to install the package onto your hard disk, and how to navigate the user interface.

Part Two, "The Norton Desktop," shows you how you can use the Desktop to manage your disks, directories, and files. Viewing, printing, and launching files are all covered in detail.

Part Three, "Personalizing the Desktop," shows you how to form your own personal computing environment, specifically designed to meet your day-to-day needs.

Part Four, "Protecting Your Disks and Files," covers the tools found on the Desktop, including how to use Norton Backup to back up essential files and directories, and how to protect files from accidental deletion. You will also learn how to diagnose and fix problems with files or disks, how to improve the performance of your hard-disk system by reducing or eliminating file fragmentation, and even how to recover the contents of your hard disk after it has been accidentally formatted.

Part Five, "Using the Desktop Utilities," describes how to use the productivity and communications tools on the Desktop, as well as describing the tools you can use to look at all the different parts of your system, both hardware and software, and how to use Norton Cache to improve your overall hard-disk performance. The last chapter contains a complete command reference to all the command-line switches you can use with the individual programs that make up the Norton Desktop package.

The Appendix contains a discussion of disk and directory structure for those who want to know more about this complex topic, and provides additional technical background to the discussion of the file and disk recovery programs described in Part IV of this book.

THE MARGIN NOTES

As you read through this book, you will come across margin notes prefaced by an icon. There are three kinds of notes:

 This symbol indicates a general note about the topic under discussion. I might use it to refer you to another chapter for more information.

 This symbol denotes tips or tricks that you will find useful when using the Norton Desktop. They might be shortcuts I have discovered, or just important techniques that need emphasis.

 Pay close attention when you see this symbol in the margin. It will alert you to potential problems and will often give advice on how to avoid them.

THE FIGURES

The figures in this book were captured with the intention of providing the clearest possible tutorial for the Norton Desktop for DOS. The default screen positions and sizes were used in most cases, but because you can configure the Norton Desktop in many different ways, do not be concerned if you see small differences between the figures in this book and the image you see on your screen.

PART ONE

The Basics of Norton Desktop for DOS

Part I introduces the Norton Desktop and describes how to install the Norton Desktop onto your hard disk. The user interface is described in detail, and information on using both the mouse and the keyboard is included. Part I closes with a description of how you can get help anywhere on the Desktop.

CHAPTER 1

An Overview of the Norton Desktop for DOS

Norton Desktop for DOS integrates the functions needed for file, directory, disk, and program management into a striking, integrated desktop display. Desktop for DOS also includes several important productivity tools— such as Norton Backup, as well as several of the file- and data-recovery programs that have elevated the name of Norton to near-legendary proportions in the PC world. There are very few tasks in home or office computing that you cannot accomplish more effectively using Norton Desktop for DOS.

NORTON DESKTOP IN BRIEF

The following sections provide a short description of the Norton Desktop package and all of the associated programs.

THE DESKTOP

The Norton Desktop is a graphical environment that integrates the functions of program and file management, and then adds even more capabilities. Norton Desktop is faster and easier to use than most shell programs, including the DOS shell. The Desktop shows disk-drive icons down the side of the screen; when you click on a drive icon, you open a window showing the disk's files and directories. You can view files made by more than 70 application programs, including files made by most popular word processors, databases, and spreadsheets; you can even view .TIF and .PCX graphics files. You can drag and drop documents directly onto the Desktop for fast, easy access, or drag documents for printing. You can also launch programs from the Desktop quickly and easily using several different methods. When you associate your document files with their application programs, you need only click on the file to open it.

Norton Desktop contains an automatic menuing system that will search your hard disk looking for applications, and then build a set of menus containing entries for those applications. You can build a Desktop that reflects your computing needs exactly by editing and refining these menus as you wish.

THE DESKTOP TOOLS

In addition to the Desktop, there are several important productivity tools in the package:

Desktop Editor is a text editor that lets you work with several files at a time.

Disk Tools provides five important features that let you make a disk into a bootable disk, recover from the DOS RECOVER command, revive a floppy disk, and create or restore a recovery disk.

Image makes a copy of the system area of a disk that can be used to help recover the disk in the event of an accident.

Norton AntiVirus protects your system against an attack by over 1,000 different strains of computer virus, and can repair any virus-infected files found on your system.

Norton Backup lets you back up files and directories to floppies or a hard disk, including network disk drives, or to a tape drive. You can schedule automatic, unattended backups that run while you are away from your computer, and you can view files before you back them up to make sure you have the right file.

Norton Disk Doctor finds and fixes all sorts of problems associated with hard or floppy disks.

Sleeper is the entertaining and amusing Norton Desktop screen saver.

SmartCan prevents erased files from being overwritten for a specified time. This greatly increases your chances of successfully recovering a file if you decide that you need that file.

Speed Disk analyzes the degree of file fragmentation on your hard disk and recommends an optimization method you can use to re-store your hard-disk performance.

SuperFind finds lost files and files that contain specific text.

UnErase searches for and recovers deleted files automatically. It also provides an advanced manual recovery technique.

UnFormat restores a hard disk when all data has been lost due to an accidental reformat.

UnFormat can not work with floppy disks formatted using the DOS FORMAT command.

THE DESKTOP UTILITIES

Finally, there are several other important utility programs in the Norton Desktop package:

Batch Enhancer extends your batch-file programming to include boxes, windows, and color manipulation.

The *Calculator* will stop you from reaching for your handheld calculator to perform those everyday calculations.

Norton Cache speeds up hard-disk access.

Norton Mail manages your MCI electronic mail account.

Remote Link lets you link up to a network or to another PC.

Scheduler automatically starts programs or batch files, or displays reminder messages at predetermined times.

System Information lets you look into the dark corners of your computer, providing 19 screens of information on the hardware and software that make up your system.

In the chapters that follow I will explore Norton Desktop programs in detail, and—with examples where it is appropriate—show you how to use the programs in the package to get the most out of your computer.

USING NORTON DESKTOP ON A NETWORK

NOTE
NOTE
Your network supervisor should install Norton Desktop on a network.

You can use Norton Desktop from a networked drive, and you can use many of the more important programs on the file server itself. However, those Norton Desktop programs that are capable of modifying the file allocation table should not be run on the file server. This is particularly true of programs like Norton Disk Doctor, Speed Disk, and UnFormat.

If you use Novell Netware or Netware Lite, make sure that you are using IPXODI drivers of version 1.13, or later. If you have Windows 3.1, you can update versions of these drivers from your Windows installation disks.

To take advantage of all the Norton Desktop's networking capabilities on a Banyan Vines network, make sure NetBIOS services are installed and running on the network file server. As this is not the usual default setting, ask your network supervisor for more information.

If you use LAN Manager, and you have configured the system for messaging, there may not be sufficient free resources to allow the Norton Desktop to connect. Update the workstation configuration to increase the number of NetBIOS commands from 11 to at least 18 using the LAN Manager Setup program.

LANtastic, the DOS-based, peer-to-peer network from Artisoft provides features that other networks do not. For example, with LANtastic, you can share the disk drives in your computer with other users on the network. Several of the Norton Desktop programs including Disk Tools, Image, Norton Disk Doctor, Safe Format, and UnFormat, may not run when the network driver software is loaded. If SmartCan was not protecting a shared drive, UnErase must also be run without the network loaded. When you want to run one of these programs, just reboot your computer without loading the network. You can reload the network again when you have finished.

HARDWARE AND SOFTWARE REQUIREMENTS FOR NORTON DESKTOP

To use Norton Desktop, you must have at least DOS 3.1, or higher. The Desktop is, of course, completely compatible with DOS 5. You will need at least 512K of conventional memory, along with a hard disk that has at least 8MB of free space for a complete installation. Norton Desktop will benefit from 1MB or more of extended or expanded memory, and you will need 2MB of free disk space (after the installation) to run Desktop most effectively. Norton Desktop supports large hard disks using Microsoft DOS 4.01 and 5.0, DR DOS 5.0 and 6.0, Compaq DOS, and Zenith DOS.

Norton Desktop, with its menus and dialog boxes, works best with a mouse, and the mouse should be Microsoft-compatible. The Desktop provides support for a complete range of printers, including dot-matrix, HP LaserJet, and PostScript printers.

You can also install Norton Desktop on a Novell file server running NetWare 286 or 386 or on an IBM PC LAN server, and there is special support for LAN Manager, Banyan, and LANtastic networks.

CHAPTER 2

Installing Norton Desktop

This chapter describes how to install Norton Desktop for DOS onto your hard disk. An essential preliminary to this installation process is making backup copies of the original program disks; this protects you in case an accident occurs with the original disks.

THE DISTRIBUTION PACKAGE

The distribution package for Norton Desktop for DOS contains either 5¼-inch or 3½-inch disks so you can get the appropriate size for your system.

Three manuals are included with the disks. *Using the Norton Desktop for DOS* describes the complete Desktop package, except for Norton Backup, which is described in a separate manual called *Using the Norton Backup for DOS*. Loading the Norton Desktop onto your system is described in the third manual, *Installing the Norton Desktop for DOS*.

Check to see if there is a README.TXT file on the Install disk. The README.TXT file contains the latest information about the package, and may contain late-breaking information not included in the manuals. To look at this file before you install the package, use the DOS TYPE command. Because the file is longer than one screen, use the DOS MORE command to display the file one screen at a time. If the Install disk is in drive A, type:

TYPE A:README.TXT ¦ MORE

You can also use the DOS PRINT command to send the README.TXT file to your printer, or you can load the file into your word processor and print it from there.

MAKING FLOPPY DISK BACKUPS

As with any new software, the first thing you should do after taking it out of the box is to make a backup set of disks. You should do this even if you plan to install the software onto your hard disk. In the event that the original disks are damaged or destroyed, these backup copies ensure that the software is still available.

To make a floppy-disk copy of all the disks in the distribution package from the DOS command line, follow these steps:

1. If you have two identical floppy-disk drives, place the first distribution, or *source*, disk in drive A and a blank disk in drive B. If you have one floppy-disk drive (or two nonidentical drives), place the source disk in the drive of your choice.

2. Type the following at the DOS prompt if you have two drives:

   DISKCOPY A: B:

   If you just have one drive, type:

   DISKCOPY A: A:

3. Follow the instructions on the screen. If you are using one drive, you will be reminded to change disks from time to time to complete the copy.

4. Repeat this procedure with all of the other disks in the package.

5. Label the disks and put them in a safe place.

INSTALLING NORTON DESKTOP ON YOUR HARD DISK

Do not install the Norton Desktop on a hard disk containing erased files or directories that you want to recover.

If you currently need to perform a recovery operation such as restoring a directory or unerasing a file, do not install the Desktop on your hard disk yet. Instead, use the programs on the Fix-It disk to recover the file or directory. When the recovery is complete, you can proceed with the installation.

If you were to install the Norton Desktop without first recovering the file, the installation program might overwrite the area of the disk occupied by the erased file, making its recovery impossible. The following programs can be run directly from the original distribution disks: Norton Disk Doctor, Speed Disk, UnErase, and UnFormat.

*See Chapter 12 for information about what **really** happens when you erase a file from your disk.*

Norton Desktop's installation program guides you step-by-step through the installation procedure, explaining the choices available at each stage. The Install program can make three different installations of the Desktop: a full installation of the complete Norton Desktop package, a minimal installation that saves space, and a custom installation where you choose the elements of the Desktop that you want to install. We'll look at each of these methods in the next three sections, starting with the full installation.

USING THE INSTALL PROGRAM

Be sure you have more than 8MB of free space on your hard disk if you plan to make a full installation of the complete Desktop package.

To start the program, insert the Install disk into drive A, and type:

A: INSTALL

Choose the appropriate display color from Black & White, Color, or Laptop. A warning screen opens reminding you not to install the Desktop on your hard disk if you want to recover an erased file. At this point, you have the choice of continuing the installation or returning to DOS.

The next dialog box describes the installation process, and it also reminds you that the Install program can modify your CONFIG.SYS and AUTOEXEC.BAT files if needed. Click on Continue or Return to DOS. Next, Install checks your system for existing versions of Norton software. If Install finds any such programs, such as the Norton AntiVirus or the Norton Backup, it recommends that you make a custom installation of the Desktop to avoid wasting disk space by installing the product twice. We will look at a custom installation in a moment. Then Install scans the memory in your system looking for traces of computer viruses. When this scan is complete, Install checks drive C for viruses. Install makes these scans so that if you are unlucky enough to have a virus on your system, Install will find it before the virus has a chance to affect the Norton Desktop files. See Chapter 15 for more information on using Norton AntiVirus to deal with computer viruses.

The next dialog box requires you to enter your name, and if you wish, your company name, to personalize your copy of the Norton Desktop. Click on OK to open the Install dialog box, shown in Figure 2.1.

MAKING A FULL INSTALLATION

The Install dialog box contains the following selections:

Full Install. Choose this option to install the whole Norton Desktop package on your system, and automatically configure your CONFIG.SYS and AUTOEXEC.BAT files. This option requires 8MB of free disk space.

Minimal Install. If space on your system is at a premium, choose this option because it only takes a little over 3MB. CONFIG.SYS and AUTOEXEC.BAT are configured for you.

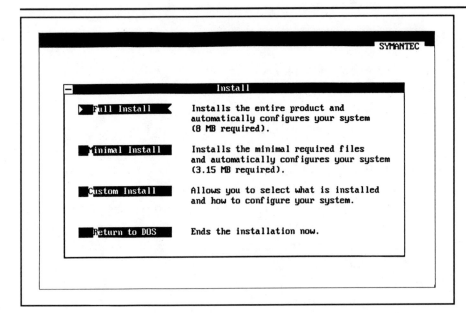

FIGURE 2.1:

Choose the installation level you want from the selections in the Install dialog box

Custom Install. If you want to install selected portions of the Norton Desktop package, choose this option.

Return to DOS. Use this option to end the installation process and return to DOS.

We'll look at each of these options in turn, starting with Full Install.

Choose Full Install to load the complete Norton Desktop package on your system. The next dialog box asks you to specify the name of the directory you want to use for the Desktop; the default is C:\ND. Install checks your hard disk to make sure there is enough room for a complete installation, and then begins the actual installation process. As the programs are copied onto your hard disk, a horizontal display on the screen shows the progress being made by moving from the left (no files copied) to the right (all files copied). After all the files on the first floppy disk have been copied, Install prompts you to insert the next disk. Don't worry, Install will tell you if you insert a disk out of sequence.

Many parts of the Norton Desktop package are in a compressed form on the original distribution disks to save space, and Install uncompresses these files as it installs them on your system.

Several of the Norton Desktop programs require you to add new commands to your AUTOEXEC.BAT or CONFIG.SYS files. For example, if you want to use SmartCan, you must add the commands SMARTCAN /ON and IMAGE. The next window, Save System Files, offers you three choices:

> **Make changes to startup files**. Choose this option if you want Install to make any changes required on your system automatically. Your existing CONFIG.SYS and AUTOEXEC.BAT files are copied to the new names CONFIG.NOR and AUTOEXEC.NOR so that you can reuse them if you wish, and any needed changes are added to the CONFIG.SYS and AUTOEXEC.BAT files in the root directory on your hard disk. This selection is the one you will probably choose.

> **Save changes in alternate files**. This option adds any changes needed into files called CONFIG.ND and AUTOEXEC.ND. You will find these files in the Norton Desktop directory on your system.

> **Do not save changes**. When you choose this option, no changes are made.

NOTE
NOTE

Don't forget to complete and return the product registration card.

At the bottom of this dialog box, you will see a list of all the Norton Desktop programs that Install can add to CONFIG.SYS or AUTOEXEC.BAT. On the left is a description of each function performed, followed by the name of the executable file; on the right of this box, you will see name of the startup file that the command will be added to—either CONFIG.SYS or AUTOEXEC.BAT (see Figure 2.2).

In some cases you will see the notation (not added) in the rightmost column. This indicates that the program *could* be added to one of your startup files if you wish, but it will not be added automatically by the Install program. This approach is a refreshing change from those programs that stuff your AUTOEXEC.BAT and CONFIG.SYS files full of programs you don't want to run.

Use the Review command button to look at the changes Install will make in your startup files if it adds these Norton Desktop programs. Another window opens listing your startup files, and you can use the Move or Delete command buttons to change the order or remove commands in these files. If you change your mind later, and decide you would rather use a different set of startup commands, you can use the NDConfig program, described in Chapter 9, to make these adjustments. Click on OK to return to the Save System Files dialog box.

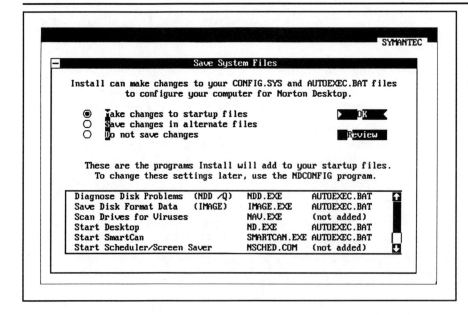

FIGURE 2.2:

Install can add these programs to your startup files if you choose Make changes to startup files

Click on OK when you have made your choice. The Install program now creates a tree file for each of your hard disks or hard-disk partitions. This saves time and speeds up many Desktop operations that use this information.

When the installation is complete, a dialog box opens containing the following choices:

Reboot. If you have made any changes to your startup files, CONFIG.SYS or AUTOEXEC.BAT, choose this option to make sure that these new files are loaded onto your system.

Go to Program. Choose this selection to go straight to the Desktop without rebooting.

Return to DOS. This option returns you to the DOS prompt.

The safest choice here is the first one, so remove the last distribution disk from the floppy-disk drive, and choose Reboot. Your computer will restart, run a quick Norton Disk Doctor test on your hard disk, create an Image data file, and open the Norton Desktop.

The first time the Desktop starts, a dialog box asks if you would like to take the Desktop Guided Tour. This Guided Tour is a good way to become familiar with the basic operation of the Norton Desktop. The tour is always available so you can take it now or at any time later.

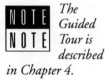

The Image program is described in Chapter 12 and the Norton Disk Doctor is described in Chapter 13.

The Guided Tour is described in Chapter 4.

MAKING A MINIMAL INSTALLATION

If disk space is at a premium on your system, you can make a minimal installation of the Desktop that only takes just over 3MB of hard-disk space. In the Install dialog box, choose the Minimal Install option. This time the Install program does not ask you to load all the distribution disks, one after another, but instead asks you to insert specific disks.

As the installation proceeds, you will see the same horizontal bar graph indicating progress as the files are uncompressed and copied onto your hard disk. When the files are copied, the installation continues just like a Full Install, and you will see the same dialog box asking if you want to reboot your system, go directly to the Desktop, or return to DOS.

The Minimal Install loads only the Desktop and associated files onto your system. The other stand-alone programs such as Norton AntiVirus, Norton Backup, Speed Disk, System Information, UnFormat, UnErase, and Safe Format are not loaded. If you need to use one of these programs, you can run them all directly from the original floppy disks. We'll see how to do this in later chapters.

Making a Custom Installation

The third and most flexible installation is the Custom Install. With Custom Install, you decide on which programs to install onto your hard disk, and which programs to install in your startup files. Experienced users will want to use this option to tailor the Desktop to their needs. Custom Install opens the dialog box shown in Figure 2.3.

All the separate components of the Norton Desktop are listed in this dialog box under the main Install Group headings:

◆ Norton Desktop

◆ Norton Mail

◆ Norton AntiVirus

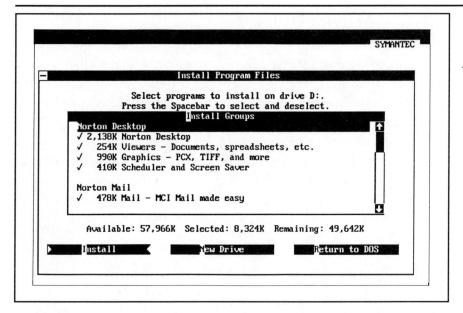

FIGURE 2.3:

Choose which programs you want to install in the Install Program Files dialog box

- ◆ Norton Backup
- ◆ Norton Menu
- ◆ Data Recovery Programs

A check mark to the left of an entry in this dialog box indicates that the program will be installed; if there is no check mark, the program will not be installed. Use the mouse or the arrow keys to move through the list, and click on the entry or press the spacebar to make your selections. Click or press the spacebar a second time to deselect an option.

At the bottom of this dialog box you will see three different measurements of disk space:

> **Available**. This number indicates the amount of free space on the hard disk before the installation.

> **Selected**. This shows the size of all the files you have selected for installation and represents the amount of disk space your selection will occupy.

> **Remaining**. This number shows the amount of disk space remaining after your selected files have been installed.

As you select and deselect files in the Install Program Files dialog box, you will see the Selected and Remaining numbers change to reflect your choices.

If you are in danger of running out of disk space, you can choose to install to a different disk drive by using the New Drive button.

Choose the Install button when you have completed your selections, and you will see the dialog box in Figure 2.4. Each of the items in the Select Configuration Options dialog box represents a different Norton Desktop program. Using the same selection methods of clicking or using the spacebar, you can choose which programs you want to be loaded automatically every time you start your system. Again, a check mark to the left of the item indicates that it will be loaded; no check mark means it will not be loaded.

When you are happy with your selections from this dialog box, select Continue to start loading and uncompressing the files. The installation continues as described under Full and Minimal Install: you are prompted for

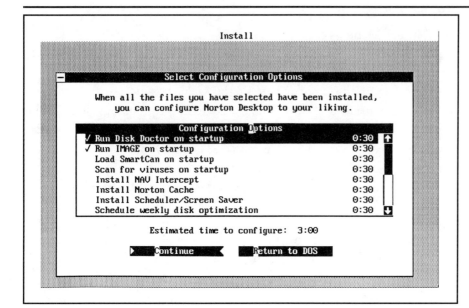

Choose the programs you
want to load from the
Select Configuration
Options dialog box

each disk as it is needed, and at the end of the installation process, you are presented with the same options of Reboot, Go to Program, or Return to DOS. If you chose any of the options in the Select Configuration Options dialog box, you should choose Reboot.

USING NORTON DESKTOP WITH MICROSOFT WINDOWS

If you are a Windows user, there is a Desktop program called INSTDOS that will create a Norton Desktop for DOS group window. Launch Windows and enter the appropriate path and file name information into the Run dialog box in the File menu. This entry might look like:

C:\ND\INSTDOS

if you installed the Desktop into a directory called ND on drive C. When you start INSTDOS, a window called Creating Group for Norton Desktop for DOS opens and you can watch the Desktop icons appear in this window one by one. When this process is complete, you will see icons for the following programs:

◆ Norton Desktop for DOS

◆ Norton Disk Doctor

◆ Norton AntiVirus

◆ Norton Backup

◆ Norton Mail

◆ Norton Menu

◆ System Information

◆ Safe Format

If you double-click on one of these icons in Windows, the regular DOS version of the program starts running; they are not Windows programs. And when you exit from one of these programs, you return to Windows, not to DOS or to the Desktop. Some Norton Desktop programs like Speed Disk should not be run in this environment; in fact, Speed Disk will politely refuse to run.

A companion product to the Norton Desktop for DOS, the Norton Desktop for Windows, is also available from Symantec. It offers very similar functions to the Norton Desktop for DOS, but contains almost all Windows programs with just a few DOS file- and disk-recovery programs.

CHAPTER 3

Elements of the Norton Desktop for DOS

This chapter reviews the major elements of the Norton Desktop for DOS user interface, and describes how you can get the most out of the Desktop using either a mouse or using the keyboard. We'll look at how to use menus and dialog boxes on the Desktop, and we'll explore command buttons, option buttons, and check boxes.

NAVIGATING THE DESKTOP

The Norton Desktop starts by opening a full-screen window. When you launch a program or open a document, another framed window opens.

In the Desktop, there are several different kinds of windows, and as you work your way through the following chapters, you will use all of them.

USING DIFFERENT KINDS OF WINDOWS

There are three main kinds of windows on the Desktop, application windows, document windows, and drive windows:

Application windows contain the work area for the program that you are working with, perhaps the Desktop Editor, or the Viewer. You will do most of your work in one of these windows.

Document windows are completely contained inside an application window, and they share the application window's menu bar. You may be able to open several document windows inside an application window. In Chapter 7 we'll look at how to open several text files, each in their own document window inside the Desktop Editor application window.

Drive windows let you access disks, directories, and files. When you open a drive window, it shows the contents—files and directories—of the drive you are using. Figure 3.1 shows a drive window for drive C open on the Desktop. The left side of the drive window shows a directory tree listing for the drive, and the right side of the window lists all the files in the highlighted directory. You can also open a view pane on a file at the bottom of a drive window, if you wish. Drive windows are described in detail in Chapter 5, and the view pane is detailed in Chapter 6.

THE MANY PARTS OF A WINDOW

We will use the Desktop and drive window shown in Figure 3.1 to describe the many parts of a window. Windows can contain many elements, but not every window has to contain all of them.

Here's a brief description of each of the major components:

◆ The *title bar* contains the name of the application, and sometimes the time of day. The title bar of the *active window* is usually a different color—or a different intensity on a monochrome screen. You may have several windows open at any time, but only one of them can be active.

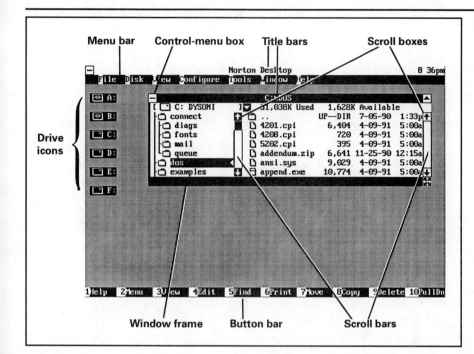

◆ The *Maximize* and *Restore* button at the right end of the title bar is a small button that controls the size of the window. Click on this button to maximize the window. When a window is maximized, it occupies as much of the screen as it can. Click on this button in a maximized window to shrink or restore the window to its original size.

◆ The horizontal *menu bar* runs across the top of the screen and contains the names of the pull-down menus. On the Desktop, these menus are, from left to right as follows: File, Disk, View, Configure, Tools, Window, and Help. You can select any of these menu items by clicking on them with the mouse; or if you prefer to use the keyboard, press F10 to turn on the menu bar, or press the Alt key along with the first letter of the menu you want to use.

◆ The *Control-menu box* sits in the upper-left corner of the window, and contains the Control menu. Click on the control box to open the Control menu—or, if you are using the keyboard, press Alt-spacebar to open the Control menu in an application window, or Alt-hyphen to open it in a document window.

◆ *Scroll bars* are used when the entire contents of a window or drop-down list box cannot be displayed all at once, as in a long document or file listing. In this case you will see a scroll bar down the right side of the window, with scroll buttons at either end and a scroll box in between. You may also see horizontal scroll bars across the bottom of certain windows.

 *The main Desktop window does not have a frame.*

◆ Each window is contained in a *frame*. To change the size of a window, place the mouse cursor on the window frame, and drag the edge of the window to the new location. You can also use the commands in the Control menu to change the shape and size of a window, as we'll see in a moment.

◆ Down the left side of the main Desktop window, you will see a vertical row of drive icons; one icon for each local disk drive on your computer or remote network drive. If you do not have a mouse on your system, these drive icons will not be present.

◆ The *button bar* is the line of buttons across the bottom of the screen. Press the appropriate function key from the keyboard (F1 for Help, F10 to access the menu bar, and so on), or click on the button to access them directly. You can change the functions associated with the button bar if you wish, and we'll see how to do this later on in Chapter 9.

USING THE MOUSE

The Norton Desktop is designed for the mouse user, and navigating your way through the Desktop with a mouse is fast and easy.

There are just a few mouse operations you have to understand:

◆ *Click.* Move the mouse cursor to the desired place in the window and click one of the mouse buttons. Most people use the left mouse button.

◆ *Double-click.* Move the mouse cursor to the appropriate place in the window, and click a mouse button twice in quick succession.

◆ *Drag.* Move the mouse cursor to the correct location, press the mouse button, and move the mouse, keeping the button pressed.

◆ *Right-click.* Move the mouse cursor and press the right mouse button. When an operation requires a right-click, I will always be sure to specify a right-click.

◆ *Mouse and key.* Hold down a key on the keyboard, perhaps the Alt key, and perform a mouse operation.

So how does all this actually work? To select a menu, click on the name in the menu bar. To select an option from within the menu, just move the mouse pointer and click on the item you want. To close a menu, click the mouse in the display area outside the menu. To change to another window, click anywhere inside the window that you want to make active. If you want to see all the options available in a drop-down list box, click on the prompt button, or if you want to select an option in a dialog box, click on the check mark to select it; if the item is already selected, click on it to deselect it.

If you are working with a long list of items, click on the scroll buttons (the small arrows at the top and bottom of the scroll bars) to move through the document or listing one line at a time, or hold down the mouse button to scroll continuously. The square scroll box indicates your relative position in the document or list; for example, when it is in the middle of the scroll bar, you are positioned in the middle of the document or list.

USING THE KEYBOARD

All the operations described above for the mouse can also be performed using the keyboard. To select a menu, press the Alt key and then type the menu's initial letter. For example, to open the File menu, hold down the Alt key and press F. You can also press F10 to turn on all the menus. Once the menus are displayed, you can use the arrow keys to display the next menu to the right or left. To select an option from within the menu, use the arrow keys, and press the Enter key when you reach the selection you want. Alternatively, you can type the highlighted letter to select an item from a menu. For example, to choose Copy from the File menu, hold down the Alt key and press F to open the menu, then press C to access Copy. Because each letter can represent only one option in a menu, sometimes the choices are less than intuitive. To close a menu, press Escape.

To change to another window, press the Tab key, or press Shift and Tab. To see all the options available in a drop-down list box, Tab to the list box, then hold down the Ctrl key and press the down arrow key. To select an option in a dialog box, use the Tab key to move to the check box, then press the spacebar to select it; if the item is already selected, press the spacebar to deselect it.

When working with a long list of items, use the PgUp or PgDn keys to move through the list a window at a time, or use the Home or End keys to go directly to the beginning or end of the list.

MOVING AND RESIZING WINDOWS

There may be times when the normal default window size is inconvenient. You can use the Control menu to change the size of a window, and then move it to another location on the screen.

Using drive windows is described in detail in Chapter 5.

When you open the Control menu in a drive window by clicking on the Control-menu box, or by typing Alt and the spacebar, you will see that it contains the following menu selections:

◆ **Restore** shrinks a maximized window back down to its original size. You can also click on the Restore button at the top right of a maximized window to achieve the same effect. If the window is not maximized, Restore is dimmed out and unavailable.

◆ **Move** lets you move the whole window to a new location on the screen. From the keyboard, use the arrow keys to move the window, and when it is in the right place, press the Enter key to anchor it there. If you want to use the mouse, just drag the window's title bar to the new location.

◆ **Size** allows you to adjust the window size by small increments. Again, use the arrow keys to change the window size, followed by the Enter key. Alternatively, if you are using the mouse, just drag the symbol in the lower-right corner of the window to change the size.

◆ **Maximize** expands a window to its largest possible size. If the window is already maximized, this command will be dimmed out and unavailable. You can also click on the Maximize button at the top right of a normal window to get the same result.

◆ **Close** lets you put a window away. You can also close a window if
you double-click on the Control-menu box or close box, at the
top-left corner of the window.

◆ **Next** makes the next window in sequence become the active window. If just one window is open, this command is dimmed out
and unavailable.

VIEWING MULTIPLE WINDOWS

It is very often very convenient to have several windows open on the Desktop
at the same time. In addition to the window manipulation commands like
Minimize and Restore described in the last section, there are two other commands from the Desktop Window menu you can use to arrange your open
windows:

◆ **Cascade** aligns all the open windows so that the title bar and edge
or corner of every open window is visible, like the drive windows
shown in Figure 3.2.

◆ **Tile** changes the shape of all the windows so that a portion of each
window is always visible, as Figure 3.3 shows.

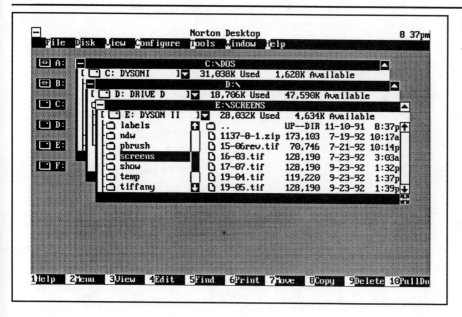

FIGURE 3.2:

*An example of cascaded
windows*

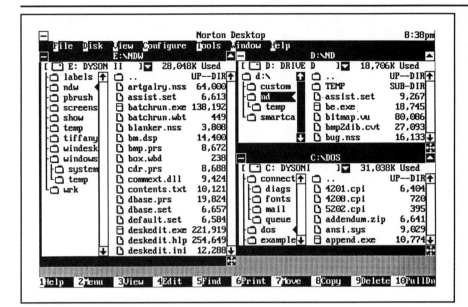

FIGURE 3.3:

*An example of tiled
windows*

USING THE MENUS

When you click on a menu name on the menu bar, a menu opens, listing the options from which you can choose. Similar functions are grouped together in the same menu; for example, the File menu contains all the entries associated with manipulating files.

There are several indicators in menus that have special meanings, as follows:

◆ *Grayed or dimmed command names.* If a command in a menu is grayed out or dimmed, it means that the command is currently unavailable. There can be many reasons why a menu item is dimmed; if a window is already maximized, the Maximize command in the Control menu will be dimmed because it has no meaning.

◆ A *check mark* before a command indicates that the command is a *toggle.* A toggle is a special kind of command; rather like a light switch, it is alternatively turned on and off each time you select it. If the check mark is present, the option is selected and turned on; if the check mark is not there, the option is not selected and is turned off. Several options in the View menu act as toggles.

◆ An *ellipsis* (…) after a menu option indicates that you will be asked for more information—usually in a dialog box—to complete the command. (Dialog boxes are described below.) Many of the commands in the File menu, Copy, Delete, and Rename are followed by ellipses.

◆ A *triangle* to the right of a menu option indicates that the command contains a submenu called a *cascading menu.* This cascading menu opens to the right of the current menu so that you can select further options. The Select and Deselect options in the File menu both open further cascading menus when they are selected.

◆ Some of the menu options list *keyboard equivalents* or *keyboard shortcuts* to the right of the options that you can use instead of opening the menu and choosing that command. For example, look at the Window menu and you will see that you can execute the Open Drive Window command by pressing the Ctrl and the W keys together.

WORKING WITH DIALOG BOXES

When you select a menu command followed by an ellipsis, a *dialog box* opens. The dialog box may ask you to enter more information, or may post a warning message if you are about to perform a potentially dangerous operation, like deleting a file. There can be several parts to a dialog box, as follows:

◆ In a *text box* you are asked to type text from the keyboard. Very often, you will find that the text box already contains an appropriate entry; if you want to keep that text, you can just move on to the next element in the dialog box. To change it, just type in the new text. If you click once on a text box, the text cursor appears (a flashing vertical bar sometimes called an *i-beam*), which you can use to edit the existing text. Text boxes are often used when you are loading or saving documents. They are also used to enter specific information, like the search string when you are searching a file for a particular segment of text.

◆ *Check boxes* usually offer a list of options that you can turn on or off. When an option is selected, it contains an X.

◆ A *list box* shows a column of choices. For example, when you are choosing a printer in the Desktop Editor, a list box shows you all the possible selections. Click on the entry you want to use, or if you are using the keyboard, use the arrow keys to move the highlight to your choice, then press the Enter key to confirm your choice. If the list box is too small to show all the possible alternatives, you will see a scroll bar down the right side of the list box. Use this scroll bar to review all the selections.

◆ A *drop-down list box* initially appears in a box with the current or default choice highlighted. The arrow, or prompt button, in the square box to the right of this opens up the list of choices when you click on it. If you are using the keyboard, press the Ctrl key followed by the down arrow key to open a drop-down list box. If there are more selections than can be displayed at once, scroll bars are also provided.

◆ *Option buttons* appear in a dialog box to present a list of mutually exclusive choices. You can only choose one option button at a time from any given number of option buttons. Any options that are currently unavailable will be dimmed or grayed out. Option buttons are sometimes called radio buttons.

◆ *Command buttons* make something happen. The most common command buttons are OK and Cancel, found in almost all dialog boxes everywhere. One command button always looks a little different; this is the command that will be executed if you press the Enter key. Pressing the Escape key has the same effect as clicking on Cancel; the dialog box disappears and no action is taken. Some command buttons are followed by an ellipsis; if you select this button, another dialog box opens so that you can choose more related settings. A command button that has a pair of greater-than symbols (>>) will expand the current dialog box when you select it, to show more detailed options.

◆ A *group box* helps to confine similar choices within the same dialog box. Figure 3.4 shows three group boxes titled "Storage Method," "General," and "Timestamp." A group box usually contains either option buttons or check boxes.

Not all dialog boxes contain all these elements, although you will find that many dialog boxes do contain most of them. For example, Figure 3.4, taken from Configure Compression on the Desktop, shows the usual OK and Cancel command buttons on the right, a set of option buttons in the Storage Method group box at the top of the dialog box, two check boxes and a text box in the General group box in the center, and three more option buttons in the Timestamp group box at the bottom of the dialog box.

Browsing for a File

Many of the Norton Desktop dialog boxes contain a Browse command button. When you choose this button, a Browse dialog box opens to help you find a drive, a directory, or a file to work with. The Browse dialog box can look slightly different depending on the major command it is associated with, but it always contains list boxes showing a file list, a directory list, and a drive list. Figure 3.5 shows the Browse dialog box that opens when you first start the Desktop Editor. Use the Edit command in the File menu to start the Desktop Editor.

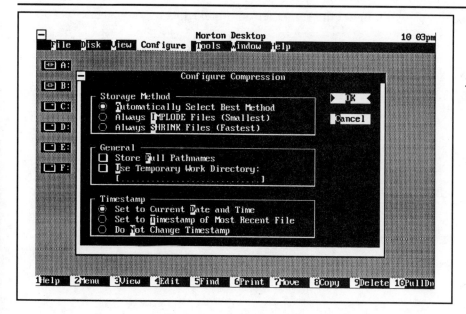

FIGURE 3.4:

The Configure Compression dialog box features option buttons, check boxes, and a text box

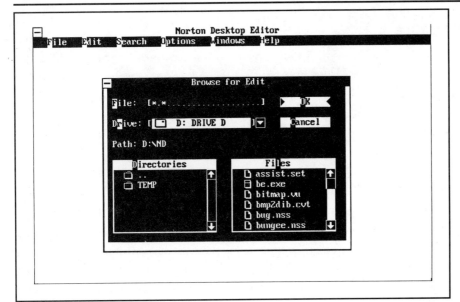

FIGURE 3.5:

*The Browse dialog box
used by the Desktop
Editor to select a file*

First choose the drive you want to work with, then the directory, and
finally, the actual file. Click on the file to select it, then click on OK to load
that file name into the File text box in the previous dialog box. Alternatively,
double-click on the file name to load the file directly.

USING WILDCARDS IN FILE NAMES

You can use the DOS wildcard characters * and ? as placeholders when you
want to specify a file or a group of files. These wildcard characters are most
helpful in text boxes where you want to select a range of files. The ? represents
one character in a file name, while the * represents several characters. For example, *.TXT specifies all the files using the file-name extension .TXT in a
directory, while MEMO??.DOC specifies a numbered group of memo files.

USING NORTON DESKTOP WITH MICROSOFT WINDOWS OR WITH DESQVIEW

Microsoft Windows and DESQview both bring multitasking capabilities to DOS. Multitasking means that you can run several different applications at the same time and switch from one to another without quitting any of them. You may run into problems if you try to run some of the Norton Desktop tools in either of these environments. The tools contain extensive error checking to avoid anything unpleasant happening if you do try to run them in these environments. In general, the tools that can modify the file allocation table are potential problems. The following programs will politely refuse to run in a multitasking setting, Disk Tools, Safe Format, Speed Disk, the Norton Disk Doctor, UnErase, and UnFormat. If you start one of them running, you will see a screen similar to the one shown in Figure 3.6.

Many of the other parts of the Norton Desktop package work well under Windows; indeed, the Norton Desktop creates its own Windows group with individual icons when you install Norton Desktop for DOS.

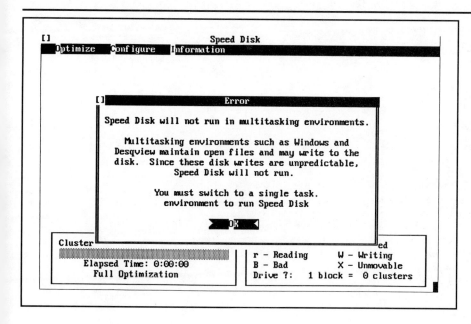

FIGURE 3.6:

You will see this message if you try to run Speed Disk under Microsoft Windows

USING THE NORTON DESKTOP WITH A NETWORK

You can use the Norton Desktop from a networked drive, and you can actually use many of the important tools on the file server itself. However, as with the multitasking environments described in the last section, those tools that are capable of changing the file allocation table should not be run on the server.

The Norton Desktop saves configuration information in files with the .INI extension. Because each user on the network may have different hardware, these .INI files should be saved in a directory on the local disk, not to a directory on the file server.

If you want the protection against accidental file deletion that the SmartCan program offers, ask your network supervisor to install the program on the network for you. When SmartCan is run for the first time, it creates a hidden directory from the root directory called SMARTCAN, and everyone on the network should have all rights (except Search) to this directory.

CHAPTER 4

How to Get Help

he Norton Desktop has an extensive system of online help, available anytime you are using the Desktop. There are several different ways you can access help:

- ◆ Open the Help menu (press Alt-H) from the Norton Desktop menu bar or from the menu bar of the Desktop application you are using, and select one of the options.
- ◆ Press F1 from any window to display the Help window, then choose a topic.
- ◆ Take the Norton Desktop Guided Tour.
- ◆ Choose the Advise entry in the Desktop Help menu to get special assistance with common disk problems and DOS error messages.

USING THE HELP SYSTEM

Let's start with the Help menu—it's always the menu farthest to the right on the menu bar. Open the menu and you will see the following entries:

Advise helps you find and fix a variety of computer hardware problems. Because Advise is different from the regular Help system on the Desktop, I will describe how to use it in a separate section later in this chapter.

Index lists all of the Help topics in alphabetical order, by group.

Keyboard describes how to use the current application from the keyboard or with the mouse.

Commands summarizes the commands available in the current application.

Procedures lists the main features available in the current application.

Using Help is a guide to the Help system itself.

Guided Tour is a conducted tour of some of the most important features of the Desktop user interface.

About shows you the program version number, the name of the registered user of this copy of the Norton Desktop, and details of the amount of memory available in your computer.

 Some of the Norton Desktop Tools, like Speed Disk or Un-Erase, do not have a Help entry on the menu bar.

When you first select the Index entry from the Help menu, or press F1, the window in Figure 4.1 opens. Terms that contain additional information are shown highlighted in a different color or intensity in this window.

The Help window has several buttons across the bottom of the window, as follows:

Go To. Tab to the highlighted entry you are interested in and click on Go To to open the associated help window. You can also just double-click on the highlighted entry to open this next help window.

Go Back When you have finished with that topic, use Go Back to return to the previous level in the Help system.

Index. Use Index to go straight to the topic index from anywhere in the Help system.

Cancel. When you are all done with the Help system, use Cancel to return to the main application screen again. You can also use the Escape key.

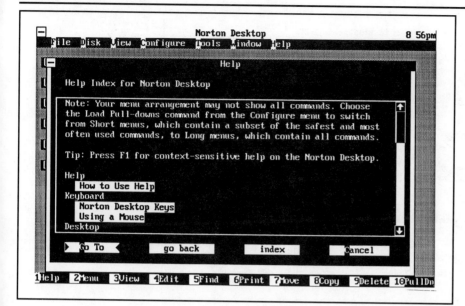

FIGURE 4.1:
There are four buttons in the Help screen

Use the Tab or the Shift and Tab keys to move from one highlighted term to another in this window, then use the Go To button to see more detailed information. You can also just double-click on the technical term to see this additional information. Use the scroll bars with the mouse to move through the help screen, or use PgUp or PgDn from the keyboard. When you have finished with this topic, click on Go Back to return to the previous level in the help system, click on Index to go straight to the listing of topics by group, or click on Cancel if you want to leave the Help system entirely and return to your application program. Using the Escape key has the same effect as clicking on Cancel.

TAKING THE GUIDED TOUR

When you complete your installation of the Norton Desktop, you are given the chance to take a guided tour of the Desktop. You can also take the tour at any other time by clicking on the Guided Tour entry in the Help menu. When you do, you will see the dialog box shown in Figure 4.2.

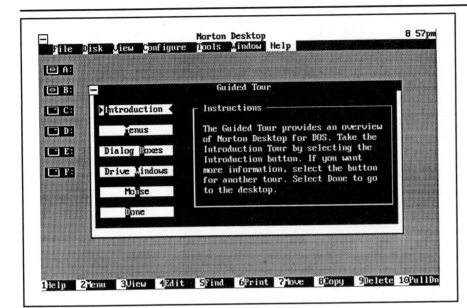

The Guided Tour dialog box lets you configure your own personal tour—you don't have to complete the tour all in one go, or, if there are parts of the tour you don't want to see right now, you don't have to watch them. Choose from:

Introduction. As it suggests, this is a brief introduction to the whole tour.

Menus. This part of the tour shows you how to use the menus in the Norton Desktop using animated examples.

Dialog Boxes. Here, the tour concentrates on using dialog boxes, and illustrates some of the major components of Desktop dialog boxes.

Drive Windows. Here the tour concentrates on how to use drive windows to manage your files.

Mouse. This part of the tour concentrates on how to use your mouse with the Desktop, highlighting the major operations of point, click, double-click, and drag.

Select the part of the tour you are interested in seeing, then click on OK to start the tour. You can also click on Done if you change your mind about taking the tour.

In most cases, all you have to do to advance to the next part of the tour, is press the spacebar when you are ready. In some cases, where the tour is making a particular point, you may be asked to press a shortcut keystroke to perform a specific operation. These keyboard shortcuts are always shown on the screen if they are needed—you don't have to remember what they are.

When you complete the tour, you should have a pretty good idea of how to use the most important parts of the Desktop—and remember, you can retake the tour any time you like.

USING THE ADVISOR

This section describes how you can use the remarkable troubleshooting facilities available in the Norton Desktop to help understand and solve your disk-related problems. We will cover the specific programs that do these tasks in later chapters; this discussion is just about how to use the Advise command in the Norton Desktop Help system to decide which program you need to use.

The selections in the Advise menu work in much the same way as the context-sensitive help available throughout the rest of the Norton Desktop. You select one topic from the list using the up and down arrow keys or the mouse, and then choose the Go To button to see a more detailed explanation. This second-level window often includes specific suggestions about which of the Norton Desktop programs you can use to help solve your problem. Technical terms are shown highlighted in a different color or intensity. Use the Tab or the Shift and Tab keys to move from one term to another, then use the Go To button to see more information. You can also just double-click on the technical term itself to see this additional information. Suggested solutions are denoted in this window by a square bullet.

If DOS reports an error that you are unfamiliar with, you can learn more about the error message from the selections in the Advise menu, and then you can run the appropriate Norton Desktop Tool to fix the problem. The first two entries in the Advise menu tell you how to use Advise; then you will see three more entries, with each category defining a different group of problems, as Figure 4.3 shows. In the next three sections, I will describe how to use each of these menu selections.

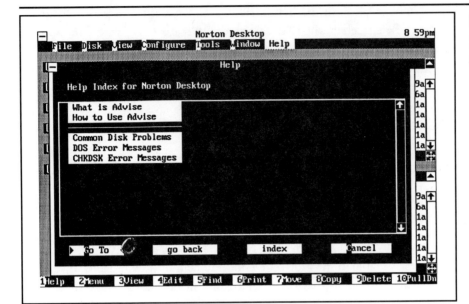

COMMON DISK PROBLEMS

Let's assume you are having disk problems, and you decide to access the Advise menu. First you choose the Advise menu, and then you select Common Disk Problems. This opens the window shown in Figure 4.4. You think the problem has something to do with cross-linked files. Move the highlight in the dialog box until it is on the third selection, Cross-linked files, and then choose the Go To button. Another window opens to display a more complete description of the proposed solution, as shown in Figure 4.5. If you choose the Run Norton Disk Doctor entry, you can actually run the Norton Disk Doctor from within the help window to diagnose the problem disk and fix the cross-linked files. Click on the Run Norton Disk Doctor entry, and you will see that the Go To button changes into the Run button. Click on Run to start the Norton Disk Doctor; you can also double-click on the Run Norton Disk Doctor entry in the Advise screen to start the program running. When you leave the Norton Disk Doctor, you return directly to the Norton Desktop.

The Norton Disk Doctor is described in detail in Chapter 13.

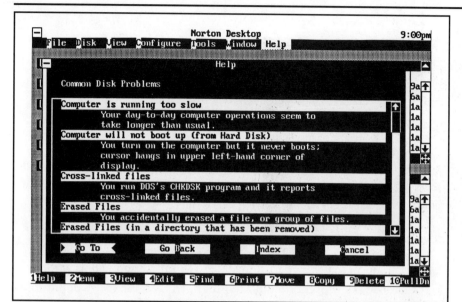

FIGURE 4.4:

The first Common Disk Problems window

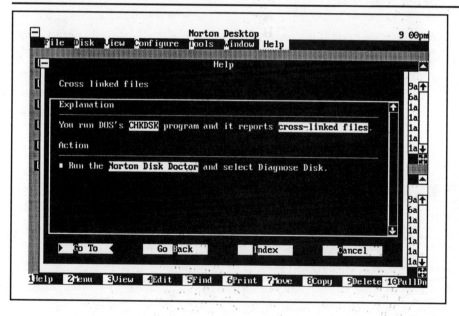

FIGURE 4.5:

You can run the Norton Disk Doctor from the Advise window if you wish

DOS ERROR MESSAGES

The next selection from the Advise menu displays a list of the common DOS errors you might see from time to time. The list includes many disk-related error messages, but it is by no means a complete list of all the DOS errors. Some of the error messages are relatively insignificant, such as:

Abort, Retry, Ignore, Fail?

which often results if you try to read a drive before you have inserted a floppy disk. However, some of the other errors can panic even the most seasoned computer user. Error messages such as:

Invalid drive specification

which can mean that your partition table has been corrupted or that the boot track has been destroyed, should not be ignored because they can indicate a deteriorating hard disk.

If you do see the error message Invalid drive specification and you know that you used to be able to access that drive, load the Norton Desktop, select the Advise menu, and choose the Invalid drive specification error message from the list of DOS Error Messages, as Figure 4.6 shows. When you select

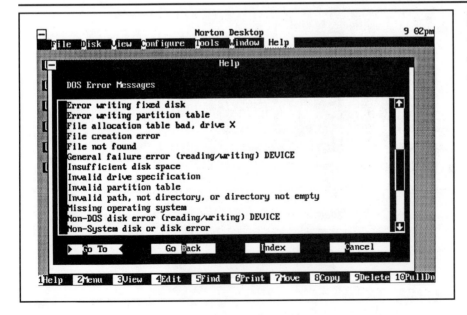

FIGURE 4.6:

Choose the appropriate error message from the list in the window

the Go To button, another window opens, as Figure 4.7 shows. This window displays more detailed information about the error message and offers two sets of reasons why the error occurred: the disk has a bad partition table or boot track, or the disk was formatted with one version of DOS, and you are trying to read it with a different version.

The next step is to run the Norton Disk Doctor directly from this window so that you can check the partition table and the boot track. You can also select the Go Back button to return to the previous window.

CHKDSK Error Messages

You can use the DOS command CHKDSK to check the formatted size and the amount of free space on a disk. CHKDSK also reports the amount of space used by hidden files, directories, user files, and bad sectors, as well as detailing the memory size and the amount of free memory available in your computer. CHKDSK tests for logical errors in the file allocation tables and the directories, and can output a series of error messages depending on what it finds.

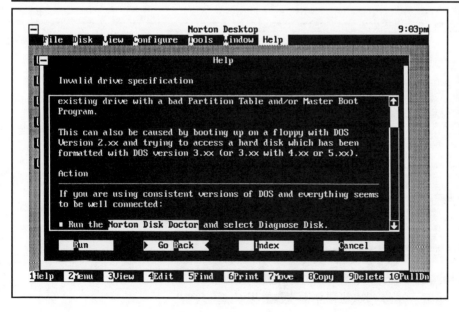

FIGURE 4.7:

The next window offers more information about the error you selected from the previous screen

You can also use the CHKDSK command to give you a report on the fragmentation of a file. CHKDSK reports that the file contains a number of non-contiguous blocks if the file is split up into pieces.

If you see this message, select CHKDSK Error Messages from the Advise menu. Move the highlight to the Contains xxx non-contiguous blocks message as Figure 4.8 shows, and select the Go To button.

NOTE
NOTE

Speed Disk is described in Chapter 14.

The next window contains a description of the CHKDSK error message telling you that the file is fragmented, or broken into several pieces. Because the file is in several different areas of the disk, it will take longer to load all the pieces than it would take to load the file if it were in only one piece. To fix this file fragmentation, the window recommends that you run the disk optimizer Speed Disk, as shown in Figure 4.9.

Highlight the Speed Disk entry and use the Run button, or double-click on the Speed Disk entry to start that program running. When you start Speed Disk, you can generate a detailed report about the fragmentation of all your files and then choose an appropriate optimization method. If you don't want to run Speed Disk, select the Go Back button to return to the list of CHKDSK errors, and then select Go Back again to return to the main Norton Desktop window.

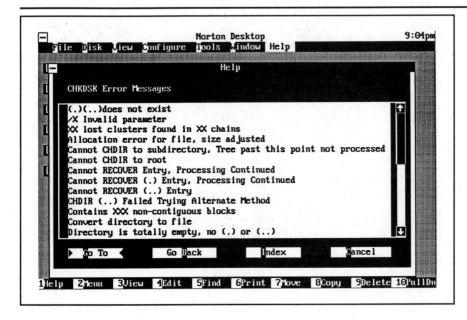

FIGURE 4.8:

Choose the appropriate CHKDSK message

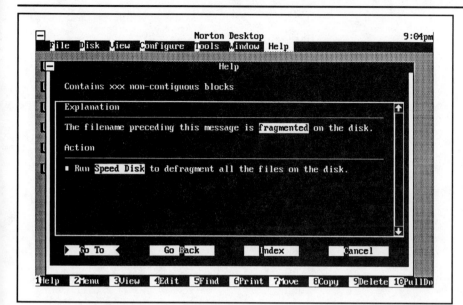

FIGURE 4.9:

You can run Speed Disk directly from the Advise window to fix file fragmentation

This brings us to the end of our discussion of Help on the Norton Desktop. In the next few chapters we'll look at how you can start to put the Desktop to use for managing files and disks, for viewing and printing files, and for launching programs.

PART TWO

The Norton Desktop

Part II shows you how manage your disks, directories, and files, and you will learn how to copy, move, delete, and rename files using Desktop's drive windows. Viewing and printing files, launching programs, and using the Desktop Editor are also described.

CHAPTER 5

Managing Your Disks, Directories, and Files

orton Desktop for DOS makes managing files, directories, and disks fast and easy. Although the Desktop package also includes important programs for file backup, file recovery, disk repair, and other important tasks, this chapter concentrates on what you see when you start Norton Desktop for DOS—the Desktop—and tells you how you can get the most out of using drive windows. Towards the end of the chapter, we'll look at the powerful file-finding capabilities of SuperFind.

OPENING AND CLOSING YOUR DESKTOP

To start the Norton Desktop, you must type

ND

at the DOS prompt.

When it is time to leave the Norton Desktop, be sure that you first close all your open application programs, then double-click on the Control-menu box or choose Exit from the File Menu. This returns you back to the DOS prompt.

DESKTOP ORGANIZATION

NOTE NOTE *If your Desktop does not match Figure 5.1 exactly, you may have changed the configuration slightly or you may have a different number of disk drives.*

NOTE NOTE *You can change and customize the entries in the short menu to fit your own personal way of working; this operation is described in detail in Chapter 9.*

When you start the Desktop, it occupies the whole of your screen, as Figure 5.1 shows. The Desktop contains many of the elements already described in Chapter 3, but we can go over them again very quickly. At the top of the screen is the title bar with the Control-menu box and the time of day. Below is the menu bar, and below that is the desktop work area. This is where you do all your work, just like on a real desktop.

Notice the Desktop drive icons down the (left) side of the screen. Figure 5.1 shows six drive icons; on your desktop you will see an icon for each hard and floppy drive on your system. RAM disks, network drives, and CD-ROMs, if you have them, are also indicated by icons.

The Desktop contains seven menus, in addition to the Control menu, and you can configure Desktop menus as either full menus or short menus. When you start the Desktop for the first time, the short menus are selected as the default configuration; short menus contain only the most often used commands. Full menus, on the other hand, contain *all* the options you can use on the Desktop. The left side of Figure 5.2 shows the full version of the File menu and the right side shows the short version. Use the first selection in the Configure menu to change from short to full menus.

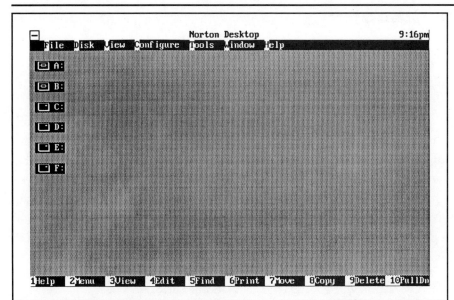

FIGURE 5.1:

The Norton Desktop occupies the whole screen

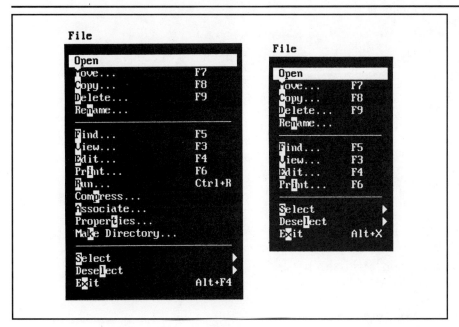

FIGURE 5.2:

The full and short versions of the Desktop File menu

OPENING DRIVE WINDOWS

One of the most important features of the Norton Desktop is the *drive window,* which lets you manage files, directories, and disks quickly and easily. It displays the contents of a disk as a directory tree and list of files; it may also show the contents of a specific file.

Just double-click on the icon of the drive you want to work with, and the drive window will open like the one shown in Figure 5.3. You can also open a drive window by selecting Open Drive Window (Ctrl+W) from the Window menu. This opens a dialog box, which defaults to the current drive; use the drive selector drop-down list box to select another drive, if you wish.

The drive window in Figure 5.3 contains several new elements not described so far, as well as the familiar title bar, Control-menu box, and Maximize button:

> ☒ **NOTE** *You can have several drive windows open at the same time on the Desktop.*

◆ Use the *drive selector* to change to another drive.

◆ The *status bar* lists important information about the drive in the window.

◆ The *tree pane* lists the directories on the chosen disk.

◆ The *file pane* lists all the files in the chosen directory.

◆ The *view pane* displays the contents of the chosen file. Select a file and use the View Pane command from the View menu to open a view pane.

◆ Speed Search lets you go directly to the file or directory of your choice. The *Search box* appears immediately after you start to type a file's or directory's name (be sure the correct pane is active). See the section headed "Speed Searches" for more information.

The active element of the drive window has a lighter border; to move to another element, press the Tab key (this cycles through the elements) or click directly on it with the mouse. Use Shift+Tab to cycle in the other direction.

SELECTING A DRIVE

The drive selector shows the letter and label of the *current drive* (if the current drive has a label). The files and directories of the current drive are listed in the tree and file panes. You can display the contents of a second disk in the

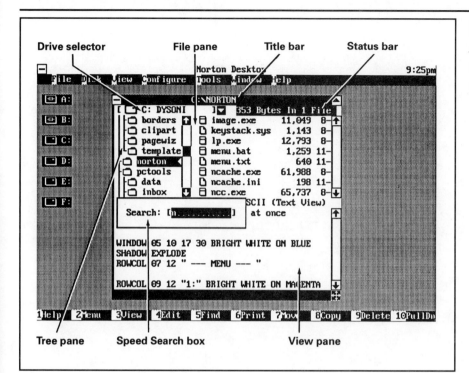

FIGURE 5.3:

A drive window opened by double-clicking on drive C

current drive window; you don't have to open another drive window. Make the drive selector active, then type in the letter of the drive you want to work with. The tree and file panes are updated automatically to reflect this change. You can also make the drive selector active, then click on the drive selector prompt button (Ctrl+↓) and select a drive from the list.

STATUS BAR INFORMATION

The status bar lists important information about the selected drive. The default information includes the disk space used and the space available. When you select files from the file tree, the status bar changes to list the number and total size of those files; when you select directories, the status information shows the number of directories you selected.

SPEED SEARCHES

Speed Search lets you specify a directory or file quickly and easily from the keyboard. All you have to do is make the appropriate pane active—either the tree or file pane—and start typing the name you are looking for. As you start to type, the Search box opens below the active pane, and the directory or file that matches the keys you have typed so far is selected. If there is no match, nothing is selected. Speed Search works by matching your keystrokes with the name in your tree or file pane. If you have many entries with similar names, you will have to enter more characters before the entry becomes unique. To find the next directory or file that matches the name you typed, press the ↓ key; to return to the previous match, press ↑. Press Enter to accept the selection and close the Search box, or press Escape to close the Search box without accepting the selection.

TREE, FILE, AND VIEW PANES

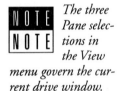

The three Pane selections in the View menu govern the current drive window.

Drive windows contain tree and file panes by default—and can contain a view pane if you wish—but, as always in the Desktop, you can change this configuration to suit your needs. You might, for example, want to close one of the panes to make room for some information about another drive. You determine which pane(s) to show by selecting one of the first three entries in the View menu. Each command is a toggle: if the command is on, you will see a check mark to the left of the menu item; if it is off, there will be no check mark.

The Tree and File Panes

The *tree pane* shows a schematic drawing of your directory structure down the left side of the drive window. Simply click on a directory icon to see the files in it appear in the *file pane* to the right. Here you can select files for copying, moving, or deleting. You can also drag files from one file pane to another in a different drive window.

There are several selections in the View menu you can use to modify the display order or actually change which of the files are displayed in the file pane: Filter, File Details, Sort By, and Show Entire Drive.

Filter This opens a dialog box that lets you choose the types of files to display in the file pane, as Figure 5.4 shows. You can choose to list a particular kind of file by selecting a particular criterion:

All Files displays all the files in the directory, bar none. This is the default setting.

Programs limits the file list to displaying files that have .BAT, .COM, .EXE, or .PIF as the file-name extension. Other files are not displayed.

Documents displays all the files associated with an application program.

Custom displays just about everything else. You can use wildcards in the Custom box to extend the scope to groups of files. Click on the drop-down list box to see a list of the last ten custom extensions you entered.

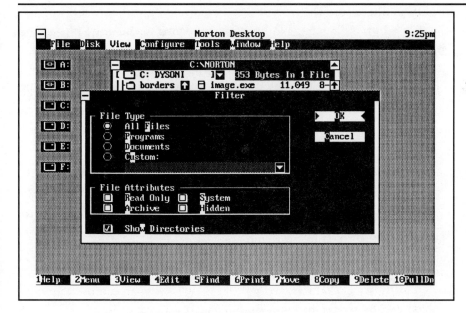

FIGURE 5.4:

Use the Filter dialog box to choose the kinds of files you want shown in the file pane

You can also use file attributes as the basis for selecting which files to display. Files can have up to four attributes or properties, as follows:

◆ A *read-only* file cannot be written to or erased by the normal commands, but it can be opened and read normally.

◆ The *archive* attribute indicates that the file should be backed up; it has been changed or modified in some way since it was last backed up.

◆ A *system* file is a hidden, read-only file that DOS uses; it cannot be written to or erased.

◆ *Hidden* files do not appear in the usual listings, nor can they be deleted or run.

The Show Directories check box displays any subdirectory names in the file pane. Remove the check mark if you don't want to see them.

File names are always shown in the file pane.

Click on OK if you want to apply the filter you just selected to the current drive window. For example, if you choose the Programs filter, then click on OK and return to the current drive window, you will only see program files listed in the file pane. Nothing has happened to the other files in the directory, they are just hidden from view.

File Details   This selects the amount of information shown in the file pane. The dialog box shown in Figure 5.5 contains the following selections:

Icon displays a small icon to the left of each file name. Different icons represent directories, documents, text files or word-processor documents, and executable programs or batch files. If you turn the icons off, the file pane lists just the file names.

Size lists the size of each file in bytes.

Date shows the file-creation dates.

Time shows the file-creation times.

Attributes shows each file's attributes.

Directory shows the name of the directory.

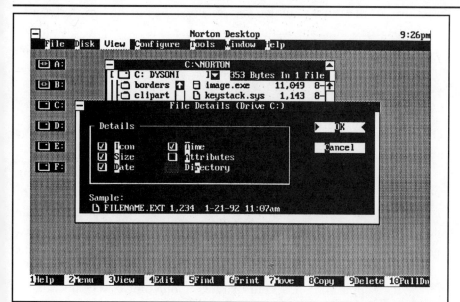

You can use the File Details dialog box to configure the file pane display

A small display at the bottom of this dialog box shows you how each file will be displayed in the file pane. Making any of these selections will change the file pane from a multicolumn list to a single column list.

Click on OK if you want this information to be shown in the current drive window.

Sort By This determines the order in which the files in the file pane are listed. Your choices are as follows:

Name sorts alphabetically by file name.

Type sorts by file extension. This selection groups like file types together first, then sorts by file name inside the various groups.

Size sorts by file size.

Date sorts by date and time.

Unsorted displays the files as they were created, saved, or copied on your disk.

Ascending sorts files in ascending order: from *A* to *Z*, from small to large, or from old to new.

Descending is the opposite of Ascending.

Show Entire Drive This lets you see *everything,* all the files on the disk. The Drive window changes into one large file pane, as Figure 5.6 shows, and the tree pane disappears. To return to the usual display, toggle Show Entire Drive off again.

The View Pane

The *view pane* is the third component of the drive window. To use it, select a file in the file pane and select View Pane from the View menu.

A third window opens across the lower portion of the screen, displaying the contents of the file without having to launch the application program that created that file in the first place. This means that you can examine the file to make sure that it is the one you want to work with and then launch the application program when you are sure you have the file you want. This simple operation can save you a lot of time if you work with some of the heavyweight application programs that take a long time to start up—and if you load the wrong data file, that translates directly into wasted time.

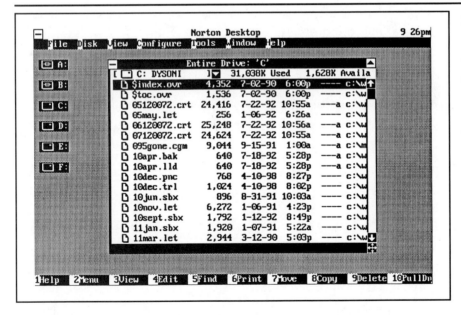

FIGURE 5.6:

To list all the files on the drive, choose Show Entire Drive

MANAGING YOUR FILES AND DIRECTORIES

Now that you understand how to work within a Desktop drive window, you can put that knowledge to work with some practical ways in which you can use the Desktop for file and directory management.

SELECTING AND DESELECTING FILES AND DIRECTORIES

Many times when you are using the Desktop for file or directory management, you must first select the file(s) you want to work with and then choose the operation you want to perform. The tree pane lets you work with directories and subdirectories; the file pane with subdirectories and files. To select a file, the file pane must be open.

To select a single file or subdirectory, click on the file (the icon or name) with the mouse; the highlight shows that the file is selected. To select a different file, just click on the new file and the highlight will jump to it. If you are using the keyboard, you can use the arrow keys as well as the PgUp, PgDn, Home, and End keys to move the highlight around the pane.

To select several adjacent files (or subdirectories) for an operation, just point to a file, click and hold the right button, and drag the mouse. Alternatively, select the first file in the sequence by clicking on the file, then hold down the Shift key as you click on the last file you want to include in the block. All the files in between, including the first and last files, will be highlighted to show that they have been selected.

If you want to select several files that are not adjacent to one another, just click on each with the right mouse button. Alternatively, hold down the Ctrl key and click on each file you want to select with the right mouse button. As you do so, each file will become highlighted in turn. With the keyboard, position the highlight over the first file you want to select, then use the arrow keys to move around the file pane, pressing the spacebar to toggle the highlight on and off over the file names as you go.

For some operations you will want to select all the files in a particular directory. The Desktop provides commands for this in the File menu.

Choose Select from the File menu to open a cascading menu containing three selections:

All (Ctrl+/) selects all the files in the file pane.

Some (+) opens a dialog box that lets you choose the files to select by name. Enter the file names you want to select into the text box. You can also use wildcards with this box to include groups of files.

Invert reverses the current selection state; it selects those files that are not selected and deselects any that are.

To deselect all files, simply click on any file with the left mouse button.

To deselect one file from a series of selected files, either click on individual highlighted files with the right mouse button, or drag the right mouse button across a group of adjacent highlighted files. Alternatively, hold down the Ctrl key and click on the file. From the keyboard, move to the file you want to deselect using the arrow keys, and press the spacebar. Repeat this process until you have deselected the right number of files.

There is also a cascading command called Deselect available in the File menu, with three options: All, Some, and Invert. These three commands work like the Select command described above. All deselects all the files in the file pane, Some opens a dialog box so you can specify the files you want to deselect, and Invert reverses the current selection.

BROWSING FOR FILES ON THE DESKTOP

Before we start to look at file and directory maintenance operations in detail, there is one more command button I should mention. Many of the operations described later in the chapter feature a dialog box that contains a Browse button. When you click on Browse, a version of the Browse dialog box opens on the Desktop. This dialog box may not always look the same— it depends on the command you are using it with—but it always contains three list boxes: a file list, a tree list (titled "Directories"), and a drive list. Figure 5.7 shows the Browse dialog box associated with the Run command from the File menu. You can use the Browse dialog box first to select the drive, then the directory, then finally the file that you want to work with. The file name is entered into the appropriate text box for you automatically. Click on OK or press Enter to call up the file into the dialog box you are in.

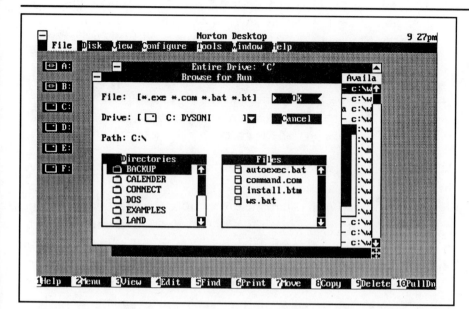

FIGURE 5.7:

The Browse dialog box lists files, directories, and drives

COPYING AND MOVING FILES AND DIRECTORIES

You can use the Desktop to copy or move a single file or directory, but you can also use it to copy or move groups of files, or even a whole segment of your directory structure. Norton Desktop displays a warning message if you are about to overwrite a file with another file that has the same name. You can then choose whether you want to overwrite the file or cancel the move or copy operation.

Copying and Moving with the Mouse

TIP *If you are moving or copying to a directory on the same drive, you may find it easier to manage the process by opening **two** drive windows, one for the source directory and another for the target directory.*

For this example, let's assume you want to copy a directory and three associated subdirectories—along with all the files in these directories—from drive C to the floppy disk in drive B:

1. Open a drive window for drive C and another drive window for drive B.

2. Select the directories you want to copy from drive C in the tree pane, so that you include all the files as well.

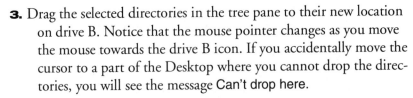

If you ever select files from the file pane, the mouse pointer will change into a single or multiple file-folder symbol, depending on whether you are copying one file or many files.

Moving *deletes the original, so use this operation with care.*

3. Drag the selected directories in the tree pane to their new location on drive B. Notice that the mouse pointer changes as you move the mouse towards the drive B icon. If you accidentally move the cursor to a part of the Desktop where you cannot drop the directories, you will see the message **Can't drop here**.

4. A dialog box opens to confirm your choice. Click on OK and a horizontal graph will show you the progress made by the copy operation. Click on Cancel any time you want to abort the copy.

When the copy is complete, you will see that an identical directory structure has been created on the disk in drive B.

You can also copy files into the current directory on a disk by dragging the files you want to copy directly to the drive icon or minimized drive-window icon on the Desktop, without having to open the drive window for that directory. The same dialog box opens as before to confirm that you want to copy the files, and the same horizontal graph shows progress made by the copy operation. You can always open the drive window afterwards to check that the copy worked as you expected.

Moving a file or directory is the same as making a copy and then deleting the original, except it is all done as a single process instead of two separate operations. To move files or directories, just follow the same steps as described above for copying, except hold down the Alt key as you perform the operation. If you don't hold down the Alt key, the move becomes a copy, and you will have to delete the original files or directories manually.

Copying and Moving from the File Menu

You can also use selections from the File menu to perform copy and move operations on files and directories. Just follow these steps to make a copy, substituting the Move command if you want to move them instead:

1. Either select Copy from the File menu, or press F8, to open the Copy dialog box, as Figure 5.8 shows.

2. Type the name of the file you want to copy into the Copy text box; you can use wildcard characters to extend the copy to include groups of files. If you selected a file before you chose the Copy selection, its name is already entered into the text box for you. If you selected several files, the Copy text box is replaced by an entry that displays the number of files you selected.

3. If you want to copy any subdirectories, click the Include Subdirectories check box.

4. Type the destination drive and directory name into the To text box. You can also open the drop-down list box to display a list of the destinations you have used most recently. This neatly allows you to avoid having to retype the destination information when you often repeat the same copy operation.

If you click on the Select button, the dialog box expands to show a drop-down list box for the destination drive and a tree list for the destination directory.

RENAMING FILES AND DIRECTORIES

To rename a file, select the file in a file pane first, then choose Rename from the File menu. The dialog box shown in Figure 5.9 opens, showing the original file name; enter the new name you want to use into the To text box, then choose OK.

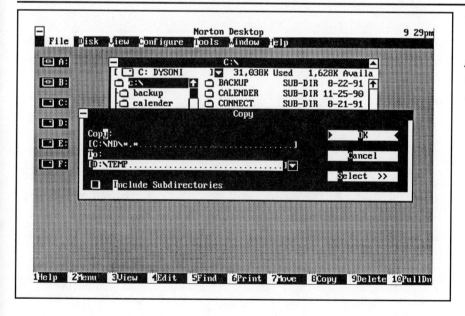

FIGURE 5.8:

Use the Copy option from the File menu to copy files from one disk to another

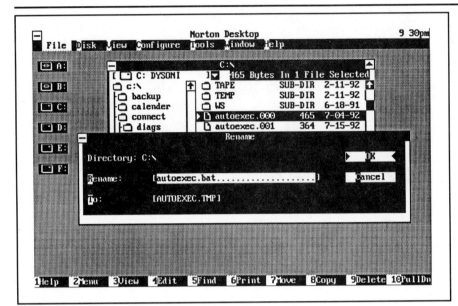

The Rename command from the File menu lets you rename files or directories

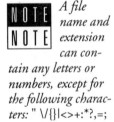

A file name and extension can contain any letters or numbers, except for the following characters: " \/{}|<>+:*?,=; *or a space.*

A file name can contain up to eight characters before the period, and the extension can contain three characters after the period.

Renaming a directory is exactly the same as renaming a file. First select the directory, choose Rename from the File menu, and type the new name into the dialog box. Directory names are also limited to eight characters before the optional extension.

MAKING A NEW DIRECTORY

You can make a new directory on any disk, as long as there is room for it, by using the Make Directory command from the File menu. The Desktop, by default, creates the new directory as a subdirectory of the current directory, unless you tell it otherwise.

To make a new directory, just follow these steps:

1. Open a drive window on the drive you want to work with.

2. Select Make Directory from the File menu.

3. When the dialog box opens, type in the name you want for the new directory. The path name of the current directory is also shown in this dialog box.

4. If you want to create the directory on another drive or in a different directory, choose Select to expand the dialog box. Now you can choose the drive where you want to make the new directory and choose the parent directory from the tree display. Click on OK when you are done.

DELETING FILES AND DIRECTORIES

Deleting files and directories is an operation that you should always be careful about. It is very easy to delete a file, but not so easy to bring it back again. Norton Desktop contains several novel and creative solutions to this problem that are described in detail in later chapters: UnErase and its companion program, SmartCan, are described in detail in Chapter 12.

In this section I discuss deleting files using the Delete command in the File menu; this is the same as clicking the Delete button on the button bar. Follow these steps:

1. Select the file, group of files, or directory that you want to remove and choose Delete. When the dialog box shown in Figure 5.10 opens, the name of the file or directory is shown in the text box.

2. Click on OK to delete the file or directory.

3. A warning window opens, asking you to confirm that you want to continue with the deletion. Select Yes to continue, or—if you have selected several files for deletion—click on Yes to All. If you are absolutely positive that you want to delete all of the selected files, clicking on Yes to All avoids having to answer the same question for every file you selected. Click on No if you don't want to delete the file, and click on Cancel to abort the whole delete operation.

The Delete dialog box also contains a Browse command button so that you can search for the file you want to delete if it is not in the current directory or on the current drive.

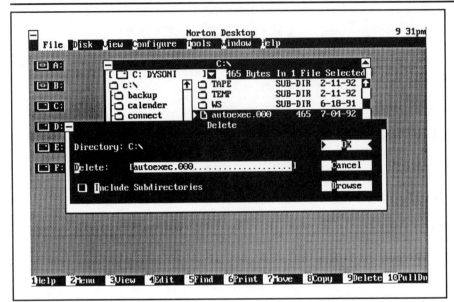

CHANGING FILE ATTRIBUTES

File attributes are characteristics or properties that you or DOS can assign to
files. You can look at and change these attributes if you choose Properties
from the File menu. A dialog box opens, showing the attributes already set
for the file indicated by a check mark, along with information on the file size
and the time and date it was last changed.

As an example, change to the root directory of drive C and select a file
called IMAGE.DAT, then choose Properties from the File menu. You can see
from Figure 5.11 that this file has the read-only attribute set, and it may or
may not have the archive attribute set, depending on how often you back up
your system.

Beware of changing many of these attributes, especially making too
many files read-only. At first glance it may seem like a good idea because
read-only files cannot be changed or deleted—right? Well, almost. Many
commercial programs write the details of your computer hardware back into
their own files. If you change these files to read-only and then reconfigure

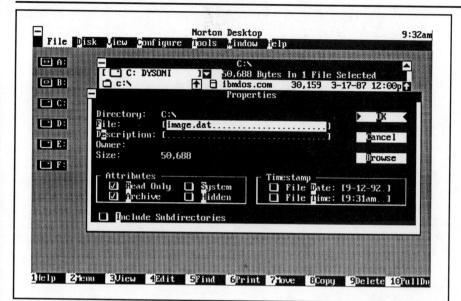

FIGURE 5.11:

Select Properties from the File menu to look at or change a file's attributes

the program when you add new hardware to your system, the program will try to update its files, find that they are now read-only, and report an error. Some programs display an understandable error message, but many programs are rather cryptic.

You should also resist the temptation to hide too many files, because the saying "out of sight, out of mind" is all too true. There is absolutely no point in hiding a program, because you will quickly forget that it is there—and when that happens, you will stop using it. If a directory is getting cluttered with files that you do not use often, do not hide them by setting the hidden attribute. Instead, copy them to another directory, or—better—back them up to floppy disk and keep them safe somewhere in case you change your mind.

EDITING FILES

The Edit command in the File menu launches the default text editor, which, if you selected it during the installation process, is the Norton Desktop

Editor. This means that you can edit text files without ever leaving the Desktop. To open a file for editing, just follow these steps:

1. Select the file in a drive window that you want to edit.

2. Choose Edit from the File menu to open the Editor containing the file you selected.

3. Edit the file using normal Editor commands. The Editor is described in detail in Chapter 7.

4. Save the file and exit from the Editor to return to the Desktop.

You can change this default editor to another program if you want to. I describe how to do this in Chapter 9.

MANAGING YOUR DISKS FROM THE DESKTOP

Several very important disk management functions are available right from the Desktop's Disk menu. In the next few sections I will describe these commands and show you how to manage your disks.

COPYING DISKS

The Copy Diskette command in the Disk menu duplicates an original, or *source,* disk onto a *target* disk. This means that both disks must be of the same capacity. For instance, you cannot use Copy Diskette to copy files from a 360K floppy to a 720K floppy disk. If this is what you want to do, then you must use the Copy or Move commands and enter the wildcards *.* into the Copy text box. This specifies that you want to copy all the files from the source disk onto the target disk.

Another important factor to remember when you use Copy Diskette is that the copy process will overwrite any files that were on the target disk before you began the copy, and you will be unable to recover them. If it is important that you preserve those files, then—again—use Copy rather than Copy Diskette.

To duplicate the contents of one disk onto another of the same capacity, follow these steps:

1. Insert the source disk into the correct disk drive. If you have a dual-drive system where both drives have the same capacity, you can insert the target disk into the other disk drive. If you have a single-drive system (or a dual-drive system where the drives are of different capacities), you will be prompted to swap the source and target disks as necessary.

2. Select Copy Diskette from the Disk menu.

3. When the Copy Diskette dialog box opens, as shown in Figure 5.12, choose the source drive in the From drop-down list.

4. Choose the target drive from the To drop-down list box and click on OK to start copying.

5. If the target disk is formatted and contains files, a dialog box will open to give you a chance to change to another target disk and avoid overwriting these files. If you don't want to preserve the files, then continue with the copy. If the target disk is *not* formatted, a dialog box will open, giving you the chance to swap the disk for one that is. To format the target disk, click on OK. (You cannot copy files to an unformatted disk.)

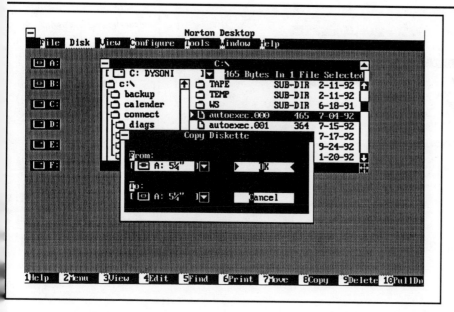

FIGURE 5.12:

The Copy Diskette command in the Disk menu makes an exact duplicate of your original disk

When the copy is complete, a dialog box opens, asking if you want to make another copy of the same source disk.

FORMATTING DISKS

You cannot format a hard disk with Format Diskette.

To format a blank floppy disk directly from the Desktop, follow these steps:

1. Insert a blank floppy disk of the appropriate capacity into the correct drive.

2. Choose Format Diskette from the Disk menu.

3. When the Format Diskette dialog box opens (see Figure 5.13), select the drive letter, formatted size, and format type from the appropriate drop-down boxes. I will explain each of the three format types in a moment.

You can also format floppy disks using this dialog box if you type SFORMAT at the DOS prompt.

4. Click on Format to start the process.

You can make several choices when you format your disk: you can choose the format type, make the disk into a bootable disk, or save information that the UnFormat program can use in the event of an accident.

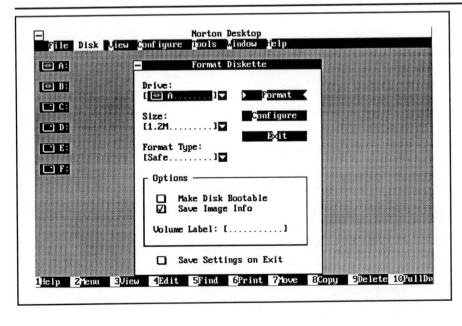

FIGURE 5.13:

Set up your formatting options in the Format Diskette dialog box

The format types are as follows:

See Chapter 12 for information on recovering files.

Safe protects against accidental data loss because it formats the disk without overwriting the existing data on the disk. It saves information about the files on the disk in a special file that later can be used by the UnErase and UnFormat programs to reconstruct the original data on the disk before it was formatted. When you select the Safe format, the Save Image Info check box is automatically checked for you. When you use this selection with a blank disk that has never been formatted before, you will be asked whether you wish to do a Destructive format.

Quick is extremely fast because it only creates a new system area on the disk and does not overwrite the data area. You cannot use Quick on a blank disk that has never been formatted before. When you select Quick, you also have the choice of saving UnFormat information or not, as you wish.

DOS overwrites and destroys all the original data on the disk, making the data unrecoverable. This is equivalent to the standard DOS format operation.

The other options include the following:

Make Diskette Bootable lets you create a bootable disk by installing the DOS system files on the disk once it has been formatted, so that you can use the disk to start your computer. This selection is optional. However, remember that the DOS files take up space on the floppy disk, so if you know you will never use the disk to start your system, there is little point in sacrificing disk space for them.

Save Image Info saves information that can be used by UnErase and UnFormat in the event that you want to recover the files originally on the disk before you formatted it. This setting is not available with the DOS format or with the Safe format option used on a new blank floppy disk.

Volume Label makes a special entry that can be up to eleven characters in length on each disk. Make the volume label descriptive: for example, you might label a floppy disk containing word-processor documents as MEMOS, or a disk that contains spreadsheet files as BUDGETS. This label is displayed in the drive windows on the Desktop. I describe adding a volume label to a disk later on in this chapter.

A NOTE ON DISK CAPACITY

It is very important that you format disks at the appropriate capacity in your drive; otherwise, sooner or later, you will lose data. The normal capacities are as follows:

◆ 360K. These are the normal 5¼-inch floppies. They have a formatted capacity of 360K. Do not format these disks as 1.2MB disks or you will lose data.

◆ 1.2MB. These 5¼-inch disks are marked in some way as *high density.*

◆ 720K. This is the normal size for 3½-inch disks. They have a formatted capacity of 720K. Do not format these disks at a higher density or you will lose data.

◆ 1.44MB. Use this capacity for 3½-inch disks marked as high-density disks. These disks have a small, square hole opposite the write-protect slide, so you can tell them apart from the 720K disks by their physical appearance. Do not format these disks at a higher capacity or you will lose data.

◆ 2.88MB. If you are using DOS 5 and have very high capacity 3½-inch disk drives, be sure to use disks marked in some way as *very* or *extra high density* in this drive.

Check the labeling on the outside of the disk box or on the disk label to be sure that you are using the correct capacity disk on your system.

ADDING A VOLUME LABEL TO A DISK

The Label Disk selection from the Disk menu lets you add or change a disk's volume label. A floppy disk has just one volume label, but a large hard disk that is divided into several partitions can have a volume label for each partition. To add or change a disk's volume label, follow these steps:

1. Select Label Disk from the Disk menu.

2. When the dialog box opens, the volume label, if there is one, is shown in a text box. Enter the new volume label into the text box and choose OK.

3. If you want to work with a different drive, click on the Drive prompt button to see a list of all the drives on your system and select a different drive.

Sometimes you know the name of the file that you want to work with, but you can't remember where it is, or which directory it is in. On other occasions you may not be able to remember the complete name of the file, but you can remember a few words or phrases that the file contains. Unfortunately, the commands available in DOS are of little use in this situation. SuperFind, however, can find a lost or misplaced file anywhere in your directory structure on any drive, and can locate specific occurrences of text inside that file. We'll look at SuperFind next.

USING SUPERFIND

SuperFind contains predefined search groups of files called *file sets,* and predefined groups of drives and directories called *location sets.* A file set is a named group of file types you can search for, and a location set is a named group of disks that you can search through. In other words, you use a file set to establish the file types you want to find, and a location set to define which disks will be searched. For example, one of the predefined file sets automatically selects just program files, while one of the location sets automatically chooses all disk drives except floppy disk drives. These sets are very convenient shorthand ways of defining a search, and we'll look at both kinds of sets later in this section.

There are several steps to follow in using SuperFind to locate a file:

1. Tell SuperFind *what* to look for in the Find Files text box. Several useful file sets are provided to help define the search.

2. Tell SuperFind *where* to look using the Where text box. This time several location sets are available to help narrow the search.

3. Tell SuperFind about any text you are looking for.

4. Select any of the advanced search criteria you want to use.

5. Start the search running.

When SuperFind locates files that match these settings, a drive window opens, listing details of the found files. You can then use the normal drive window commands to work with the files you have just located.

LOCATING FILES WITH SUPERFIND

To launch SuperFind, choose Find from the File menu, or click on Find (F5) on the button bar. However you start the program, you will see the Super-Find dialog box shown in Figure 5.14.

There is one entry on the SuperFind menu bar, Options, but you can use SuperFind in its simplest mode—to locate one or more misplaced files on your disks—without using the Options menu at all. Enter as much of the file name as you can remember into the Find Files text box; then use the wildcard characters ? or * to represent the part of the file name that you cannot remember. You can also choose one of the predefined file sets in the Find Files drop-down list box:

All Files is equivalent to the wildcard statement *.* and finds all types of all files.

All Files Except Programs finds all files except files that have .EXE, .COM, or .BAT file-name extensions.

Database Files finds all files made by dBASE or other programs that use dBASE file-name extensions, and all files made by Symantec's Q&A database program.

Documents finds all document files with file-name extensions of .DOC, .TXT, and .WRI.

Programs finds all files that have extensions of .EXE, .COM, or .BAT, excluding all others.

Spreadsheet Files finds all files that use Lotus 1-2-3 and Microsoft Excel compatible file-name extensions: .WK?, .WQ?, and .XLS.

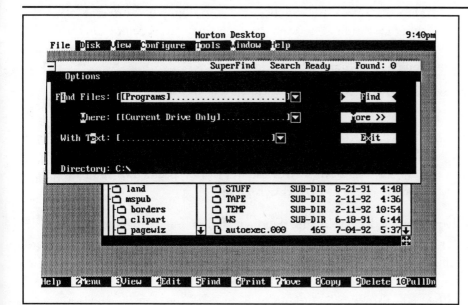

FIGURE 5.14:

*Use the SuperFind
dialog box to enter your
file-search criteria*

*Searching
a large
disk like a
network
file server can take a
long time. Be sure
that you want to use
this option before you
start the search.*

For the next step, choose where you want SuperFind to look for the lost file, and enter it into the Where text box. You can also choose from several predefined location sets:

Current Drive Only includes just the current drive. This is the setting you will probably use most often.

All Drives includes all drives accessible to your system including floppy disks, CD-ROMS, and network file servers. This kind of search can take a long time to complete.

All Drives Except Floppies excludes only floppy disks from the search.

Current Dir and Subdirs restricts the search even further, searching only the current directory—and subdirectories if there are any.

Current Directory Only restricts the search to just the current directory. This is another location set that you will use quite often.

Floppy Drives Only searches only your floppy disk drives. Make sure that you have inserted the appropriate disks before you start to use this location set; otherwise, you will see a warning message when you click on Start to begin the search.

Local Hard Drives Only excludes any network drives from the search.

Network Drives Only searches just your network drives, and ignores your local hard disk.

Path searches all the drives and directories specified by the Path statement in your AUTOEXEC.BAT file.

Now that you have told SuperFind which files to look for, and how to look for them, you can click on the Find command button to start the search running. The Find button changes into the Stop command button during the search, and you can click on Stop if you want to halt or abort the search early. When you first start SuperFind, it displays the current directory, but as a search proceeds, this changes to show the directory being searched, and a count of the number of files found is also shown. When the search is complete, you will see the message **Search Done**, unless you stop the search in which case you will see the message **Search Aborted**. If files are found that match the search criteria, a drive window will open that lists all the files and their locations. In fact SuperFind opens a new drive window for each search you complete, and these drive windows are individually numbered in sequence so that you can tell them apart. You can use the Desktop Window menu to change from one window to another.

SEARCHING FOR TEXT

*You cannot use the wildcard characters ? and * in a search string because Super-Find will look for these specific text characters instead of interpreting them as wildcards.*

If you want to find a specific piece of text that you think is in one of your files, enter that string into the With Text text box. SuperFind now searches through your files looking for the text you entered as the search text, or *search string*. Any files found that match the Find Files specification and contain the With Text search string will be displayed in the SuperFind drive window. The default setting for SuperFind text searches is not case-sensitive, so *NORTON, Norton,* and *norton* will all match. If you want to make the text search more specific, turn on Match Upper/Lowercase in the Options menu to force the search to be case-sensitive.

ADVANCED FILE SEARCHES

There are several advanced search options you can access if you click on the More command button to open the lower portion of the SuperFind dialog box. Figure 5.15 shows this expanded SuperFind dialog box. After you expand the dialog box, the More command button is relabeled Less, and you can use it to shrink the dialog box back down to its former size.

SuperFind lets you select criteria to focus the search even further by selecting one or more of the following:

◆ Date

◆ Time

◆ Size

◆ Owner (network only)

◆ Attributes

Let's look at each of these selections in turn.

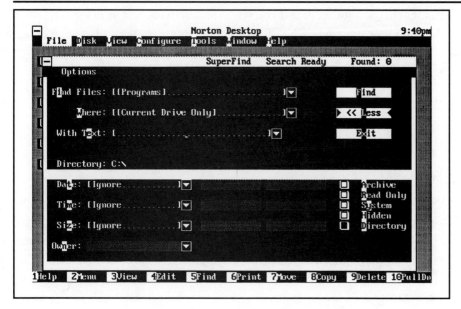

FIGURE 5.15:

The SuperFind dialog box contains several advanced search options

Searching by File Date

You have the following options in the Date drop-down list box:

◆ Ignore

◆ On

◆ Not On

◆ Before

◆ Before or On

◆ After

◆ After or On

◆ Between

◆ Not Between

The default setting is Ignore, but you can choose any one of these settings. One or two additional dialog boxes appear when you make a selection. You are asked to enter either a single date or a pair of dates depending on your choice. The current system date is shown in this dialog box, but you can change that to another date if you wish. The Between selection includes only the dates you enter, while Not Between does not include the dates you enter.

Searching by File Time

You have a similar set of selections in the Time drop-down list box:

◆ Ignore

◆ At

◆ Not At

◆ Before

◆ Before or At

◆ After

◆ After or At

◆ Between

◆ Not Between

The default setting for Time is Ignore, but you can choose any setting. The Between and Not Between time options work just like their counterparts under the Date heading described above.

Searching by File Size

The Size options include:

◆ Ignore

◆ Less Than

◆ Greater Than

◆ Between

◆ Not Between

The default for Size is Ignore. The acceptable range of file sizes goes from 0 to 65MB.

Searching by File Owner

If you are currently logged on to your network, you will see another entry for Owner at the bottom of the SuperFind dialog box. If you are not logged on to the network, this box is dimmed and unavailable. The default setting is Ignore. The drop-down list box contains a list of user names specific to your network, and you can search for files belonging to just one user at a time.

Searching by File Attributes

You can also search for files using the setting of specific file attributes as search criteria. Each file can have different settings for each of the four attributes: archive, read-only, hidden, and system. The Attribute check boxes can have one of three possible states:

Checked. A check mark appears in the box, and SuperFind searches for files with this attribute set.

Blank. There is nothing in the check box and SuperFind searches for files with this attribute *cleared* or *not set.*

Gray. The check box is grayed out. SuperFind ignores this attribute during a search.

TIPS FOR OPTIMIZING A SEARCH

Using advanced options can make a search extremely specific, and that is a good way to make the search run as fast as possible, or to *optimize* it. There are also several other things you can do to optimize a search:

◆ Turn on Match Upper/Lowercase in the Options menu to make the search as specific as possible.

◆ Use as many of the advanced options as you can.

◆ Use wildcards carefully in the Find Files text box to limit the search as much as possible.

◆ Select the smallest and most restricted choice in the Where text box.

CREATING YOUR OWN FILE AND LOCATION SETS

You can have up to 16 file sets and 16 location sets active at the same time.

If you find yourself using particular file specifications in the Find Files or Where text boxes over and over again, you can create your own file sets or location sets to automate this part of the search process. Click on Search Sets in the Options menu to open the dialog box shown in Figure 5.16.

The process of creating a file set or a location set is essentially the same. In the dialog box, click the File Sets option button to add or edit a file set, or click the Location Sets option button to add or edit a location set.

Adding or Editing a File Set

To delete a file or location set, highlight the victim and click on the Delete command button.

Figure 5.17 shows the dialog box that opens when you click on Add for a file set; the Edit dialog box is very similar. Enter the name you want to use for the file set into the Name text box (the brackets are added automatically). This is the name you will see in the Find Files drop-down list box in the main SuperFind dialog box.

Enter one or more file specifications into the Definitions text box. You can enter several file specifications into this text box if you want to search for different types of files at the same time, or you can just enter one specific

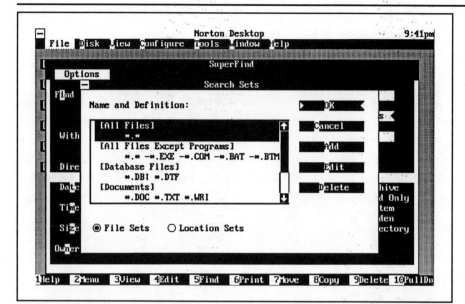

FIGURE 5.16:
*Use the Search Sets
dialog box to customize
your own file or
location sets*

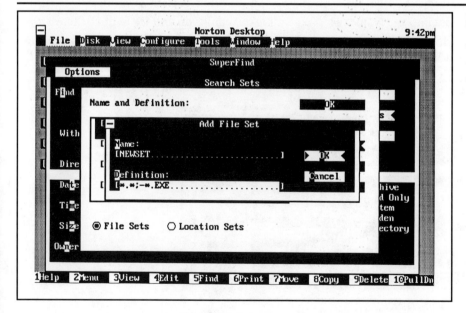

FIGURE 5.17:
*Define a new file set
in the Add File Set
dialog box*

entry. If you use more than one, separate them with a space, a comma, a plus sign, or a semicolon. If you want to exclude a file specification from the list, place a minus sign before the entry. For example, to include all possible file types except .EXE files, type:

.;–*.EXE

The *.* wildcard statement includes all file types, while the –*.EXE specifically excludes all files with the .EXE extension. You can use the single character wildcard symbol, ?, the multiple character wildcard, *, or the wildcard character ¦, which represents one or fewer characters. An example might make this clearer. In SuperFind, ????.EXE finds all executable files with exactly four characters in their file names, whereas ¦¦¦¦.EXE finds all executable files with four or fewer characters in their names. To make the ¦ character appear on your screen, type the ¦ key.

Click on OK to add your new file set to the list available in SuperFind.

Adding or Editing a Location Set

When you click on Add for a location set, you will see the dialog box shown in Figure 5.18. Enter the name you want to associate with this new location set into the Name text box. This is the name you will see in the Where drop-down list box in the main SuperFind dialog box. In the Definition text box,

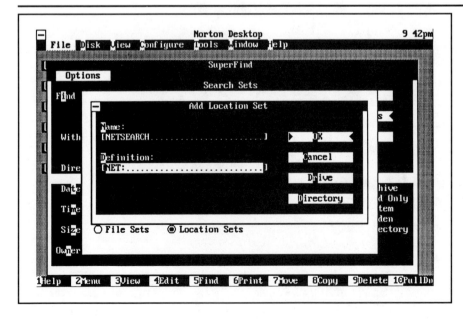

FIGURE 5.18:

Create a new location set in the Add Location Set dialog box

specify the disk drives and directories to use in this new location set; you cannot specify files in this definition box. SuperFind supports the following shorthand disk-drive specifiers:

Floppy:	All floppy disk drives
Hard:	All local nonnetwork hard disks
Net:	All network hard disks
*:	All drives
d:	Drive *d*
d1:–dn:	All disk drives from *d1* to *dn,* inclusive
d1:,d2:	Two or more named disk drives. Separate the entries by a comma

as well as the following shorthand directory specifiers:

.	The current directory
..	The parent directory of the current directory
d:\path	A specific directory
d:\path+	A specific directory and all its subdirectories
path1, path2	Two or more directories. Separate the entries by a comma or a space
%name%	All the directories included in the DOS environment variable specified by *name.* This is usually of special interest to programmers using SuperFind

You can also use the Drive command button to open a dialog box containing two group boxes. One contains icons for all the drives on your system, and the other contains check boxes for the following groups: all floppy disks, all hard disks, and all network drives. Make your selections, then click on OK to return to the Add Location Set dialog box.

There is a command button called Directory that you can use to open the Select Directory to Search dialog box. Here you can select a drive and directory to add to the location set. Check the Include Subdirectories box if you want to include the subdirectories of the selected directory. Click on OK to return to the Add Location Set dialog box.

Now you should have a name for the location set, as well as path and directory entries, each separated by commas in the Definition text box. Click on OK to add this new location set to the list in SuperFind.

Now you can use your own file and location sets next time you want to use SuperFind to search for that elusive lost file.

CREATING BATCH FILES FROM A FILE LIST

The Create Batch entry in the Options menu creates a DOS batch file that runs on each of the files that SuperFind locates. Select Create Batch to open the dialog box shown in Figure 5.19.

See Chapter 18 for more information on using batch files.

The batch file will contain one line for each file listed in the SuperFind drive window, and you can use this dialog box to add commands before and after each file name. You must first enter a name for the batch file; then enter any commands you want to use before or after all the file names that SuperFind locates. If you just want to create an ASCII file containing the names of the found files, leave both of these text boxes empty. Several of the steps involved in converting this list of files into a useful batch file can be automated by clicking

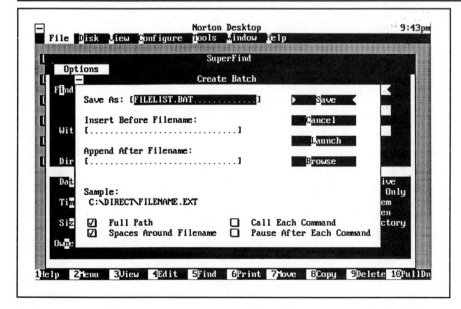

FIGURE 5.19:

The Create Batch dialog box lets you create a DOS batch file using the results of a SuperFind search

on one or more of the check boxes in the lower part of this dialog box:

Full Path. Check this box if you want to use the full DOS path before each file name. Leave this box unchecked if you want to use just the file name and extension without any path information.

Spaces Around Filename. Check this box to add a space before and after each file name. This can make the batch file easier to read. However, there may be times when you want a character like a quote mark to be placed right against the file name. If this is the case, leave this box unchecked.

Call Each Command. In DOS 3.3, and later, there is a batch command called CALL that you can use to invoke other batch files from inside a batch file. If you want to insert a CALL command at the beginning of each line in the batch file, check this box.

Pause After Each Command. When you check this box, the DOS PAUSE command is inserted between every line in your batch file. This means that you can stop your batch file running if you press Ctrl+C when you see the Press any key to continue... prompt.

To create and test your batch file, click on the Launch command button. This runs the batch file in a DOS window. If there are errors in the batch file, it will be aborted. When you are happy that you have everything in place, click on OK to save the batch file and return to the SuperFind dialog box. This does not have to be the end of the road for your batch file. You can use the Edit command from the File menu to open the Desktop Editor on the file to continue development.

By now it should be clear that you can perform all your file, disk, and directory work, without ever leaving the Norton Desktop. In the next chapter we'll look at how you can print or view files from the Desktop.

CHAPTER 6

Viewing and Printing Files

This chapter describes the different methods you can use with the Desktop to view and print files. It used to be that if you wanted to check the contents of a particular file—to see if it was worth keeping or not—you first had to load the application that created the file, and then load the file itself. With several files from big application programs, this could take forever. With the Desktop, you can view files in several different formats without invoking the application program that originally made them.

In fact, you don't even have to know which program made them. Many different data formats are available to help make sense of the data. The files are displayed in what is called their *native format,* a format that closely approximates the way that you are used to looking at the data. The

Desktop contains formats, or *viewers,* for over 50 different applications, including Microsoft Word, dBASE, Excel, and Quattro, as well as graphics files such as CompuServe's .GIF files, Windows bitmaps, .PCX files, and even .TIF files.

USING THE DRIVE WINDOW VIEW PANE

The fastest way of looking at the contents of a file is to use a view pane in a drive window. Here are the steps:

1. Open a drive window for the disk.

2. Select the file you want to view in the file pane.

3. Select View Pane from the Desktop's View menu. A view pane will open below the tree and file panes as a third part of the drive window.

If the file is too large to be displayed all at once, use the scroll bars to move through the file. You can also drag the drive window border and make the window bigger, but this increases the size of the whole drive window, not just the view pane.

The view pane shows the contents of the file you just selected in the file pane. If you leave the view pane open and choose another file, its contents will appear in the view pane replacing the first file. You can only look at one file at a time, unless you open a second drive window.

Desktop knows how to load the correct viewer format by looking at the file-name extension of the file you select. If Desktop decides that the file is a dBASE file, then the file is displayed in the database format; if Desktop decides that the file is a spreadsheet file, it will use the spreadsheet format; and so on. If the Desktop does not recognize the file you select, it uses the default viewer. When the view pane is active, you can force the Desktop to use a different viewer by selecting Viewer from the View menu, then choosing Change Viewer from the Viewer submenu. The Change Viewer list box opens, containing the selections shown in Table 6.1. Make your selection from the list and click on OK. The contents of the file are now displayed in the new viewer format. Be aware that some of the formats are just plain unsuitable for certain file types.

COMPRESSION PROGRAM VIEWERS
ARC
LHARC
ZIP
ZOO

DATABASE VIEWERS
Clipper
dBASE
FoxBase/FoxPro
Paradox
Q&A
Reflex

GRAPHICS VIEWERS
CompuServe GIF
Micrografx Charisma
Micrografx Designer
Micrografx Draw
PCX
Pictor
TIF
WordPerfect Bitmap
WordPerfect Clipart

TABLE 6.1:
*File Viewers Available
in Norton Viewer*

MISCELLANEOUS VIEWERS
DESQview PIF
EXE
Hex

SPREADSHEET VIEWERS
Excel
Lotus
Microsoft Works
Mosaic Twin
Multiplan
Quattro
Symphony
VP Planner Plus
Words & Figures

WINDOWS VIEWERS
Bitmap
Clipboard
Icon
Metafile
Paint
PIF
Word for Windows

TABLE 6.1:
File Viewers Available in Norton Viewer (continued)

WORD PROCESSOR VIEWERS
Ami/Ami Pro
ASCII (Text View)
Lotus Manuscript
Microsoft Word
Microsoft Works
Professional Write
Q&A Write
Volkswriter
WordPerfect
WordStar
XyWrite

TABLE 6.1:
File Viewers Available in Norton Viewer (continued)

Use the ASCII (Text View) viewer if you want to look at text files such as AUTOEXEC.BAT, CONFIG.SYS, or any of the Windows .INI initialization files. The dBASE viewer displays files made by dBASE or by programs that make a dBASE-compatible file format. The Hex viewer can display the contents of any type of file, but is best suited to displaying the contents of binary, or program, files.

Although several different graphics file viewers are shown in the Change Viewer list box, you cannot use them in the view pane. To view a graphics file, you must use the Norton Viewer, described next.

VIEWING FILES WITH THE NORTON VIEWER

The view pane is fine for some tasks, but to take a closer look at a file, or to look at a graphics file, the Norton Viewer is what you need.

There are several ways you can start the Norton Viewer to look at a file:

◆ Click on the View (F3) button on the Desktop button bar.

◆ Choose the View option from the Desktop File menu.

◆ Double-click on the file VIEW.EXE.

◆ Run the program VIEW.EXE from the DOS prompt.

SELECTING FILES

To select a file from inside the Norton Viewer:

1. Choose Open from the Viewer's File menu.

2. Select the file you want to look at in the Browse for a File to View dialog box using the list boxes, or you can type the name of the file directly into the File text box.

3. When you have made your choice, click on OK to view the file.

Figure 6.1 shows the Browse for a File to View dialog box.

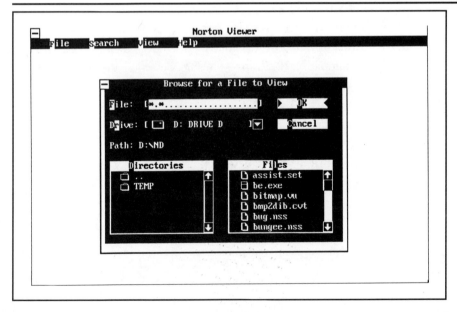

FIGURE 6.1:

Select the file you want to view using the Browse for a File to View dialog box

VIEWING SPREADSHEET FILES

Figure 6.2 shows part of a spreadsheet file displayed in the Norton Viewer. Cells in the file are arranged just as they are by the application program that created the spreadsheet in the first place. Use the arrow keys, the mouse, or the scroll bars to move around the spreadsheet. The line at the top of the spreadsheet, just under the menu bar, indicates the current cell address, as well as the contents of the cell—whether it is a text entry, contains a formula, or is just an empty cell.

The full name of the file you are viewing is shown at the bottom of the window, along with the name of the viewer being used to display the file.

If there is a particular cell you know you want to go to directly, use the Go To selection from the Search menu. This opens a dialog box for you to enter the reference for the cell you are interested in seeing. Enter a cell reference, click on OK, and you will go straight to the right place in the spreadsheet. Using Go To can be a great timesaver if you often use very large spreadsheets.

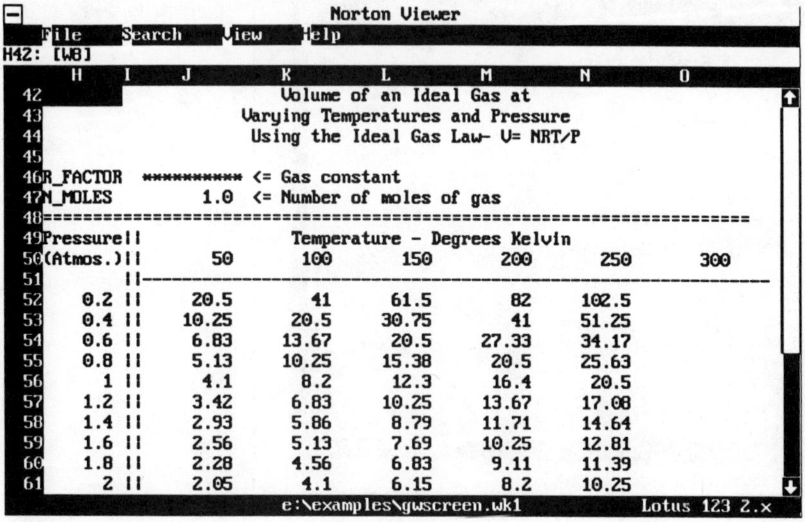

| NOTE NOTE | *If you are not viewing a spreadsheet, ASCII, word-processing or database file, the Go To option in the Search menu is dimmed out and unavailable.* |

FIGURE 6.2:

A spreadsheet file displayed in the Norton Viewer

VIEWING DATABASE FILES

Figure 6.3 shows part of a database file in the Norton Viewer. The line under the menu bar shows the database record number and the currently selected database field name.

As with the spreadsheet viewer, use the arrow keys, the mouse, or the scroll bars to move around and inspect the database file. Use the Goto command from the Search menu to go straight to a specific record in the database. This time a dialog box opens asking you to specify a record number. Enter a number, click on OK, and you will go straight to that individual record.

One of the commands in the Search menu is only available if you are viewing a database file, and you can use it to swap between a view of a single record, to a view of the whole database showing all the records that will fit in the View window. Use View Record to switch into single-record view mode, and click on View List if you want to return to the list of all records.

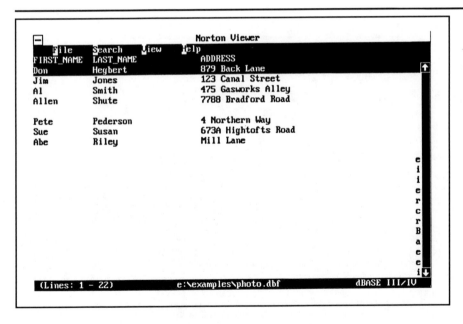

FIGURE 6.3:

A database file in the Norton Viewer

VIEWING BINARY FILES

The Hex viewer displays files in a special format, as Figure 6.4 shows. It allows you to look at any kind of file, including .EXE files, files made by your word processor, even files made by your spreadsheet. In Figure 6.4, the leftmost column of hexadecimal (hex) numbers on the screen shows the location of the data in terms of a byte count from the beginning of the file. The central part of the window shows the actual data in the file as two-digit hex numbers, and each line displays 16 bytes of information. On the right side of the window, these same 16 bytes are shown in ASCII form.

From the display of the Norton Desktop README.TXT file in Figure 6.4, it is easy to see the correspondence between the hex and ASCII parts of the window. This correspondence may not be so easy to see if you view an .EXE file in the Hex viewer; in fact some of the data will be completely unreadable. This is because an .EXE or program file is a *binary* file, not an ASCII text file, and contains statements that were never intended to be read as text. These nondisplayable characters are shown as dots in the text portion of this window.

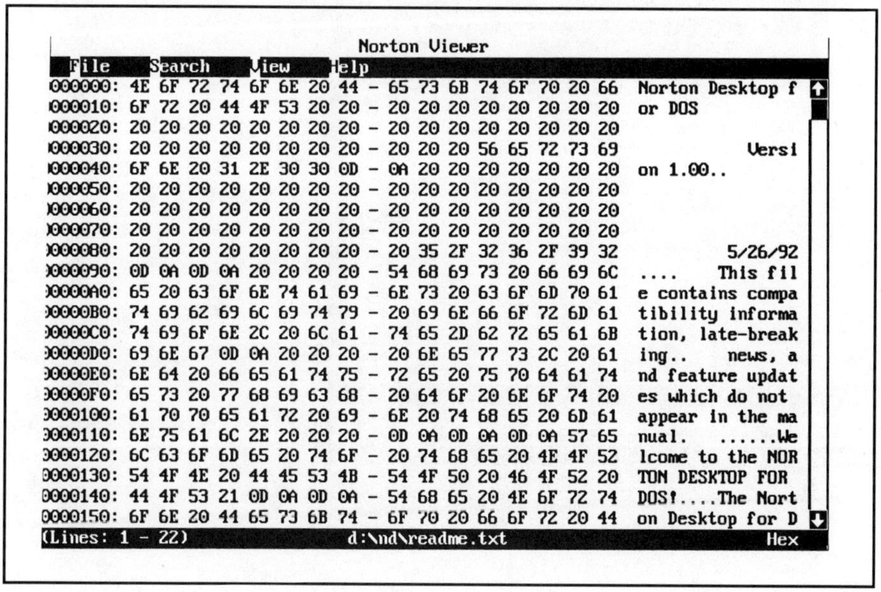

FIGURE 6.4:

Part of the README.TXT file shown in the Hex viewer

If the file you are working with was made by one of the popular file-compression utility programs like ARC, LHARC, PKZIP, or by the Compress option in the Desktop's File menu, you will see another file viewer, as Figure 6.5 shows. The ZIP viewer lists information, line by line, for each of the original files inside the ZIP file, including the original file name, original size in bytes, compressed size in bytes, the file time and date, the compression method, and the CRC (Cyclical Redundancy Check)—a kind of checksum. The other compressed-file viewers show very similar information.

VIEWING GRAPHICS FILES

The Norton Viewer also simplifies looking at bit-mapped and .TIF image files. Figure 6.6 shows a sample .TIF file containing part of a dog training company logo displayed in the TIF viewer.

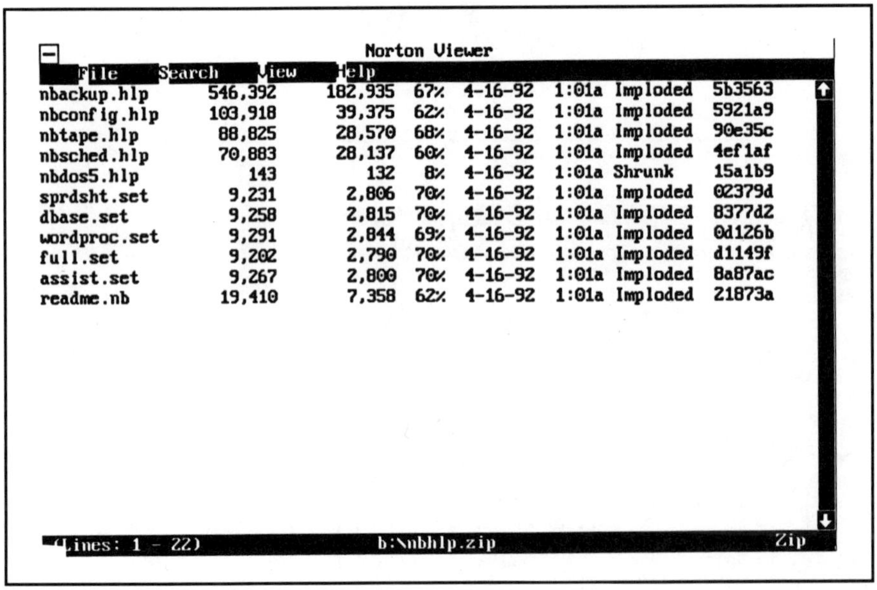

FIGURE 6.5:
A PKZIP file displayed in the ZIP viewer

```
                            Norton Viewer
    File      Search      View      Help
nbackup.hlp    546,392   182,935  67%  4-16-92  1:01a  Imploded  5b3563
nbconfig.hlp   103,918    39,375  62%  4-16-92  1:01a  Imploded  5921a9
nbtape.hlp      88,825    28,570  68%  4-16-92  1:01a  Imploded  90e35c
nbsched.hlp     70,883    28,137  60%  4-16-92  1:01a  Imploded  4ef1af
nbdos5.hlp         143       132   8%  4-16-92  1:01a  Shrunk    15a1b9
sprdsht.set      9,231     2,806  70%  4-16-92  1:01a  Imploded  02379d
dbase.set        9,258     2,815  70%  4-16-92  1:01a  Imploded  8377d2
wordproc.set     9,291     2,844  69%  4-16-92  1:01a  Imploded  0d126b
full.set         9,202     2,790  70%  4-16-92  1:01a  Imploded  d1149f
assist.set       9,267     2,800  70%  4-16-92  1:01a  Imploded  8a87ac
readme.nb       19,410     7,358  62%  4-16-92  1:01a  Imploded  21873a




(Lines: 1 - 22)             b:\nbhlp.zip                        Zip
```

FIGURE 6.6:

Norton Viewer can display several different types of graphics files, including the .TIF file shown here

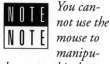

You cannot use the mouse to manipulate a graphical image, and while the image is on the screen, the Norton Viewer menus are not available.

If you press F1 for Help when you have a graphics image displayed in the viewer, you will see a list of keystrokes you can use to manipulate the image. These keystrokes are listed in Table 6.2. Some of the operations you can perform on graphics images are complex and may take some time to complete. If this is the case, Norton Viewer will put a message on the screen to reassure you that something is happening. For example, if you press the [key to rotate an image in a counter-clockwise direction, you will see a short message appear on the screen, and a moment or two later, your rotated image will appear on the screen.

SEARCHING FOR TEXT

If you want to find a particular piece of text that you think is in one of your files, open a viewer for the file and use the commands in the Search menu to look for the text or the *search string*.

KEYSTROKE	ACTION
Up arrow	scrolls image up
Down arrow	scrolls image down
Left arrow	scrolls image left
Right arrow	scrolls image right
PgUp	scrolls image up one page
PgDn	scrolls image down one page
Del	scrolls image left one page
End	scrolls image right one page
+	zoom in
−	zoom out
]	rotates image clockwise
[	rotates image counter clockwise
C	enables/disables screen refresh
I	inverts colors of the image
Home	returns the image to its original position and size
Esc	quits the graphical screen and returns to the Viewer window; you can also use the /q key

TABLE 6.2:

Viewer Commands for Manipulating Graphical Images

As an example, select the Norton Desktop README.TXT file in the SND directory, and open the Norton Viewer. Now choose Find from the Search menu. When the dialog box shown in Figure 6.7 opens, enter the text you want to search for into the Search Text text box. There are four check boxes in this dialog box, as follows:

◆ **Ignore Case** when checked will find all occurrences of the specified text regardless of the case of the letters. This means that norton, Norton, and NORTON will all be considered to be the same text. Clear this check box if you want to be specific about case.

◆ **Multiple Finds** lets you tell the Norton Viewer that you want to search for more than one occurrence of the specified text. When this box is checked the Find Text dialog box stays on the screen until you put it away by clicking on the Cancel command button. If you clear this check box, the Find Text dialog box will close when the first occurrence of your search text is located.

◆ **Forward** starts the search at the current cursor location and searches towards the end of the file. If you want to search though the whole file, make sure you are at the beginning of the file when you start the search running.

◆ **Backward** starts the search at the current cursor location, and searches backward towards the beginning of the file.

Enter **norton** into the Search Text box, check the Ignore Case and Forward check boxes, then click on Find when you are ready to start the search.

When a match is found, the matching text is highlighted. You can either click on the Find command button again to look for more matches, or you can use the Find Next or Find Previous commands from the Search menu. If no match is found, you will see the message No more matches found.

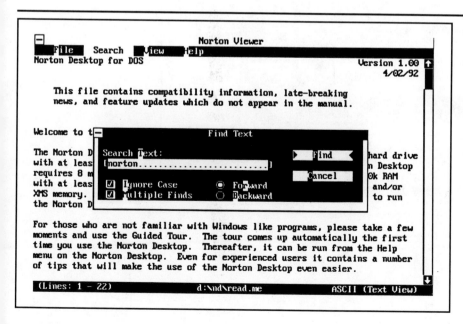

FIGURE 6.7:

This Find Text dialog box will search for a text string in the README.TXT file displayed in the Norton Viewer

If you are working with a binary file in the Hex viewer, you can also use Find, but this time the Find command opens a slightly different dialog box as Figure 6.8 shows. The Hex Search Dialog box shown in Figure 6.8 lets you enter your search text in either ASCII or as hex. Type your search text into the Text box if you want to specify the string as ASCII characters. You can enter up to 30 characters into the Text box. As you enter them, notice that they are automatically translated into hex and written into the Hex box.

If you prefer to enter the search string as hex instead of ASCII, tab to the Hex box and enter the string as pairs of hex characters. This time the search string is automatically translated from hex into ASCII and appears in the upper text box.

Use the Ignore Case, Multiple Finds, Forward, and Backward check boxes to narrow down the search, then click on Find when you are ready to start.

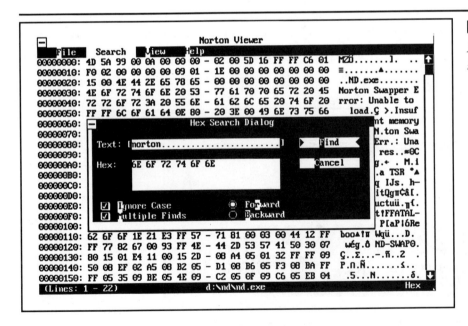

Enter the search string in either hex or ASCII

PRINTING FILES FROM THE DESKTOP

To finish this chapter, we'll take a look at how you can use the Norton Desktop to print text files quickly and easily. You cannot use this feature of the Desktop to print files generated by your word processor.

USING THE PRINT COMMAND

If you want to print a text file like AUTOEXEC.BAT or a file created using the Desktop Editor, follow these steps:

1. Open a drive window for the disk that contains the file you want to print.

2. Select or highlight the file from the list in the file pane.

3. Choose the Print command from the File menu, or use the Print (F6) button on the button bar.

4. Select OK to start printing the file.

If you are using the keyboard, follow these steps:

1. Choose the Print command from the File menu, or press Print (F6).

2. Enter the name of the file you want to print, or use Browse to find the file you want to print.

3. Select OK to start printing the file.

The steps you should follow to set up your printer for the Desktop are described in Chapter 9.

CHAPTER 7

Using the Norton Desktop Editor

This chapter looks at the Norton Desktop Editor, a powerful replacement for the DOS EDIT or EDLIN editors that you can use to look at and modify text files such as CONFIG.SYS, AUTOEXEC.BAT, or any of the Microsoft Windows .INI initialization files. You can work with just one file or several files at the same time, and you can cut and paste text to and from the Clipboard.

WORKING WITH THE DESKTOP EDITOR

To launch the Desktop Editor, click on Edit in the File menu, or use F4 from the button bar. Whichever method you choose, a standard browse dialog box opens so you can choose a drive and a file. When you have chosen a file, the Desktop Editor window opens as Figure 7.1 shows.

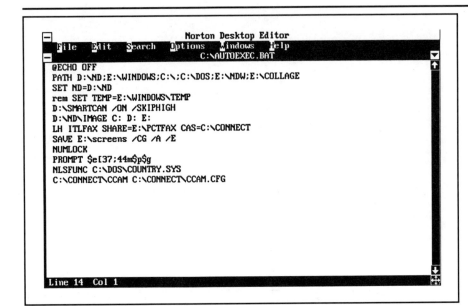

FIGURE 7.1:

The Desktop Editor containing the file AUTOEXEC.BAT

When you open the Desktop Editor on a single text file, one document window opens inside the Desktop Editor window. If you open several text files, each individual file occupies its own document window inside the main Desktop Editor window. You will also find an entry in the Windows menu that corresponds to each document window you open. Click on these entries to change from one document to another.

Each document window has its own Control menu, and you can use the selections in the Control menu to move, resize, or close your document windows as follows:

Restore zooms the window back to its original size.

Move lets you use the arrow keys to move the window to a new location. Press the Enter key when the window is in the right place.

Size lets you change the size of a document window. The up and down arrow keys move the bottom of the window, and the left and right arrow keys move the right side. Press the Enter key when the window is the correct size.

Maximize zooms a window to fill the whole screen.

Close closes the current document window. You can also use the Ctrl and F4 keys together to close a window.

Access the Control menu by clicking on the Close button, or by pressing the Alt key and the hyphen key at the same time.

You can also use the Ctrl key with PgUp or PgDn to maximize or restore the window if you toggle the Num Lock key off.

Next switches to the next document window. You can also use the Ctrl and F6 keys together to switch to the next window.

Figure 7.2 shows two small document windows open at the same time in the Desktop Editor. This way, you can refer to one document as you edit the other.

Just as with a drive window, you can click on the button at the top-right corner of a document window to maximize or restore the window.

At the bottom of the Desktop Editor window you will see a status line showing the current line and column cursor position. As you move through your document, you will see these numbers change to reflect the new cursor position.

OPENING AND SAVING FILES

There are several commands you can use in the File menu to open or save files:

New creates a new empty document window called UNTITLED.1, UNTITLED.2, and so on. You can use the Save As command to give the file a more meaningful name.

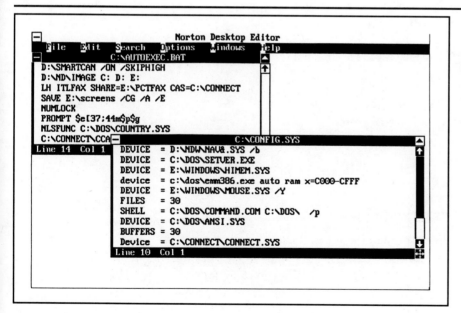

FIGURE 7.2:

Two document windows open at the same time in the Desktop Editor

Open loads an existing text file using a browse dialog box for file-name entry. The contents of the file are displayed in the active window.

Close closes the current document window. If you have made changes to the file but not saved them yet, a dialog box opens telling you the file has changed, and asking if you want to save these changes. Click on Yes to save the changes, No to abandon them, or Cancel if you want to give yourself time to think.

Save saves the contents of the current document window using the original file name, and keeps the document open so that you can continue editing. If you plan a long session, make sure you use this command from time to time to save your work, so in the event of an accident, you will loose as little work as possible.

Save As saves the contents of the current document window under a different file name. This can be especially useful if you want to create several similar, but not identical, files. After the file has been saved, the new name you used appears at the top of the active window, instead of the original file name.

Inserting a File

To add a file into your current document, use the Insert command from the File menu. The whole file is read from disk and is inserted at the cursor location. Here are the steps to follow:

1. First place the cursor at the location where you want to insert this file.

2. Select Insert from the File menu.

3. When the File text box opens, enter the name of the file you want to read from disk and insert into your current document.

4. Click on OK to import the file, and the contents of the file will appear at the cursor location.

ENTERING TEXT

Most of the time you spend working with an editor like the Norton Desktop Editor you are entering or editing text, or manipulating text in some other way. Many of the commands that the Desktop Editor uses for handling text are standard commands, so you will have no trouble working with the Desktop Editor.

There are several keyboard commands you can use to change the relative position of text in a Desktop Editor window, in addition to using the regular scroll bars. These commands do not change the text in any way, nor do they change the position of the text in the file, they just move the text inside the window so that you can work on it more easily.

End first moves the cursor to the end of the current word; then when you press it again, you move to the end of the current window; and if you press End a third time, you move right to the end of the file.

Home first moves the cursor to the beginning of the current word; then when you press it again, you move to the beginning of the current window; and if you press End a third time, you move right to the beginning of the file.

PgUp and **PgDn** move the contents of a window one page at a time.

These commands are not available from any menu, so you can use them at any time directly from the keyboard.

Adding Text

Creating a new text file from scratch couldn't be simpler; you just open the Desktop Editor and start typing. Similarly, if you want to add to an existing text file, just go to the end of the file and start typing. You can use the Backspace or Delete keys to correct any mistakes you make as you go along.

If you type past the right margin, the word wrap features of the Desktop Editor will move the word to the beginning of the next line automatically, so there is no need to press the Enter key at the end of each line. You will only have to use the Enter key when you want to create a blank line in your text or when you want to end a paragraph. Word wrap is handled on a document-by-document basis and is controlled through the Options menu, described later in this chapter.

You can use the Reformat option in the Edit menu to reformat a marked section of your document, according to the current Page Width setting. To reformat a part of a document, mark it first by dragging the mouse over the text you want to rework, then click on Reformat in the Edit menu. The Desktop Editor realigns your chosen text.

Deleting Text

You can also mark a block of text using the keyboard: use the Shift key with the arrow keys or the PgUp and PgDn keys.

There are several different techniques you can use to delete text from the Desktop Editor; you can delete anything from a single character to a large piece of text. You can use the Backspace key to remove the character to the left of the cursor, or the Delete key to delete the character at the cursor. If you mark a block of text first, by dragging the mouse over the text, then using the Delete key or the Clear command from the Edit menu, you can remove the whole block with a single keystroke. Finally, if you decide to throw everything away and start again, you can use Select All from the Edit menu to mark all the text in the current document window, and then use Clear to delete in a single operation.

Cutting, Copying, and Pasting Text Using the Clipboard

No editor would be complete without a set of commands to move text to and from the Clipboard, and you will find the Cut, Copy, and Paste commands in the Edit menu. To copy text from the Desktop Editor to the Clipboard so that you can transfer the text into another document, follow these steps:

You must mark text first before using Cut or Copy; otherwise, nothing happens.

1. Select the text you want to transfer by dragging the mouse across it or by using the Shift key and the appropriate arrow key on the keyboard.

2. Choose the Copy command in the Edit menu, and the text is copied onto the Clipboard. If you use the Cut command instead of the Copy command, the text is still transferred to the Clipboard, but the original text is deleted from your document.

3. Now open your second document window, and position the cursor at the appropriate place in the document to receive the text from the Clipboard.

4. Choose the Paste command with this second document window active to transfer the text across from the Clipboard into your document and complete the process.

SEARCHING FOR AND REPLACING TEXT

As you work with your document in the Desktop Editor, you can use the options in the Search menu to search for, or to search for and then subsequently replace certain strings of text in your file. You can search for single characters or whole words, and you can even search forward through the file or backward from back to front.

SEARCHING FOR TEXT

Use the Find (Ctrl+F) command in the Search menu when you want to look for a specific set of text in a document, and you will see the dialog box shown in Figure 7.3.

If you want the search to be case-sensitive, check the Match Case check box. Using Match Case is a good way to make the search more specific and therefore faster. Choose either Forward to specify a search from the current cursor location to the end of your file, or Backward to specify a search from the current cursor location to the beginning of your file. The Desktop Editor beeps when the Find operation reaches the end or the beginning of the file.

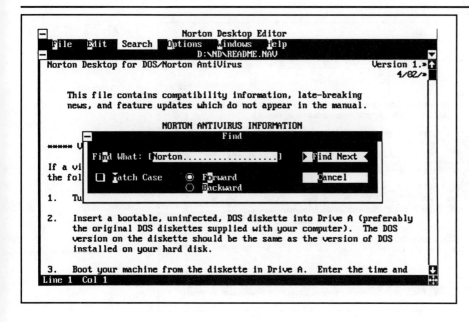

FIGURE 7.3:

Specify your search string text in the Find dialog box

Start the search by clicking on the Find Next button. The search ends when the Desktop Editor reaches the beginning or the end of the file, or when a match is found. Matching text is highlighted in the document window, and to look for more occurrences of the same text, select Find Next once again from the Find dialog box.

Take a moment to experiment here, and open the Desktop Editor on the README.NAV file that is a part of the Norton Desktop package. Enter the text **Norton** as the search string, specify a forward search, and then click on Find Next to start the search. Each time the search string is found, the search stops and the word *Norton* is highlighted. Use Find Next to search for the next occurrence of the string.

REPLACING TEXT

When you are working in a text file, you often want to do more than simply find all the occurrences of a particular set of text. You may want to replace one or more of those occurrences of text with something else. To do this, you need the Replace command. Choose Replace (Ctrl+R) from the Search menu to open the dialog box shown in Figure 7.4.

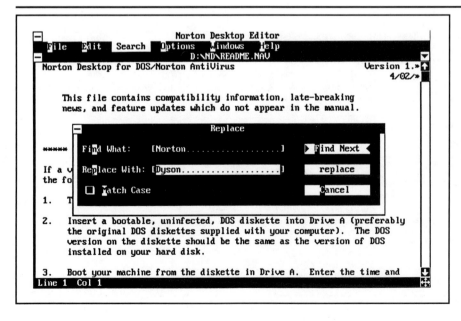

FIGURE 7.4:

Enter both the text you want to search for and the replacement text in the Replace dialog box

Enter the text you want to search for into the Find What text box, and the alternative text into the Replace With text box. Again, as in a Find operation, you can use the Match Case check box to make the search case-sensitive. Click on Find Next to start the search for candidates.

A replacement operation always starts at the current cursor location and moves forward through your file. If you want to search the entire document, be sure that you are at the beginning of the file when you start the replace operation. When a match is found, the search text is highlighted. Click on the Replace button to confirm that you want to replace this occurrence of the search text, or click on Find Next to look for another occurrence. The Desktop Editor beeps when the Replace operation reaches the end of the file.

There are many different ways you can use the Replace command, ranging from correcting a consistent spelling error throughout a document to changing one command into another with just a few straightforward keystrokes.

USING THE OPTIONS MENU

Some of the settings in the Desktop Editor are default settings that you can change if you wish, by using the two selections in the Options menu.

The first selection, Page Width, sets the width of your document as the number of horizontal characters across the screen or page. The normal maximum is 80 characters.

Word Wrap (Ctrl+W) is a toggle—it is either on or off. If you see a check mark to the left of this menu item, then Word Wrap is turned on. As you type, the word wrap feature of the Desktop Editor will automatically move a word that is too long to fit at the end of one line to the beginning of the next line, according to the setting established for Page Width. With Word Wrap on, there is no need to press the Enter key at the end of each line. You will only have to use the Enter key when you want to add one or more blank lines to your document, or when you want to end a paragraph.

PRINTING YOUR WORK

Before you print your document, you must make several important decisions about page layout and whether you want to include headers and footers in your printed output. You can also choose which printer to use and configure several different printer options. The Print Setup option from the Desktop Editor File menu helps you establish the page format you want to use and set up your printer; the Print command actually prints your document. We'll look at these commands next.

ESTABLISHING THE PAGE FORMAT

The Print Setup option from the Desktop Editor File menu opens the exact same dialog box as the Printer option in the main Norton Desktop Configure menu does. This means that you can easily set up different printer configurations for Desktop printing and for printing from the Editor if you want to; just select the appropriate configuration. Because Chapter 9 describes the Configure Printer dialog box and how to use it in some detail, we'll just look at the process very quickly here.

Choose Print Setup from the File menu to open the Configure Printer dialog box shown in Figure 7.5.

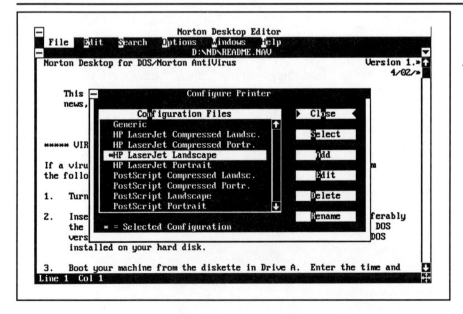

FIGURE 7.5:

Choose your printer from the list in the Configure Printer dialog box

You can create several special configurations if you find yourself using certain settings over and over. For example, you could use one for condensed landscape-mode printing, and another for numbered lines in portrait mode if these are the options you use most often.

See Chapter 9 for a detailed description of the options available in the Printer Settings dialog box.

Select a printer configuration file from the list in the dialog box; the Generic printer at the top of the list supports most dot-matrix printers. If you have a LaserJet or PostScript printer, you can select a configuration file for that printer type. The current selection is marked with a star to the left of the list box. Click on Select to choose a new configuration.

If you don't see a configuration file for your printer or you want to create a special configuration, click on the Add button, and you will see the Printer Settings dialog box open as Figure 7.6 shows.

This dialog box lets you control both your printer and the appearance of text on the printed page. You can compress the text, wrap the text, number the lines, add a header, control your printer by including printer-specific commands in a printer setup file, set all the page margins, and even select the port on your computer you want to use to output the file. You can also print directly to a file if you wish.

Click on OK when you are happy with your choices in this dialog box, and your new printer configuration file will take its place along with all the other printer configurations in the list box.

If you change your mind about any of these settings at a later date, just come back to the Print Setup option in the File menu, choose the appropriate printer configuration from the list box, and click on the Edit

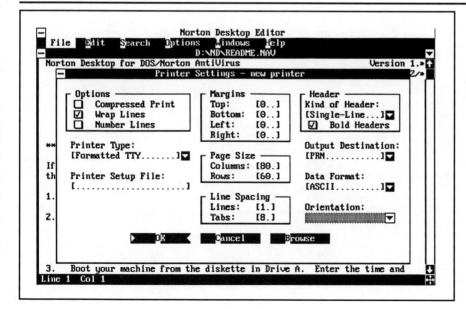

FIGURE 7.6:

Set up your configuration file using the Printer Settings dialog box

button. This opens the same Printer Settings dialog box and allows you to change your printer configuration information. You can also click on Rename if you want use a different name for your printer configuration. To remove a configuration from the list, highlight it first, then click on Delete.

Printing Your Document

Now you are ready to print your document. Choose Print from the File menu, and the Desktop Editor will initiate document printing. As your document is printed, a small percentage bar graph on the screen shows you printing progress.

CHAPTER 8

Launching Programs

he Norton Desktop features several different ways you can use to start, or *launch*, your application programs, including launching directly from a drive window file pane and using the Norton Menu.

LAUNCHING PROGRAMS FROM THE DESKTOP

Later in this chapter we'll look at some more advanced topics and explore how to create associations between application programs and the documents they create.

LAUNCHING DIRECTLY FROM THE FILE PANE

When you open a drive window, the file pane lists all the files and subdirectories contained in the selected directory. There are two ways you can launch a program directly from the file pane:

◆ Double-click on the program file name in the file pane.

◆ Use the arrow keys to move the highlight to the right file, then press the Enter key.

Whichever method you use, the selected program starts running and replaces the Desktop on the screen. When you have finished using the program, close it in the usual way, and you will return directly to the Desktop once again, without having to interact with DOS.

USING THE RUN COMMAND

You can use Run to execute any DOS command.

If you remain a devotee of the DOS command line, you can still use it from inside the Desktop to start your favorite program. Here's how you can use the Run command to launch a file:

Use the Run command if you don't want to open a drive window.

1. Select the Run command from the Desktop File menu or type Ctrl+R.

2. When the dialog box shown in Figure 8.1 opens, type in the correct file name to start the application. Include a related data file name too, if you wish. If the directory containing the application you want to use is not part of your DOS path statement, you must include complete path information in the text box. For example, to start WordPerfect and open the file 10MAY.LET, enter:

C:\WP51\WP 10MAY.LET

into the text box. To reenter a command you just recently used with this text box, click on the drop-down list box to select the entry. The Desktop keeps a history of your previous commands so that you don't have to reenter them every time.

3. Select how you want the program to return to the Norton Desktop. If you want to pause before returning to the Desktop, be sure and check the Pause on return check box. When you close the application, you will see the message:

Press any key to return to the Norton Desktop.

If you clear this check box, you will immediately return to the Norton Desktop when you close your application.

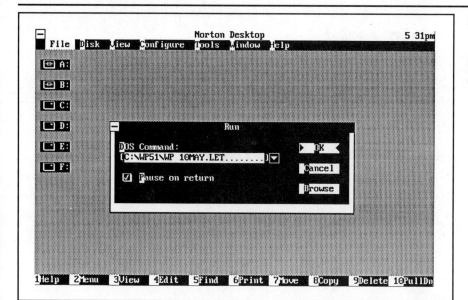

FIGURE 8.1:
*You can launch any file
using Run from the
Desktop File menu*

You can also use the Browse button in this dialog box to search for the file you are interested in running. When you click on Browse, a standard Browse dialog box opens. Choose the drive, directory, and file name you are interested in, then return to the Run dialog box to start the application.

USING THE DOS SESSION COMMAND

Sometimes you might want to run DOS from right inside the Desktop rather than exit from the Desktop, run a program, then return to the Desktop. The DOS Session (Ctrl+D) command in the Tools menu lets you do just that, and so helps you save time. When you choose DOS Session, the Desktop is cleared, and the DOS prompt appears on your screen. You can now run any DOS command or any application program on your system. To return to the Desktop, just type **EXIT** at the DOS prompt, and press the Enter key to go right back to the Desktop.

If you forget that you are using the Desktop in this way, and try to start the Desktop again, you will see the message:

ERROR: Another copy of ND.EXE is already running.

Don't worry, just type EXIT to return to the Desktop.

LAUNCHING FROM NORTON MENU

One of the major new features included in the Norton Desktop brings is the Norton Menu system, described in detail in Chapter 10. Norton Menu automatically creates a custom-built menuing system based on the applications that you have on your system. Figure 8.2 shows the Norton Desktop with the Norton Menu window open in the center of the Desktop.

The Norton Menu creates headings that include Utility Programs, Database Programs, Spreadsheet, and Word Processing programs, and you can launch your applications directly from this menuing system without ever leaving the Desktop. See Chapter 10 for a complete description of how you can set up and use Norton Menu on your system.

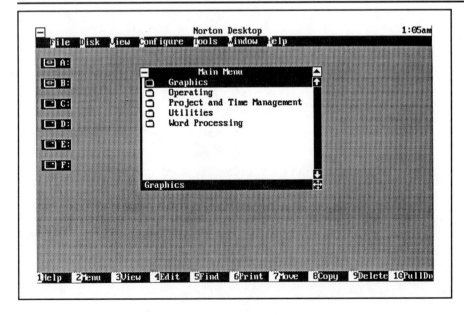

FIGURE 8.2:

The Norton Main Menu window open on the Desktop

USING THE SCHEDULER

The Norton Desktop also includes a Scheduler in the Tools menu. You can use the Scheduler to start a program running on your system at a specific time. You can also use it to send yourself reminder messages. The Scheduler is described in Chapter 16.

ESTABLISHING ASSOCIATIONS

The Associate command in the Desktop File menu lets you look at or change your *associations*. You can associate documents that have a given file-name extension with the application program that created them in the first place. Most programs create these extensions automatically; for example, some word processors use the extension .DOC, Lotus 1-2-3 uses .WK1, and dBASE uses .DBF.

By establishing an association, you can simplify the program launching process even more. All you have to do is double-click on the document file name in a drive window file pane to start the application program running the associated document.

For example, if you associate file names with the .DOC extension with Microsoft Word, then when you click on any .DOC file, the Desktop will open Word and automatically load the document file you clicked on.

ADDING AND EDITING ASSOCIATIONS

To add a new association or look at the associations already established on your system, choose the Associate command from the Desktop File menu. The dialog box shown in Figure 8.3 opens, listing all of the current associations.

There are two option buttons at the bottom of this dialog box that you can use to display your associations in two different ways:

Program Name. Choose Program Name to see your associations listed alphabetically by application program name. Some programs, particularly graphics or illustration programs, might have more than one file-name extension associated with them. For example, many illustration programs can load both .PCX and .TIF format graphics images.

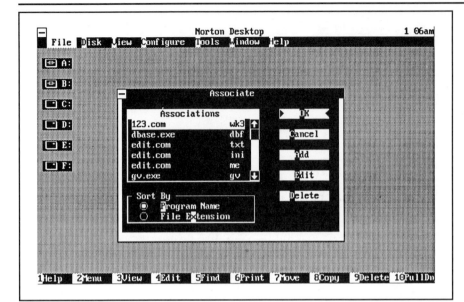

File Extension. Select this option to see your existing associations listed alphabetically by file-name extension.

If you just want to look at the existing associations on your system, this is as far as you need to go. Use the scroll bars or the arrow keys to move through the list shown in the Associations list box.

To create a new association between an application program and a file-name extension, choose the Add command button from this dialog box. If you want to modify an existing association, highlight it, then click on the Edit command button. The Add Association dialog box shown in Figure 8.4 is very similar to the Edit Association dialog box.

There are three text boxes in this dialog box. To create a new association:

1. Enter the full path name of the application program into the Program text box, including the drive letter and directory name, if this information is not already part of your DOS path statement.

2. Enter the file-name extension you want to associate with this application program into the Extension text box. An extension can be one, two, or three characters, but you do not have to enter the

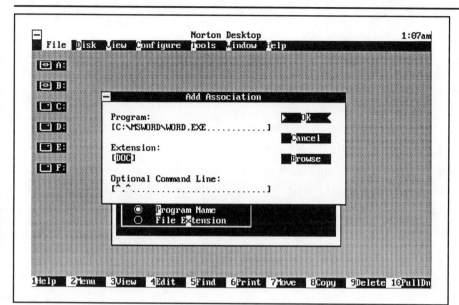

FIGURE 8.4:

Add new associations to your system in the Add Association dialog box

leading period that precedes the extension. Remember that you can only associate one particular extension with one program at a time (for example, .DOC only with Microsoft Word), although an application program can have several extensions associated with it (for example, .PCX and .TIF files associated with an illustration program).

3. Any text you enter into the Optional Command Line text box is appended to the program name at the time you actually double-click on the document to start the program running. (See "Invoking a Custom Startup Command" later in this chapter.)

This dialog box also contains a Browse command button you can use to open a Browse dialog box. When you select a file using this particular Browse dialog box, the path and file name information are loaded directly into the Program text box.

Now that an association is established, all you have to do is double-click on the document file in a drive window file pane to start the application program running your chosen document. If you associated file names that have the .DOC extension with Microsoft Word, you can click on any .DOC file anywhere on your system to open Word and automatically load the document file you clicked on.

Alternatively, you can enter the name of a document file into the Run dialog box in the Desktop File menu, and as long as an association exists, the correct application will automatically open the file whose name you typed.

DELETING ASSOCIATIONS

If you remove an application program from your system because you don't plan on using it any more, you can delete any residual associations that remain. Open the Associate dialog box, highlight the entry you want to delete, and click on the Delete command button.

INVOKING A CUSTOM STARTUP COMMAND

NOTE *The Delete command button is dimmed until you select one of the entries in the Association list box.*

You can use the Optional Command Line text box in the Add or Edit Association dialog boxes to open your application in a particular way. For example, if your application supports macros, and you always use the same macro with your files, add its name to the Optional Command Line text box and it will be executed as your chosen application starts running.

You can include any normal DOS command-line entry in this text box. For example, if you are a WordPerfect user and you share your computer with other users, you might want to add the /X startup option for WordPerfect. This tells WordPerfect to restore all the default values that you can change with the Setup key (Shift+F1). By using this /X option, you can be sure that the regular default values are in effect, not those of any previous user.

PART THREE

Personalizing the Desktop

Part III describes how you can use the Norton Desktop to form your own personal computing environment, specifically designed to meet your day-to-day needs. You will learn how to configure the Desktop and how to create and maintain your own menu system.

CHAPTER 9

Customizing Your Desktop

! n working with the Desktop in previous chapters, we have used it pretty much as it was installed, without configuring or customizing it. The Desktop is a very flexible environment, however, and it offers many opportunities to tailor it exactly to your needs and work habits. If there are features of the Desktop that you use constantly, there may be ways that you can get even more performance out of your system. On the other hand, if there are Desktop options that you dislike or never use, there may be a way to turn them off so they don't get in the way.

In this chapter we will look at all of these configuration options and point out some of the pros and cons of using them on your system. We'll begin by looking at the NDConfig program, and then examine the entries available from the Desktop Configure menu.

USING NDCONFIG

All of the Desktop-wide configurations are made using the NDConfig program; things such as use of screen colors, mouse responsiveness, Desktop-wide passwords, and so on.

To start NDConfig from the DOS prompt, change to the Norton Desktop directory, and type:

NDCONFIG

Alternatively, you can enter this program name into the Run command from the Desktop File menu. Either way, you will see the opening dialog box, as Figure 9.1 shows.

There are five command buttons in this dialog box:

Video and Mouse. Use this selection to configure screen and mouse characteristics for the whole Desktop.

Temporary Files. With this selection, you can specify the directories you want the Desktop to use for temporary files.

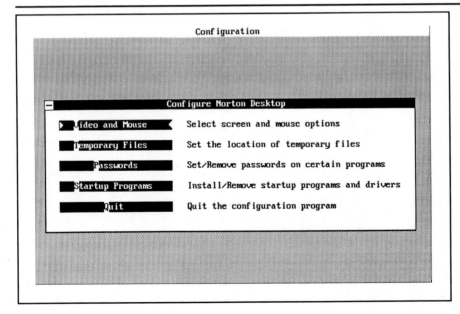

FIGURE 9.1:

You can set many Desktop-wide parameters by using NDConfig

Passwords. Use this to set passwords on some of the Desktop programs.

Startup Programs. This setting lets you configure the Norton Desktop terminate-and-stay-resident programs.

Quit. Use this selection when you have configured your system, and you are ready to return to DOS.

In the next part of this chapter, we will look at each of these selections in turn.

VIDEO AND MOUSE

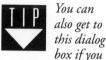

You can also get to this dialog box if you use the Video/Mouse selection from the Desktop Configure menu.

Choose Video and Mouse to open the dialog box shown in Figure 9.2. This dialog box is divided into two parts; the left side lets you configure your screen options, while the right side lets you set up your mouse. The following drop-down list boxes are available:

Screen Colors. Choose a set of screen colors from a selection of color sets, including Black and White, Monochrome, CGA Colors, Grayscale (for laptops), and two color sets for an EGA/VGA. You can also choose Custom Colors if you want to fashion your own color combinations.

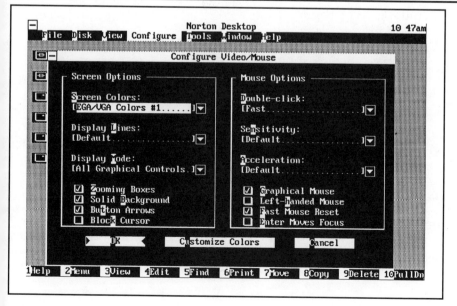

FIGURE 9.2:

Use the Configure Video/Mouse dialog box to set up your screen and mouse options

Display Lines. Choose the number of display lines you want to see on your screen, from 25, 28, 43, or 50 for a VGA monitor, or 25 or 43 for an EGA monitor; you must have the correct display adapter to use these settings.

Display Mode. Select the display mode you want to use from Standard, Some Graphical Controls, or All Graphical Controls. Some Graphical Controls displays graphical icons for files and disk drives, and uses graphical dialog boxes. Standard displays a solid mouse cursor and uses text characters inside dialog boxes to define command buttons and check boxes. All Graphical Controls displays square check boxes, as well as other graphical controls.

 You must have an EGA or VGA monitor to use Some Graphical Controls or All Graphical Controls.

This part of the dialog box also has four check boxes:

Zooming Boxes. Choose between zooming dialog boxes or pop-up dialog boxes.

Solid Background. Check this to see a solid background on the Desktop; otherwise, the background will appear to be textured.

Button Arrows. This selection turns the triangular arrowhead characters on the command buttons on or off.

Block Cursor. Changes the normal text cursor into a block cursor.

Over on the mouse side of this dialog box, you can choose settings in these drop-down dialog boxes:

Double-click. Set the double-click rate you want to use from Slow, Medium, or Fast.

Sensitivity. Select the mouse sensitivity from Default, Low, Medium, or High.

Acceleration. Choose the appropriate acceleration from Default, None, Medium, or Fast. This setting controls how fast the mouse cursor responds to mouse movements.

It is very difficult to suggest settings for these mouse options, because of the hardware differences between mice from different manufacturers, and the individual way in which you use your mouse. Experiment with the different settings in this dialog box to find the combination that suits you best.

At the bottom of the mouse side of this dialog box, you will find four check boxes:

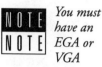

You must have an EGA or VGA monitor to use Graphical Mouse.

Graphical Mouse. Check this box to turn the mouse cursor into an arrow pointer.

Left-handed Mouse. This selection reverses the mouse buttons.

Fast Mouse Reset. Check this box if you have a serial, IBM PS/2, or Compaq mouse.

Enter Moves Focus. Check this box to make the Enter key work in the same way that the Tab key does. That is, when this box is checked and you press the Enter key on the Desktop, you can move through a list of choices, rather than using the Enter key to accept the default (or highlighted) option.

If you selected Custom Colors from the Screen Colors list box, choose the Customize Colors command button to open the dialog box shown in Figure 9.3; otherwise, choose OK to return to the NDConfig opening dialog box to make your next selection.

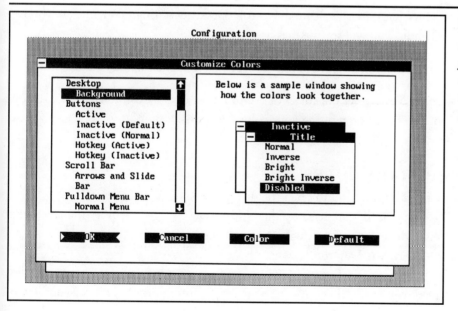

FIGURE 9.3:

Select the screen element first, then choose the colors you want to use in the Customize Colors dialog box

The Customize Colors dialog box is split into two parts. The left side of the screen contains a list of all the elements on the Norton Desktop for which you can specify a color, while the right side of the screen offers a selection of display attributes—you can choose from Normal, Inverse, Bright (sometimes referred to as bold), Bright Inverse, or Disabled.

Choose the Desktop screen element you want to work with, perhaps the scroll bar arrows and slide, or the active command button. When you are ready to specify your colors for this element, choose the Color command button, and a dialog box opens that contains two horizontal color bars, one for the foreground color and the other for the background color. Above these bars you will see a box that illustrates how the current color choices will look on your screen. Use this box to test your color combinations; some will be pleasant and restful, others will be quite the opposite, and several color combinations will just be completely unusable. Just click on the foreground or background color you are interested in using, and this text box will change accordingly. Alternatively, use the arrow keys to change your color settings.

Choose OK when you are happy with our choices and you will return to the Customize Colors dialog box. If you don't like the colors you have chosen, use Color to change them again, or select Default to change *all* the colors back to the normal Norton Desktop settings. When you choose Default, you will see the message:

Are you sure you want to restore ALL colors to their default state?

Select Yes to reset the colors or No to return to the Customize Colors dialog box to continue refining your color selections.

Your color settings are stored in a file called NORTON.INI, along with other important configuration information.

If you have enough free memory space in your computer and you want to make the Desktop run as fast as possible, create a RAM drive to use for your swap files.

TEMPORARY FILES

Choose this option to open the dialog box shown in Figure 9.4.

Swap files are used by the Norton Desktop for memory management tasks during program operation, and they are automatically deleted when you leave the Desktop.

Temporary files are used to store program information as you use the Desktop, and they are also deleted automatically when you leave the Desktop.

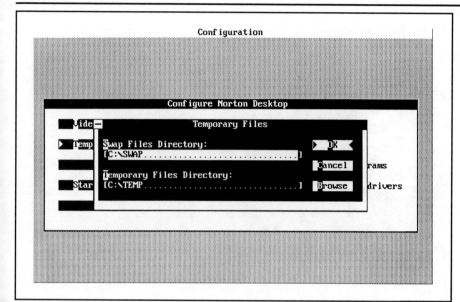

FIGURE 9.4:
Specify the drive and directory you want the Norton Desktop to use for temporary files

Enter the drive and directory you want the Norton Desktop to use for its swap file into the first text box, and the drive and directory you want to use for temporary files into the second text box. This dialog box also contains a Browse command button, so you can search your system for exactly the right place for these files.

PASSWORDS

 *You assign one single password to be used with all the selected programs.*

You can assign a password to several of the more potent Norton Desktop file and disk recovery programs to prevent unauthorized access to these potentially dangerous programs.

Select Passwords from the opening NDConfig screen to open the dialog box shown in Figure 9.5. Use the arrow keys or the mouse to highlight the program you want to protect, then press the spacebar to add a check mark opposite the program name on the left side of the dialog box. If you want to protect all of these programs, choose the Protect All command button; or, if you are removing a password from all of the programs, choose the Remove All command button. When you have made your selections, click on the Set Passwords command button to actually enter your password.

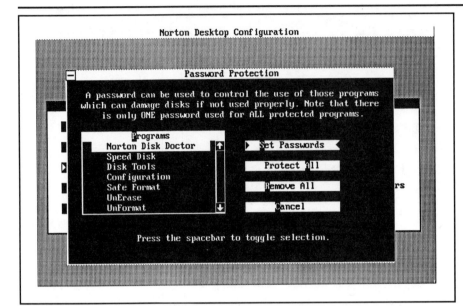

FIGURE 9.5:
Select the programs you want to password protect in this dialog box

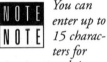
You can enter up to 15 characters for your password, including both letters and numbers.

You are asked to enter your password twice to confirm that you typed it correctly. As you type, you will see asterisks in this dialog box, for security reasons. If you make a mistake, an error box opens with the message:

Does not match!

just click on OK and try again.

Now, when you start one of the password-protected programs, a dialog box opens asking you to enter the password. If you forget the password, you will have to reinstall the Norton Desktop for DOS from the original installation disks; you cannot bypass this password.

STARTUP PROGRAMS

Several of the programs in the Norton Desktop package are terminate-and-stay-resident (TSR) programs, also called memory-resident programs. You load TSR programs using a command in either your CONFIG.SYS or your AUTOEXEC.BAT file, and they stay loaded onto your system all the time, waiting to go to work. This is in sharp contrast to the normal way of working with a program: you load the program, use it, and when you are done, DOS takes care of unloading the program and recovering that memory space for use by the next program.

Norton Desktop does not load these TSR programs onto your system automatically during the installation because they can take up quite a lot of memory if they are all loaded onto your system. Depending on how you use your computer, you may not need to load all of them. Also, the Norton Desktop designers are sensitive to different user's needs and usage of scarce memory space, and so provided the Startup Programs option to allow you to configure these TSR programs to create your own individual computing environment.

Select Startup Programs from the opening NDConfig screen to open the dialog box shown in Figure 9.6.

The list box displays the TSR programs you can select and also shows the amount of memory space each of them takes when loaded onto your system. If there is no memory requirement listed for the entry (as for Diagnose disk problems), the program is run as a part of your start-up process, but is not installed as a TSR program. Highlight the option or options you want

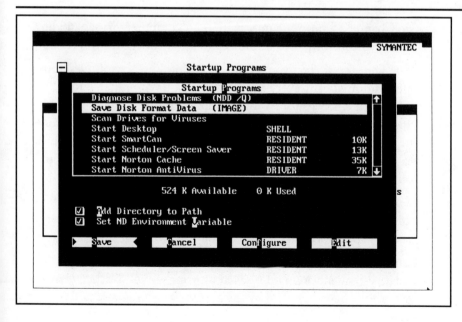

FIGURE 9.6:

Select the TSR programs you want to use in the Startup Programs dialog box

to use in this list box. If the program needs additional configuration information, the Configure command button becomes available, and you should use it to select settings appropriate for your system. The dialog box presents the following choices:

See Chapter 17 for information on how to configure Norton Mail.

Diagnose Disk Problems. This selection runs the Norton Disk Doctor as a part of your start-up sequence. See Chapter 13 for more information on the Norton Disk Doctor.

Save Disk Format Data. This selection runs the Image program every time you start your computer. Use the Configure command button to specify the drive letters you want Image to protect. See Chapter 12 for more information.

Scan Drives for Viruses. This option runs Norton AntiVirus as a part of your start-up sequence. Use Configure to choose a scan method:

◆ Do Not Scan for Viruses

◆ Scan All Drives for Viruses

◆ Scan Selected Drives for Viruses

See Chapter 15 for more information on computer viruses and how to use Norton AntiVirus to protect your system against infection.

Start Desktop. When you select this option, the Norton Desktop opens automatically every time you start your computer. This means that when you start your computer running, you will see the Norton Desktop instead of the DOS prompt, and all the features of the Desktop will be immediately available for use. If you use the features of the Norton Desktop often, this is the best way for you to run your system.

Start SmartCan. This selection installs the terminate-and-stay-resident program SmartCan on your system. SmartCan takes 10K of memory space. See Chapter 12 for information on using SmartCan.

Start Scheduler/Screen Saver. This selection installs the terminate-and-stay-resident program Nsched on your system. Nsched is used by both the Scheduler and by the Screen Saver program, and occupies 13K of memory.

Start Norton Cache. This option installs the Norton Cache program, a program that acts as an intermediary between you and your hard disk. Norton Cache can increase the performance of your hard-disk system, at the cost of a very modest 35K of memory. You can invoke Norton Cache from either your CONFIG.SYS file *or* from your AUTOEXEC.BAT file—one or the other, but not both. Norton Cache is a complex program, so to configure and tune it for best performance, I recommend that you read Chapter 18 before changing any of the default settings.

Start Norton AntiVirus. This last option lets you install the terminate-and-stay-resident portion of Norton AntiVirus onto your system. This takes approximately 7K of memory space.

Your Norton AntiVirus configuration options include:

◆ Comprehensive Scan with System Area Protection

◆ Comprehensive Scan

◆ Boot Sector and Execution Scan

◆ Execution Scan Only

◆ Do Not Check Files for Viruses

See Chapter 15 for more information on how to use Norton AntiVirus.

In addition, there are two check boxes at the bottom of this window:

Add Directory to Path. Check this box if you want to add the directory name you used to install Norton Desktop into your path statement in AUTOEXEC.BAT.

Set ND Environment Variable. Check this box to set the ND environmental variable to include the Norton Desktop program directory.

Some TSR programs can be very sensitive to the order they are loaded, so you may need to experiment a little to get the best possible compromise. Choose the Edit command button to position the new commands in your CONFIG.SYS and AUTOEXEC.BAT files.

To move a line, follow these steps:

1. Highlight the line you want to move.

2. Select Move, and you will see an arrowhead appear at both ends of the highlighted line.

3. Move the line to its new location with the arrow keys.

4. Select Drop or press the Enter key to anchor the line.

When you have completed your selections, remember to click on Save before you quit the NDConfig program to store your choices into the NORTON.INI file and save the new versions of AUTOEXEC.BAT and CONFIG.SYS.

If you do make additions or changes to either CONFIG.SYS or to AUTOEXEC.BAT, remember that you must reboot your computer to make the changes take effect.

CONFIGURING YOUR DESKTOP

NOTE *The rest of this chapter assumes you are using the long menus; all possible options will be described.*

The remainder of this chapter will detail how to configure the Norton Desktop using entries from the Desktop Configure menu. This menu, shown in Figure 9.7, lists the options you can use to configure your Desktop.

Using this menu you can:

◆ customize the appearance of your desktop

◆ select a set of menus from several predefined options

◆ customize the button bar at the bottom of the main Desktop window

◆ configure network settings

◆ establish printer parameters

◆ select file-compression options

◆ save your settings for future use

I will go through each of the selections shown on this menu and describe ways that you can use them to get the best out of your system.

The Configure menu contains selections you can use to tailor the Desktop to your needs

CUSTOMIZING DESKTOP MENUS

The most obvious way to customize your Desktop menus is to select the first entry in the Configure menu. Desktop maintains two main sets of menus, known as long menus and short menus. Short menus are used by default until you change to long menus. The short menu contains just the most commonly used commands you need for day-to-day use, whereas the long menu contains every Desktop command. Choose Load Pull-downs from the Configure menu, and select the menu set you want to use. If other menu sets are available, you can load one of them if you wish.

Using the Edit Pull-downs selection from the Configure menu, you can customize your own Desktop even further. You can do the following:

◆ change the menu bar text or any text in a menu

◆ remove a menu from the menu bar or a command from a menu

◆ add standard menu commands to your custom menu structure

◆ change the sequence of menus on the menu bar

◆ add your own application programs or commands to the menu system

NOTE NOTE *These Desktop menus are not the same as the Norton Menus described in Chapter 10.*

The Edit Pull-downs command in the Configure menu opens the Edit Pull-down Menu dialog box shown in Figure 9.8. This dialog box looks a little complicated, so let's look at it piece by piece. The Available Commands list box on the left contains all the commands contained in the long menus in the same order that they appear in each menu. After a couple of custom entries, this list starts with the first commands in the File menu (usually on the left of the Desktop menu bar), and ends with the last command in the Help menu (always on the right of the menu bar). You will also see a menu item separator line (–), used to distinguish between different types of commands in the same menu. Below this Available Commands list box is a small help box that contains a brief description of the currently highlighted command.

The Your Menu list box on the right side of this dialog box lists the structure of your current menu. Items that are left-justified in the list box are menu names—they appear on the Desktop menu bar (such as the File menu). Items indented once are menu selections (such as Open in the File menu) or cascading menu titles (such as Select in the File menu). Items indented twice are cascading menu selections (such as All, Some, and Invert in the Select cascading menu in the File menu).

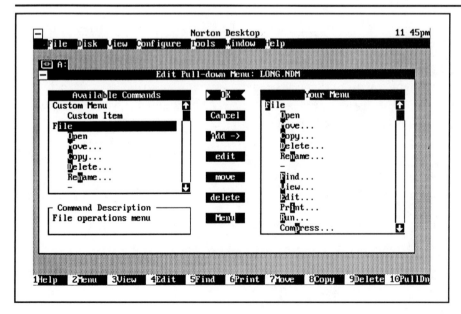

FIGURE 9.8:

You can make all sorts of changes to the Desktop menu system using the Edit Pull-down Menu dialog box

There are several command buttons between the Available Commands list box and the Your Menu list box, as follows:

Add adds a command to your custom menu. First click on the place in the Menu list exactly where you want to place this new command, then highlight the item you want to add from the Available Commands list at left. Choose Add to add your new command.

Edit allows you to edit the text of an item in your custom menu or change the keyboard shortcut keys.

Move lets you move the highlighted item in the Your Menu list up or down in the menu order. If you move a menu title, all the indented menu options below it will move, too. Highlight the entry you are interested in, then choose Move. Now use the arrow keys to move the entry to a new location, and press the Enter key when you are done. You cannot use the mouse in a Move operation.

Delete removes the currently highlighted item from the Your Menu list. Remember that the Available Commands list always contains all the Desktop commands; you cannot add to or delete from this list, only from the Your Menu list.

Desktop menus are stored in files with the file-name extension .NDM.

Menu opens the Menu Operations dialog box. In this dialog box you can specify the overall menu title and enter a description for the menu. You can also set the reset mode, which specifies whether your custom menu resets to the original default long menu or short menu. The Menu Operations dialog box also contains three command buttons: Save As, so you can modify an existing menu and save it under a new name; Load, so you can load another menu; as well as the Reset command button.

A couple of examples will make this clearer; in the next three sections we will add a standard Desktop command to the custom menu, create and add a custom command to the custom menu, and then look at how we can edit these additions.

Adding Standard Desktop Commands

You can use this technique to add the same command into more than one menu if you wish.

In this first example, imagine you like using the short Desktop menu because it offers all the functions you need—except one, the DOS Session command. To add this command, follow these steps:

1. Highlight the item in the Your Menu list box that is immediately above where you want this new command. For example, click on Rename in the File menu to add it beneath Rename.

2. Highlight the DOS Session command in the Available Commands list box.

3. Click on the Add command button to add the new command.

4. Click on OK to save your changes.

Use this technique to add separator bars to delineate your own menus.

Now when you use Short Menus in the Desktop, you'll have the DOS Session command available in the File menu.

Adding Your Own Custom Commands

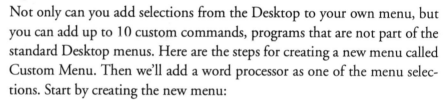

The Norton Desktop knows how long the menu bar is, and will not let you add more menus than will fit.

Not only can you add selections from the Desktop to your own menu, but you can add up to 10 custom commands, programs that are not part of the standard Desktop menus. Here are the steps for creating a new menu called Custom Menu. Then we'll add a word processor as one of the menu selections. Start by creating the new menu:

1. Select Edit Pull-downs from the Configure menu.

2. Place the highlight in the Your Menu list box immediately above the place where you want to add this new menu. For example, highlight File.

3. Click on the Custom Menu selection in the Available Commands list box.

4. Click on the Add command button. The new menu has been added to the Your Menu list box, but at the moment, it is below the end of the File menu.

5. Use the scroll bars in the Your Menu list box to bring the new menu into view, then highlight it, and choose the Move command button. Move the Custom Menu entry to the top of the Your Menu list box, above the File menu. This will place this new menu at the left end of the Desktop menu bar.

Next, we have to add an entry into this menu for the word processor. Imagine you use WordPerfect from a directory called WP51 on drive C. Here are the steps:

1. Click on Custom Menu in the Your Menu list box. This will place our new entry in this menu.

2. Choose Custom Item from the Available Commands list box, and use the Add command button. The Edit Custom Item dialog box opens, as Figure 9.9 shows.

3. Using a Shortcut Key is optional; just press the shortcut key combination you want to use with this command. You can use any of the following:

   ◆ any function key except F1 or F10

   ◆ the Shift key in combination with any function key

   ◆ the Ctrl key in combination with any function key

   ◆ the Ctrl and Shift keys together, in combination with any function key, letter, or number. You cannot use Ctrl+M—this is equivalent to pressing the Enter key.

   ◆ a combination of the Alt key in combination with any function key, letter, or number

   The shortcut combination you choose is shown in this dialog box.

4. Enter the text you want to see when you open this menu into the Menu Item Name text box. If you want to highlight a letter in this command name, type a caret (^) immediately before the letter. This allows you to type the highlighted letter as a shortcut key when you open the menu. In our example, this might be **Word^Perfect**.

5. In the Command Line box, enter the path and file name needed to start the word processor. Again, for our example, this might be:

C:\WP51\WP.EXE

You can also include any command-line options or switches that you use; you can even include a file name if you know you will be working with this file on a regular basis.

6. Click on OK to dismiss this dialog box, then click on OK in the Edit Pull-down menu dialog box to return to the Desktop.

Now you should see a new menu, Custom Menu, at the left end of the Desktop menu bar. When you open this menu, you should see a single entry for your word processor. Using this technique, you can add more of your own frequently used programs.

There are other ways of making an application program easily available; see the description of the Norton Menus in Chapter 10.

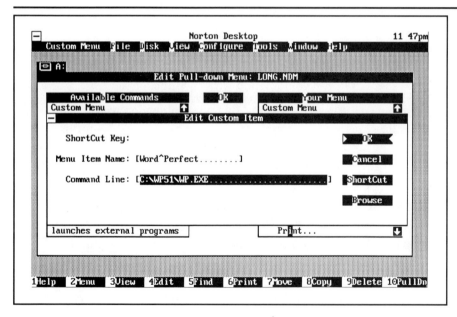

FIGURE 9.9:

Create your word processor entry using the Edit Custom Item dialog box

Editing Your Commands

Once you have added a standard or custom menu item to your Custom Desktop menu, you can edit or change the entry if it is not to your liking. Choose Edit Pull-downs in the Configure menu, highlight the entry you want to edit, and then click on the Edit command button. If you are editing a menu title, then the menu name and shortcut key (if available) are shown in their respective text boxes. If you are editing a menu command, the Edit Custom Item dialog box we just described at the end of the last section opens so you can work with the shortcut keys, menu item name, or command-line options, as required.

WORKING WITH PASSWORDS

Passwords restrict users to certain areas of the Desktop. Choose Password from the Configure menu to establish a password. Enter your choice of password into the text box and then enter it again into the next dialog box to confirm your password. As you type, only asterisks appear in these two text boxes, for security reasons.

To disable the password, choose Password from the Configure menu, enter your current password into the text box, and click on OK. When the Change Password dialog box opens, enter the password; leave the text box blank, but click on OK. The Change Password dialog box opens; click on Yes.

SELECTING PREFERENCES

Select Preferences in the Configure menu to open the Configure Preferences dialog box shown in Figure 9.10. By using selections from this dialog box, you can establish many important Desktop settings, including the following:

◆ create a shutdown routine to save important information when leaving the Norton Desktop

◆ choose the Desktop mode

◆ decide how drive icons are presented on the Desktop

◆ establish several advanced Desktop configuration settings

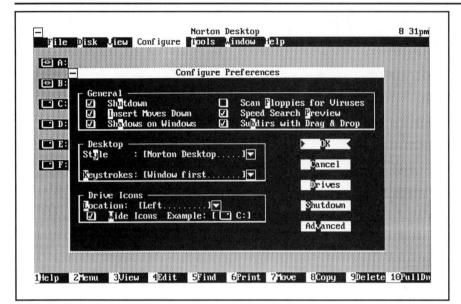

The first group box in this dialog box contains several useful settings, including a shutdown routine option. The shutdown routine is so important that I will devote the whole of the next section to this topic. Meanwhile, let's take a look at the other settings in this group first:

Insert Moves Down. Many of the operations you perform on the Desktop involve files in some way—moving, copying, or deleting them. If you check this box, the cursor will move down one line in a drive window when you use the Insert key to select a file. This means that the cursor is now positioned ready to select the next file; you don't have to move the highlight with the arrow keys. If you are a keyboard user, selecting this option will save you many keystrokes; it is less important if you use a mouse.

Shadows on Windows. This selection adds or removes shadows to your Desktop windows.

Scan Floppies for Viruses. Check this box if you want Norton Anti-Virus to scan the files on your floppy disks when you open a drive window on a floppy disk drive. Many computer viruses are inadvertently transferred from computer to computer via floppy disks, and this is a good way to prevent viruses from infecting your system. See Chapter 15 for complete information on virus protection.

Speed Search Preview. Check this box if you want the Desktop to update the file pane immediately as a Speed Search match is found in the tree pane, or to update the view pane when a Speed Search match is found in the file pane.

Subdirs with Drag & Drop. Check this box if you always want to include all subdirectories (and their files) in any drag-and-drop mouse operation. If this box is not checked, subdirectories and their files are not automatically included when you select a directory.

Creating Your Own Shutdown Routine

You can create a personalized shutdown routine that consists of all the operations you want to perform each time you leave the Norton Desktop. Check the Shutdown check box, then choose the Shutdown command button to open the dialog box shown in Figure 9.11.

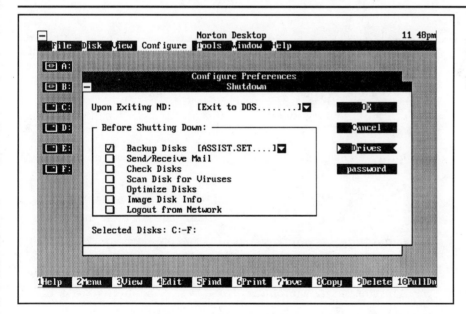

FIGURE 9.11:

Select options for inclusion in your personal shutdown routine

The Shut-down command button stays dimmed until you use the Shutdown check box.

First, use the Upon Exiting ND drop-down list box to establish what you want to happen when you quit the Norton Desktop:

Exit to DOS returns you to DOS.

Secure Computer locks your computer and waits for you to enter a password. Select this option first, then use the Password command button to specify the password.

Reboot reboots your computer.

The remaining check boxes in this dialog box determine the actions to take just before leaving the Norton Desktop:

Backup Disks runs Norton Backup. Choose the appropriate Norton Backup Set file from the drop-down list box. Chapter 11 details Norton Backup.

Send/Receive Mail runs Norton Mail. Once a connection is made, documents in your Out directory are sent, and new messages are copied into your In directory. See Chapter 17 for more on Norton Mail.

Check Disks runs the Norton Disk Doctor, which checks your hard-disk partition table, boot record, and root directory, and also checks the rest of your hard disk for lost clusters. Norton Disk Doctor is described in Chapter 13.

Scan Disk for Viruses runs Norton AntiVirus. See Chapter 15 for more information on computer viruses.

Optimize Disks runs Speed Disk. See Chapter 14 for more on Speed Disk and disk optimization.

Image Disk Info runs the Image program. Creates an updated Image file for each drive you choose. See Chapter 12 for more information.

Logout from Network disconnects your computer from the network.

Use the Drives command button to specify which hard disks you want checked by your shutdown routine. The drives you specify will be displayed at the bottom of the Select Local Drives dialog box.

Choose the options that you want to use in your shutdown routine, then click on OK to return to the Configure Preferences dialog box. The Norton Desktop keeps the list of options you chose for your shutdown routine in a file called SHUTDOWN.BAT; you can look at this file using the Desktop Editor if you wish.

Choosing the Desktop Style

The Desktop group box in the Configure Preferences dialog box allows you to operate the Desktop in one of two different modes: the Norton Desktop mode or the Norton Commander mode. Commander mode is provided for previous users of the Norton Commander who want an easy migration path to the Desktop. Choose the mode you want to use from the Style drop-down list box, then click on OK.

Choosing Keystrokes Preferences

You navigate your way through your drive windows using the Home, End, and arrow keys. If you turn on DOS Background from the View menu, you can use these keys with the DOS command line as well.

For example, open a drive window on drive C, then turn on DOS Background. As you move the highlight from directory to directory in the tree pane, notice that your current directory, as shown at the DOS prompt, also changes to this directory.

You can choose whether you want these navigation keys to act on the drive window first or on the DOS command-line first by choosing an option from the Keystrokes drop-down list box. Choose the Command line first selection to make the navigation keys act on the DOS command line when the DOS background is on, or choose the Window first selection to make the keys act on the current drive window.

If you choose Command line first, you can still navigate through a drive window if you press the Shift key along with the navigation key. Also, if you choose Window first, you can still work at the DOS prompt by pressing Shift and the navigation key.

Working with Drive Icons

You can alter both the position and the appearance of your drive icons on the Desktop by using options from the Drive Icons group box. To change the position of your drive icons, make a selection from the Location drop-down list box. Left places the icons vertically down the left side of the Desktop (this is the default setting), while Right places them on the right side. Bottom places the icons at the bottom of the Desktop, starting from the left side. Off turns the drive icons off so that they do not appear anywhere on the Desktop. Check the Wide Icons check box to display drive icons labeled with the drive letter and a small graphic that indicates the disk drive type—either a floppy disk, a hard disk, or a network drive. If you clear this check box, drive icons only contain the drive letter.

Choose the Drives command button to select which drives are displayed on the Desktop as icons. Either select the drives individually, one at a time, or by type: all floppy drives, all local hard disks, or all network drives. Click on OK to save your settings and return to the Configure Preferences dialog box.

Setting Advanced Options

Click on the Advanced command button to work with several more Desktop configuration options:

Show Free Disk Space Statistics. Check this box if you always want to see the summary information at the top of the file pane in a drive window. This information includes the amount of space occupied by files as well as an indication of the amount of free disk space remaining. Clear this check box to remove this information.

Refresh Windows Automatically. If you check this box, the Desktop rereads your hard disk when you return to the Desktop after running an external program. This ensures that the information in the file pane is correct and up to date, and reflects any changes that were made by the external program. However, the information in the tree pane is not updated.

Refresh Drive Icons Automatically. When this box is checked, all drive icons are refreshed when you return to the Desktop from an external program.

Display Wait…When Busy. During a long operation on the Desktop, the mouse cursor turns into an hourglass icon indicating that the computer is busy and cannot respond to mouse or keyboard input. If you don't use a mouse, you will not see this visual feedback telling you the system is busy. Check this box, however, and you will see the word Wait appear in the upper-left corner of the main Desktop window during any long operation.

Always Update Master Environment Area. When you check this box, the Desktop uses the DOS interrupt 2EH when an external command is executed, which allows changes to take place to the master copy of the DOS environment. You should not use this option if you are using an alternative command shell like NDOS from Symantec or the shareware product 4DOS, or if you are running the Norton Desktop from a batch file.

Update Button Bar to Match Pull-downs. When you check this box, the Desktop button bar is automatically changed so that the F2 through F9 function keys reflect the menu items with those function keys in the current set of menus. This reset occurs when you open the Desktop, when you load a new set of pull-down menus, or when you assign a function key to a command on the current set of pull-down menus.

Click on OK to return to the Configure Preferences dialog box.

STARTUP PROGRAMS

When you select Startup Programs from the Configure menu, you open the same dialog box described earlier in this chapter under the heading "Startup Programs" in the discussion of the NDConfig program (see Figure 9.6). Because both these Startup Programs dialog boxes are identical, the discussion of how you use them will not be repeated.

CUSTOMIZING THE BUTTON BAR

At the bottom of the main Desktop window is a row of buttons you can use to perform certain commands without using the menus. It should come as no surprise to you that you can change these functions and specify your own commands. You may assign any Norton Desktop commands to your own button bar.

For example, if you find that you don't use the Move command button very often, you can replace it with one of the other Desktop commands, perhaps with Rename—or even with a Desktop tool such as UnErase. Two of the button bar functions cannot be changed: F1 for Help and F10 for access to the pull-down menus. But if you don't use the button bar at all, you can turn it off completely.

Choose the Button Bar selection from the Configure menu to open the Configure Button Bar dialog box, as Figure 9.12 shows. The Available Commands list box on the left side of this dialog box shows all the Desktop commands you can assign to a button. The current button assignments are shown on the right side of the dialog box. To associate a different command with a button, follow these steps:

1. Highlight the button you want to change on the right side of this dialog box.

2. In the Available Commands list box, highlight the command you want to use with this button, and click on the Assign command button. In our example, this is Rename. A short description of Rename appears in the box below the Available Commands list box. You can also double-click on the new command in the Available commands list box to complete the assignment.

The command you selected is now available from the button bar, and the cursor automatically moves to the function key text box so that you can confirm the text you want to see on the button when it is displayed on the desktop. If the original command name is too long to fit (only the first six characters can be displayed), edit the name down to six characters.

3. Repeat these steps until you have configured the button bar to your satisfaction.

4. Click on OK to accept these changes.

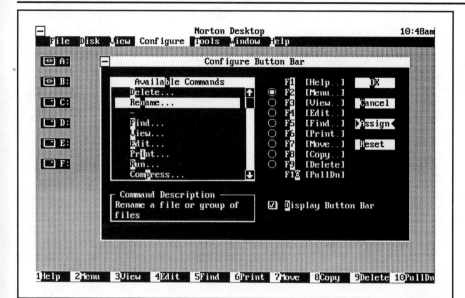

Add your own choice of functions to the button bar using the Configure Button Bar dialog box

If you want to put any of the commands from a cascading menu (such as the File Select or Deselect menu selections) onto the button bar, change the command names to something more meaningful so that you are not confused. Both the Select and Deselect menus contain commands called All, Some, and Invert, and their precise meaning depends on the context.

If you don't want to see the button bar at all, remove the check mark from the Display Button Bar check box in the Configure Button Bar dialog box. When you click on OK, the button bar will be removed from the Desktop. Just check the box again to restore the button bar.

To restore the button bar commands back to their original default assignments, use the Reset command button in the Configure Button Bar dialog box. Another dialog box opens asking you to confirm that you want to reset the button bar; click on OK.

When you have made all your changes to the button bar, click on OK in the Configure Button Bar dialog box to save these changes for future Desktop sessions.

SETTING CONFIRMATION OPTIONS

The Norton Desktop often asks you to confirm that you want to complete a potentially dangerous operation such as deleting a file or removing part of your directory structure, just to be on the safe side. Some people find these messages annoying, so the Desktop provides a way to turn them off. Select Confirmation in the Configure menu to bring up the Configure Confirmation dialog box, shown in Figure 9.13. Each one of the five check boxes in this dialog box controls a confirmation dialog box relating to the operation you are about to perform.

The check boxes are as follows:

Delete. Check this box if you want to see a warning before deleting any files that are not protected by SmartCan. SmartCan is described in Chapter 12.

Subdirectory Delete. Check this box if you want to see a warning before removing directories. This is independent of the Delete check box, which refers only to files.

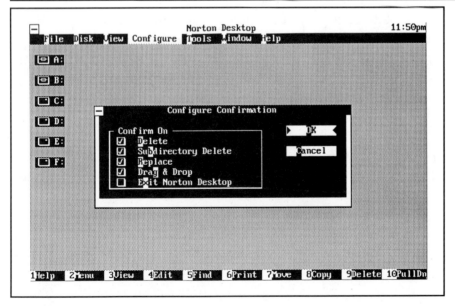

FIGURE 9.13:

If you find the Desktop's confirmation messages annoying, you can turn them off in the Configure Confirmation dialog box

Replace. Check this box if you want to see a warning before you write over an existing file. I suggest you always leave this option checked; overwriting operations can often introduce more problems (some of them subtle and complex) than just deleting a file. For instance, you wouldn't mistakenly want to overwrite an existing file that has the same name—but completely different content—without knowing about it!

Drag & Drop. Check this box if you want to see a warning before completing a mouse operation such as copying, moving, or deleting a file, or launching an application.

Exit Norton Desktop. Check this box if you want to see a confirmation box before leaving the Norton Desktop. You can safely leave this option turned off, because if you have not saved all your work when you try to exit, the Desktop will always remind you.

Click on OK to make these changes for your current Desktop session; see "Saving Your Changes" at the end of this chapter to make them permanent.

SETTING THE CLOCK

The Norton Desktop displays the current time according to your computer in the top right corner of the title bar. If the time is wrong, or you want to change the display format, choose Clock from the Configure menu. The Configure Clock dialog box opens as Figure 9.14 shows.

If the time is wrong, enter the correct time into the Current Time text box; or if the date is off, enter the correct date into Current Date text box.

To turn off the Desktop time display, clear the Display Time check box, or if you want to see the time displayed in military format, check the 24 Hour Time check box.

VIDEO AND MOUSE SETTINGS

When you choose the Video/Mouse option from the Configure menu, you open the same dialog box described under the heading "Video and Mouse" and shown in Figure 9.2 earlier in this chapter. Please refer to that discussion

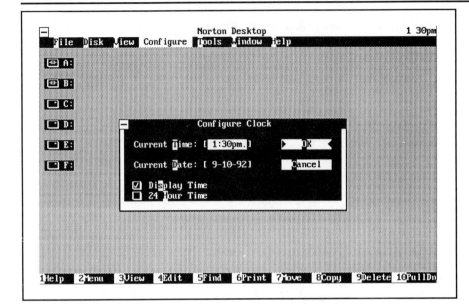

Set the clock in your computer, or change the display format with the Configure Clock dialog box

for a complete description of all the Norton Desktop video and mouse configuration options.

SPECIFYING THE DEFAULT EDITOR

When you select a document on the Desktop, then choose the Edit command from the Desktop File menu, the Desktop opens the default editor on the file. When you first install the Desktop, the Desktop Editor is configured as the default editor. If you have another editor that you would rather use instead, however, you can use the Editor command from the Configure menu to change this default.

When the Configure Editor dialog box opens, as Figure 9.15 shows, choose either the Built In option button to use the Norton Desktop Editor or the External option button to use a different editor. If you choose External, enter the program file name and extension of the editor you want to use into the text box. If the editor's path is not specified in your path command in the AUTOEXEC.BAT file, you must include full path information in this text box. There is also a Browse button in this dialog box that you can use to search for the file name you want to use.

WORKING WITH THE SCREEN SAVER

Use only one screen saver program at a time. If you have another such program, make sure it is turned off before you use Sleeper.

When an image is displayed on your computer screen for a long period of time, there is a danger that it may be burned in on the screen and become permanently visible as a ghost image. You can often see this kind of ghost image on screens used by automatic teller machines outside banks. Many application programs always leave a title bar and a menu bar visible at the top of most of their windows, so there is the chance that these elements could become burned in on the screen.

The screen saver Sleeper is meant to prevent burn-in. It blanks your screen when you are not using your computer and displays a constantly moving graphic image rather than a static display.

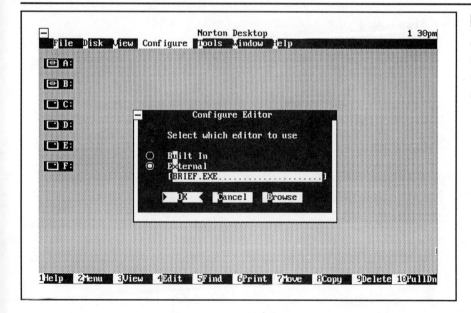

FIGURE 9.15:

Select the editor you want to use in the Configure Editor dialog box

There is also a more serious side to Sleeper. You can use it to hide confidential information on your screen, in case someone not privy to this information unexpectedly comes into your office, or in case you have to move away from your computer for a few moments and don't want anybody to look over and see your screen. Using Sleeper is much faster than closing your application program and then reopening the same file and finding your place after your visitor has left. You can also use a password with Sleeper, so that you are the only person who can turn Sleeper off before returning to your application program.

Before using Sleeper, you must have installed the terminate-and-stay-resident program Nsched on your system. If you did not include Nsched when you made your initial installation, see the section called "Startup Programs" earlier in this chapter for more information. If you try to use the Screen Saver option from the Configure menu without Nsched on your system, a dialog box opens giving you instructions on how to install Nsched.

Choosing the Right Sleeper Image

To start Sleeper, choose Screen Saver from the Configure menu. The dialog box shown in Figure 9.16 opens so that you can choose the screen saver image you want to use. When you first use Sleeper, the default setting is Time and Date. At the top of the Configure Screen Saver/Sleeper dialog box is a drop-down list box containing the names of all the screen savers. You can choose one of the many animated images in this list, such as the Message, RoboMice, or the ever popular Fish Tank.

If your chosen Sleeper image accepts a message or if you want to use your own .PCX image as the screen saver, the Configure command button becomes available, and opens the control dialog box for the specified screen saver. The controls shown in this dialog box will change as you select different screen savers.

Sleeper is not compatible with Microsoft Windows.

To choose a screen saver, just highlight your choice in the Screen Saver Type list box. Then, to demonstrate the screen saver, click on the Test command button. Press any key or move the mouse when you are ready to return to the Configure Screen Saver/Sleeper dialog box.

Use the Screen Blank Delay drop-down list box to set the time period you want to elapse before Sleeper clears your screen and starts the screen saver running.

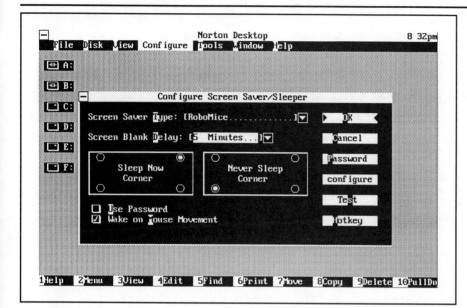

FIGURE 9.16:

Set up your screen saver in the Configure Screen Saver/Sleeper dialog box

 *Sleeper images not supported by your computer video hardware are dimmed in this list.*

The Sleep Now Corner lets you select one corner of your screen so that when you move the mouse into this corner, Sleeper will blank your screen immediately. The Sleep Never Corner turns all the other triggers off, so if you park your mouse in this corner, Sleeper will *not* invoke the screen saver.

You can also use a hotkey to trigger Sleeper if you prefer; just press the Ctrl, Alt, and Z keys simultaneously.

To prevent mouse movements from turning Sleeper off, clear the Wake on Mouse Movement check box. Alternatively, if you want to turn Sleeper off when you move your mouse, check this box instead.

Using a Password

The Sleeper password does not protect your files and directories, it just prevents people from looking at the current document displayed on your screen.

You can prevent unauthorized people from looking at the screen that Sleeper is hiding by using a password. Select the Use Password check box, then use the Password command button from the Configure Screen Saver/Sleeper dialog box. You can use your network password if you have one, or you can enter a custom password of your own. If you *do* specify a password, Sleeper asks you to enter your password before you can regain use of your screen.

If you don't work on sensitive or confidential information, I do not recommend using a password with Sleeper. If you forget the password, the only way to turn Sleeper off and get back to work will be to reboot your computer—and this means that you might lose your unsaved work in any currently open documents.

Using a PCX File as a Sleeper Image

You can add your own images to Sleeper's repertoire as long as they are contained in .PCX format files. Choose PCX File as the screen saver in the Screen Saver Type drop-down list box, then use the Configure command button to enter the name of the file you want to use. You must enter complete information for the file, including drive and directory name, if this information is not part of your DOS path statement.

Using Sleeper with the Desktop Tools

Do not use Sleeper while using an application that you do not want to interrupt, such as a communications program, even if there are long periods of inactivity on your system.

Several of the file- and disk-recovery programs included in the Norton Desktop package can detect the presence of Sleeper and can turn Sleeper off until they have finished their work. It is critical that these programs not be interrupted during the course of their operation; otherwise, data might be lost. The following programs can detect and disable Sleeper:

◆ Disk Tools

◆ Image

◆ Norton Disk Doctor

◆ Safe Format

◆ UnErase

◆ UnFormat

SETTING UP YOUR NETWORK

The Norton Desktop is very good at detecting your network automatically, and configuring itself accordingly. This makes using features like Network Link a breeze. However, there are a few, usually complex, occasions when you may have to configure Norton Desktop manually for a certain configuration. For example, if your computer is attached to two networks at the same time, perhaps LANtastic and Novell, the Desktop will default to Novell, and you will have to configure the Desktop manually to use LANtastic.

Choose Network from the Configure menu to open the Configure Network dialog box shown in Figure 9.17. Select the appropriate network from the Network Type drop-down list box. If you are using any network other than Novell, you can enter a new name into the Workstation Name text box. On a Novell network, this text box is grayed out. You can enter a new timeout period in seconds into the Network Timeout box; the larger this timeout, the longer Desktop attempts to attach to the network. If your network is heavily used, response can be slow, so use a longer timeout.

Check the Trap Network Messages check box if you want network messages displayed in a dialog box; clear the box to let the network manage your messages. Finally, click on OK to save these settings.

CONFIGURING YOUR PRINTER

Choose Printer from the Configure menu to open the Configure Printer dialog box shown in Figure 9.18.

Select a printer configuration file from the list in the dialog box. The Generic printer at the top of the list supports most dot-matrix printers. If you have a LaserJet or PostScript printer, you can select a configuration file

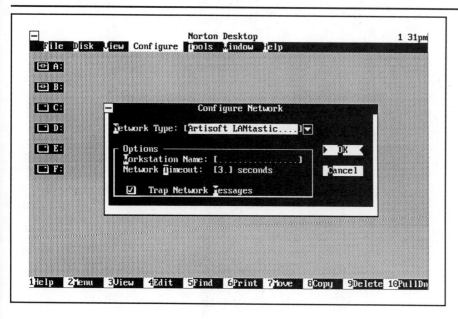

FIGURE 9.17:

You can manually configure your network settings from the Configure Network dialog box

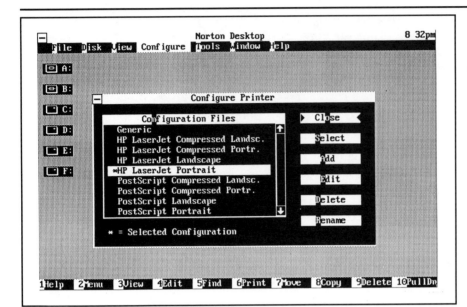

FIGURE 9.18:

*Choose your printer
from the list in the
Configure Printer
dialog box*

*The Print
Setup op-
tion from
the
Desktop Editor File
menu opens the same
dialog box as the
Printer option in the
Norton Desktop Con-
figure menu does.
This means that you
can easily set up dif-
ferent printer con-
figurations for
Desktop printing
and for printing
from the Editor if
you want to.*

for that printer type. The current selection is marked with a star to the left of the list box. Click on Select to choose a new configuration.

If you don't see a configuration file for your printer, or you want to create a special configuration, click on the Add button, enter a name for this configuration, then you will see the Printer Settings dialog box open as Figure 9.19 shows.

This dialog box lets you control both your printer and also the appearance of the printed page:

Options contains three check boxes to control compressed printing, line wrap, and whether or not the lines are numbered as they are printed. Numbered lines are useful if you are a programmer or are working with legal or advertising documents.

Printer Type lets you choose from a range of different kinds of printers. If your printer name is not in this list, there is a very good chance that your printer can work like, or *emulate*, one of these printers.

Printer Setup File allows you to enter the file name you want to use for a printer setup file. You can also use the Browse command button to find the right file. You can use a printer setup file to send a

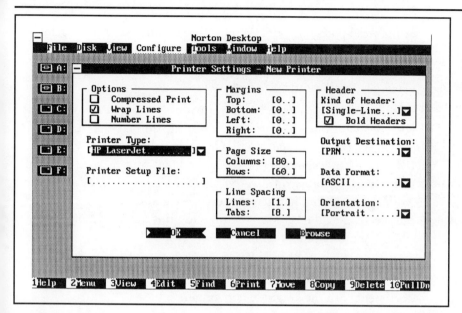

FIGURE 9.19:
Set up your configuration file using the Printer Settings dialog box

You can create several special configurations if you find yourself using certain settings over and over. For example, you could use one for condensed landscape-mode printing, and another for numbered lines in portrait mode if these are the options you use most often.

specific sequence of characters to your printer before printing starts. This way you can access specific printer functions that may not be available from the Printer Settings dialog box. See your printer manual for more details. The setup characters must be contained in a small text file, and you can use the Desktop Editor to create one.

Margins sets the top, bottom, left, and right margins in terms of character positions. For example, enter 5 if you want to use a 5-character left margin. All margins are initially set to zero.

Page Size sets the page size in terms of rows and columns.

Line Spacing sets the line spacing and the number of spaces used for a tab. If you want to double-space your document, enter 2 as the line spacing.

Header selects the type of header used. A header is text that is always printed at the top of every page, and you can choose None, Single-Line, or Double-Line. Single-Line is the default, and prints the file name, along with the page number and the current time and date. Double-Line adds the file's creation date, or last modification date to the information contained in the Single-Line header.

Output Destination selects the name of the port on your computer that the document will be sent to. Normally this will be LPT1 for the default printer port, but you can direct your document to one of the serial ports on your computer, or you can specify a file name and send the document to a disk file. If you choose to send your document to a disk file, you will be asked to enter the file name when you start printing the document.

Data Format lets you specify the format of the data in the document you are about to print. Most simple text files just contain ASCII characters, but if you transfer files between your computer and an IBM mainframe computer, you may find that your files are coded in EBCDIC (pronounced *ebseedick*) rather than ASCII. Similarly, when working with WordStar files that use the eighth bit for their own purposes, select the WordStar setting to print the file. Choose from ASCII, Wordstar, or EBCDIC.

Orientation sets the paper alignment. Portrait prints your document with the long side of the page vertical, while Landscape prints your document with the long side horizontal.

Click on OK when you are happy with your choices in this dialog box, and your new printer configuration file will take its place along with all the other printer configurations in the list box.

If you change your mind about any of these settings at a later date, just come back to the Printer option in the Configure menu, choose the appropriate printer configuration from the list box, and click on the Edit button. This opens the same Printer Settings dialog box, and allows you to change your printer configuration information. You can also click on Rename if you want use a different name for your printer configuration. To remove a configuration from the list, highlight it first, then click on Delete.

SELECTING FILE COMPRESSION OPTIONS

Chapter 18 contains a detailed description of how to use file compression on the Desktop.

You can use the Compress option from the Desktop File menu to compress files you don't use very often so that they take up less space. To specify how you want your files compressed, choose the Compression option from the Configure menu, and you will see the Configure Compression dialog box, as Figure 9.20 shows.

There are two ways to compress files: Implode or Shrink. Implode produces the greatest degree of compression, but runs slower than Shrink. Shrink, on the other hand, is faster, but does not compress the file quite so

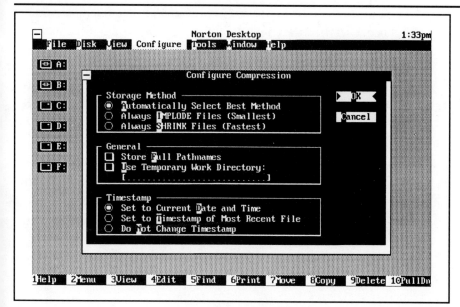

FIGURE 9.20:
Select the file-compression options you want to use in the Configure Compression dialog box

much. You can specify which method you want to use, or as a convenient alternative, you can let the Desktop decide by choosing the Automatically Select Best Method option button. To store the full path as well as the file name, check the Store Full Pathnames check box.

As a file is compressed, a temporary storage area is used to contain interim information as the process proceeds. When the compression is complete, this temporary information is deleted. This means that you have to have more free disk space available during compression than that used by the original and the compressed versions of your file after compression. To use a different drive for this temporary interim information, check the Use Temporary Work Directory check box, and enter the name of the drive and directory.

Finally, you must decide how you want to handle the timestamp on your compressed file. There are three choices:

Set to Current Time and Date assigns the current system time and date to the compressed file. This is the default setting, and is the one you will use most often.

Set to Timestamp of Most Recent File uses the time and date from the most recent file as the time and date for the compressed file, and ignores all earlier files.

A timestamp is the combination of time and date assigned to a file when it is created or modified.

Do Not Change Timestamp keeps the original timestamp, and does not change it when the compressed file is updated.

CONFIGURING THE DESKTOP LINK

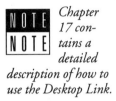

Chapter 17 contains a detailed description of how to use the Desktop Link.

The Desktop Link allows you to connect two computers together and transfer files between them without using a network or swapping endless floppy disks. The hardware configuration for this process is designed to be as automatic as possible, and most of the time reconfiguration is not required. If you are curious about these communications parameters or if line problems demand that some of the settings be adjusted, choose Desktop Link from the Configure menu to open the dialog box shown in Figure 9.21.

This dialog box contains drop-down list boxes for the following communications settings:

Port. Select the parallel or serial port you want to use for communications.

Baud Rate. Choose the baud rate for communications; be sure that both computers are set to the same rate. If you select a rate too high for your computer hardware, Desktop Link will lower the rate automatically until communications are established.

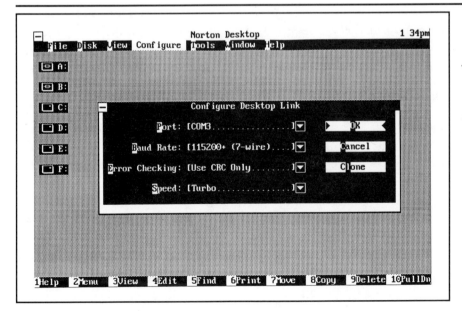

FIGURE 9.21:

Use the Configure Desktop Link to fine-tune communications parameters

Error Checking. Desktop Link always checks data integrity; if errors are detected, the data is retransmitted. Two types of error correction are available: Use Checksum Only or Use CRC Only. With Checksum, the ASCII values of all the data transmitted are added together, and this value is also transmitted to the receiving computer. CRC, short for *Cyclical Redundancy Check*, is a more complex method designed to detect transposition errors that Checksum cannot detect.

Speed. The Speed drop-down list box contains three choices: Turbo (the default setting), Normal, and Slow. Turbo divides the data into transmission blocks of 4K, Normal uses blocks of 2K, and Slow uses the smallest block size of 512 bytes.

All these drop-down list boxes have an initial setting called Auto. Desktop Link will start by using the most efficient method your computer hardware can support. If problems are encountered, Desktop Link will modify the communications parameters until the problems disappear.

When you have adjusted the settings to your satisfaction, click on OK to save these settings for your current Desktop session; see the next section for information on how to make these changes permanent.

SAVING YOUR CHANGES

If you have made changes using selections from the Configure menu, and you want to preserve these changes for future Desktop sessions, make sure the Desktop looks just how you like it, then select Save Configuration from the Configure menu. There is no dialog box associated with this command.

If you do not use this command, any changes you have made to the Desktop will only be available for the duration of your current session, and when you exit from the Desktop, these changes will be lost.

CHAPTER 10

Creating Your Own Menus

The Norton Desktop package contains a menuing system completely independent of the familiar Desktop menus that we have been working with so far. You can automatically create menus specifically tailored to the programs you use on your own computer system, or you can create or edit these menus manually if you wish. Once the menu is in place, you can use it to access any program on your hard disk. You can even use it to access programs on your network. In this chapter we'll be looking at the program that makes all this possible, Norton Menu, and we will work our way through several examples of how you can use these menus to the best advantage on your system.

CREATING MENUS AUTOMATICALLY

The first time you choose the Menu selection from the Desktop Tools menu after installing the Desktop package on your system, a dialog box opens giving you three choices:

Autobuild. Choose this option to create a menu system automatically for your system.

Create. If you want to create the menu system manually, select this option, and see the section in this chapter, "Creating Menus Manually."

Cancel. Select Cancel to return to the Norton Desktop.

Choose the Autobuild command button, and the program will scan your hard disk or disks looking for application programs. When the Desktop recognizes one of your programs, it organizes them into one of the following categories:

◆ Accounting
◆ Communications
◆ Database
◆ Education
◆ Graphics
◆ Home Applications
◆ Integrated Software
◆ Network
◆ Operating
◆ Programming
◆ Project and Time Management
◆ Spreadsheet
◆ Utilities
◆ Word Processing

When the menu is complete, you will see a menu list similar to the one shown in Figure 10.1. This figure shows the menu on my computer system; yours will probably look very different.

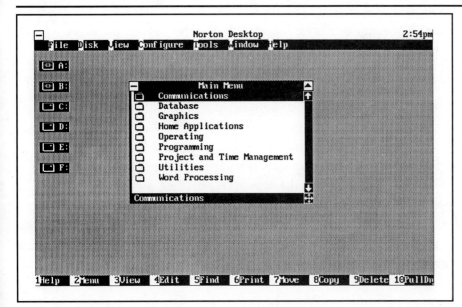

If you don't have any accounting or check-balancing programs, then you won't see the Accounting menu selection in your menu; if you don't have access to a network, you won't see the Network option.

USING YOUR MENUS

When you have created a menu for your system, you can open that menu by selecting the Menu option from the Desktop Tools menu or by using F2 (the Menu key). When the menu opens on the screen, you will see that the top level is headed Main Menu, and any of the major program categories described in the last section that are represented by programs on your system are listed in the menu.

These menu windows behave just as you would expect. Click on the close box at the top-left corner of the menu or press the Escape key from the keyboard to open the menu's Control menu. This Control menu contains the usual selections: Restore, Move, Size, Maximize, Close, and Next. You can move the Main menu around on the screen by dragging the title bar, and you can resize the menu if you drag the bottom-right corner. If some of the Main menu entries are hidden from view because the menu is too small, you can use the scroll bars to see the other entries.

If you open several menus at once, you can use the commands in the Window menu to control them. Use Cascade Menus to arrange the windows, or use Close All if you want to close all the menus at once. Any open menus appear as numbered items at the end of the Window menu; just select an item to make it current.

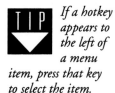

If a hotkey appears to the left of a menu item, press that key to select the item.

Menu items either open a submenu or run a program. To select an item from the menu, highlight the entry and press the Enter key. With the mouse you can just double-click on the entry you want to use. For example, if you have WordPerfect installed on your system, you will see the category Word Processing at the end of your Main Menu. If you select Word Processing, a second window opens, containing the entry WordPerfect. To start your word processor running, select or double-click this entry; the screen clears and the next thing you see is WordPerfect's opening screen. Type your document, and then, when you exit WordPerfect, you return directly to the menu system on the Desktop. Using these menus is much easier than remembering the name of the directory where you installed WordPerfect, and then remembering the correct command-line syntax to open the program. You should be able to do all your work without ever leaving the Norton Desktop or the Norton Menu system on your computer.

CREATING MENUS MANUALLY

If you want to control the menu-creation process on your computer, choose Create from the opening Menu screen to load the Norton Menu program. When Norton Menu opens, choose New from the File menu, and you will see the dialog box shown in Figure 10.2.

Enter a title for your menu, up to 32 characters long, into the New Menu Title text box. A file name must be assigned to this new menu, so choose Auto if you want Norton Menu to choose the name, or check the File option button if you want to specify a name and enter the name into the text box yourself. Click on OK, and your new menu appears in the main Norton

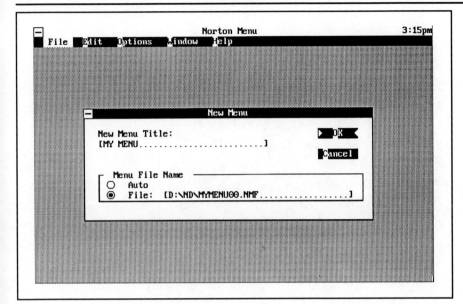

FIGURE 10.2:

Enter a title for your menu using the New Menu dialog box

Menu window as an empty title bar with no menu entries. Now you are ready to add items into the menu from one of the following categories:

Program. You can run a program or execute a DOS command from the menu.

Submenu. You can open a submenu within the menu.

Batch. You can also run a DOS batch file from the menu.

We'll look at each of these options in turn, starting with a program.

CREATING A PROGRAM MENU ITEM

Here are the steps to follow to create a program menu item:

1. Choose the Add option from the Norton Menu Edit menu to open the Add Menu Item dialog box shown in Figure 10.3.

2. Select the Program option button in the Item Type group box.

3. Enter a name for this menu selection, up to 32 characters long, into the Name text box. This entry is what appears in the final menu, sorted into alphabetical order.

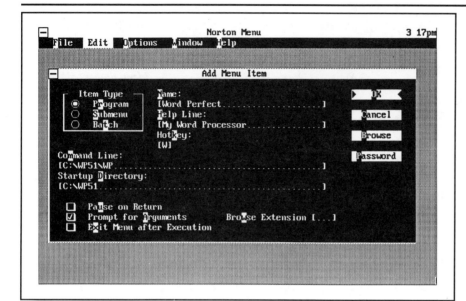

FIGURE 10.3:

Use the Add Menu Item dialog box to create program, submenu, or batch menu items

4. In the Help Line text box, enter any additional information that you want to appear with the menu item, again up to 32 characters long.

5. If you want to use a hotkey with this program, enter the hotkey into the Hotkey box. This hotkey will appear to the left of the menu item, and you can type this hotkey rather than highlighting the item and pressing the Enter key.

6. Enter the sequence of keys that you usually use at the DOS prompt to start this particular program into the Command Line text box. Include complete path information if the directory is not already included in the path statement in your AUTOEXEC.BAT file. For example, if you are a WordPerfect user and the program is in a directory called WP51 on drive C, you might enter:

C:\WP51\WP.EXE

You can also use the Browse command button in the Add Menu Item dialog box to locate the program and directory you are interested in using.

7. Certain DOS programs must be started from a particular directory. If you are using one of these programs, enter the name of this directory into the Startup Directory text box.

8. If the program you are using posts important information on the screen, check the Pause on Return box. This information then stays on the screen so that you can read it.

9. You may want to add more command-line arguments at the time you actually run the program, and you can do this if you check the Prompt for Arguments check box. When you select a menu item with this box checked, the Enter Program Arguments dialog box opens to allow you to enter any additional information. If you would like to pass a file name to the program, you can specify the extension in the Browse Extension text box.

10. If you want to return directly to the Norton Desktop when you quit the program, rather than return to the menu, check the Exit Menu after Execution check box.

11. Use the Password command button to enter a password if you want to use one with this menu selection.

12. Choose the OK command button to return to the main Norton Menu window, then use either the Save or the Save As selections from the Norton Menu File menu to save your new menu.

CREATING A SUBMENU

A submenu is another level of menu that you call from the main menu. You can also call a submenu from another submenu. Using submenus is a good way of grouping similar programs together, and you can create submenus easily using Norton Menu. Here are the steps for creating a submenu:

1. Choose the Add option from the Norton Menu Edit menu to open the Add Menu Item dialog box.

2. Select the Submenu option button in the Item Type group box. The Add Menu Item dialog box changes as Figure 10.4 shows, ready to receive submenu information.

3. Enter a name for this submenu, up to 32 characters long, into the Name text box. This entry will appear in the final menu, arranged in alphabetical order. Alternatively, you can use the Browse command button to select a submenu file from the Files list in the Browse dialog box.

4. In the Help Line text box, enter any additional information that you want to appear with the menu item, again up to 32 characters long.

5. If you want to use a hotkey with this program, enter the hotkey into the Hotkey box. This hotkey will appear to the left of the menu item, and you can type this hotkey rather than highlighting the item and pressing the Enter key.

6. Use the Password command button to enter a password if you want to use one with this menu item.

7. Select the OK command button to return to the main Norton Menu window, then use either the Save or the Save As selections from the Norton Menu File menu to save your new submenu.

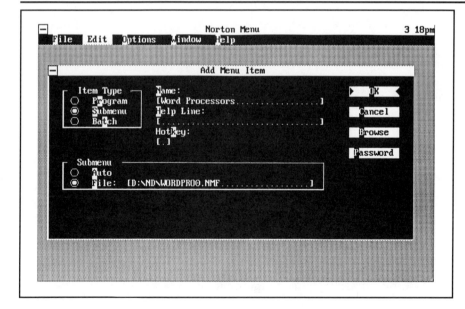

FIGURE 10.4:

The Add Menu Item dialog box ready to receive submenu information

CREATING A BATCH MENU ITEM

NOTE
NOTE

See Chapter 18 for more information on the DOS and Norton Desktop programming commands you can use in your batch files.

You can also add a DOS batch file into a menu if you follow these steps:

1. Choose Add from the Norton Menu Edit menu to open the Add Menu Item dialog box.

2. Select the Batch option button. The Add Menu Item dialog box changes again as Figure 10.5 shows, this time ready to receive batch file information.

3. Enter the name of the menu item, up to 32 characters long, into the Name text box.

4. Enter any help information you want to include into the Help text box.

5. If you want to use a hotkey with your batch file, type the key in the Hotkey text box.

6. Use the Password command button to enter a password if you want to use one with this menu item.

7. Type the text of your batch file into the Batch File Text box. Batch files can contain up to 127 characters per line and must have the file-name extension .BAT. If you plan on entering a long batch file, use Ctrl+PgUp or the Zoom command button to expand the Batch File Text box to fill the screen and become the Norton Menu Editor. This editor is very similar in function and operation to the Desktop Editor described in Chapter 7. Ctrl+PgDn will shrink the text box back to its original size, and you can also use the Exit to NMenu command from the Norton Menu Editor File menu to return to the Add Menu Item dialog box. Remember to use the Save As command from the Norton Menu Editor File menu to save your batch file, and use the .BAT file-name extension. Also, if you try to leave Norton menu without saving your work, a dialog box opens asking if you want to save or discard your changes.

Repeat the steps in these last three sections of this chapter as many times as necessary to build up a complete menu system made up of the application programs, submenus, and batch files you want to use. The steps may seem long and complex at first, but after you have used them a couple of times, they will rapidly become second nature.

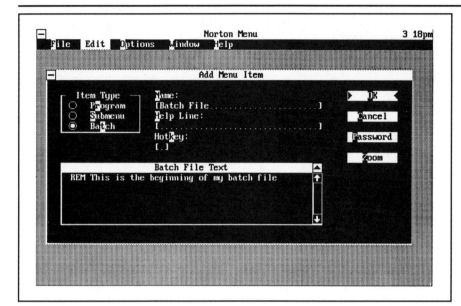

FIGURE 10.5:

*The Add Menu Item
dialog box ready to
receive batch file
information*

IMPORTING MENUS

If you are already using menus made by the Norton Commander or by
Direct Access, you can import them for use with Norton Menu. Choose the
Import selection from the Norton Menu File menu to open the Menu Import dialog box, then select the appropriate option button for either the Norton Commander or for Direct Access. You can use the Browse command
button in this dialog box to select the file you want to import. Select OK,
and a dialog box opens asking if you want to append this menu to the end
of your current menu or replace the current menu; choose Append or
Replace, and the menu will be imported into Norton Menu.

EDITING YOUR MENUS

Norton Menu may appear to make a mistake during the automatic menu-
generation process if one of your application programs has the same executable file name as one of the names in the Norton Menu database. Also,
you may decide that the current arrangement of items in your menus does
not fit your way of working. As you might expect, there are commands in

Norton Menu to edit, delete, move, or copy menu items; you can even change the menu title if you get tired of it.

EDITING OR DELETING MENU ITEMS

Use the selections in the Norton Menu Edit menu to modify your menus. To edit a menu item, first highlight the item, and then choose Modify (Ctrl+E) from the Edit menu. This opens the Edit Menu Item dialog box shown in Figure 10.6. This figure shows the dialog box open on a program entry. The Edit Menu Item dialog box will contain different entries when you edit a program, submenu, or batch entry.

This dialog box works in the same way as the Add Menu Item dialog box described in previous sections, with one notable exception. You cannot change the item *type*: program, submenu, or batch. All the entries in the Item Type group box at the top-left corner of this dialog box are dimmed out and unavailable. You can edit or change anything else in this dialog box, however, including the menu name, the help information, or the hotkey. Just type in your changes, then choose the OK command button and you will see the new menu in the Norton Menu main window.

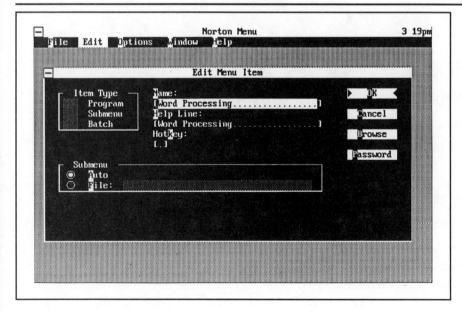

FIGURE 10.6:

Use the Edit Menu Item dialog box to modify your menu entries

To remove an item from your menu, highlight the item you want to delete, then use the Clear command from the Edit menu or press the Delete key on the keyboard. A dialog box opens asking if you are sure that you want to delete the selected item. Choose OK to complete the deletion, or choose Cancel to return to the main Norton Menu window.

To change the title of a menu, use the Menu Title (Ctrl+T) command from the Edit menu to open the Edit Menu Title dialog box where the current menu title is displayed in the Menu Title text box. Type in the new title, then use the OK command button to dismiss this dialog box and return to the main Norton Menu window.

As time goes by you will undoubtedly make changes to the programs and directories on your hard disk. You could modify your menu structure by hand to reflect these changes, but it is much easier to have the Norton Menu program do it for you. Choose the Autobuild option from the File menu to open the dialog box shown in Figure 10.7.

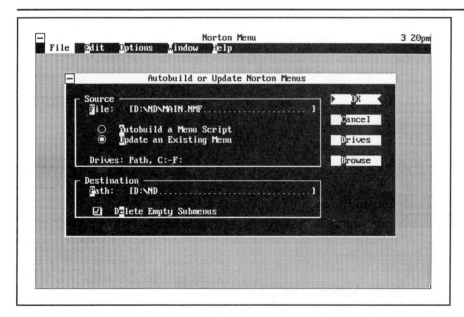

FIGURE 10.7:

Select Update an Existing Menu in the Autobuild or Update Norton Menus dialog box to make Norton Menu update your menus automatically

Select the Update an Existing Menu option button in the Autobuild or Update Norton Menus dialog box to make Norton Menu update your menus automatically. The program scans your hard disk looking for the new disk and directory path information and updates your menu automatically. For more information on the Autobuild feature, see the section called "Creating and Maintaining Corporate Menus" later in this chapter.

MOVING AND COPYING MENU ITEMS

If you want to create a new menu that will be very similar to an existing menu, it is faster to copy that menu and change it than it is to enter the new menu from scratch. To do this, highlight the menu item you want to copy, then choose the Copy (Ctrl+C) command from the Edit menu. The Copy command temporarily stores a copy of the menu item in an area of computer memory called the *paste buffer*. This concept is very similar to the Clipboard used by many programs, including the Desktop Editor. Once the menu is in this paste buffer or Clipboard, you can use the Paste (Ctrl+V) command to recall the menu item and copy it into its new location.

Once the menu item is in its new location, you can use the Edit command to modify it to suit the new location.

 *If you have worked with the Clipboard in the Desktop Editor, then using the Cut, Copy, and Paste commands in Norton Menu will be easy.*

If you want to move a menu item to a new location, rather than create a copy of it, use the Cut (Ctrl+X) command. Cut also uses the Clipboard to store the menu item until you use the Paste command to install the menu item into its new location. Highlight the menu item that you want to be below the item you are moving, then use the Paste command. In other words, Paste inserts the menu item from the Clipboard *before* the menu item you highlighted.

If you want all your menu items arranged in alphabetical order, don't bother to arrange them by hand, use the Sort Menu Items command from the Options menu instead. This command does not open a dialog box, but you will be able to see that the menu items have been rearranged.

CUSTOMIZING NORTON MENU

There are several commands you can use from the Options menu to customize or configure Norton Menu so the program works the way you like.

SETTING PREFERENCES

Select Preferences from the Options menu to open the dialog box shown in Figure 10.8. Settings in this dialog box control Norton Menu features such as how menu item icons are displayed, and whether or not you will be prompted to confirm delete operations. The Preferences dialog box contains the following check boxes:

Confirm on Delete. Check this box if you always want to be prompted to confirm a delete operation. Some people find these confirmation boxes annoying; leave the box blank and Norton Menu will delete the menu item immediately, without asking for your permission.

Autosave Files. When you check this box, menu files are saved automatically when you make changes to them. This is a good safety feature, and I suggest that you leave this box checked.

Ask for Edit/Run Password. When this box is checked, you will be asked to enter a password if you switch between Norton Menu's Run and Edit modes. Run and Edit modes are described in the section called "Creating and Maintaining Corporate Menus," later in this chapter. The Password command button is dimmed and unavailable until you check the Ask for Edit/Run Password check box.

Check Program Names. Check this box to make Norton Menu check for the existence of a program before attempting to launch that program. This is another useful safety option, so check this box now.

Menu Item Icons. Check this box to place small icons to the left of all your menu items—the icon precedes the hotkey if there is one.

NOTE NOTE *Menu file names are built from the first eight letters of the menu plus the file-name extension .NMF. For example, the main menu is stored in a menu file called MAIN.NMF.*

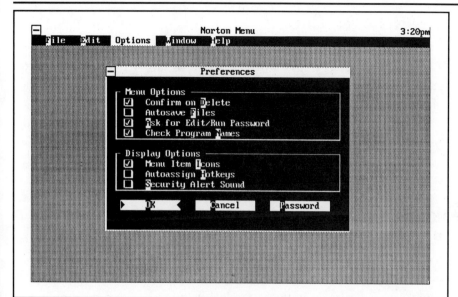

Use the settings in the Preferences dialog box to customize your Norton Menu program

Autoassign Hotkeys. By checking this box, you can have Norton Menu assign hotkeys to menu items automatically. Hotkeys are assigned from A to Z, then from 0 through 9, for a total of 36 hotkeys. If your menu contains more than 36 items, Norton Menu cannot automatically assign hotkeys to items 37 and higher.

Security Alert Sound. When this box is checked, an alert will sound when a user makes three consecutive unsuccessful login attempts. The alarm lasts for several seconds.

When you have completed your selections using the Preferences dialog box, use the OK command button to return to the main Norton Menu window.

USING A SCREEN SAVER

See Chapter 9 for a complete description of Sleeper, the Norton Desktop Screen Saver.

Just as you can invoke Sleeper, the Norton Desktop Screen Saver, on the Desktop, you can use the Screen Saver selection in the Options menu to set Sleeper up to work with Norton Menu. The steps you use to set up Sleeper and the screen saver images you can use with Norton Menu are exactly the same as those described in Chapter 9, and so they will not be repeated here.

CHANGING THE CLOCK

Use the Clock selection from the Options menu to set the system clock on your computer. It is important that the clock be set properly for several reasons, but particularly to ensure that the date and time associated with a file are correct.

You can also choose the format of the time displayed by Norton Menu—either 12- or 24-hour style. If you don't want to see the clock in Norton Menu, just clear the Display Time check box.

LOOKING AT MENU INFORMATION

Use the Menu Info selection from the Norton Menu Options menu to open the dialog box shown in Figure 10.9. The Menu Info dialog box displays information about the selected menu item, including the menu title and file name. You will also see information about the menu item type: program, submenu, or batch. If the item is a batch file, Script Data gives a count of the bytes in the file.

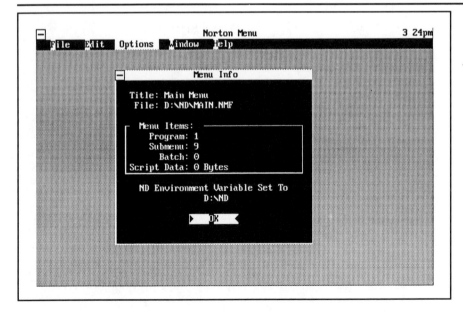

FIGURE 10.9:

Use Menu Information from the Options menu to display information about your menu items

CREATING AND MAINTAINING CORPORATE MENUS

If you are in charge of a number of computers in your office, you might consider setting up a Norton Menu system for each user. There are several features in the Norton Menu program that make this process much easier than you might imagine.

For example, you can almost guarantee that no two computer systems in your office are identical in every respect; some will have one hard disk, others will have two or more, and almost all of your users will have different directory structures. To set up menus for all these users may seem an impossible task, but it is really quite straightforward. Here is a summary of the major steps:

1. Install Norton Menu on your computer.

2. Build a menu system.

3. Use the Export command from the Norton Menu File menu to create and export a menu symbolic text file (more on this in a moment).

4. Install Norton Menu and this symbolic text file on a user's computer system.

5. Use the Autobuild function from the File menu to automatically update the menu system for this user, adding each user's particular disk and directory path information into the user's menu file.

And that's all there is to it; just repeat steps 4 and 5 on all the other computers in your office, and everyone can use Norton Menu.

A menu is usually stored in a binary file, but when you use the Export selection from the Norton Menu File menu, you translate that binary file into an ASCII file humans can read. You can look at or edit this ASCII file with the Desktop Editor if you wish. This ASCII file is referred to as a *symbolic text file*. Figure 10.10 shows a listing of the symbolic text file created by exporting WORDPROC.NMF to the symbolic text file WORDPROC.NAB. All the menu items, command-line options, and passwords and hotkeys (if they were used) are present in this file.

```
           nabfile

           ;****************************
           menufile      "wordproc.nmf"
           ;****************************
           menutitle     "Word Processing"


           item          "WordPerfect"
           ;------------------------
           type          PROGRAM
           command       "wp.exe"
           assoc         "wphelp.fil"
           help          "WordPerfect Corporation"
           startupdir    "c:\wp51"
```

FIGURE 10.10:
A listing of the symbolic text file WORDPROC.NAB

In the next section, we'll look at the steps needed to export this symbolic text file, and in the following section, we'll examine how you can specifically customize that file for each of your users.

EXPORTING THE SYMBOLIC TEXT FILE

Here are the steps to follow to create and export a menu file:

1. Select Export from the File menu to open the Export Menu dialog box shown in Figure 10.11.

2. Highlight the menu file you want to export.

3. Use the Directory command button to change to a different drive or directory if you wish.

4. Select the OK command button to start the export process.

5. When the export process is complete, you will see a dialog box open confirming that the selected menu was exported successfully.

The menu file you selected is transformed into a symbolic text file with the file-name extension of .NAB. You can use the Desktop Editor (or any other text editor) to change this file if you wish. Do not change the file using normal word-processor commands, unless your word processor is in text-only mode, as you may accidentally introduce hidden formatting characters into the file that will cause problems for Norton Menu.

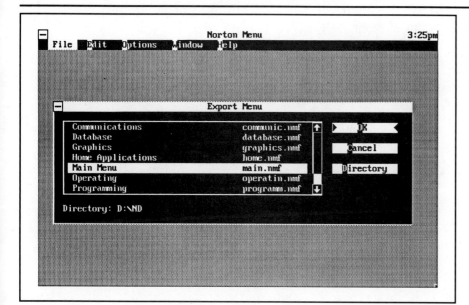

FIGURE 10.11:

Select a menu file to export using the Export Menu dialog box

USING AUTOBUILD TO CUSTOMIZE THE MENU SYSTEM

The next step in this process is to convert the symbolic text file back into a form that Norton Menu can work with. The symbolic text file with the .NAB file-name extension must be converted back into a binary file with the file-name extension .NMF. This binary file must also contain correct directory information if the menu system is to function correctly. You can accomplish both of these tasks using Autobuild from the File menu. Here are the steps:

1. Create a directory for Norton Menu on the target computer. The default Norton Menu directory is \ND. It makes good sense to create this same directory on all the computers that you plan to use with menuing systems to simplify future operations and maintenance.

2. Install Norton Menu and the symbolic text file on the target computer.

3. Choose Autobuild from the File menu, and you will see the dialog box shown in Figure 10.12.

4. Select the Autobuild a Menu Script option button.

5. Select a symbolic text file, either the file you just exported or the default file MASTER.NAB. MASTER.NAB will scan your system looking for application programs and install them in a menu organized by category.

6. You can also use the Browse command button to look for NAB files.

7. Enter the name of the directory you want to use with the menus on the target computer into the Path text box.

8. Choose OK to start the autobuild process running. Autobuild translates the symbolic text file into a binary file, and automatically customizes this binary file to adjust for any differences in drive or directory structure on the target computer.

When Norton Menu completes the autobuild process, the new menu appears, and your user can start working with this menu immediately.

If you are concerned about your users tampering with the menu system after you have installed it, you can turn off the menu bar in Norton Menu with the Choose Run Mode selection in the Options menu. This allows your users to launch application programs from the menu system but prevents them gaining access to the File, Edit, Options, Windows, or Help menus. To

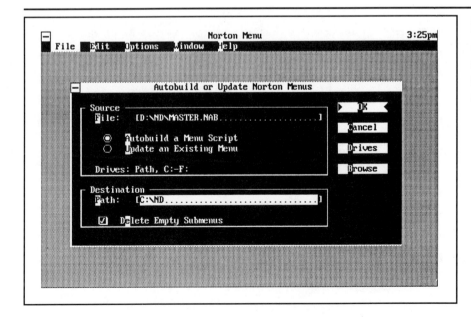

FIGURE 10.12:

Use the Autobuild option from the File menu to customize the menu system

turn the menu bar on again, type Alt+R from the keyboard or double-click the close box in the upper-left corner of the main Norton Menu window.

USING NORTON MENU FROM THE DOS COMMAND LINE

Chapter 19 details all the command-line switches you can use with the programs that comprise the Norton Desktop package.

You can also run Norton Menu from the DOS command line using several different switches or command-line arguments. The usual syntax is:

NMENU *pathname /switches*

where *pathname* should include both a file name and directory details if the directory is not specified in your path command in AUTOEXEC.BAT, and *switches* can be either /edit or /run. If you use /edit, Norton Menu will let you run and edit your menus, but if you use /run, all editing ability is removed and all you can do is run the menus.

PART FOUR

Protecting Your Disks and Files

Part IV shows you how and why you should use Norton Backup to back up essential files and directories, and how to protect your files from accidental deletion or a computer virus attack. Part IV also covers how to speed up your disk system by reducing or eliminating file fragmentation, and how to diagnose and fix disk-related problems.

CHAPTER 11

Backing Up Your
Hard Disk

A *backup* is an up-to-date copy of all your files that you can use to reload your system in case of an accident. It is an insurance policy against anything happening to the hundreds or possibly thousands of files you might have on your hard disk. If the unthinkable were to occur—losing all your files due to a hard-disk problem and not having any back-up copies—it would take you weeks or even months to recreate all those files, if indeed they could be recreated. If you run your own business or work on your computer from home, it is crucial that you make regular, consistent backups—because no one will do it for you, and it is a sad fact that hard disks do fail occasionally, usually at the most inconvenient moment.

PLANNING YOUR BACKUPS

You should get into the habit of backing up your system regularly, so that you never have to do any extra work as a result of a damaged or missing file. How often you make a backup depends on how much you use your computer and how often your files change. If you use your computer for entertainment on weekends, you don't have to back up very often. If your business depends on data in the computer, then you should back up at least every day. If you are a programmer, a writer, or the person in charge of the finance department, who is concerned with up-to-date and accurate accounts payable and receivable, then consider backing up your new data twice a day.

WHY SHOULD YOU MAKE A BACKUP?

There are several reasons for making a backup of the files on your hard disk:

◆ Protection against hard-disk failure is the most common and important reason for backing up your hard disk. A hard disk can fail at almost any time, but it is always at the most inconvenient moment. You can install an up-to-date backup in a few minutes and be back in business very quickly. Your bank, utility company, and city, county, and state government agencies are constantly backing up their disk systems on all their computers to avoid having the downtime and expense involved in recreating their data.

◆ Protection against accidental deletion is another prime reason for making a backup. UnErase and SmartCan (described in Chapter 12) can provide protection up to a point, but after the file has been purged from the SMARTCAN directory, you may not be able to recover it using UnErase; you will have to go to your backup set to find a copy of the file.

◆ Moving files from one computer to another can be done by means of a backup, particularly if you are working with files that are too large to fit onto a single floppy disk.

◆ You can use a backup as a way of freeing up valuable disk space on your computer. This is safer than just deleting the files; you can always recover and restore the files if you decide that you needed them after all.

◆ You can also use a backup to make a permanent archive at the end of a project, when a person leaves your company, or at the closing of the company's books at the end of the fiscal year.

◆ If you are going to use the hard-disk optimizing program Speed Disk to defragment your hard disk, it is a good idea to make a complete backup of all your important files before using it for the first time; your hard disk and the optimizing program may be incompatible. Power outages and brownouts can also occur at any time. Speed Disk is discussed in Chapter 14.

◆ You should make a precautionary backup of your files before you perform any maintenance work on your files and directories, such as cleaning out old demonstration software that you have decided you don't need and removing games that you don't play anymore. No matter how careful you are, there is always the possibility that you will accidentally delete a file that really belongs to a different application program. If you find that this application program won't start after your housekeeping session, you can restore the missing file from your backup.

WHEN SHOULD YOU MAKE A BACKUP?

One of the most neglected topics in discussing backups is the emphasis on a consistent backup plan. Plan your strategy and—most important—stick to it! With no backup plan, you'll accumulate disks haphazardly, waste disks, and waste valuable time looking for that elusive file.

The first decision to make is how often you should make a backup. To arrive at a conclusion that fits the kind of work you do, ask yourself the following questions:

◆ How fast does the data in your files change: every minute, ten minutes, day, week, or month?

◆ How important to your day-to-day operations is this data? Can you work without it, and how long would it take to recreate the data?

◆ How much will it cost to recreate the data in terms of time spent and business lost?

It all comes down to a very simple rule: back up all the files that you cannot afford to lose.

In our computerized world, it may take hours or days to create and maintain a file, but it can be lost or destroyed in just microseconds. A hard-disk failure, a mistaken delete command, overwriting a long file with a short one with the same name—these can destroy a file just as completely as fire or flood. You just have to lose one file to become a convert to regular, planned backups.

WHAT KIND OF BACKUP SHOULD YOU MAKE?

A common backup strategy is to make a complete backup every Friday, and then make partial backups each day or even twice a day of all the files that have changed since that backup. This ensures that you have all your files on a backup disk somewhere. For example, if your hard disk crashed on Thursday, you could restore last Friday's full backup, and restore all the incremental backups made since then.

It is a very good idea to keep one full backup of your system in storage somewhere for at least six months; a year is even better. The file that you most want to recover may be the file you deleted three months ago, and your most recent backups won't show a trace of it.

You may reuse disks for future backups, but be sure to replace them regularly (for example, every six months) with brand new disks.

If you use disks as your backup media, use 3½-inch disks if you can, rather than 5¼-inch disks, because the smaller disks are much more robust and less prone to mechanical damage. They also hold more data. Don't try to save money by using generic or secondhand disks for your backup; this will turn out to be a false economy. Use the best quality disks you can afford for your backups.

HOW IS A BACKUP MADE?

When you create a new file or modify an existing file on your system, DOS uses one of the file's attributes, the archive attribute, to tell the rest of the world that the file has changed in some way. Norton Backup looks at this archive attribute and uses it to decide whether to back up the file or to leave it alone, depending on the backup method you have selected. When the backup is complete, Norton Backup resets this archive attribute so that it knows that the file has been backed up.

For some files this is a one-time operation; the file is created, the archive attribute tells Norton Backup to back up the file the next time you run it, and Norton Backup obliges. Other files that you or an application program change—such as a company inventory database, a set of personnel records at your dentist, or a long report that you have been working on for weeks— change so often that they are backed up every time you run Norton Backup.

When you use Norton Backup to make a backup of the files and directories on your system, there is a definite sequence that you should follow in configuring the program to your specific hardware and then testing that the backup was successful. Here is a summary of the major steps involved in making a backup. These steps also provide the outline for the main part of this chapter:

1. Because of the many possible hardware configurations, you have to tell Norton Backup about the hardware you have on your system. Norton Backup provides a function for this purpose called Configure, which performs a short series of tests to confirm that the chosen settings will work and produce a good backup.

2. Go ahead and back up the files and directories on your system. This you do with the Backup feature.

3. After the first backup, and again after you change any of the hardware on your computer, you should make a comparison between the files in the backup and the original files on your disk. This safety measure, called Compare, is designed to ensure that if and when you ever need to restore files from your backup, perhaps many months after you originally made the backup, your files will be usable.

4. In the event of an accident of some kind, you can make a claim on your backup insurance policy and use Restore to reload your files from the backup floppy disks onto your hard disk again.

ON-SITE OR OFF-SITE STORAGE?

If you use a computer as part of your business, consider rotating one of your backup sets to a safe, off-site storage location, just as you would for any other important company documents such as financial records, photographs, drawings, and patent or trademark applications. People often back up their hard disk and put the backup disks right next to the computer. If the computer is damaged by an accident—be it fire, earthquake, flood, or vandalism—there is a good chance that the backups will be damaged, too.

If you *do* decide to keep your backups on location, remember that not all fireproof safes and strong boxes are rated for storing magnetic media. Most are meant for papers, but disks can become unusable at much lower temperatures than 451°F, the temperature it takes to ignite paper. You should also protect your backup set against extremes of temperature, the presence of magnetic fields, and contaminants, such as dust and dirt, moisture, smoke, and chemicals. Very often the damage after a small fire does not come from smoke and flames but from the water used to fight the fire.

If you decide to use off-site storage, however, you will find that many companies specialize in the safe, secure storage of magnetic media; see if there is one in your area that will pick up and return your backups on a regular schedule. Look in the yellow pages under "Computer Data Storage" or "Business Records Storage."

The usual way that businesses rotate backups through an off-site storage location is to label all the disks for week one as Backup Set 1 and send them off to the storage company. Then during week two they make Backup Set 2 and send it out for storage, too. They start making Backup Set 3 and ask the courier company to return the disks that make up Set 1 so that they can be reused during week four. This way, as they are creating a new backup set, there is always one set in secure storage, and another, older set in the process of being returned to them for reuse.

CONFIGURING NORTON BACKUP

The first time you use Norton Backup, you must go through a series of steps that test your computer to make sure that you can take advantage of your hardware in making your backups. This process defines the types of floppy-disk drives you have attached to your computer as well as the kind of disks you plan to use for your backups. Norton Backup also performs a backup compatibility test to check that your chosen configuration works. This information is stored in a file on your hard disk so that the next time you run Norton Backup, this file automatically loads your default settings.

It is not difficult to complete this configuration process; just follow the instructions given in the dialog boxes. Also, you must complete the configuration before you can actually make a backup.

Start Norton Backup from the Tools menu on the Desktop or type:

NBACKUP

at the DOS prompt.

An alert box opens to tell you that Norton Backup has not been configured for this computer yet. Click on the Start Configuration command button to continue or Quit to leave Norton Backup. You have to complete four main configuration groups before you can use Norton Backup: Program Level, Video and Mouse, Backup Devices, and Configuration Tests. In the sections that follow, we'll look at each of these groups in turn, starting with the program or user level choices.

Choosing Your User or Program Level

Norton Backup has three user levels: basic, advanced, and preset. When you first install Norton Backup, the program is configured at the basic level. When you change this user level, you change the number of options available to you in the Backup, Compare, and Restore windows. Norton Backup selects the safest settings and automatically configures them for you at the basic level. At the advanced level, you can choose how these same settings are made. The preset level is for nontechnical people who want to see a simpler program interface, and who want to use a backup strategy set up by someone else. As you become more familiar with Norton Backup you will probably want to change your user level from basic or preset to advanced. The two sections in this chapter that describe making full and partial backups will be done at the basic level. The preset level is described under the heading "Using Setup Files" near the end of the chapter. The advanced options are described in the sections called "Choosing Backup Options" and "Choosing Restore Options" later on in this chapter.

VIDEO AND MOUSE OPTIONS

If you have already used Norton Desktop or NDConfig to set up your video and mouse options, these settings are loaded by Norton Backup and presented as the current defaults. This means that you don't have to reselect the same information again in Norton Backup. See Chapter 9 for a full description of all the video and mouse settings, and how to choose custom screen colors.

DEFINING YOUR BACKUP DEVICES

If you use an external tape drive, make sure it is turned on before you configure Norton Backup, otherwise the program may not be able to see the tape drive.

Norton Backup checks your floppy-disk drives and shows you what it recognizes in a dialog box. Make sure that the disk-drive capacities are correct, then click on OK. Next, Norton Backup performs two configuration tests on your hardware, a Disk Change test and a Direct Memory Access (DMA) test. Remove any floppy disks from your drives before starting the Floppy Drive Change Line test, then click on the Start Test button.

DMA is a method of data transfer that does not involve the computer's microprocessor—and because of this, the transfer is very fast. Unfortunately, some PC-compatibles may not support high-speed DMA transfers due to hardware limitations. The DMA test is designed to find out whether or not your computer can do this. If these tests fail, Norton Backup can compensate for them and still make reliable backups; if your computer passes these tests, no changes will be necessary.

Under certain circumstances it is possible that failing the DMA test will stop your computer running; if this happens just restart your computer and start the Norton Backup again. You will find that Norton Backup has checked the Slow DMA check box to indicate the change from high-speed to low-speed DMA. Click on OK to close this dialog box.

SELECTING A DISK LOG STRATEGY

Before Norton Backup starts to back up your disk, the program makes a list of all the files and directories on your hard disk. This is called a *log*, and there are two ways Norton Backup can make one:

Fastest. If you choose this setting, Norton Backup reads your hard disk directly. This works very quickly, but cannot work on substituted or network disk drives.

Most Compatible. This setting is somewhat slower, but will be able to read information from any kind of hard disk.

Many computers can run at more than one speed, and sometimes Norton Backup can experience problems running at the fastest speed. This typically occurs when microprocessors are *pushed* or run at a clock speed faster than the one they were designed for. If the High Speed CPU Caution box is checked, you will see a warning dialog box open when you next start Norton Backup, reminding you to engage the lower speed before continuing with the backup.

Norton Backup is now configured. The next stage of this process is to run the compatibility test.

RUNNING THE BACKUP COMPATIBILITY TEST

Run another compatibility test if you change any of the hardware in your computer, especially hard disks or expansion boards. These additions can sometimes have subtle effects on the way the DMA works, and you should know about them before you realize that you cannot restore lost files from your backup. This step is described at the end of this section.

The floppy-disk compatibility test actually performs a short backup to a floppy disk, thus eliminating any doubts about Norton Backup's effectiveness or compatibility. It starts up automatically. Be sure to run and complete this test on your computer before you try to make a backup. You need to use two floppy disks or one tape during this test. The disks do not have to be formatted, but if they contain any files, Norton Backup will alert you before it overwrites and destroys them. It also needs full and exclusive access to the floppy disk or tape drive during this test, so you will not be able to access your drives with another program until this test is complete. Most of this test is performed automatically in a hands-off mode; however, you will be asked to choose the disk drive or tape you want to use with the backup.

If you are using a tape, insert a tape cartridge into your drive. If you don't have a formatted tape, Backup will format the tape for you; however, be aware that the format can take up to 45 minutes to complete. If the tape already contains data, you can choose to overwrite the data, append the test to the end of the tape, or use a different tape. The test only takes about 2MB of tape space. Only one tape is used, so you will not be asked to change tapes.

Click on the OK command button to start the test, and then sit back and watch Norton Backup run the test. The Backup Progress window opens to show progress made. Follow the prompts that tell you when to insert the disks. If the disks were not formatted, Norton Backup formats them first, then makes a test backup. When the backup part of the test is complete, follow the prompt on the screen and insert the first disk once again for the compare part of the test, then click on Continue. The Compare Progress window opens, prompting for the second disk as necessary. At the end of this phase of the test, you will see one of the following messages in an alert box on the screen:

The compatibility test completed successfully. You can now make reliable backups. This message indicates that your computer will work with Norton Backup without any problems of any kind.

Compatibility test was interrupted. Rerun the compatibility test to verify your configuration. This message indicates that the tests were interrupted. You must complete the tests before you can be sure of making reliable backups on your system. Be sure to run the tests next time you start Norton Backup.

Compatibility test failed. This message indicates that your computer failed the test for some reason. Press F1 to display a Help screen that suggests some things you can try to solve the compatibility problem on your computer. A dialog box will open the next time you start Norton Backup to remind you that the compatibility test failed. You must correct any problems and pass the test before you can use Norton Backup.

Norton Backup works best when both the Files and the Buffers settings in your CONFIG.SYS file are set to 30. Use the CONFIG.SYS Modification dialog box to confirm these settings, then choose which of the following options you would like to add to your AUTOEXEC.BAT file:

Add Norton Backup directory to the PATH statement. Check this box to add the Norton Backup directory to your path statement. If you used the Install program to load the Norton Desktop package, there is a very good chance that Norton Backup is installed in the Norton Desktop directory, and that the appropriate information is already present in your AUTOEXEC.BAT file.

Set the NBACKUP environment variable. Check this box to establish a DOS environment setting for Norton Backup.

Load the Backup Scheduler TSR. Check this box if you want to load the Norton Scheduler each time you start your computer.

The Norton Backup files are stored on your hard disk in a compressed form to save space, and they are automatically expanded each time they are used. On a slow computer, you may experience a large time delay during this file-expansion process; however, you can choose to expand these files permanently—they will take up more disk space, but the Norton Backup program will run faster. In the Expand Program Files dialog box, choose the Expand command button to permanently expand the Norton Backup program files or the Cancel command button to continue with the configuration.

Click on Save to save your configuration settings on disk, and then open the main Norton Backup window. Your computer has passed all the tests, and you are now ready to make your first real backup.

Norton Backup contains a Configure button that opens the Configure window in Figure 11.1. Once you have established your initial operating settings, you will probably never need to use Configure, except under the following circumstances:

◆ to change the program or user level.

◆ to store catalog files in a different directory.

◆ to check that newly installed disk drives or other hardware configuration changes do not affect Norton Backup.

If you need to rerun any of the tests you've already run, choose either the Backup Devices or the Configuration Tests command buttons in the Configure window. The tests work in the same way I have already mentioned, so I will not describe them here again.

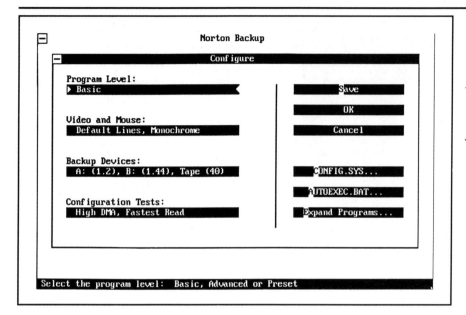

Use the Configure window to change the program or user level, and to rerun the Configuration tests if you change your disk hardware

BACKING UP YOUR HARD DISK

Start Norton Backup by selecting it in the Tools menu or by typing:

NBACKUP

from the DOS command line. There are four entries on the menu bar as Figure 11.2 shows. Not all these menu selections are available at all times:

File lets you work with setup files. Setup files are described later in this chapter.

Macro lets you create or run Norton Backup macros, which are described later in this chapter.

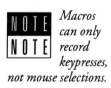

Macros can only record keypresses, not mouse selections.

Tape Tools contains selections that help you work with your tape drive. See the section called "Making Tape Backups" later in this chapter for more information.

Help contains context-sensitive help appropriate to your user level. The menu also contains specific entries for the major components of Norton Backup: Backup, Compare, Restore, Schedule and Configure.

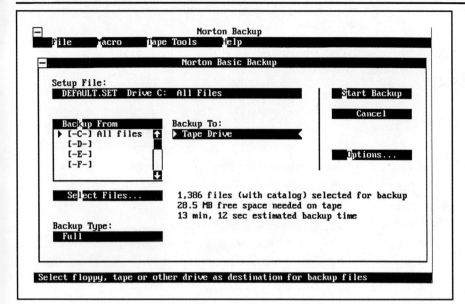

There are also six command buttons in the center of the Norton Backup opening window that handle the main program functions:

Backup

Compare

Restore

Backup Scheduler

Configure

Quit

Choose the Backup command button to open the Backup window. The major elements of the Backup window are the following:

◆ The Setup File button lets you select the setup file you want to use for the backup. Click on this button and you will see a listing of all the setup files on your system.

◆ The Backup From button lets you select the hard-disk drive to back up. Highlight the drive letter and press the spacebar, or click on the drive letter using the right mouse button.

◆ The Select Files command button lets you choose the directories and files to back up.

◆ The Backup Type button tells Norton Backup the type of backup to make.

◆ The Backup To button lets you tell Norton Backup where to put the backup set. The information below this box shows the number of files selected for inclusion in this backup, and the amount of space these files occupy. When you back up to floppy disks, you will see an estimate of the number of disks needed to hold the backup, along with an estimate of how long the backup is expected to take.

◆ The Options command button lets you choose backup options, such as whether to use data compression or error correction, and whether Norton Backup should quit when the backup is finished.

◆ The Start Backup command button actually starts the backup process.

All of these options are described in more detail later in this chapter.

MAKING A COMPLETE BACKUP

The first thing you should do after configuring Norton Backup is make a full backup of all the directories and files on your hard disk. Here are the steps to follow:

1. Make sure you have enough floppy disks and labels for the backup set. You can find out how many to use by reading the estimate at the bottom of the Backup window.

2. Launch Norton Backup and select the Backup command button.

3. Choose the Setup File button, and select the FULL.SET file from the list.

4. Use the right mouse button to click on the drive you want to back up in the Backup From list box. The words All files appear to the right of the drive you select.

5. Select Full using the Backup Type button.

6. Choose the floppy-disk drive you want to back up to with the Back-up To button.

7. Select the Start Backup command button to start the backup operation running, and then just follow the directions on the screen for changing disks.

Figure 11.3 shows the Backup Progress window. The four main parts of this window are:

◆ At the top left, the tree display indicates the directory being backed up.

◆ At the top right, the file display shows individual files as they are backed up.

◆ At the lower left, this window shows how the current floppy disk is filling up and how the whole backup is proceeding.

◆ At the lower right, the panel shows the name of the setup file, the catalog file, and the estimated and actual tapes or disks, files, bytes, and time used for this backup.

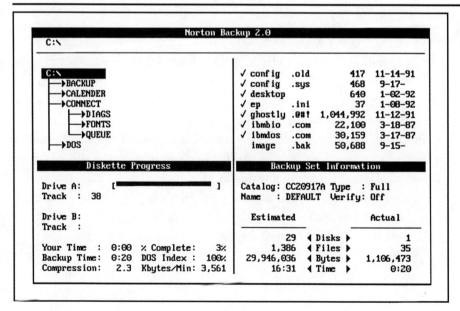

FIGURE 11.3:

The Backup Progress window shows information about the current backup operation

Be sure to label your disks in the proper order (for example, Disk 1 of 25...).

If you wait more than approximately 15 seconds before inserting a floppy disk, a dialog box will open and prompt you to insert the next disk. As the backup proceeds, the bar graphs in the bottom left panel of the window indicate the progress of the backup. You will find that the floppy-disk drive light on your computer may stay on during the backup; this is normal and is nothing to worry about. As you remove the disks, be sure to label them with the disk number and time and date of the backup, and note the fact that this is a full backup. If you have to restore this backup set at any time, you will have to use the disks in the same sequence that you used to make the backup.

When the backup is complete, the catalog for the entire backup set is written onto the last disk of the set, and a message indicates the number of files that were selected and backed up. Click on OK to return to the main Norton Backup window. Put the backup disks in a safe place.

Now is an excellent time to make a comparison between the files backed up to the floppy disks and the original files still on your hard disk. This ensures that the backup was complete. Use the Compare function for this. This is described later in this chapter under the heading "Comparing Files."

MAKING A PARTIAL BACKUP

You may not always want to back up your whole disk. Often you will want to back up only the files that have changed, the files that changed after a certain date, or certain file types.

When DOS creates or modifies a file, the archive attribute is automatically turned on to indicate that the file should be backed up the next time a backup is made. This archive attribute may or may not be turned off by Norton Backup, depending on what kind of backup you make.

The steps you follow in making a partial backup are much the same as those described above for your first full backup, except that you have more choices to make and more flexibility in how you actually make the backup.

Deciding on the Backup Type

> **NOTE** *The back-up files and copy files are written in a special format; you must use Norton Backup to restore them again.*

You can select the following different types of backup using the Backup Type button:

Full backs up all the selected files, ignoring the current setting of the archive attribute. When the backup is complete, Full resets the archive attribute for all files. Use this method to make your first backup.

Incremental backs up those selected files that are new or have changed in some way since the last backup. When the backup is complete, the archive attribute of all the backed up files is off. If you use this setting, use new disks for each incremental backup, otherwise you will write the changed files over the older versions on the backup disks.

Differential backs up all new files or all files that have changed since the last full or incremental backup. The status of the archive attribute is not changed.

Full Copy makes a copy of all the files you selected, whether the files have changed or not. Full Copy does not change the archive attribute, so it is useful for copying files from one system to another because it will not disturb your normal backup strategy. Remember, though, that this backup is not a copy of the files in the DOS or Windows sense of the word. You must use Restore to extract any data from (or open or view) a file; you cannot use DOS or Windows.

Incremental Copy is similar to the above selection, except that it copies just the files that have changed—again, without changing the status of the archive attribute.

The backup type you choose should depend on your individual circumstances and the goals that your backup strategy defines. You are not confined, however, to just these five methods; you can also choose the individual directories and files you want to back up.

Selecting Files to Back Up

Now that you have chosen the type of backup you want to make, you can further specify the directories and files that you want to include in the backup. If you are working at the basic level in Norton Backup, certain mechanisms are available to you; if you are working at the advanced level, you have more options.

Click on the Select Files command button in the Backup window to open the Select Backup Files window in Figure 11.4. This window has two panes just like a Desktop drive window—a tree pane on the left that lists directories and a file pane on the right that list files. The file pane lists the file name, extension, size in bytes, date and time, and attributes.

If the attribute is set for a particular file, you will see a letter representing that attribute in the right-most column in the file pane. Attributes are shown in the following order: read-only, hidden, system, and archive. You can use the drive icons at the top left of this window to change to another drive.

The menu bar now contains just one selection: File. The File menu contains options you can use to view and copy or delete files. To view a file, highlight it in the file list, then choose View. A window opens displaying the contents of the file. See Chapter 6 for more information on viewing files and changing viewers.

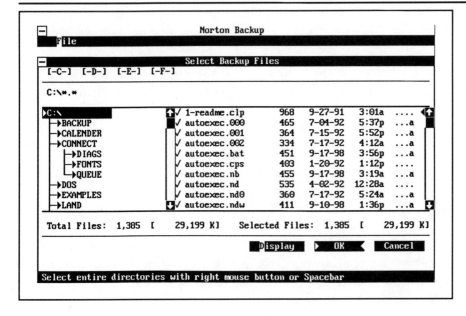

FIGURE 11.4:

Choose the directories and files you want to back up in the Select Backup Files window

At the bottom of the window you can see a summary line containing a count of the files on the current drive and the number of files selected for this backup, as well as three command buttons, Display, OK, and Cancel. If you are working at the advanced level, you will see three more command buttons: Include, Exclude, and Special.

Display This lets you decide on the information that is shown in the Select Backup Files window. It opens the Display Options dialog box. In the Sort Files By group box, you can choose to sort the files in the file pane by:

◆ file name

◆ file extension

◆ file size

◆ file date

◆ file attributes

And in the Other group box, you can choose the following:

Group Selected Files lets you collect all the selected files in each directory at the top of the file pane. This is particularly useful if you only want to back up a few files from each directory.

File Filter lets you select groups of files based on a wildcard specification in this text box. The default of *.* selects all files in the current directory. For example, to show just the executable files in the current directory, enter *.**EXE** into this text box. Files that you selected before applying this filter remain selected.

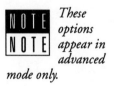

These options appear in advanced mode only.

Include/Exclude Select the correct drive in the Backup From list in the main Backup window *before* using Include/Exclude; otherwise your Include/Exclude list will be cleared. Click on either the Include or the Exclude command buttons in the Select Backup Files window to open the Include/Exclude Files dialog box shown in Figure 11.5. This dialog box includes the following:

Path contains the directory path of the files and/or directories you want to include or exclude. To use a different path, just type it into this text box.

File specifies the filter to use for including or excluding files; use the usual ? and * DOS wildcard characters.

Include/Exclude All Subdirectories adds or removes subdirectories from the backup.

Edit Include/Exclude List opens a dialog box that contains the actual statements that tell Norton Backup which files to include and exclude. These statements are executed in sequence, so if you want to back up all files in a directory except the .EXE files, for example, first specify that you want to include *all* files, then add another statement that excludes the files with an .EXE extension.

To add a line to the Include/Exclude list, follow these steps:

1. Choose the appropriate drive using the Backup From button in the main Backup window, make sure you are using the advanced level, then click on Select Files.

2. Click on either the Include or Exclude command buttons at the bottom of the Select Backup Files window to open the Include/Exclude Files dialog box. Enter any new directory path information into the Path text box, if necessary, and the new file filter you want to use into the File text box.

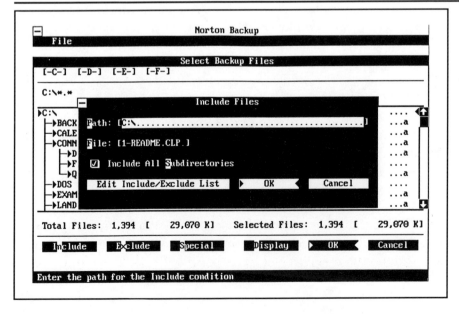

FIGURE 11.5:

Use the Include/Exclude Files dialog box to refine your selection of files for backup

3. Check the Include/Exclude All Subdirectories check box if you want to include or exclude all subdirectories.

4. Click on the Edit Include/Exclude List command button to open the Edit Include/Exclude List dialog box. This dialog box contains a list of include/exclude statements, as well as three more buttons:

   ◆ The Delete button removes the highlighted entry from this dialog box

   ◆ The Copy button duplicates a highlighted entry. This can be very useful if you want to create a new entry that is very similar to an existing entry.

   ◆ The Edit button opens the Edit dialog box, so you can alter the highlighted entry.

5. Click on the OK command button when your entry is complete. This new entry will be added at the end of the list in the Include/Exclude List box.

Once you have made an Include/Exclude filter, all the files selected will show a selection icon in the tree or file pane. You then can fine-tune that selection manually, if you wish, before selecting more files or deselecting others.

This option only appears at the advanced level.

Special This sets up separate conditions for including or excluding files in your backup. Click on this button to open the Special Selections dialog box shown in Figure 11.6. Here you can select all files that fall between a specific range of dates, as well as exclude copy-protected files, read-only files, system files, or hidden files. When you check the Exclude Copy Protected Files box, the five text boxes immediately to the right become active; type the name of one copy-protected file to exclude from the backup into each of these text boxes (wildcards are allowed).

Choosing the Drive to Back Up To

You use the Backup To drop-down box in the main Backup window to tell Norton Backup where to put the backup, either drive A or drive B—or any storage device that uses a DOS path, such as another hard disk somewhere. If drives A and B are of the same type, there is an option in this drop-down

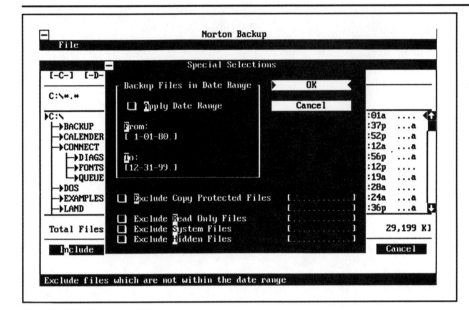

Set up criteria for including or excluding files in your backup using the Special Selections dialog box

Your network system manager may not be too keen on you backing up your hard disk onto the network, partic- ularly if server disk space is at a premium.

list that allows you to use both drives during the same backup. You can be backing up to one drive while you are changing and labeling the other.

The DOS path option lets you specify your backup to be sent to any storage medium that has a DOS path, such as a network drive, a Bernoulli box from Iomega Corporation, or a tape drive if it can be configured as a DOS device.

There are four check boxes at the bottom of the Backup To dialog box when you are using the basic user level and backing up to disks:

Prompt Before Overwriting Used Diskettes. Check this box to open a warning dialog box if you try to backup to a disk that already contains files. This is a good safety precaution, so be sure to check this box.

Use Error Correction on Diskettes. Norton Backup's error-correct- ing code greatly increases your chances of making a successful back- up and subsequent restoration. This setting is enabled by default, and I recommend that you leave it turned on.

Proprietary Diskette Format. This allows you to use a special disk format that is unique to Norton Backup. This format is not compatible with normal DOS files, but it does squeeze more information onto the disks. All disks will be reformatted when you first select this option, so you cannot change to this format in the middle of a backup set; the master catalog requires that the same disk format be used throughout the backup. If you want to use these disks with a regular DOS application, reformat the disk using the Desktop.

Always Format Diskettes. With this setting you can force Norton Backup to format every backup disk every time. This procedure will slow down the backup, but it helps prevent problems associated with misaligned floppy-disk read/write heads.

If you backup to a DOS Drive and Path, you have different check boxes:

Backup to a Single DOS Component File. Norton Backup stores backup data in files called component files, and a single component file fits exactly onto one floppy disk. At the basic user level, the component size is equal to the capacity of your largest floppy disk.

Display Directory Listing Prior to Backup. Check this box if you want to see a directory listing of the selected DOS path before the backup starts.

And there are different check boxes if you back up to tape:

Append Backup Data to Tape. Check this box if you always want to append backups onto the end of the current tape. This is the safest setting at the basic user level.

Display Directory Listing Prior to Backup. Check this box if you want to see a directory listing of the selected DOS path before the backup starts.

Store Copy of Catalog on Tape. Check this box if you want to store a copy of the catalog file onto the tape.

Always Format Tapes. Check this box if you plan to make lots of unattended backups to tape; the backup can be completed even if a used tape is inserted. If you don't work this way, then leave this box unchecked because formatting a tape can take a very long time.

At the advanced user level when backing up to disks, you have more choices with Overwrite Caution and Error Correction.

Overwrite Caution. Norton Backup opens an alert box if it finds you are trying to use a disk that already contains data. You can then choose to continue with this disk and overwrite these files or change to another disk. You can also choose the specific kinds of disks that you want to see a warning for; choose from Off, Regular DOS Diskettes, Norton Backup Diskettes, or Any Used Diskette. The safest option is Any Used Diskette. This opens a warning box when Norton Backup finds a disk containing any kind of file.

Error Correction. Norton Backup's error-correction code greatly increases your chance of making a successful backup and subsequent restoration. This setting is set to Enhanced by default and I recommend that you leave it selected. Your other choices are Off or Standard.

When backing up to a DOS drive, you now have more choices:

Backup File Size. You can choose the component file size at the advanced user level. The most flexible setting is Use DOS Best Fit. This setting can adapt according to the disk type you use. As well as the Use DOS Best Fit setting, you can choose from a component size that represents a 360K, 720K, 1.2 MB, or 1.44 MB increment.

And finally, if you are working at the advanced user level with a tape drive:

Tape Overwrite/Append. Choose from Always Append, Always Overwrite, or Overwrite on Full Backup Only. Always Append ensures that existing backups are never overwritten. Always Overwrite makes the fastest backup because the backup is always written at the beginning of the tape. Overwrite on Full Backup only overwrites existing backups if you are making a full backup. Partial backups such as incremental or differential backups are always appended to the end of the tape.

CHOOSING BACKUP OPTIONS

Norton Backup lets you configure your backup settings. The number of settings changes as you change your user level from the basic to the advanced level. When you click on the Options button in the Backup window at the basic level, you open the Norton Basic Backup dialog box; when you are at the advanced level you open the Norton Advanced Backup dialog box, and this adds more settings. We'll look at the basic level options first.

Basic Options

The Basic Disk Backup Options dialog box is shown in Figure 11.7. You can make the following settings:

Verify Backup Data (Read and Compare). When you check this option, Norton Backup compares the original data in the files against the backup. This may slow down your backup slightly, but I recommend that you use it every time you make a backup, as protection against making an unusable backup.

Compress Backup Data (Save Time). Use this setting to invoke Norton Backup's data-compression option. Not all files can be compressed to the same extent; word-processor files and spreadsheets show the largest amount of compression, while .EXE files show less. If you check this box, you select the Save Time compression setting described next under Advanced Options.

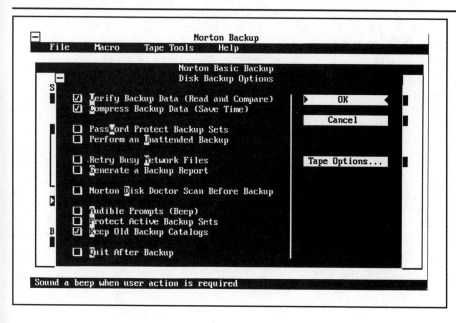

FIGURE 11.7:

Use the Basic Backup Options dialog box to select the basic backup settings

Password Protects Backup Sets. With this setting you can protect your backup by using a password.

Perform an Unattended Backup. Check this box if you plan to make unattended backups, and Norton Backup will use a predetermined response if you do not reply to requests for input within 15 seconds. The backup will stop automatically, however, if existing files are found on the backup disk or if the disk itself is found to be defective.

Retry Busy Network Files. When you use Norton Backup on most networks, busy files are skipped automatically; however, if you use a Novell network, you can check this box if you want Norton Backup to retry busy files until they are not busy. Be aware that files can stay busy for a long time, and by checking this option, you can slow down the whole backup.

Generate a Backup Report. Check this box if you want to generate a backup report. This is a good idea if you are making backups in a corporate setting and need to be able to show when a specific file was backed up for audit trail reasons. Reports are stored as text files named after the current setup file, and have the file-name extension .RPT.

Norton Disk Doctor Scan Before Backup. Check this box if you want to run the Norton Disk Doctor just before you make a backup.

Audible Prompts (Beep). This setting allows Norton Backup to beep every time the program opens an alert box to tell you about an error or ask you to make a choice. You can turn this option off right now.

Protect Active Backup Sets. Check this box to avoid writing over any of your active backup sets.

Keep Old Backup Catalogs. Norton Backup writes the backup catalog onto the hard disk, as well as onto the final floppy disk in the backup set. The next time you make a full backup, Norton Backup usually deletes all the interim catalogs to conserve disk space. If you want to keep all these catalogs, check this box. Remember that you can always rebuild a catalog from the actual backup disks themselves. (Catalogs are described later in the section on comparing files.)

Quit After Backup. Use this setting if you want to exit Norton Backup when the backup is complete; otherwise, you will return to the main Backup window. This option may save you several keystrokes at the end of a backup.

If you are using a tape drive as your backup medium, click on the Tape Options command button to open the Tape Backup Options dialog box. This dialog box is the same as the dialog box shown in Figure 11.7 for disk options.

Most of the important settings in the Norton Basic Backup dialog box are already set to their preferred settings by default, so there may be no need to change any of them. To change a setting, click on the check box of the appropriate option, then click on OK to return to the Backup window.

Advanced Options

The Options command button at the advanced level gives you control over a wider range of settings than at the basic level. This dialog box is shown in Figure 11.8. You have the following choices:

Data Verification. This increases the reliability of the backup, so you should use it. There are three possible settings for this option: Off, Sample Only, and Read and Compare. Off turns data verification off completely. Sample Only checks every eighth track written to the backup floppy disk. Read and Compare is the most comprehensive data-verification method in Norton Backup—all the files written to the backup disks are checked.

Data Compression. Using data compression does not affect the reliability of the backup, but it can certainly affect the number of floppy disks needed or the length of time the backup takes. There are four settings available for data compression: Off, Save Time, Save Space (Low), and Save Space (High). Off turns data compression off completely, so no compression is performed. Save Time optimizes the backup speed to reduce the amount of time it takes to complete the backup. The faster your computer runs, the bigger time saving you will see. Save Disks (Low) attempts to increase the amount of compression to minimize the number of disks needed for the backup. Save Disks (High) offers the maximum amount of compression and saves the largest amount of disk space, but usually increases the time that the backup takes.

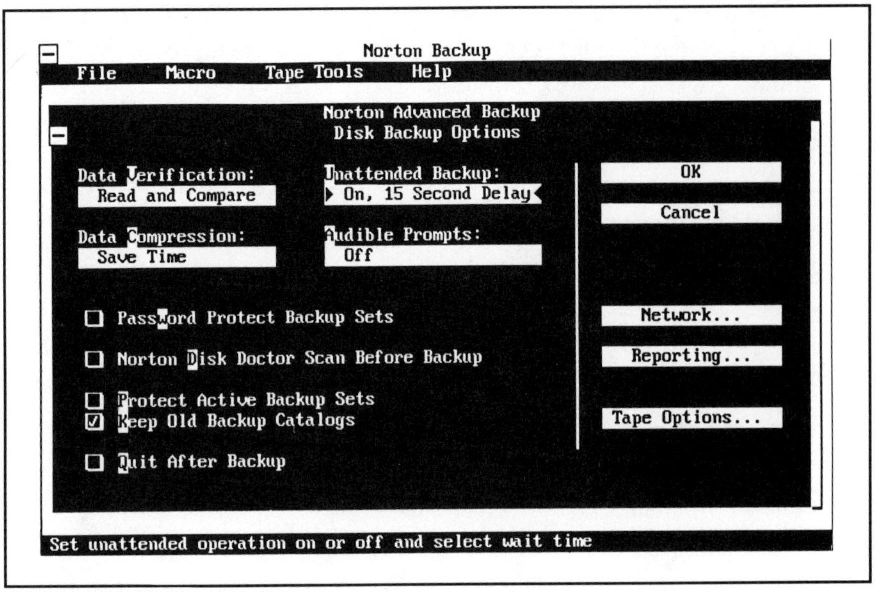

```
 ┌─                    Norton Backup                          ─┐
 │ File    Macro    Tape Tools    Help                         │
 │ ┌─                 Norton Advanced Backup                    │
 │ │                   Disk Backup Options                      │
 │ Data Verification:      Unattended Backup:        ┌─────────┐│
 │   Read and Compare      ▶ On, 15 Second Delay ◀   │   OK    ││
 │                                                   └─────────┘│
 │ Data Compression:       Audible Prompts:          ┌─────────┐│
 │   Save Time               Off                     │ Cancel  ││
 │                                                   └─────────┘│
 │  ☐ Password Protect Backup Sets                   ┌─────────┐│
 │                                                   │Network..││
 │  ☐ Norton Disk Doctor Scan Before Backup          └─────────┘│
 │                                                   ┌──────────┐│
 │  ☐ Protect Active Backup Sets                     │Reporting.││
 │  ☑ Keep Old Backup Catalogs                       └──────────┘│
 │                                                   ┌──────────┐│
 │  ☐ Quit After Backup                              │Tape Opti.││
 │                                                   └──────────┘│
 │ Set unattended operation on or off and select wait time     │
 └─────────────────────────────────────────────────────────────┘
```

FIGURE 11.8:
You can control a wide range of backup settings at the advanced level

Unattended Backups. Choose Off, or select a time interval that Norton backup must wait for user input before proceeding.

Audible Prompts. Choose Off, Low Tone, High Tone, or Chime for your audible prompt. You can hear a sample of each tone as you move from one option button to the next. The best choice here is Off.

To set the advanced network options, choose the Network command button:

Retry Busy Files. At the advanced level, you can be much more flexible when you encounter a busy file. You can choose to retry until a specified period of time elapses or until a specific time is reached. You can even tell Norton Backup to retry until the file is not busy—and that could take a long time. You can also specify that Norton Backup not retry a busy file. In this case the backup continues with the next available file.

Send message to user of busy file. Check this box to send the user of the busy file a message that Norton Backup is attempting to open the file. This option is available only on Novell 286 networks, and also assumes that the network user has messaging turned on. If messaging is turned off, the user will never see this message.

To set the advanced report options, choose the Report command button:

Include in Report. At the advanced user level, you have more control over the information selected for inclusion in the report. The report always begins with the date and time that the backup began, the name of the setup file, and the user's description of the setup file. You can also include the following:

◆ Backup Option Settings

◆ List of Processed Files

◆ All Error Messages

◆ Summary of Backup Statistics

Append. Check this box if you want to append each backup report to the previous report to produce a running log of all your backups.

The other selections—Password Protect Backup Sets, Norton Disk Doctor Scan Before Backup, Protect Active Backup Sets, Keep Old Backup Catalogs, Quit After Backup, and Disk Options—are the same as those described under Basic Options.

COMPARING FILES

If you add a new expansion board to your computer, make a test backup and then use the Compare command to make absolutely sure that the new board has not affected your backup in some subtle way.

After you have made a backup, you should compare the files contained in the backup against the original files on your hard disk. In this way, you can be sure that the files you backed up match the files on your hard disk, and that they can be restored successfully.

Start Norton Backup in the usual way. When you choose the Compare button from the Norton Backup program, the Norton Basic Compare window opens, as Figure 11.9 shows. The major elements of the Compare window are summarized as follows:

◆ The Backup Set Catalog button displays information for the catalogs created during previous backups. Select the catalog for the backup set that you want to compare.

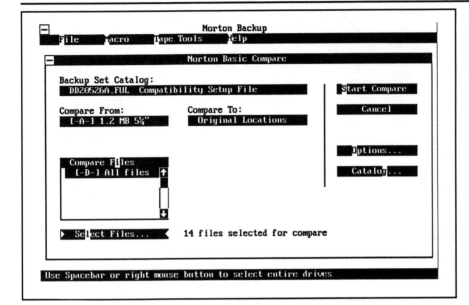

FIGURE 11.9:

The Compare window checks your backup against the original files on your hard disk and looks for problems

◆ The Compare From button contains the list of devices that can be used for backups on your system. Select the drive originally used to make the backup, usually one of your floppy-disk drives or a tape drive.

◆ The Compare Files box contains disk icons for the drives that were fully or partially backed up. If you double-click on a drive icon, you select all the files on that drive.

◆ Use the Select Files button to compare only specific files.

◆ The Compare To button specifies the location of the original files for this comparison. This is usually your hard disk.

◆ The Options button lets you specify whether a beep will sound when an alert box appears and whether to quit Norton Backup when the comparison is complete.

◆ The Catalog button lets you find a catalog file in any directory, then load or delete it. You can also use this button to rebuild a catalog using the original backup disks in the event that the catalog is damaged or to retrieve a catalog from a floppy disk.

◆ The Start Compare button starts the comparison process running.

MAKING A COMPLETE COMPARISON

To make a comparison between the files you have just backed up and the original files on your hard disk, using either the basic or the advanced level, follow these steps:

1. Collect all the floppy disks that comprise the backup set together in numerical order, then click the Compare button in the main Norton Backup window.

2. Select the appropriate catalog file with the Backup Set Catalog button in the Compare window.

3. Choose the appropriate drive in the Compare From box. This is the drive you will use to load your backup disks for the comparison.

4. Use the Select Files command button if you want to compare specific parts of the backup.

5. Click on the Compare To list box to select the files on your hard disk you want the backup set compared against.

6. If you want to use a different catalog file in this comparison, click on Catalog to select another.

7. Click on Start Compare to begin the actual comparison process.

The Compare Progress window will open. This is very similar to the Backup Progress window mentioned before. You will be prompted to load the next disk for the comparison in the bottom-left pane, and summary information is presented in the other panes. At the end of the comparison, an information box opens to list the number of files selected and the number of files compared.

There are several Compare options and selections that it is important for you to know about. These are detailed in the next few sections:

Backup Set Catalog The backup set catalog file contains an index to the backup and contains the information needed to compare or restore the files in the backup. Two catalogs are created for each backup, one stored on the last backup disk of a backup set and the other on your hard disk.

Use the Backup Set Catalog button to look at all the catalogs on your hard disk; click on the one you want to use. Norton Backup gives each catalog file a unique name, based on the drive being backed up, the date, and a special sequence code. The file-name extension reflects the backup type: .FUL for a full backup, .INC for incremental, .DIF for differential, and .CPY for a copy.

A master catalog is created or updated for each setup file when you make a full, incremental, or differential backup; it is not created for a full or incremental copy backup. The master catalog has the same name as the setup file and the file-name extension .CAT, and is used when you make a comparison of a full backup. Norton Backup automatically merges all the catalogs made during full, incremental, and differential backups for the same set.

Compare From Use the Compare From drop-down list box to tell Norton Backup where to look for the backup set used in the comparison. If you have two floppy-disk drives of the same size, you can choose to use both of them. In this case, Norton Backup compares data in one, then in the other, speeding up the compare operation by quite some time. You can also use a DOS path here for any device that uses one: a Bernoulli box, network drive, and a tape drive, and so on.

Compare Files The Compare Files selection tells Norton Backup which drives contain the files against which you want to compare the backup set. When you select a drive, *all* the files on that drive are selected for the comparison. If you just want to compare a few files, use the Select Files command button described in a moment.

Compare To You use the Compare To button to tell Norton Backup where the original files are that you want to compare against the backup set. This is almost always the same drive and directory from which the files were originally backed up. You can choose from the following:

> **Original Locations.** Directories and files in the backup are compared against those from which they were backed up.
>
> **Other Drives.** Use this selection to specify a directory of the same name as the original, but located on a different drive. A dialog box opens for the name of the drive.

Other Directories. With this selection you can specify that the comparison be made against files in a different directory. This can be a different drive as well as a different directory.

Single Directory. This last specification is used to compare the backup set against a specific directory, no matter what the original drive and directory. A dialog box appears for you to enter the name of the directory you want to use.

Options There are several options you can elect to use during basic user level tape or floppy-disk comparison:

Perform an Unattended Compare. Check this box if you want to make the comparison in unattended mode.

Retry Busy Network Files. Busy network files cannot be compared, so check this box if a comparison is vital; otherwise leave this box blank and busy network files will be skipped.

Generate a Compare Report. Check this box if you want to make a report on the comparison.

Audible Prompts (Beep) beeps every time an alert box opens. Check this box to turn the beep off.

Quit After Compare lets you save your settings and exit to the Norton Desktop when the comparison is complete. If this box is not checked, you'll stay inside the backup program.

At the advanced user or program level, these choices are expanded somewhat, as you might expect:

Unattended Compare. Choose Off, or choose On and select a time interval that Norton Backup must wait for user input before proceeding.

Audible Prompts. Choose from Off, Low Tone, High Tone, or Chime for your audible prompt. You can hear a sample of each tone as you move from one option button to the next. The best choice here is Off.

Quit After Compare. When this box is checked, you will exit Norton Backup as soon as the compare is complete.

Tape and disk options are both the same at the advanced level, and the network and reporting options are the same for Compare as they were for Backup, and so will not be described again here.

COMPARING SPECIFIC FILES OR DIRECTORIES

Click on the Select Files command button to open the Select Compare Files window. This window is very similar to the Select Backup Files window described earlier and works in much the same way. You select the directories and files for the comparison, close the window, then click the Start Compare command button.

There are several buttons available at the bottom of this window that you can use to select specific files for comparison, depending on the program level you are using. At the basic level you can use the following:

Version. When you load a master catalog, files from several backup sets will be available, and it is quite possible that the same file may be represented several times. By default, the latest version of a file will be compared, but if you use the Version command button, it is possible to compare a specific version of the file. If there is only one version of the file available, the Version button is dimmed and unavailable. But if there are several, choose the Version button to display a list of the available files. Highlight the version of the file you want to use for the comparison and click on OK.

Display. This button lets you decide on the information to show in the file pane. It opens the Display Options dialog box. You can sort the files in this window by name, extension, size, date, or attribute(s). Besides being able to apply a file filter so that only certain files are shown in the window, you can also opt to group all the selected files together at the top of the file pane, irrespective of where they are actually located in the directory.

At the advanced level, you have access to two more command buttons:

Print. When you have chosen the files you want to compare, you can print the list now or send the list to a file using the Setup command button in the Printer Setup dialog box. If you print to a file, the default file name is DEFAULT.TXT.

Special. Use this to exclude files from any comparison. Clicking on Special opens the Special Selections dialog box. Here you can exclude files that fall into a specific range of dates, as well as files based on their copy-protection status and status of their read-only, hidden, or system attributes.

By using these Select Files options carefully, you can proceed to compare all files in your backup, or just compare those specific files that you are most interested in.

WORKING WITH CATALOGS

A catalog contains all the information about a particular backup, including a copy of the directory structure of the backed-up hard disk, the names of all the files included in the backup, the total number of files backed up, and the name of the setup file used to make the backup. The catalog is saved in two places for safety reasons: on your hard disk and on the last floppy disk in a set of floppy-disk backups. Before you can do a backup comparison or restoration, you must select the appropriate catalog to use. If the correct catalog is not already shown in the Backup Set Catalog drop-down list box, you can use the Catalog command button to open the Select Catalog dialog box to find or recreate it. The Files list at the left side of this dialog box lists all the catalogs for all the backup sets on the current drive, including any master catalogs. If the file you want to use is not shown in the list, change to a different directory or drive using the Directories list box in the center of this dialog box.

The following command buttons are available from the Catalog Select dialog box:

Load. This selection loads the highlighted catalog and returns to the main Compare window. If you elected to use a password with your backup, you will be asked for that password before the catalog is loaded.

Retrieve. If the catalog file you want to use is no longer available on your hard disk through accidental deletion or other mishap, you can reload it from the last floppy disk or tape of the backup set using this command. Norton Backup prompts you to load the last floppy disk in the backup set.

If you are backing up to tape and did not check Store Copy of Catalog on Tape, the catalog will not be present—you will have to use the Rebuild command button instead of Restore.

You must use the same speed for the restoration that you used when you made the original backup.

Rebuild. If the catalog file is missing from both your hard disk and the last floppy disk or tape, you can use the Rebuild command to reconstruct as much as possible of the catalog file. Norton Backup reads the directory structure and file name information from the backup floppy disks and adds it to a new catalog file, one disk at a time. If a disk is missing from the middle of the backup set, you will have to create two new catalogs, one that describes the files up to the missing disk and one that describes the files after the missing disk.

Find Files. Use this option to search through your catalog files for information about a specific file that you backed up previously. This is especially useful if you want to compare a file but can't remember when the file was backed up or which catalog the file is in. You will still have to use the Load button to use the appropriate catalog in a compare operation.

Delete. You can remove obsolete catalogs from your hard disk with the Delete command. Highlight the catalog you want to delete, then click on the Delete command button. You will be asked to confirm that you want to delete the catalog before it is actually removed from your hard disk.

No Catalog. Norton Backup can make a comparison without using a catalog if you select this option. Without a catalog loaded, you can use the Select Files button to open the Edit Include/Exclude List window, and specify the files for this comparison. Then Norton Backup will scan the backup set for just those files specified in the list.

RESTORING FILES

Start Norton Backup by selecting it in the Tools menu. Select the Restore button from the main Backup window when you are ready to restore files to your hard disk or load them to another disk somewhere. You will see the Restore window shown in Figure 11.10. This window shares much in common with the main Backup window; just remember, however, that you are doing things the other way around when you restore files to your system. The main elements of the window are as follows:

◆ The Backup Set Catalog button shows the names and descriptions of existing catalogs corresponding to existing backup sets. Select the catalog that corresponds to the backup set that you want to restore.

◆ The Restore From button shows the drives you can use to restore the backup.

◆ The Restore Files list box contains icons for the drives that were fully or partially backed up.

◆ Use the Select Files command button to restore only specific files. This is discussed in the next section.

◆ The Restore To button lets you select where you want to put the restored files.

◆ The Catalog command button lets you load, retrieve, rebuild, or delete a catalog, as I described previously under the heading "Working with Catalogs."

◆ The Options command button lets you specify several restoration settings, depending on your user level. These settings are described later in this section under the title of "Choosing Restore Options".

◆ Use the Start Restore button when everything is set to your liking and you are ready to start the restoration.

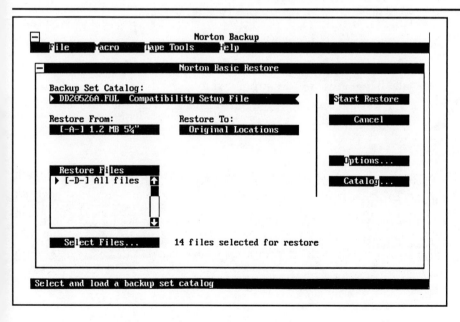

FIGURE 11.10:

Control the restoration of files to your system using the Restore window

If you are planning to restore your hard disk to the same state it was in after your last backup, you must restore the backups in the following order:

◆ If you made a full backup, restore the latest full backup set.

◆ If you made a full backup followed by several incremental backups, restore the full backup first, followed by each of the incremental backups in order, starting with the oldest set.

◆ If you made a full backup, followed by differential backups, restore the full backup first, followed by the most recent differential backup.

To restore previously backed up files to your hard disk:

1. Collect all the disks that are included in the backup set.

2. Select the catalog for the backup set that you want to restore.

3. Choose a floppy disk or tape drive using the Restore From button, or specify a DOS path.

4. Select the disk drive you want to restore these files to with the Restore Files button. This selects all files.

5. Click on the Start Restore button to begin the process of restoring your files and open the Restore Progress window.

The Restore Progress Window is similar to the other two progress windows in Norton Backup, and it shows how the restoration is progressing with horizontal bar graphs. You are prompted to insert disks as necessary. At the end of the restoration, a message box opens, showing the number of files selected and the number restored.

RESTORING SPECIFIC FILES OR DIRECTORIES

Often a partial restoration may be all you need to recover, for example, a file or directory deleted by accident. Follow the steps given above for a complete restore, but use the Select Files command button to choose the files you want to

If the Start Restore command button is shown in lowercase letters, you have not selected any files to restore.

restore. This button opens the Select Restore Files window containing several file-selection command buttons. At the basic level you can use the following:

Version. Files from several different backup sets may be available for you to restore, and it is quite possible that the same file may be represented several times. By default, the latest version of a file will be restored, but if you use the Version command button, it is possible to restore a specific version of the file. If there is only one version available, the Version button is dimmed and unavailable. But if there are several, choose the Version button to display a list of the available files. Highlight the version of the file you want to restore and click on OK.

Display. This button lets you decide on the information to show in the Select Restore Files window, and opens the Display options dialog box. You can sort the files in this window by name, extension, size, date, or attribute(s). Besides being able to apply a file filter so that only certain files are shown in the window, you can also opt to group all the selected files together at the top of the file pane, irrespective of where they are actually located in the directory.

If you are at the advanced level, you can also use the following command buttons:

Print. You can print the current catalog now or send the list to a file using the Print command button.

Special. Use this button to exclude certain files from the restoration. Click on Special to open the Special Selections dialog box if you want to restore files that fall between two specific dates. This does not restore files from within this range, so you must still select the individual files to restore. This selection just excludes files that are outside the range of dates from being restored. You can also exclude files based on their copy-protection status, as well as on the status of their read-only, hidden, or system attributes.

RESTORING FILES AFTER A HARD DISK FAILURE

One of the prime reasons for backing up your files is so that you can reload them again after an accident, such as a hard disk problem. There may be several important steps that you must go through first, however, before you

Use Image to store vital disk information in case of an accident; use Disk Tools to create a rescue disk to use if your hard disk refuses to boot.

can get to that point. You have to get your computer to the state where it can run a program before you can think about restoring your data, and that may mean repartitioning your hard disk and reinstalling your DOS files.

In the event of serious disk damage, you must first install all your DOS files and then install the Norton Desktop, before you can even load Norton Backup. Once Norton Backup is loaded, then you can start restoring your backed-up files.

CHOOSING RESTORE OPTIONS

Norton Backup lets you configure your restore settings in the Restore Options dialog box. The number of settings depends on your user level. When you click on the Options button in the Restore window at the basic level, you open the Norton Basic Restore Options window; when you are at the advanced level you open the Norton Advanced Restore Options dialog box, and this adds more settings.

Basic Options

When you choose the Options command button at the basic level in the Restore window, the Norton Basic Restore Options dialog box opens, as shown in Figure 11.11. Choose from the following settings:

Verify Restore Data (Read and Compare). When you check this option, Norton Backup compares the files restored onto your hard disk with the files in the backup set to make sure the files are restored properly. This may slow down your restore slightly, but I recommend that you use this setting, as a protection against serious disk problems.

Perform an Unattended Restore. Check this box if you want to perform an unattended restore with default 15-second delays on all requests for user input.

Retry Busy Network Files. Check this box if you want Norton Backup to retry busy network files. This can slow the restore down quite considerably.

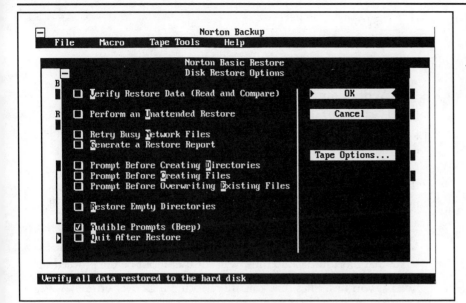

*Select the Restore options
you want to use in the
Norton Basic Restore
Options dialog box*

Create a Restore Report. Check this box to make a restore report.

Prompt Before Creating Directories. Turn this option on to see a
message before the restore creates any new directories on your hard disk.

Prompt Before Creating Files. Turn this option on if you want to be
prompted before any new files not on the target disk are created
from the backup.

Prompt Before Overwriting Existing Files. Select this to see a
prompt before overwriting a file of the same name.

Restore Empty Directories. This setting lets Norton Backup restore
empty directories, even if they do not contain any files.

Audible Prompts (Beep). Turn the beep off with this option.

Quit After Restore. You can also make Norton Backup return to the
Desktop at the end of the restoration, if you wish.

Click on the options you want to use, then click on OK to return to the main
Restore window.

Advanced Options

At the advanced level, the Restore options contain additional selections besides those described at the basic level:

Data Verification. Data restored to your hard disk can be compared against the data in the backup to ensure that there were no problems. You can choose one of three settings: Off, Sample Only, or Read and Compare. Off turns data verification off. Sample Only reads every eighth track on the hard disk and compares it to the floppy-disk backup. Read and Compare is the most rigorous method because it compares all the data written to your hard disk against the data in the backup set.

Unattended Restore. Choose Off, or choose On and select a time interval that Norton Backup must wait for user input before proceeding.

Overwrite Files. Files that you are restoring may overwrite files with the same names already on your disk. You have three choices: Never Overwrite Files, Overwrite Older Files Only, and Always Overwrite Files. Never Overwrite Files tells Norton Backup not to restore a file if it already exists on your hard disk. Overwrite Older Files Only makes Norton Backup restore the backup file only if it is more recent than the file already on your hard disk. Always Overwrite Files restores all files to your hard disk, irrespective of the file's creation date.

Audible Prompts. Choose from Off, Low Tone, High Tone, or Chime for your audible prompt. You can hear a sample of each tone as you move from one option button to the next. The best choice here is still Off.

Archive Flag. This selection tells Norton Backup how to treat the archive attribute on each file. The choices are as follows: Leave Alone - Do Not Change, Clear - Mark As Backed Up, and Set - Mark As Not Backed Up. Leave Alone - Do Not Change does not alter the archive attribute; Clear - Mark As Backed Up sets the archive attribute to indicate that the file has been backed up; and Set - Mark As Not Backed Up sets the archive attribute to indicate that the file has not been backed up. These settings obviously have an effect on subsequent backups you make. Files whose archive attribute indicates that they have been backed up will only now be backed up by the Full and Full Copy backup types. Files whose archive attribute indicates that they have not been backed up will always be backed up.

The network and reporting options are the same as those described at the advanced user level for backup and compare, and so will not be described again here. Select the options of your choice and click on OK to return to the main Restore window.

MAKING TAPE BACKUPS

With more and more people using larger and larger hard disks, and networks becoming much more common, backing up to floppy disks is no longer the preferred method; it takes too long, and it uses too many floppy disks. Today's backup media of choice is the tape backup system.

Norton Backup supports tape drives that conform to the QIC 40 or QIC 80 tape format standards; QIC 40 is the lower-density 40MB standard, and QIC 80 is the higher-density 80MB standard. You can use preformatted tapes, but you may find that you get better results by formatting the tape on the same drive that will read and write to the drive. Formatting a tape can take from 40 minutes for a standard-length 40MB tape to almost 2 hours for an extended-length tape.

If you have a tape drive installed on your system, it becomes a selectable option with the Backup To, Compare From, and Restore From buttons, just like your floppy-disk drives.

USING THE TAPE TOOLS MENU

There are several selections in the Tape Tools menu you can use to help you manage your tapes:

Identify. Use this selection to confirm tape information such as tape name, type, number of volumes on the tape, and used and remaining space on the tape. Norton Backup creates a new volume on a tape for each backed-up drive, as well as a copy of the catalog if that was specified in the Advanced Tape Backup Options dialog box.

If you try to access the Tape Tools menu and you don't have a tape drive on your system or your tape drive is turned off, Norton Backup opens an error window to tell you that it cannot complete the requested operation. Just click on OK to dismiss the error window, no damage is done.

Erase. This selection deletes the header from the beginning of the tape, making the data on the tape inaccessible, but does not overwrite all the data on the tape. This selection works very quickly.

Security Erase. Use this selection when you want to obliterate and actually overwrite all the data on the tape. Data is overwritten with zeros—this can take a considerable length of time to complete, as every part of the tape is overwritten. All data is lost, permanently.

Format. Use this option to format a blank tape. Formatting is actually a two-part process. First the entire tape is formatted; then, on a second pass, the tape is certified, and bad areas of the tape are marked so that they are never used.

Delete Volumes. This selection deletes a volume from the tape. You can only delete volumes from the end of the tape, and all volumes selected for deletion must be sequential.

Retension. This is a particularly useful feature of Norton Backup that is used to check the tape's tension. If you are experiencing difficulty in reading to or writing from a tape, use this selection to wind the tape all the way to the end and then back again, resetting the tension. Norton Backup automatically retensions a tape before formatting.

When a tape backup is complete, you should slide the record tab on the tape cartridge to the right to write-protect the tape and protect it from accidental erasure.

USING BACKUP WITH NORTON ANTIVIRUS

The Norton Backup needs a special setup when used with Norton AntiVirus. Norton AntiVirus prevents any program, including Norton Backup, from accessing the two special files, NAV_.SYS and NAV&.SYS. There are at least two ways around this problem that let you backup your files when you want to but still provide appropriate virus protection.

The easiest and safest way to avoid conflict with Norton AntiVirus is to indicate that these two files should be considered copy-protected files, and therefore should not be backed up. You can do this using the Special box from the Select Files window. When Norton Backup encounters these files, they will not be backed up; if you ever do need to restore them after a disk problem, you can reload them from your original Norton Desktop disks. In many ways this is the best solution, because you can make unattended backups, and still have the best in virus protection available at all times.

The second method that you might consider, is to disable Norton Anti-Virus for the time it takes to make the backup, then start Norton AntiVirus running again when your backup is complete. You can disable Norton Anti-Virus if you hold down both the Shift keys after you hear the first beep from your computer as it boots up. You will see a message indicating Norton Anti-Virus has not been loaded. Now make your backup, then reboot your computer to reload Norton AntiVirus again.

AUTOMATING YOUR BACKUPS

There are several ways you can automate and streamline your backup operations. You can use setup files, invoke macros, use command-line switches from the DOS command line, and use the built-in Norton Desktop Scheduler. We will look at each method in turn, starting with setup files.

USING SETUP FILES

Any time you use Norton Backup you are actually using a *setup file*. Setup files contain backup program settings and file selections, and are a fast way of loading a preset configuration, so that you don't have to reconfigure Norton Backup every time you want to use it. When you change something in one of the main windows—Backup, Compare, or Restore—or make different selections using Select Files, you are changing information in the setup file. These changes will only apply to the current backup session unless you explicitly save them back into a setup file. You can either save them in the current setup file to modify that file, or save them in a different file to create a new setup file. If you want to perform different types of backup, you can have a different setup file for each type of backup.

| NOTE | *At the preset level, you can load a setup file using the Preset Backups list box, but the selections in the File menu are unavailable.* |

Use the commands in the File menu to work with setup files when you are at the basic or advanced levels. You can use Open Setup and choose a file from any drive or directory on your system. Use any Norton Backup commands to change this setup file, then save it using Save Setup. Or if you want to change the name of the setup to something different, use Save Setup As.

Use the Print command to make a hard copy of the contents of a setup file.

Using a setup file is one of the easiest ways that you can configure a backup strategy for someone else who is perhaps less technical than you are. Then that person can use the preset level with the setup file, rather than the basic or advanced levels, to make his or her backup. In this way, you can reduce a complex operation to just a few choices, and the backup can be run with a minimum of interaction with the program.

Norton Backup comes with several useful setup files already configured for you:

NOTE
These precon-figured setup files all perform attended backups.

FULL.SET	Runs a full backup when launched, backing up all files on the first hard disk to a high-capacity floppy disk in drive A, and quits when the backup is complete.
DEFAULT.SET	Is a duplicate of FULL.SET.
ASSIST.SET	This setup file is used with the Scheduler to make a full backup at 4:00 pm on Friday, and then incremental backups Monday through Thursday. All files on drive C are backed up to a high-capacity disk in drive A. ASSIST.SET quits when the backup is complete.
DBASE.SET	Makes a full backup of all dBASE and Q&A files it can find.
SPRDSHT.SET	Makes a full backup of Lotus 1-2-3 and Microsoft Excel files.
WORDPROC.SET	Makes a full backup of files made by Microsoft Word (for Windows and for DOS), Ami, Ami Pro, WordPerfect, and JustWrite—as well as plain text files.

If you find that your requirements are very close to one of these precon-figured files, open the setup file and modify it to your own needs by making the necessary changes, then save the file to a new name using Save Setup As from the File menu. This way you don't have to create the setup file from scratch.

MAKING AND USING MACROS

Another way you can speed up your backups is by using a *macro,* which is a series of keystrokes stored in a file that you play back at a later date to automate the backup, compare, or restore procedure. Norton Backup stores a macro with the setup file in effect when you created the macro, and you can only use one macro with each setup file.

You must be in the main Norton Backup window when you start recording your macro because this is the reference point that Norton Backup uses as its starting point for running the macro.

You must also use the keyboard to generate the keystrokes needed for the macro; you cannot use mouse clicks. If a letter in a menu name or a command button is underlined, you can press the Alt key and the underlined letter together to select the item directly from the keyboard. Most of these underlined letters are easy to associate with their corresponding functions, such as *B* for Backup, *C* for Compare, and *R* for Restore. Others, however, are less than intuitive, like *N* for Configure and *r* for Printer Setup.

Use the Insert key to select a file or to turn an option on in your macro, use the Delete key to deselect a file or to turn an option off, and use Ctrl+Enter to represent pressing the Start Backup or Start Restore buttons. Do not use the spacebar to toggle check boxes or option buttons on or off while you are recording your macro. The toggle will reverse every time you run the macro; use the Insert or Delete keys to turn options on or off. This way it does not matter what the setting is when the macro is run.

To record a macro:

1. Start Norton Backup and select the program level you (or someone else) will use when running the macro.

2. Return to the main Norton Backup window, the one containing the Backup, Compare, Restore, Configure, and Quit command buttons.

3. Choose Record from the Macro menu or press F7. If a macro already exists for this setup file, Backup will ask if you want to overwrite it. The macro recording starts, waiting for your keystrokes. You will see the Recording indicator in the lower right of the window to remind you that the macro recorder is running.

TIP *Run the procedure you plan to automate with the macro a few times in manual mode first, so that you are familiar with the required steps—and to make sure the program is going to do what you expect it to do.*

TIP *In a Norton Backup macro the Insert key will always turn an item on and the Delete key will always turn an item off.*

NOTE *You cannot use a macro with any of the entries in the Tape Tools menu. The macro recorder will pause when you choose one of these commands, and then resume when you exit the tape operation.*

4. Press the keystrokes needed to run the procedure. You cannot record mouse selections.

5. You can make a Norton Backup macro pause and wait for input from the keyboard if you press Alt+F7 when you are in a dialog box. When the macro is played back, the word Waiting is displayed at the lower-right corner of the screen. The macro will continue running when the user selects OK or Cancel to close the current dialog box.

6. Press F7 to stop the recording, then use Save Setup or Save Setup As from the File menu to save your macro.

When you have finished making the macro, run it a few times to make sure it does what you think it should. This is particularly important if you are going to give the macro to someone else! You can use any program user level when making a macro, and you must use that same level to play the macro back again.

To play a macro:

1. Launch Norton Backup and select the setup file that contains the macro you want to use.

2. Make sure that you are in the main Norton Backup window before starting your macro.

3. Choose the Run command from the Macro menu (or press F8).

Norton Backup turns the mouse and keyboard off when it runs a macro, so make sure you are familiar with a procedure before you turn it into a macro.

Using Command-Line Switches

NOTE
NOTE

See Chapter 19 for a complete list of all the command-line switches you can use when making a backup or a restore with Norton Backup.

There are several important command-line options you can use with Norton Backup:

@

runs a macro associated with a setup file. For example, to play a macro associated with DAILY.SET, enter the following in the Run command in the Desktop File menu or from the DOS command line: **NBACKUP.EXE @ DAILY.SET.**

/a

launches an unattended backup immediately, just as though you had clicked on the Start Backup command button. The /a and @ options are mutually exclusive; you can specify one or the other on the command line, but you cannot use them together. To start Norton Backup using the setup file called DAILY.SET, for example, enter **NBACKUP.EXE DAILY.SET /a** in the Run dialog box in the Desktop File menu. The .SET file-name extension is optional here.

/tc

specifies a Full Copy backup.

/td

specifies a Differential backup.

/tf

specifies a Full backup.

/ti

specifies an Incremental backup

/to

specifies an Incremental Copy backup

You can combine macros with command-line switches to make Norton Backup a very powerful program that is very easy for the inexperienced user to use.

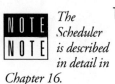

The Scheduler is described in detail in Chapter 16.

USING THE SCHEDULER

You can use the Norton Desktop Scheduler to post a message on your screen at a certain time—reminding you that it is time to make a backup, or to launch an unattended backup at a preset time—even if you are nowhere near your computer. You must remember, however, that if Norton Backup encounters an error, or enters a state that requires your intervention, the program will stop and wait for your input just as if you were making a regular attended backup. Try to anticipate those conditions and use Norton Backup options to configure the program so that these stops don't occur. Also make sure that the files you want to back up will fit on one floppy disk (or two if you have two identical floppy disk drives). Here are several things to watch out for when making an unattended backup:

A successfully completed unattended backup can return to the Desktop or to DOS if you select the Quit After Backup check box in any of the basic or advanced options dialog boxes.

◆ Make sure the system time and date are correct in your computer. If they are not correct, the Scheduler will not start your backup when you expect it to.

◆ Ensure that your backup files will fit onto the backup medium. This is especially important if you back up to floppy disks; it is less important if you back up to a DOS path, to a tape drive, or to a local or networked hard disk.

◆ Turn off the overwrite warnings, so that Norton Backup will not stop if it encounters existing files on your backup disks.

◆ Make sure that the backup floppy disks are formatted to the correct capacity, or turn on Always Format Backup Diskettes.

CHAPTER 12

Recovering Files and Disks

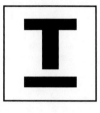

There are several programs available as part of the Norton Desktop for DOS that provide a high degree of protection against accidents happening to disks or files. Some of these programs have been part of the Norton series of products for several years and have earned their near-legendary status in the PC world through exceptional performance. In this chapter, we'll look at four of these programs:

NOTE *Although Image and UnFormat can provide a high degree of protection for your files and directories, you should still perform regular backups.*

Image takes a snapshot of vital disk information.

SmartCan holds deleted files in a special directory for a period of time as a safety measure.

UnErase recovers deleted files.

UnFormat recovers a hard disk after an accidental reformat with the DOS FORMAT command.

SAVING HARD DISK INFORMATION WITH IMAGE

The Image program makes a copy of the system area of your hard disk—the boot track, the file allocation tables, and the root directory. If you reformat the disk by accident, the UnFormat program uses the information saved by Image to reconstruct the files on your disk.

To run Image from the DOS prompt, type:

Image can be used from a network, but you cannot use Image to protect a network file server.

IMAGE

The program executes very quickly. While it runs, it flashes the message:

Updating IMAGE for Drive C:

on the screen. When it's done, it prints

Finished Updating IMAGE for Drive C:

over the first message. Each time you run Image, the program updates two files in the root directory of your disk with copies of the current boot track, the file allocation tables, and all the entries in the root directory. These files, named IMAGE.DAT and IMAGE.BAK, must stay in the root directory if they are to be effective. (Image sets the read-only bit on all the Image data files so you cannot delete them by accident.) Do not copy them to another disk or directory. IMAGE.BAK is a backup of the main Image file, IMAGE.DAT; if you don't have the space for these two files on your hard disk, run Image with the /NOBACKUP switch. From the DOS prompt, type:

IMAGE / NOBACKUP

and only the IMAGE.DAT file will be created or updated.

UnFormat and Un-Erase are both described later in this chapter.

If you accidentally reformat your hard disk, UnFormat uses the information stored in IMAGE.DAT to recover your files and directories. Other Norton Desktop Tools such as Speed Disk and Safe Format also update the IMAGE.DAT file if one is present on your disk.

In addition, the UnErase utility uses information from IMAGE.DAT to recover deleted files that have become fragmented or broken into several small discontinuous pieces.

You can run Image every time you start your computer by adding the line:

IMAGE /NOBACKUP

to your AUTOEXEC.BAT file using the Desktop Editor.

To ensure that the information in IMAGE.DAT is as accurate as possible, you should really run Image at the end of your session rather than at the beginning. See the section called "Creating Your Own Shutdown Routine" in Chapter 9 for a description of how you can run the image program. An accurate, up-to-date IMAGE.DAT file increases the chances of a complete recovery of all the files on your hard disk if it is reformatted.

PROTECTING FILES WITH SMARTCAN

Have you ever hesitated before deleting a file that you were not quite sure about, but that you didn't think you would need again? The SmartCan program lets you delete that file with confidence because it actually delays the deletion. When SmartCan is active, it intercepts the commands that usually delete files and—instead of carrying out the delete operations—moves the files into a directory called SMARTCAN. This procedure has the added benefit of protecting the files from being overwritten, which in turn makes them easier to recover if you change your mind and decide that you want to keep them after all.

Throughout the discussion that follows, SmartCan (mixed upper- and lower-case) refers to the program name, and SMARTCAN (upper-case only) refers to the name of the directory used to hold the deleted files.

The files are held in the SMARTCAN directory for a period of time that you specify, and then they are deleted. You can also specify the amount of disk space you want to reserve for the SMARTCAN directory.

SmartCan offers several very handy and important features:

◆ You can easily recover deleted files from the SmartCan directory using the Desktop's UnErase program, even if the files were deleted by another application program.

◆ You control when and how often the SMARTCAN directory is emptied.

◆ You can specify the drives and file types you want to protect with SmartCan.

The Un-Erase program can recover files from the SMARTCAN directory very quickly.

◆ You can open SmartCan and look at the deleted files held in the SMARTCAN directory, and also see how full this directory is.

All these features will do a great deal for your piece of mind, especially when combined with a regular routine of hard-disk backups made with Norton Backup, described in Chapter 11. If the file is still in the SMARTCAN directory, you can recover it using UnErase. If the file is no longer in the SMARTCAN directory, restore the file from your backup.

CONFIGURING SMARTCAN

SmartCan consists of two parts: a configuration program you use to establish how you want SmartCan to operate and a terminate-and-stay-resident portion that actually does all the work. We'll look at how to configure SmartCan first, then at how to load the terminate-and-stay-resident portion using AUTOEXEC.BAT.

To run SmartCan from the DOS prompt, type:

SMARTCAN

and you will see the opening dialog box shown in Figure 12.1. Check the Enable SmartCan check box to activate SmartCan; otherwise SmartCan will not be active, even if it is loaded into memory.

Next, select an option from the Files to Protect group box, as follows:

All Files. This option extends protection to all files on the chosen drives. This is the most extensive level of protection, and is the option you will probably use most of the time.

Only the Files Listed. Use this selection if you are sure that you only want to protect specific files. You can enter up to nine file-name extensions into the File Extensions text box.

All Files Except Those Listed. This option lets you reverse the sense of the previous choice. Enter the file-name extensions for those files that you do *not* want to protect.

Protect Archived (Backed Up) Files. SmartCan does not automatically save files that have already been backed up—after all, you can reload these files from your backup if you ever need them again. Check this box if you want to make SmartCan protect these files too.

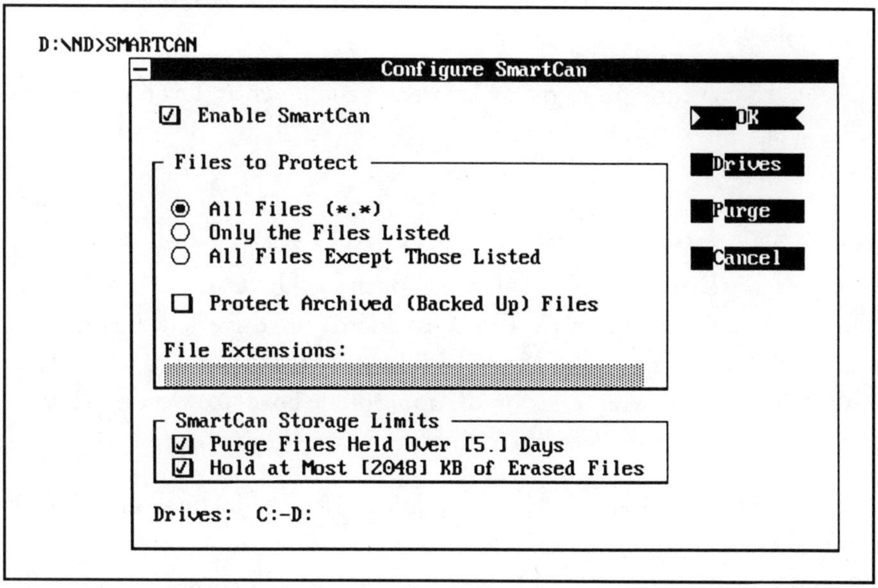

```
D:\ND>SMARTCAN
┌─────────────────── Configure SmartCan ──────────────────────┐
│ ─                                                            │
│   ☑ Enable SmartCan                          ▷  OK  ◁        │
│                                                              │
│  ┌ Files to Protect ──────────────┐          Drives          │
│  │                                 │                          │
│  │  ◉ All Files (*.*)              │          Purge           │
│  │  ○ Only the Files Listed        │                          │
│  │  ○ All Files Except Those Listed│          Cancel          │
│  │                                 │                          │
│  │  ☐ Protect Archived (Backed Up) Files                     │
│  │  File Extensions:               │                          │
│  │  ▒▒▒▒▒▒▒▒▒▒▒▒▒▒▒▒▒▒▒▒▒▒▒▒▒▒▒▒▒▒  │                          │
│  └─────────────────────────────────┘                         │
│  ┌ SmartCan Storage Limits ────────────────┐                 │
│  │ ☑ Purge Files Held Over [5.] Days        │                 │
│  │ ☑ Hold at Most [2048] KB of Erased Files │                 │
│  └──────────────────────────────────────────┘                │
│  Drives:  C:-D:                                              │
│                                                              │
└──────────────────────────────────────────────────────────────┘
```

FIGURE 12.1:
The SmartCan opening dialog box

File Extensions. Into this text box, enter the file-name extensions that you want to either protect or not protect, depending on the option you picked above. You can enter up to nine different extensions if you separate them by a single space or comma. You can mix upper- and lowercase letters, and you don't have to use the star (*) and the dot before the extension (as you do in DOS). For example, you can just enter **EXE** to specify all executable files or **DBF** to specify all your dBASE files. If you select All Files, this text box is dimmed.

With the next two entries, you can also specify the storage limits for the SMARTCAN directory:

Purge Files Held Over [XX] Days. Enter the number of days, from 1 to 99, that you want to preserve files held in the SMARTCAN directory, before they are automatically removed. The default is 5 days, and you can enter 0 to specify no time limit.

Hold at Most [XX] KB of Erased Files. Enter the maximum amount of disk space you want to reserve for the SMARTCAN directory, in kilobytes, from 16 to 9,999. When the SMARTCAN directory fills up, the oldest files will be purged first to make room for later files. If you don't want to set an upper limit, do not check this box and your deleted files will be held until you run out of disk space.

The drives currently protected by SmartCan are shown at the bottom of this dialog box.

SELECTING DRIVES FOR PROTECTION

Click on the Drives command button to open the Drives dialog box. Use the Tab or arrow keys to move from drive letter to drive letter, and press the spacebar to turn on the check mark for each drive you want to protect. With the mouse, merely click on the appropriate boxes to select the drives.

There are three selections in the Drive Types group box:

All Floppy Disks. Check this option to protect files on your floppy disks.

All Local Drives. Use this selection if you want to protect files on all your local drives—hard disks as well as floppy disks.

All Network Drives. This selection protects files on all of the drives on your network.

Choose the selections most appropriate to your current environment. You can always revise these settings later if you change your mind.

MANUALLY PURGING FILES

As I have said, SmartCan copies the files you delete into the SMARTCAN directory, giving them names that start with the @ character and end with the .SAV file-name extension. The files will be purged automatically as the specified time period expires; however, if you want to remove them earlier, just click on the Purge command button to open the Purge Deleted Files window, as shown in Figure 12.2.

The files you have deleted are listed in the window, along with their sizes and creation dates and times. Below the window, the screen displays the

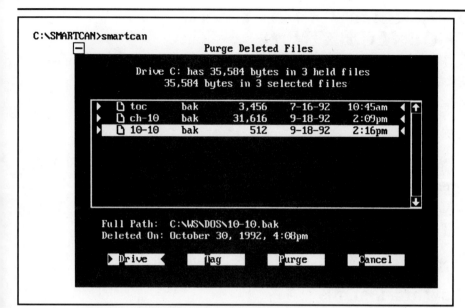

C:\SMARTCAN>smartcan

```
┌─┐              Purge Deleted Files
│─│
    Drive C: has 35,584 bytes in 3 held files
           35,584 bytes in 3 selected files

  ▶  ▯ toc      bak      3,456    7-16-92    10:45am  ◀  ▲
  ▶  ▯ ch-10    bak     31,616    9-18-92     2:09pm  ◀
  ▶  ▯ 10-10    bak        512    9-18-92     2:16pm  ◀

                                                        ▼

  Full Path:  C:\WS\DOS\10-10.bak
  Deleted On: October 30, 1992, 4:08pm

  ▶ Drive ◀      Tag          Purge          Cancel
```

FIGURE 12.2:
The Purge Deleted Files window lets you choose the files you want to remove manually from the SMARTCAN directory

original path name and the time and date you deleted the file. There are four selections available to you in this window, as follows:

◆ **Drive.** Select this option to specify the drive or drives from which you will purge files.

◆ **Tag.** You can mark, or *tag*, a group of files that meet a particular file specification, or you can tag a group of files by specifying a common file-name extension. Then you can purge the entire group at once instead of deleting each file one at a time.

◆ **Purge.** This selection removes the files you selected or tagged.

◆ **Cancel.** Select this option to return to the main dialog box.

Using the Purge command button is the *only* safe way to remove files from the SMARTCAN. Remember, if you use the DOS DEL or ERASE commands to remove them, SmartCan will carefully make another copy of them as long as they meet the File Protection criteria.

Click on OK when you are ready to return to the DOS prompt.

ADDING SMARTCAN TO YOUR AUTOEXEC.BAT FILE

The first time you run SmartCan, you should run it as I described above. If you add the line:

SMARTCAN /ON

to your AUTOEXEC.BAT file, SmartCan will load your settings from disk and take its place in the memory of your computer without invoking the program's full-screen mode. This loads the program with your settings each time you boot up your computer, so you don't have to remember to do it yourself.

Once SmartCan is installed on your system, you can examine the program's configuration from the DOS command line by typing:

SMARTCAN /STATUS

which displays a summary screen similar to the one shown in Figure 12.3. If you want to turn SmartCan off for a while, use the command:

SMARTCAN /OFF

or, if you want to remove SmartCan from memory, type:

SMARTCAN /UNINSTALL

> **NOTE** *If you are a network user, load the network driver and shell (IPX.COM and NET3, NET4, or NET5) before you load SmartCan.*

```
C:\>SMARTCAN /STATUS
SmartCan, Norton Desktop 1.00, Copyright 1992 by Symantec Corporation

SmartCan Status:      Enabled
Drives Protected:     C: (SmartCan contains 784K in 22 files)
                      D: (SmartCan is empty)
Files Protected:      All files
Archive Files:        Not Protected
Files Deleted After:  5 days


C:\>
```

FIGURE 12.3:

You can access the SmartCan status screen from the DOS prompt

RECOVERING DELETED FILES WITH UNERASE

Deleting files is easy, sometimes *too* easy. If you use wildcards in file names in a DEL operation, you might specify more files than you intended and end up deleting too many files, maybe even the entire contents of a directory. For example, both EDLIN and WordStar create .BAK files when files are modified and saved. Most people delete these files to save space, relying on their backup disks for copies of the original files. Suppose, in this case, you mistype

DEL *.BAK

as

DEL *.BAT

Instead of deleting your .BAK files, you have just deleted all your batch files!

Careful disk organization can help prevent some of these accidental erasures. To protect your batch files, for example, you should keep them in a separate directory, away from your EDLIN or WordStar files. No matter how good your organization is, however, sooner or later you will accidentally erase a file or want to recover a file that you erased intentionally, and this is where the UnErase program comes into play.

Before we look at UnErase, I want to take a moment to describe what actually happens when you delete a file or add a new file onto one of your disks.

WHAT REALLY HAPPENS WHEN YOU DELETE A FILE?

If you delete a file using the DOS commands DEL or ERASE, the Delete button on the Desktop button bar, or the Delete command from the Desktop File menu, the deleted file's entries are cleared from the file allocation table. DOS also changes the first character of the file name to a Greek lowercase sigma character (ASCII E5 hex or 229 decimal) to indicate to the rest of DOS that the file has been erased. However, the file's entry, including its starting cluster number and its length, remains in the directory, hidden from view because DOS added the sigma character in the file name. The data itself remains in its original location on the disk. No data on disk is actually changed until DOS is instructed to write a new file over the space formerly occupied by the deleted file. Thus, the first cluster of a file can be found and recovered quite easily as long as it has not been overwritten.

WHAT HAPPENS WHEN YOU ADD A NEW FILE?

To learn how to reduce file fragmentation, see the discussion of the Speed Disk program in Chapter 14.

When you add a new file to your disk, DOS looks for the next available cluster of free disk space. If the file is small enough to fit into this space, DOS simply inserts it. However, if the file is larger, DOS splits it up into several pieces, recording it into clusters that are not numbered consecutively. In other words, the file becomes *fragmented.*

Thus, saving a new file on the disk destroys a deleted file's data. If the new file is larger than the old one, the old file is completely obliterated. If the new file is smaller than the old one, some unknown amount of the old file will remain on the disk until it is finally overwritten during another write-to-disk operation.

The most important point to remember about file recovery is you must not save anything on the disk until you have completed the recovery operation. Do not even install the Norton Desktop on your hard disk; instead, you should run UnErase from the original distribution disks. Install the complete Norton Desktop package onto your hard disk only when the recovery operation is completely finished. By following this rule, you will not overwrite the erased file's data and you will increase the chances of a complete recovery.

USING UNERASE TO RECOVER DELETED FILES

If the deleted file is a short file or is on a floppy disk, there is an excellent chance that UnErase will be able to restore it on the first attempt. If the file is badly fragmented or part of it has been overwritten by another file, the chances of a complete recovery are substantially less.

To demonstrate how UnErase works, we will create a small text file, delete it, and then recover it using UnErase from the original floppy disk. Follow these steps:

1. Use the Desktop Editor to create a small text file containing the text:

This is a short section of text

2. Use the Save As command from the Desktop Editor File menu to call the file MYFILE.TXT.

3. Return to the Norton Desktop, click on the drive icon that contains this new file, highlight the file, then use the Delete command from the File menu or the Delete button on the button bar to delete the file. You could also use the DOS DEL command from the DOS command prompt.

4. Now exit from the Desktop, insert the disk containing the UnErase program into a drive, make that drive the current drive, and type:

UNERASE

to start the program running. We are starting UnErase from one of the original floppy disks for the purposes of this example, but if you installed the Norton Desktop package *before* you decided to recover a deleted file, you can run the program directly from the Desktop Tools menu.

UnErase can recover deleted files from a network drive only if Smart-Can is installed for that drive.

The main UnErase screen is shown in Figure 12.4. In the center of the screen you can see the information for the file you just deleted, MYFILE.TXT. Notice, however, that the screen shows the first character of the file name as a **?** character. This reminds you that UnErase does not know what that first character should be (recall that DOS replaced this character with the sigma symbol), and you will have to supply the original character during the next part of the recovery process. (If you are using the SmartCan utility, you will see the complete file name, with no missing letters.) Also in the display you can see the file size, creation date and time, and the prognosis for recovery, which in this case is described as **good**.

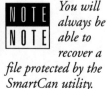

You will always be able to recover a file protected by the SmartCan utility.

To see more information about this file, choose the Info button below the main window. This displays a screen similar to Figure 12.5, showing the file name, creation time and date, file size in bytes, and file attributes. All of this information helps you to identify this file as the correct file to unerase.

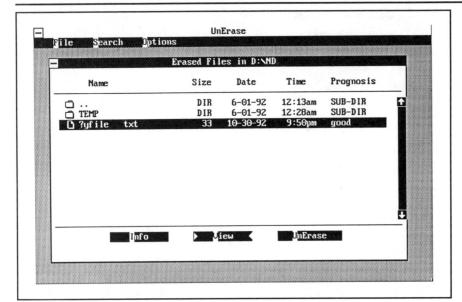

FIGURE 12.4:

The main Unerase window lists information about deleted files.

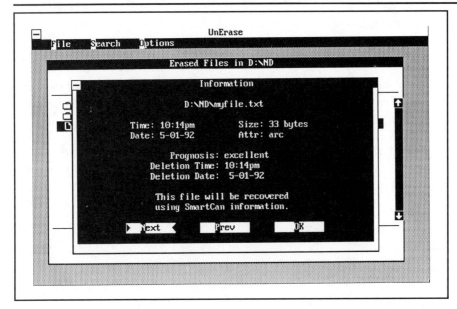

FIGURE 12.5:

The Information screen displays details about the deleted file

The recovery prognosis is shown; UnErase describes the chances of recovery, or *prognosis,* of a file as Excellent, Good, Average, or Poor, in decreasing order of the likelihood of a success. (This column also might display the messages Not Applicable, Recovered, non-erased, or SUB-DIR, depending on the status of the recovery process.)

UnErase also displays a short message describing the current status of the file. This message may be relatively optimistic about the recovery, such as:

This file can be recovered in one piece,
but it may not contain the correct data.

or rather more ominous, as in the following case:

The first cluster of this file
is now being used by another file.

The message is directly related to the entry in the prognosis column.

Choose View to look at the contents of the file as text or in hex. For the sample MYFILE.TXT, you will see a display similar to the one shown in Figure 12.6. The View selection shows that the original data is still on the disk. Use the Text or Hex button to change the format of the display. The hex view shows the numeric values of the bytes on the left, and the equivalent ASCII characters on the right. Figure 12.6 shows the file in text view. Select the Next or Previous box to examine other deleted files on the disk, or select OK to return to the main UnErase screen.

To unerase the file, choose the UnErase option, and you will be prompted to supply the first character of the file name. Use the correct character if you can remember it; otherwise, use any character as the first letter. Remember, you can always use the Rename option from the File menu or the DOS RENAME command to change the name later. As soon as you type the first character, the file is unerased, and the Prognosis column displays the status as RECOVERED.

If you want to recover several files from the same directory, you can use the Select Group option from the File menu. Alternatively, you can use the + key on the numeric keypad. The Select window opens and prompts you to select the files. You can use file names, extensions, or any of the DOS wildcard characters to specify the files. For example, specify *.* to recover all of the deleted files in the directory, or specify *.WK? to recover only your

NOTE *See Chapter 5 for a description of file attributes.*

FIGURE 12.6:

The View selection lets you look at the contents of the file as text or in hex

Lotus 1-2-3 spreadsheet files. When you select OK to return to the main Un-Erase screen, you will see arrowhead characters to the right and left of the files matching your file specification. To remove files from the list, press the – key on the numeric keypad, or choose Unselect Group from the File menu.

After your selection is complete and you choose the UnErase button, a window opens to confirm the number of files you want to attempt to recover. This window also asks if you want to be prompted to supply the missing first character of the file name. When this box has a check mark, UnErase prompts you to supply a beginning character for each file. If you clear the check mark from the box, UnErase does not prompt for a character—it simply inserts the first letter of the alphabet that results in a unique file name for each file. These names might look a little strange at first because most of them will begin with the letter *a* or *b*. You can use the Rename command from the File menu to change the names to something more appropriate.

There are several options in the File menu that you can use to look at erased files in other directories or on other disks. If you want to change to another drive, select Change Drive (Alt+ D) and choose a drive from the list in the Change Drive window. Use View Current Directory (Alt+C) to display files in the current directory, or use View All Directories (Alt+A) to look at all the erased files on the current drive. To change to a specific directory, first select Change Directory (Alt+R); then locate the appropriate directory in the graphical display of directory names, or type the first few letters of the name into the Speed Search window. Remember that the Change Directory screen does not show deleted directories.

If the main window displays a large number of files, you can use the selections from the Options menu to arrange the files in the most convenient order. You can sort the files by name, extension, time, size, or by prognosis, and you can choose to include or exclude existing files in the directory that have not been erased. A check mark appears next to your current selection in the menu. This sorting applies only to the files shown in the main UnErase window; the order of the files on your disk remains unchanged.

You have now completed a simple file recovery by unerasing MYFILE.TXT. As long as you start the recovery process soon after you have deleted the file, and the file is not badly fragmented or overwritten, the chances for recovery are usually quite good.

MANUALLY UNERASING FILES

Now that you are familiar with unerasing files automatically, you are ready to learn how to unerase files manually. You should only use manual recovery methods if the automatic recovery mode did not work. Although it is considered an advanced technique, always remember that UnErase will provide help at every stage. In the following example, we will delete the README.TXT file supplied with the Norton Desktop, and then we will use UnErase's manual recovery methods to restore the file. First, change to the Norton Desktop directory on your hard disk. Then type:

TYPE README.TXT¦MORE

to display the beginning of the README.TXT file, as shown in Figure 12.7.

Press Ctrl+C to break out of the display, and then erase the READ.ME file by typing:

DEL README.TXT

```
Norton Desktop for DOS                           Version 1.00
                                                     5/26/92

    This file contains compatibility information, late-breaking
    news, and feature updates which do not appear in the manual.


Welcome to the NORTON DESKTOP FOR DOS!

The Norton Desktop for DOS requires DOS version 3.1 or later and a hard
drive with at least 3.2 megabytes free.  A full installation of the
Norton Desktop requires 8 megabytes of disk space.  The Norton Desktop
requires 640k RAM with at least 512k free, but will benefit from 1 meg
or more of EMS and/or XMS memory.  You must have an additional 2mb of
free disk space in order to run the Norton Desktop for DOS.

For those who are not familiar with Windows like programs, please take a
few moments and use the Guided Tour.  The tour comes up automatically
the first time you use the Norton Desktop.  Thereafter, it can be run
from the Help menu on the Norton Desktop.  Even for experienced users it
contains a number of tips that will make the use of the Norton Desktop
even easier.

-- More --
```

FIGURE 12.7:
The contents of the Norton Desktop README.TXT file

If you want to unerase the file to a new file name, directory, or disk, press Alt+F and then T.

To restore README.TXT, start UnErase from the DOS prompt by typing:

UNERASE

or select UnErase from the Norton Desktop Tools menu. The top of the screen shows that you are in the NORTON directory, and a line within the window describes the ?EADME.TXT file.

Position the highlight over the ?EADME.TXT file, and then press Alt+M or choose Manual UnErase from the File menu. UnErase asks you to enter a character to complete the file name. Enter an **R** and you will see the Manual UnErase screen shown in Figure 12.8.

At the left side of the Manual UnErase screen, the File Information box displays information about the README.TXT file, including the file name, attributes, creation date and time, and size in bytes. Below this information is the starting cluster number for README.TXT from the file allocation table. Next, the Clusters Needed field reports the number of clusters that the file occupied before it was deleted; this represents the number of clusters that you must recover to unerase the file. On the last line, the Clusters Found

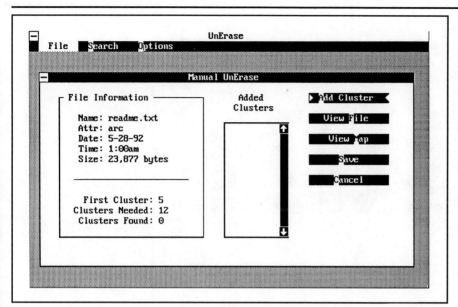

FIGURE 12.8:
The Manual UnErase screen provides detailed information about the erased file

count keeps track of the clusters you add to the file. This number is zero now, but it will increase as you recover clusters and add them to the file.

In the center of the screen, the Added Clusters box displays the actual cluster numbers as you add clusters to the file.

From the selections at the right of the screen, choose Add Cluster, and you will see the display shown in Figure 12.9. You use the Add Clusters screen to specify the clusters you want to include in the file you are recovering. Use the arrow keys to move the highlight from one box to another. Not all the clusters in the original file may be recoverable, of course.

To find the file's clusters, you can choose from the following options:

UnErase does not let you add clusters that are already allocated to another file.

◆ **All clusters** automatically adds the most likely clusters to the file and provides the most straightforward method of recovering the file's data.

◆ **Next probable** lets UnErase choose the next likely cluster to include. (Clusters are chosen one at a time.)

◆ **Data search** lets you enter a search string of as many as 28 characters in either ASCII or in hex. If you enter the search string in ASCII, it is translated into its hex equivalent and displayed in the hex window. To enter the search string in hex, use the Tab key or

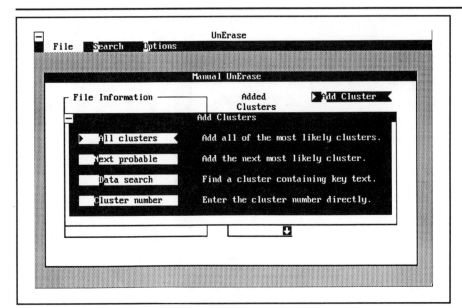

the arrow keys to move to the hex box, and type in the search characters. Place a check mark in the Ignore Case box to find the search string irrespective of case, or clear the check mark to make the search case-specific.

◆ **Cluster number** requires that you know which cluster to add. At the top of the Add Cluster Number screen, UnErase lists the valid range of clusters for your drive. You can specify a single cluster or a range of clusters. Enter a starting cluster number and an ending cluster number. If the range you specify contains clusters already in use in another file, UnErase finds the first free cluster within the range.

The simplest way of finding the data for the file is to select All clusters. Choose that option now. The program will find all the clusters that the README.TXT data occupies and list them in the Added Clusters box. Before completing the recovery process by actually saving the file, you can examine the information contained in the found clusters or even remove or rearrange the clusters.

VIEWING OR UNSELECTING FOUND CLUSTERS

Be sure that the highlight is on the first cluster in the Added Clusters box, then select View File to examine the contents of this cluster. You will see a display similar to the one shown in Figure 12.10, but remember that your cluster numbers will be different because they refer to your own disk. Figure 12.10 shows the data as text; to see the display in hex, select or click on the Hex box. Use the up and down arrow keys, the PgUp or PgDn keys, or click on the scroll bars to move through the file. Cluster boundaries are marked in the file. Compare this figure with Figure 12.7 to confirm that what you see is indeed the start of the README.TXT text file. Select OK to return to the main Manual UnErase screen.

Select View Map to see the relative location and size of the data you have recovered so far. This information for our example is shown in Figure 12.11. The space occupied by this file is shown as an F character. Disk space occupied by other files is shown as a block with a dot in the center, and unused disk space is shown as a solid block. Select OK to return to the main screen.

> NOTE NOTE
> *Each block in the Disk Map display represents several clusters.*

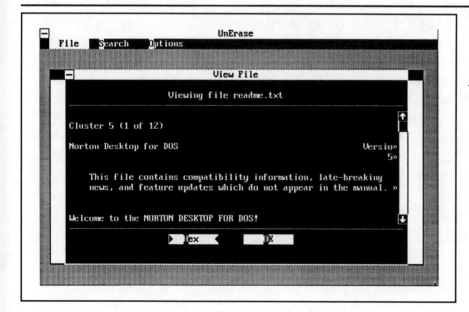

FIGURE 12.10:
View File shows the contents of the first cluster in the README.TXT file

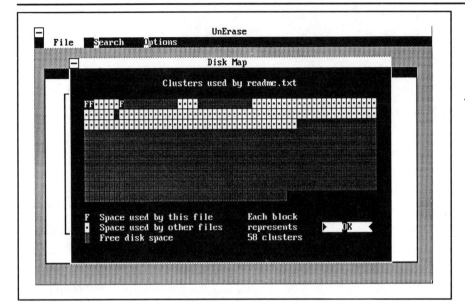

The Disk Map display shows the size and location of the clusters you have recovered so far

You can move a cluster within the Added Clusters box if you are unhappy with its current location. Move the highlight to the Added Clusters box, position the highlight on the cluster you want to move, and press the spacebar. A small arrowhead appears to the right of the cluster number and confirms your choice. Now, use the up and down arrow keys to move the cluster to a new location in the list. Press the spacebar again to unselect the cluster at its new location. Select View File again to be sure that this new position is consistent with the rest of the file's contents.

Now that you're sure that you have selected the correct clusters to unerase, use Save to complete the recovery process. This menu selection stores the data in the README.TXT directory entry and also restores the file allocation table data so that DOS can find the file again. Recovery of README.TXT is now complete.

RECOVERING PARTIAL FILES

Often, recovering files is not as straightforward as it was in the previous examples. DOS may have overwritten all or part of the erased file with another file before you realize that you want to recover the erased file. Several factors determine whether recovery is possible, including the length of the new and erased files, and the existence or nonexistence of the erased file's directory entry.

If the file has been partially overwritten, you still might be able to recover some portion of the file, but there is a good chance that its original directory entry will have been overwritten. If this is the case, you can use Create File from UnErase's File menu to create a new directory entry to use with the recovery process. You can now use Manual UnErase to search for clusters to add to the file. Note that in this kind of recovery, the Add Cluster screen contains only three selections: Next Probable, Data Search, and Cluster Number. You cannot use automatic recovery techniques under these circumstances.

If you are recovering files from a badly damaged disk, you probably don't want to store the recovered clusters on the same disk. Select the UnErase To option from the File menu to save the file to another disk. Choose the drive from the list of available drives shown in the UnErase To window, or merely type the letter of the drive you want to use. At the end of your recovery attempt, the clusters will be written to the drive you selected.

The single most important aspect of this kind of file recovery is how much you know about the contents of the erased file. If you know nothing about the file, it may be impossible to determine whether you have recovered it completely. If the file is a program file, running only the recovered portion can lead to unpredictable—and sometimes unpleasant—results. The only safe way to proceed in this case is to delete the partial file, and restore the entire file from your backup set.

SEARCHING FOR LOST DATA

If you can't remember which directory an erased file was in, or if you are unable to recover the directory it was in, you can use the selections in the Search pull-down menu to locate clusters containing certain types of data. The Search menu contains the following options:

◆ **For Data Types** lets you choose from Normal Text, Lotus 1-2-3 and Symphony, dBASE, or Other data types. Use the spacebar to make your selection, or click on the appropriate box with the mouse. Select Stop to abandon the search.

◆ **For Text** lets you enter a text search string. If you check the Ignore Case box, both upper- and lowercase strings are checked. The text you are searching for is shown at the top of the Search Progress window. A percentage-complete display shows the progress being made by the search. Select Stop to abandon the search.

As the search proceeds, the screen shows a list of the file fragments. UnErase names these fragments FILE0001, FILE0002, and so on. You can press the Escape key to stop the search at any time; then you can highlight a file fragment, and use View to examine it. If the file fragment is the beginning of a file you want to recover, select UnErase.

◆ **For Lost Names** searches for inaccessible file names. Files may be lost if the directories that they were in are overwritten. Names of erased files are displayed on the screen; when you see a file name you recognize, highlight the file name, and select the UnErase button in the lower-right corner of the screen.

◆ **Set Search Range** lets you specify the starting and ending cluster numbers for the search. The range of valid cluster numbers is shown on the Search Range window. You can use this selection to restrict the area of the disk that will be searched if you have an idea of where the missing file is located on the disk. You probably should use this selection first to restrict the search, and then specify the type of data you want to search for with one of the other selections.

◆ **Continue Search** resumes an interrupted search so you don't have to reenter the search criteria.

To save the file fragments found in this way, use the Append To selection from the File menu. Append To adds these clusters to an existing file.

RECOVERING AN ERASED DIRECTORY

To recover files, you must sometimes first recover a directory so that you can gain access to the files. Note that if a directory contains *any* files, it cannot be deleted.

You can use UnErase to restore deleted directories; in fact, the procedure is the same as for restoring deleted files. After you have recovered the directory, you can restore all of its files.

DOS removes a directory in the same way that it removes a file. The first character is set to the same special character (a lowercase sigma), and the removed directory's entry remains in its parent directory (unseen, of course), exactly like a removed file's entry. UnErase lists directories that have not been deleted using their full names in uppercase letters, and it lists the names of deleted directories in uppercase letters with a question mark as the first character.

Let's look at an example to review this procedure briefly. Suppose you erased all your spreadsheet files that were in the 123 directory on drive C, then erased the directory itself, and later realized that this was not the directory you had intended to delete. The UnErase program will not be able to find the spreadsheet files to restore them, because their names, starting cluster numbers, and file lengths are all stored in the 123 directory that has also been deleted. You must first recover the directory before attempting to recover the files. To run UnErase on the 123 directory, change to the directory that was the parent of the 123 directory (the root directory, in this example) and type:

UNERASE

This displays the screen shown in Figure 12.12.

UnErase asks you for the first character of the directory name, or uses information provided by SmartCan to complete the entry. After you have recovered the directory, you can proceed to recover the files that were in the 123 directory. Because the files were all small, each a single cluster, your chances of recovering them are relatively good. Select Change Directory from the File menu, and using the graphical directory that is displayed, change to the recovered 123 directory. Select each of the files individually, or if you want to recover all of them at the same time, use Select Group to specify all the files.

As you now know, file recovery is by no means certain. Many aspects of the process influence the success of any recovery attempt, most of which you examined in this chapter. Although the file-recovery process can be more difficult than was shown in this chapter's examples (for example, recovering

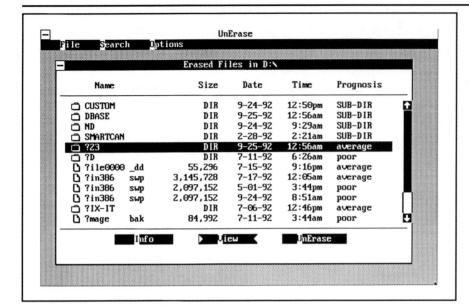

*Unerasing a directory
before recovering the
files in that directory*

program files can be messy), you should have enough knowledge of the Norton Desktop UnErase program to attempt difficult recoveries on your own. If you can't rescue the file with the Norton Desktop, chances are that the file *can't* be recovered.

UNERASING FILES WITH DOS 5

*Delete
Tracking
will not
work on a
network or on any
drive that has been
redirected using the
JOIN or SUBST
commands.*

DOS 5 provides several utilities that assist in the file-recovery process:

◆ Mirror. This program creates a copy of the bookkeeping information on a disk, just like the Norton Image program.

◆ Delete Tracking. Mirror also installs a memory-resident program called Delete Tracking. Delete Tracking is similar in operation to SmartCan, with one vital difference: Delete Tracking stores information about the deleted file, including the file name and starting cluster number, into a file called PCTRACKR.DEL, but it does not protect the file's data. The Norton Desktop SmartCan program stores the actual file itself, hence guaranteeing a complete recovery.

UnErase checks for files made by both Image and Mirror, and if both file types are present, UnErase uses the most recent file. UnErase can also use information stored in the Delete Tracking file PCTRACKR.DEL to help in recovering files.

The Norton Desktop SmartCan and UnErase programs, used together with a complete, up-to-date backup of all your important files, offer the most complete solution to recovering deleted files.

RECOVERING FROM FORMATTING PROBLEMS

One of the most appalling prospects for a hard-disk user is accidentally reformatting a hard disk, an operation that destroys all data and programs. With UnFormat, however, you can now recover data from a reformatted hard disk. Some PC manufacturers have even invented another command for formatting the hard disk, just to make reformatting more difficult to do by accident.

Using UnFormat

When you run the DOS FORMAT command on a hard disk, it clears the root directory and the file allocation table of their entries, but it does not overwrite the data area on the disk. The data is still there, but because the root directory and the file allocation table have been cleared, you normally have no way of getting to it. The UnFormat program provides an easy way of recovering these files. Note, however, that UnFormat will not recover floppy disks formatted with the DOS FORMAT command because the original data is actually overwritten. However, UnFormat *can* recover floppy disks that have been formatted using the Norton Desktop Format Diskette command.

 *Some versions of DOS, including Compaq DOS 3.1, and DOS 2.11 from AT&T, actually overwrite all the original data when they format a hard disk. UnFormat cannot recover files under these circumstances.*

You should run the Image program as a part of your daily operation. Doing so creates a file called IMAGE.DAT (and a copy called IMAGE.BAK) that UnFormat can use to recover the disk. Although these files' entries will be cleared from the root directory and file allocation table if the hard disk is reformatted, running the UnFormat program from a floppy will let you recover their data and thereby recover your hard disk completely. You should add an Image statement for the logical disk drives on your computer. For

Include the Image utility in your AUTOEXEC.BAT file so that IMAGE.DAT is updated regularly.

example, if you have a large hard disk divided into three logical drives—C, D, and E—you need one Image drive statement in your AUTOEXEC.BAT file. Add the line:

IMAGE C: D: E:

to protect all three disk drives.

After Image has created these files, you cannot delete them by accident—they are read-only files. If you try to delete them with the DOS DEL or ERASE command, you will receive an **Access denied** error message. The IMAGE.DAT file is also used by the UnErase program when you recover files and directories.

If you run UnFormat on a hard disk when the information contained in IMAGE.DAT is not up to date, the recovery will be incomplete. If you have added or removed files and these changes were not stored in IMAGE.DAT, UnErase will not know about them. For example, if you deleted files, UnFormat will assign data to those files even though they no longer exist. Furthermore, data in files created since IMAGE.DAT was updated will not be recovered. After UnErase has done all it can to recover data with an outdated IMAGE.DAT file, run the Norton Disk Doctor from the original Norton Desktop floppy disks to sort out the few remaining file fragments.

You can run UnFormat from a network, but you cannot unformat a network file server.

If your hard disk has been accidentally reformatted with the DOS FORMAT command, insert the Norton Desktop original floppy disk (or a copy of this disk) that contains UnFormat into drive A. You have to run UnFormat from a floppy disk because your hard-disk copy of UnFormat can't be accessed. Do this immediately—before you load any files from your backup onto the reformatted hard disk. If you try to load programs first, you may overwrite the IMAGE.DAT file, in which case a complete recovery will be impossible.

Always run Un-Format on an accidentally reformatted hard disk before writing anything else to the disk—otherwise you may overwrite IMAGE.DAT, making recovery difficult.

The UnFormat program is automatic and easy to use. You don't need to select options from pull-down menus; simply choose from two or three simple alternatives shown on the screen. To run the program, select UnFormat from the Tools menu in the Norton Desktop, or at the DOS prompt, type:

UNFORMAT

The program displays the startup screen shown in Figure 12.13.

```
┌─────────────────────────────────────────────┐
│─          UnFormat                           │
│                                              │
│   UnFormat will recover a hard disk or floppy│
│   diskette that has been accidentally        │
│   formatted.                                 │
│                                              │
│   UnFormat can also rebuild a disk that has  │
│   been destroyed by a virus or corrupted due │
│            to a power failure.               │
│                                              │
│      ▶ Continue ◀          Quit              │
│                                              │
└─────────────────────────────────────────────┘
```

Choose Continue to change to the drive selection window from which you can select a drive to unformat. In this example, we will use drive E.

The next window asks if you used IMAGE to save IMAGE.DAT for drive E. Answer Yes if you did or if you are not sure. If you answer No, the disk will be unformatted from scratch.

Recovering Data with IMAGE.DAT

If you previously used the Image utility to save a copy of the system area of your disk, recovery after an accidental format should be fast and easy. The next window that opens is a warning screen that contains a list of the files in the root directory of the selected drive. These files will be lost if you unformat the disk.

Next UnFormat looks for a copy of IMAGE.DAT on the disk. If it finds a copy, it opens the IMAGE Info Found window.

The window shows both the most recent time that Image saved the IMAGE.DAT file and the previous time, and asks you which version you want to use to unformat your hard disk. If you want to use the most recent copy of IMAGE.DAT to recover the contents of your disk, select Recent. If you want to use the previous copy, select Previous; otherwise, select Cancel.

The combination of an up-to-date IMAGE.DAT file and a complete set of current backup disks greatly increases the chances of a complete recovery of all the files on your reformatted hard disk. Be prepared.

If damage occurred to your disk after the last IMAGE.DAT file was created, you may not always want to use the most current version of this file to recover the hard disk. Obviously, any changes you made to the disk after the IMAGE.DAT file was created will not be recovered.

Restoring the data will overwrite the current data; if this is acceptable, select OK to continue. UnFormat now gives you the choice of a full restore or a partial restore.

◆ **Full** restores the entire system area, including boot record, file allocation table information, and the root directory. If you are unsure of how to proceed at this point, selecting Full is safest option.

◆ **Partial** lets you select the parts of the system area you want to restore—boot record, file allocation table, or root directory.

UnFormat reconstructs the data, and then opens a window to inform you that drive E has been successfully restored. It also advises you to run Norton Disk Doctor with the /QUICK switch selected as a final precaution against lost clusters or cross-linked files. If the Norton Disk Doctor reports errors on your disk, the errors are a result of creating files after you last ran the Image utility. In other words, IMAGE.DAT was not completely up to date.

Recovering Data without the IMAGE.DAT File

If you are prompted for a DOS disk during the recovery process, copy COMMAND.COM to your root directory to make the hard disk a bootable disk.

Even if you do not have a copy of IMAGE.DAT, you can still use UnFormat to recover much of the data on your hard disk.

When UnFormat asks if you have saved IMAGE.DAT for the drive, choose No. UnFormat then shows a map of the disk and displays the progress made during the unformatting process. When UnFormat is finished, subdirectories will be called DIR0, DIR1, DIR2, and so on. All the files in your root directory will be missing. Use the manual UnErase techniques described earlier in this chapter to recover these files.

Remember to run the Norton Disk Doctor to find any remaining file allocation errors when UnFormat has finished. Then, check to see if all your files and subdirectories are on the hard disk.

UnFormat cannot recover files in the root directory; however, it can recover files in all other directories.

Finally, copy any of the files that you need for normal operation to the root directory. Then be sure that AUTOEXEC.BAT, CONFIG.SYS, and COMMAND.COM are all present. If they are not there, copy them to the root directory from your backup floppy disks.

UnFormat returns to the opening screen to ask if you want to unformat another disk. Select Quit to return to DOS.

UNFORMAT AND DOS 5

DOS 5 provides protection against accidents in the form of the Mirror command. Mirror files are similar to Image files, in that they both save important information about a drive for use if the drive suffers an accident. UnFormat has the best of both worlds, because UnFormat can use files made by Image or files made by Mirror to recover a disk. If both types of files exist on a drive, UnFormat makes use of the most recent file.

If you want UnFormat to use a particular type of file, you can include a command-line switch, as follows:

UNFORMAT *drive* /IMAGE

This forces UnFormat to use information contained in an Image file and ignore any Mirror files, while

UNFORMAT *drive* /MIRROR

tells UnFormat to use a Mirror file for the recovery process, and ignore any Image information. The *drive* variable represents the drive letter of the disk you are recovering.

TAKING CARE OF YOUR DISKS

In this final section, we'll take a look at ways to avoid mechanical damage to disks, since extended use can cause both hard and floppy disks to deteriorate. Floppy disks are especially prone to damage through mistreatment and careless handling.

SAFEGUARDING FLOPPY DISKS

The following suggestions for handling floppy disks will help you protect your data and prevent problems:

◆ When you are not using a floppy disk, keep it in its jacket in a disk storage tray or in its box.

◆ Do not expose floppy disks to high temperatures; for example, do not leave them on a window sill, on top of your monitor, or in a car parked in the sun. The disks will warp and become unusable.

◆ Keep disks away from magnetic fields, such as motors, paper clip holders, stereo speakers, magnetized screwdrivers, and magnetic keys.

◆ Do not touch the recording surface of the disk. This can transfer dirt and body oils to the disk's surface and destroy data.

◆ Label all your disks. Write on the label before attaching it to the disk. If you must write on the label after it is on the disk, use a soft felt-tip pen—not a ballpoint pen or a pencil. Add a volume label to each of your disks.

◆ Keep backup copies of all distribution disks, preferably in a different place from the original disks. Often, a local company will specialize in archiving data. Such places use precisely controlled temperature and humidity to ensure long life to the media in storage. They also usually have excellent security and fire protection.

PROTECTING HARD DISKS

Your hard disk is not immune to problems either. The following suggestions relate to its care:

◆ When you are using the hard disk, do not move the disk unit (if the drive is external) or the computer cabinet (if the drive is internal).

◆ Before you turn off your computer or move the system, use a head-parking program to stabilize the heads on the hard disk.

◆ To protect your system against power outages or "brownouts," use a voltage regulator, a surge suppressor, or a small uninterruptable power supply (UPS).

◆ Do not obstruct the air flow to the back of the computer; the air flow cools your system.

◆ Keep the card slots at the back of your computer covered. If you remove a card, replace the plate. An open slot directs hot air over the motherboard.

◆ Perform timely backups.

In the next chapter, we'll look at how you can use the Norton Desktop package to find and fix disk problems.

CHAPTER 13

Diagnosing and Fixing
Disk Problems

hat do you do if your disk contains files that you cannot read? You can use the Norton Disk Doctor to diagnose and fix the unreadable files.

DOS provides the CHKDSK command for finding and fixing file Allocation Table (FAT) errors and the RECOVER command for accessing files that contain bad sectors. However, DOS does not include programs that can find or fix physical errors on a floppy or hard disk. The diagnostics program disk supplied with some computers may be able to locate errors, but it usually can't fix them. Fortunately, Norton Disk Doctor (NDD) finds and fixes any logical or high-level physical errors on your floppy or hard disk. I do not go into great depth about the cause and nature of disk errors in this chapter. Suffice it to say, you should run Norton Disk Doctor after DOS reports a disk error.

FINDING AND FIXING DISK PROBLEMS
WITH NORTON DISK DOCTOR

You can run Norton Disk Doctor from the DOS prompt or by selecting it from the Tools menu in the Norton Desktop. If you are using the Advise

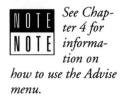

See Chapter 4 for information on how to use the Advise menu.

menu from the Desktop, you can also run the Norton Disk Doctor directly from some of the Advise help screens.

To run Norton Disk Doctor from the DOS prompt, type:

NDD

with no parameters or switches. The opening screen is shown in Figure 13.1.

You can select five options from the main Norton Disk Doctor screen: Diagnose Disk, Surface Test, Undo Changes, Options, and Quit Disk Doctor.

FINDING PROBLEMS WITH DIAGNOSE DISK

Diagnose Disk is the most important part of the Norton Disk Doctor. After choosing this selection, you are asked to select a disk drive from the list of active drives, as shown in Figure 13.2.

```
D:\ND>NDD
```

```
┌─ ─────────────────── Norton Disk Doctor ───────────────────┐
│                                                             │
│   ▶ Diagnose Disk ◀        Test the integrity of a disk.    │
│                                                             │
│      Surface Test          Test the surface of a disk.      │
│                                                             │
│      Undo Changes          Undo Norton Disk Doctor changes. │
│                                                             │
│      Options               Set Norton Disk Doctor options.  │
│                                                             │
│      Quit Disk Doctor      Exit Norton Disk Doctor.         │
│                                                             │
└─────────────────────────────────────────────────────────────┘
```

FIGURE 13.1:
The Norton Disk Doctor opening screen

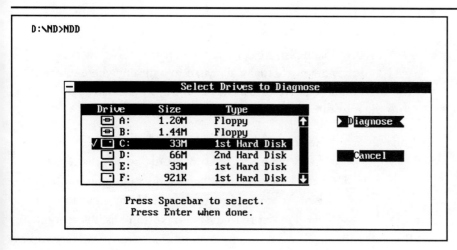

*Norton Disk Doctor's
Select Drives to
Diagnose screen*

*NDD will
not work
on disks
that have
more than 1,024
cylinders.*

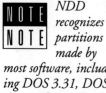

*NDD
recognizes
partitions
made by
most software, including DOS 3.31, DOS
4.0, Disk Manager,
and SpeedStor.*

Use the arrow keys to move the highlight and press the spacebar to select the drive(s) you want to check, or click on the appropriate drive with the mouse. This inserts a small check mark next to the drive letter. Press Enter to start the analysis.

Norton Disk Doctor analyzes the following areas of your disks:

◆ Partition Table. If the disk you specified is a hard disk, Norton Disk Doctor checks the partition table.

◆ DOS Boot Record. NDD examines the boot record to ensure that it is not damaged. The BIOS Parameter Block is also checked to verify that the media descriptor byte is correct for the type of disk being checked.

◆ File Allocation Tables. The file allocation table (FAT) is a list of the addresses of all the files and directories on a disk. Because this is the index to all your program and data files, DOS keeps two copies of the FAT on each disk. Norton Disk Doctor checks for read errors in both of the copies of the FAT. If it finds a read error, NDD copies the good FAT over the FAT containing the read error. Next, both tables are checked to see that they are identical and that they only contain legal DOS entries.

◆ Directory Structure. Norton Disk Doctor reads every directory on the disk, searching for illegal file names and file sizes, FAT errors, and cross-linked files.

◆ File Structure. NDD also checks the file structure in the same way as it checks the directories.

◆ Lost Clusters. These disk clusters are marked as "in use" by the FAT, but they are not actually allocated to a file anywhere. Norton Disk Doctor converts lost clusters into files and writes them into the root directory.

If it finds an error, Norton Disk Doctor describes the problem and asks whether you want to fix it. Figure 13.3 shows the dialog box that NDD displays when it finds an error in the FAT. When NDD asks if you want to correct the problem, click on Yes to fix the problem or No to move to the next set of tests. Choose Cancel to return to the main Norton Disk Doctor menu.

If you use the Stacker file-compression program from Stac Electronics and you are experiencing disk problems, be sure to run the Stacker utility SCHECK.EXE before you run the Norton Disk Doctor. SCHECK can deal with certain problems that Norton Disk Doctor may not be able to repair. Once SCHECK has finished, you can go ahead and run the Norton Disk Doctor.

If you are having problems with a read-only Stacker drive, you should run SCHECK first, then run the Norton Disk Doctor.

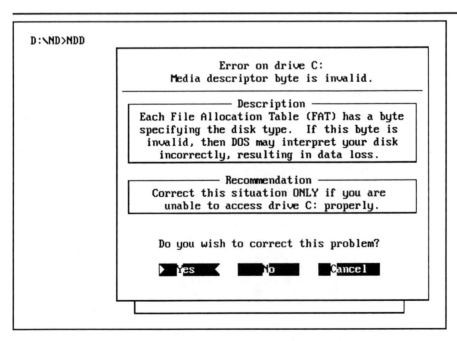

FIGURE 13.3:

A file allocation table error found by Norton Disk Doctor

```
D:\ND>NDD

                    Error on drive C:
              Media descriptor byte is invalid.

   ┌─────────────── Description ───────────────┐
   │ Each File Allocation Table (FAT) has a byte │
   │ specifying the disk type.  If this byte is  │
   │ invalid, then DOS may interpret your disk   │
   │    incorrectly, resulting in data loss.     │
   └─────────────────────────────────────────────┘

   ┌──────────── Recommendation ────────────┐
   │ Correct this situation ONLY if you are  │
   │  unable to access drive C: properly.    │
   └─────────────────────────────────────────┘

      Do you wish to correct this problem?

      ▶ Yes          No          Cancel
```

RUNNING THE SURFACE TEST

Next, you have the option of running a complete sector-by-sector test of the entire disk. If you have a large hard disk, this test can take some time to run. Disk Doctor can check a 65MB hard disk in less than ten minutes if it doesn't find any bad clusters. It will take longer if it finds errors.

Disk errors can take a variety of forms, and Norton Disk Doctor is especially helpful for isolating, and in some cases curing, problems associated with *read errors*. Because Norton Disk Doctor actually reads or attempts to read the data from each cluster on the disk, it differs from the DOS CHKDSK command, which tests only for logical errors in the data contained in the file allocation table and the directories.

When a disk-read error occurs, DOS responds with a variety of messages. The typical DOS prompt following such a device error is likely to be Abort, Retry, Ignore, Fail?; however, the actual selections in this sequence vary according to which version of DOS you are using and the nature of the error. This prompt is the way DOS gives you the choice of how to deal with the error. If you choose Abort, DOS stops executing the program that initially performed the read. Retry tells DOS to try the operation again. Choosing Fail causes DOS to return control to the original application with an error code indicating failure. Selecting Ignore causes DOS to return control to the application without such a code, presenting the illusion that the operation has already been performed. Disk errors occur for a variety of reasons, usually at the most inconvenient moment; Surface Test is a good way to find and isolate them. The Surface Test selection dialog box is shown in Figure 13.4. Set up the appropriate Surface Test parameters by making selections from this dialog box.

The test criteria you can specify from the Surface Test dialog box include the following:

> **NOTE** *A cluster already marked as bad is not usually an indication of a deteriorating disk; most hard disks have a small number of clusters containing sectors that are marked as bad by the low-level formatting program.*

◆ **Test.** Choose from Disk Test or File Test.

> **Disk Test.** This test reads every part of the disk, including the _system area and the data area. Because it is so thorough and it checks the entire disk, the disk-read test can take a long time to run.

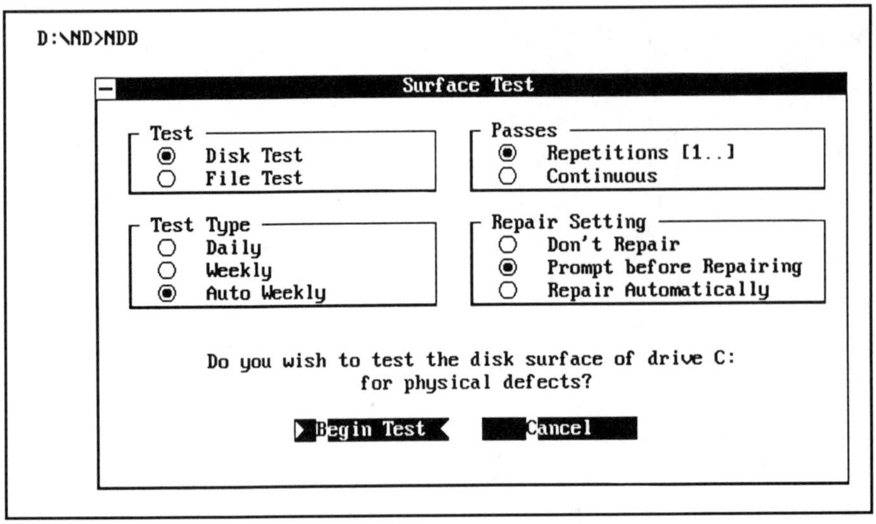

```
D:\ND>NDD
 ┌─┬──────────────────── Surface Test ────────────────────┐
 │ ─ │                                                      │
 │  ┌ Test ──────────────────┐  ┌ Passes ──────────────────┐
 │  │  ◉  Disk Test           │  │  ◉  Repetitions [1..]    │
 │  │  ○  File Test           │  │  ○  Continuous           │
 │  └────────────────────────┘  └──────────────────────────┘
 │                                                          │
 │  ┌ Test Type ─────────────┐  ┌ Repair Setting ──────────┐
 │  │  ○  Daily               │  │  ○  Don't Repair         │
 │  │  ○  Weekly              │  │  ◉  Prompt before Repairing│
 │  │  ◉  Auto Weekly         │  │  ○  Repair Automatically │
 │  └────────────────────────┘  └──────────────────────────┘
 │                                                          │
 │      Do you wish to test the disk surface of drive C:    │
 │                 for physical defects?                    │
 │                                                          │
 │         ▶ Begin Test ◀        Cancel                     │
 └──────────────────────────────────────────────────────────┘
```

FIGURE 13.4:

Norton Disk Doctor lets you select the test criteria to use for the surface test

File Test. This checks all current data and program files and directories for errors. However, it does not check the erased file space, the unused file space, or the system area, which is why it usually takes less time to run than Disk Test.

◆ **Passes.** Enter the number of times you want the test repeated, from 1 to 999 times, or select Continuous to run the test until you press Escape.

◆ **Test Type.** Choose the type of test you want to run:

Daily runs a fast check of the disk.

Weekly runs a comprehensive disk test that takes at least twice as long to run as the daily selection. It also detects errors that the daily test might miss.

Auto Weekly. The default setting for Norton Disk Doctor, this test runs the Weekly test if it is run on any Friday, otherwise it runs the Daily test.

◆ **Repair Setting.** This option lets you choose how you want NDD to respond when it finds an error.

Don't Repair. This setting tells NDD to ignore any read errors. You are not likely to use this setting.

Prompt before Repairing. When NDD finds an error, the program informs you of the error and then asks you if you want to move the file to a safe area on the disk. This is the setting you will use most often.

Repair Automatically. This selection makes the repair process as automatic as possible; use it when you want to run NDD unattended. Bad sectors are moved without delay.

The actual test screen is shown in Figure 13.5. Sectors in use by files are shown as a light box with a dark center, and unused sectors are shown as darker boxes. Bad sectors are marked with a B, and the actual area under test is shown by a special character.

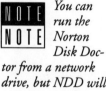

You can run the Norton Disk Doctor from a network drive, but NDD will not test a network file server.

While the disk test is being made, an analog display shows the progress of the test (as percentage completed) at the bottom left of the screen, as shown in Figure 13.5. The program updates this display as the test proceeds. The number of the sector currently being tested and the total number of sectors on the disk are shown on the screen. The estimated and elapsed time are also shown to give you an idea of how long this test will take. The disk test first checks the system area of the disk, then it checks the data area. Any errors encountered are displayed on the screen.

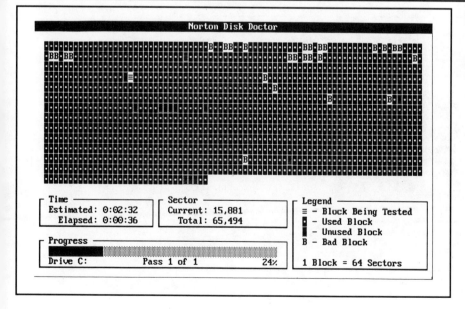

FIGURE 13.5:

The Norton Disk Doctor display while running Disk Test

The names of any files that contain unreadable clusters are displayed on the screen, along with an error message. If a data sector is found to be bad, but is not in use by a file, NDD marks it as bad so that it will not be available for use in the future. If a data sector is bad and is being used by a file, the program copies the file to a safe location on the disk, and the sector is marked as bad. Norton Disk Doctor displays the names of any files that it moves. You must check the list afterward to ensure that all your files are safe.

When the test is done, NDD lists the areas of the disk that were tested, along with the status of the test. The test status codes include the following:

◆ OK. No problems were found.

◆ Fixed. A problem was found and fixed.

◆ Not Fixed. A problem was found, but it was not fixed.

◆ Skipped. The test was not performed.

◆ Canceled. The test was interrupted and did not run to completion.

An example of this screen is shown in Figure 13.6.

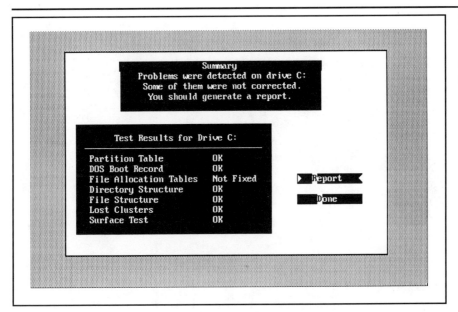

The Norton Disk Doctor screen at the end of the test run for drive C

Don't save the report on the disk you are testing, because if the disk is in poor condition, you may never be able to load the report to read it.

NDD also generates a tabulated report suitable for printing or capturing as a file, as shown in Figure 13.7. You can examine the report on the screen: just use PgUp or PgDn to move through the report, or click on the scroll bars with the mouse. To print the report, select the Print button. If you don't have time to look at the report now, select the Save As button to save the report in a file. When the Save Report window opens, enter the name you want to use for the report file. After the file is saved, another window opens to confirm that the report was written to the specified file name.

UNDO CHANGES

The Norton Disk Doctor contains a major advance in disk-testing capability. Unlike other disk-repair programs, Norton Disk Doctor can actually reverse the repair process and remove the changes made during the repair cycle. Details of any changes made to a disk by NDD are saved in a file called NDDUNDO.DAT located in the root directory. To restore a disk to its original condition, select Undo Changes from the main menu. When the disk selection window appears, choose the drive letter of the disk that contains NDDUNDO.DAT. Norton Disk Doctor uses the information in NDDUNDO.DAT to reverse the changes and return the disk to its original condition.

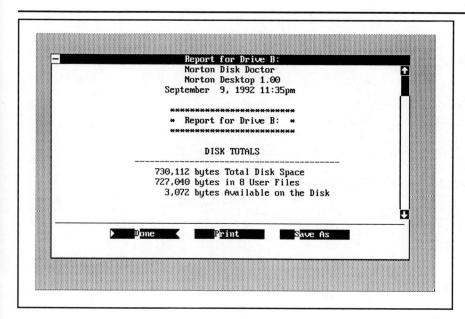

FIGURE 13.7:

A Norton Disk Doctor report for a 720K floppy disk

CONFIGURING NORTON DISK DOCTOR OPTIONS

Choose the Options selection from the main Norton Disk Doctor menu to display the Norton Disk Doctor Options window shown in Figure 13.8. Here, you can configure the program to your own requirements. Three selections are available: Surface Test, Custom Message, and Tests to Skip.

Surface Test

Select this option to enter your choices for the Surface Test. This dialog box is exactly the same as the screen shown in Figure 13.4. Make your selections from Test, Test Type, Passes, and Repair Setting.

Custom Message

If you are a network manager or are in charge of several computers in a department, you will find the Custom Message selection very useful. You can enter a message here that Norton Disk Doctor will display if the program finds an error in the system area of a disk. Because this is the most important part of a disk, you might not want your users to proceed with repairs on their own. You can enter a message including your name, department name, and extension number, as shown in Figure 13.9. After you have entered the text,

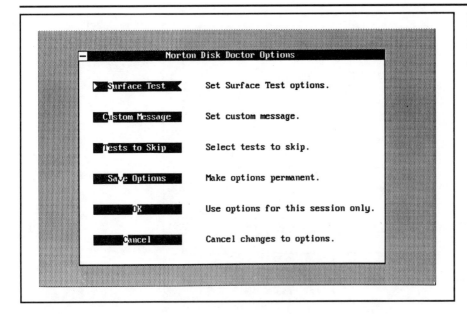

FIGURE 13.8:

Disk Doctor Options selection dialog box

use the F2 function key to set the display attribute of your message. Choose from Normal, Reverse, Bold, or Underline. This will add even more impact to your message. Don't forget to check the Prompt with Custom Message box, and then save this message by choosing or clicking on the Save Options button in the Disk Doctor Options window.

After you have saved your custom message, the user's only option when Norton Disk Doctor encounters an error is to choose the Cancel Test button at the bottom of the error screen. The user cannot continue with the other tests.

Tests to Skip

The Tests to Skip selection provides more configuration choices so that you can customize the program even further. This is particularly useful if your computer is not a true IBM compatible. There are four options in Tests to Skip, as Figure 13.10 shows.

◆ **Skip Partition Tests**. If you use nonstandard hard-disk partition software, Norton Disk Doctor might not recognize your partitions. Check this selection to turn off the partition table tests.

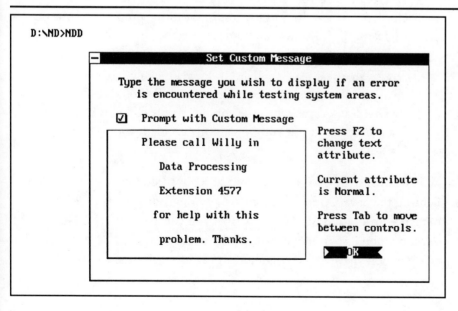

FIGURE 13.9:

Use Custom Message if you are a system manager for a group of computers

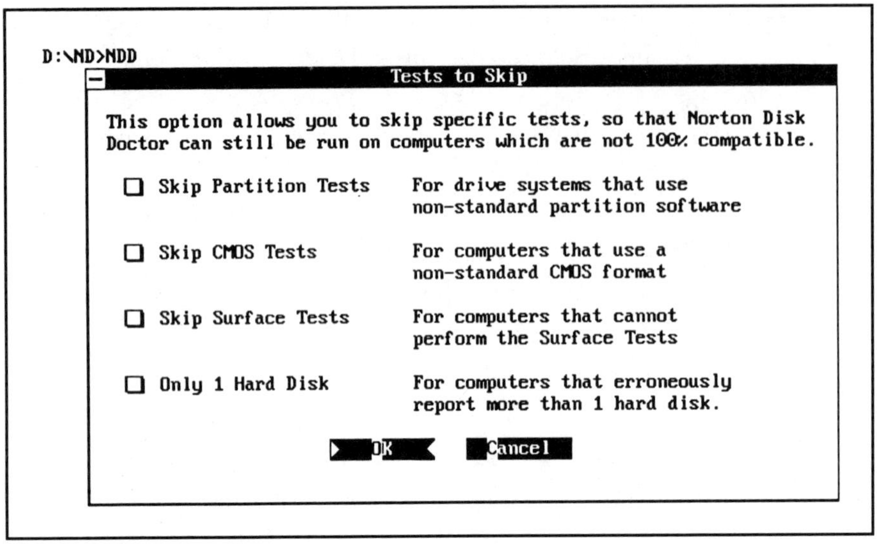

```
D:\ND>NDD
┌───────────────────────────── Tests to Skip ─────────────────────────────┐
│ [-]                                                                      │
│   This option allows you to skip specific tests, so that Norton Disk     │
│   Doctor can still be run on computers which are not 100% compatible.    │
│                                                                          │
│     [ ] Skip Partition Tests    For drive systems that use               │
│                                 non-standard partition software          │
│                                                                          │
│     [ ] Skip CMOS Tests         For computers that use a                 │
│                                 non-standard CMOS format                 │
│                                                                          │
│     [ ] Skip Surface Tests      For computers that cannot                │
│                                 perform the Surface Tests                │
│                                                                          │
│     [ ] Only 1 Hard Disk        For computers that erroneously           │
│                                 report more than 1 hard disk.            │
│                                                                          │
│                     ► OK ◄        ■ Cancel                               │
│                                                                          │
└──────────────────────────────────────────────────────────────────────────┘
```

FIGURE 13.10:

The Tests to Skip screen lets you configure NDD to your particular computer hardware

◆ **Skip CMOS Tests.** If your CMOS settings are nonstandard, check this selection to turn off the CMOS tests. (See Chapter 18 for details about CMOS.)

◆ **Skip Surface Tests.** If you never intend to use the Norton Disk Doctor Surface Test, select this option. I recommend you do not check this box—the Surface Test is one of the program's most useful features, and you should not forget about it.

◆ **Only 1 Hard Disk.** Check this box if your computer consistently reports that you have two hard disks when you know you only have one. For example, if you use an AT&T 6300, NDD finds two hard disks even when the computer only contains one. This is a problem with the computer, not a problem with Norton Disk Doctor.

When you have finished making your selections, you can save them by highlighting the Save Options button and pressing Enter or by clicking on the button with the mouse. The next time you run Norton Disk Doctor, the selections you just saved will be loaded into the program automatically. This way you don't have to reconfigure the program each time you run it.

QUITTING THE NORTON DISK DOCTOR

The final Norton Disk Doctor menu selection is Quit Disk Doctor. Use this selection to return to the Norton Desktop or, if you started Norton Disk Doctor from the command line, to return to DOS.

UNDERSTANDING DISK ERRORS

If Norton Disk Doctor discovers an increasing number of errors, you should replace or repair your hard disk or controller as soon as possible. How critical an error is depends on the location of the bad sector on your disk. If the error is in the system area of the disk, in the boot record, in the file allocation table, or in the root directory, you may lose all the data on the disk. In the case of a hard disk, this can represent a great deal of data. (This is another reason to be sure that your floppy-disk or tape backups are always up to date.) If the bad sector contains the boot record, the hard disk may refuse to boot. If Norton Disk Doctor reports errors on a floppy disk, try cleaning the disk heads. Then reformat the disk and run Norton Disk Doctor on it again to see if the problems have cleared up. If that does not work, throw the disk away. Never use a dubious disk as a backup disk for archive storage. Make your backups on error-free disks or tapes, and replace them periodically. When you need to reload your system from your backup disks, you can't afford to have any errors.

RUNNING NORTON DISK DOCTOR FROM THE DOS COMMAND LINE

NOTE
NOTE *See Chapter 19 for a complete list of all the DOS command-line switches you can use with the Norton Disk Doctor.*

You can also run the Norton Disk Doctor from the DOS prompt with one of two switches: /COMPLETE tests every sector on the disk, and /QUICK tests only the system area of the disk. To run NDD on drive C without the data sector tests, type:

NDD C: /QUICK

To run NDD on drive C and test all of the data area, type:

NDD C: /COMPLETE

You can use NDD on your hard disk every time you start your computer if you include the following line in your AUTOEXEC.BAT file:

NDD C: /QUICK

This will perform a brief analysis of your hard disk every time you boot up your computer.

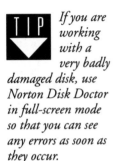 *If you are working with a very badly damaged disk, use Norton Disk Doctor in full-screen mode so that you can see any errors as soon as they occur.*

The Norton Disk Doctor finds and fixes most of the disk-related problems you are likely to encounter. It fixes bad or corrupted partition tables, bad or missing boot records, and a corrupted BPB (BIOS Parameter Block). In the area of file-structure problems, Norton Disk Doctor can repair bad or corrupted file allocation tables, reconstruct cross-linked files, and fix physical problems that prevent you from reading directories or files. Finally, this program can also reverse any changes that were made during the repair process and return the disk to its original state.

RECOVERING, REVIVING, AND REPAIRING DISKS WITH DISK TOOLS

The Disk Tools program does not just do one thing, it can perform five important disk-recovery procedures:

◆ make a disk bootable

◆ recover from the DOS RECOVER command

◆ revive a defective disk

◆ create a rescue disk

◆ restore a rescue disk

All of these selections are available from the main Disk Tools dialog box. To run the program, type:

DISKTOOL

from the DOS command line. The Disk Tools main menu is shown in Figure 13.11. Use the arrow keys to make your choice and press Enter, or click on Proceed to run the program.

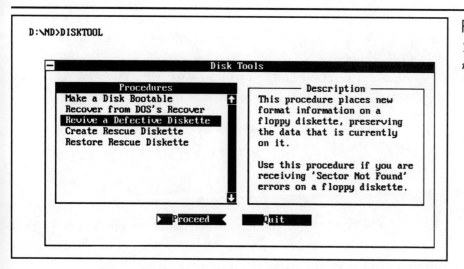

```
D:\ND>DISKTOOL
```

┌─────────────────────── Disk Tools ───────────────────────┐

```
        ┌──────── Procedures ────────┐   ┌──── Description ────┐
        │ Make a Disk Bootable     ↑ │   │ This procedure places new
        │ Recover from DOS's Recover │   │ format information on a
        │ Revive a Defective Diskette│   │ floppy diskette, preserving
        │ Create Rescue Diskette     │   │ the data that is currently
        │ Restore Rescue Diskette    │   │ on it.
        │                            │   │
        │                            │   │ Use this procedure if you are
        │                          ↓ │   │ receiving 'Sector Not Found'
        └────────────────────────────┘   │ errors on a floppy diskette.

                    ▷ Proceed ◁        Quit
```

FIGURE 13.11:
*The Disk Tools
main menu*

MAKING A DISK INTO A BOOTABLE DISK

This selection does whatever is needed to make a disk bootable, including modifying the partition table if necessary—so use it with care.

First, select the disk you want to make bootable from the list of available disks. If the disk is a floppy disk, insert the disk into the drive. Disk Tools then copies the system files from your hard disk onto the floppy disk. When this process is complete, a window opens to tell you that the specified disk is now bootable.

RECOVERING FROM THE DOS RECOVER COMMAND

You can use the DOS RECOVER command to try to recover data from a file after DOS reports a "bad sector" error message. Although you might recover some information from the file, the data contained in the bad sectors will be lost. If you use RECOVER on a disk that has bad sectors in the directory, the program gives each recovered file the following name:

FILE*nnnn*.REC

in which *nnnn* represents the order in which the files were recovered. You will then have to rename each generic FILE*nnnn*.REC file on the disk by looking at the contents of each file and specifying a more meaningful name. You will also have to recreate the disk's directory structure.

RECOVER does not restore deleted files.

Disk Tools lets you restore your disk to the state it was in before you ran RECOVER. You can also use this option instead of the DOS RECOVER command.

After you select the disk you want to work with, a warning dialog box appears to remind you that you should only use this procedure if:

◆ you have already run the DOS RECOVER command

or

◆ your root directory has been destroyed

A final warning dialog box reminds you that all files on the drive will be lost and asks if you still want to continue. Select Yes to continue. The program displays a disk map that shows you the progress made in the recovery.

At the end of this process, Disk Tools checks for cross-linked files on the disk. Directories are renamed DIR0000, DIR0001, and so on, and files in the root directory are renamed FILE0000, FILE0001, and so on. You can rename your directories by using the Norton Desktop Rename command described in Chapter 5.

REVIVING A DEFECTIVE DISK

Run the Norton Disk Doctor on any floppy disk you must revive—just to be sure the disk is not damaged.

This option revives a floppy disk by reformatting it. The original data will not be lost during this reformat—it will remain on the disk.

After you choose the floppy disk you want to revive, the program displays the dialog box shown in Figure 13.12. This dialog box shows the progress being made as an analog display; it also shows the percentage of the task completed.

CREATING A RESCUE DISK

A rescue disk is a real life-saver; make one now.

Creating a "rescue disk" lets you store vital information from your hard disk on a floppy disk that you can keep in a safe place in the event of an accident. It is the disk you wish you had the moment after you see the terrifying DOS message

Invalid drive specification

on your screen.

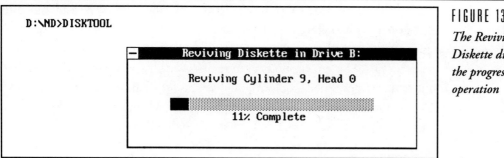

```
D:\ND>DISKTOOL
```

┌─ Reviving Diskette in Drive B: ─┐

Reviving Cylinder 9, Head 0

11% Complete

FIGURE 13.12:
*The Reviving a Floppy
Diskette display shows
the progress of the
operation*

The information stored on a rescue diskette includes partition table information, boot record information, and CMOS configuration information.

Partition Table Information

Every formatted hard disk contains at least one partition. Some people divide large hard disks into smaller partitions and may install different operating systems in each. The information on how your hard disk is partitioned is saved in a table on your hard disk. If this table is ever lost or damaged, DOS may not recognize the drive and you will see the Invalid drive specification error message when you try to access the drive or boot your system.

Boot Record

The boot record is a small portion of all disks reserved for the DOS bootstrap loader program, a small machine-language program that loads the DOS operating system. The boot sector also contains information that the computer needs to be able to read and write data to and from your hard disk. If the boot record is ever damaged, your system will not be able to access your hard disk.

CMOS Values

CMOS (pronounced *sea-moss*) is an acronym for complementary metal-oxide semiconductor. Many PCs use a small battery backed-up CMOS chip to store essential system parameters, including the date and time, and the type and number of the disks used on your system. This information is held in the CMOS chip when you turn your computer off at the end of a session, and the battery back-up ensures that this vital data is preserved and available the next time you start your computer. CMOS devices are high speed and consume very little power, so the battery in your computer may last for several years. Some computers even include small recharging circuits so that the batteries never need replacing. However, if the battery voltage falls below a certain level, the data contained in the CMOS chip may be lost. Your computer may just refuse to boot up from the hard disk, or you may see the message

CMOS Checksum Failure

when you try to boot your computer. This indicates that the data held in CMOS is now inconsistent in some way.

Preparing the Rescue Disk

I recommend that you prepare a freshly formatted disk containing the DOS system files for use as your rescue disk. Use the Norton Desktop Format Diskette option described in Chapter 5 or use the DOS FORMAT command from the DOS prompt to prepare this disk. With the system files present on your rescue disk, you will be able to boot from the disk if anything happens to your hard disk—and because the rescue disk does not contain the AUTOEXEC.BAT or CONFIG.SYS files, you will be starting a clean system with no memory-resident programs loaded.

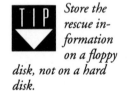

Store the rescue information on a floppy disk, not on a hard disk.

The Create Rescue Diskette dialog box is shown in Figure 13.13. From the list of available floppy disks, choose the disk to which you want to write the rescue information. After Disk Tools writes all the information to the disk, remove the disk, label it carefully, and store it in a safe place. The information is stored in three files: PARTINFO.DAT, BOOTINFO.DAT, and CMOSINFO.DAT. If you change your setup information by adding an additional floppy disk or if you upgrade to a new version of DOS, remember to run Create Rescue Diskette again to keep your vital information current.

RESTORING A RESCUE DISK

This selection lets you reload vital configuration information from the rescue floppy disk in the event that your hard-disk drive is damaged. It is the reverse process of creating a rescue disk. The Restore System from Rescue Diskette dialog box is shown in Figure 13.14. Select or click on Yes to restore

```
D:\ND>DISKTOOL
```

```
┌─────────────────────────────────────────────────────┐
│ [─]            Create Rescue Diskette                 │
├───────────────────────────────────────────────────────┤
│                                                         │
│   This procedure will save extremely important         │
│   information about your hard disk system to a floppy   │
│   diskette.  If your computer ever loses this          │
│   information, you will have a copy of it to restore    │
│   from.  If you ever change this information,           │
│            be sure to run this procedure again.         │
│                                                         │
│        The following information will be saved:         │
│        1.  Partition Tables (changed by FDISK)          │
│        2.  Boot Records     (changed by FORMAT)         │
│        3.  CMOS Values      (changed by SETUP)          │
│                                                         │
│              ▶ OK ◀        ▶ Cancel                     │
└─────────────────────────────────────────────────────┘
```

FIGURE 13.13:

The Create Rescue Diskette dialog box

```
D:\ND>DISKTOOL
```

```
┌─────────────────────────────────────────────────────┐
│ [─]        Restore System from Rescue Diskette        │
├───────────────────────────────────────────────────────┤
│                                                         │
│   This procedure will restore extremely important       │
│   information about your hard disk system from a floppy  │
│   diskette.  This information must have been previously  │
│         saved using the Create Rescue Diskette          │
│                      procedure.                         │
│                                                         │
│    You should only run this procedure if you can no      │
│    longer access partitions on your hard disk and you've │
│         already tried running the Norton Disk Doctor.   │
│                                                         │
│      Are you absolutely sure you wish to restore from    │
│                  the rescue diskette?                   │
│                                                         │
│              ▶ Yes ◀       ▶ No ◀                        │
└─────────────────────────────────────────────────────┘
```

FIGURE 13.14:

The Restore System from Rescue Diskette dialog box

the CMOS, partition table, or boot record information back onto your hard-disk system again.

The combination of the Norton Disk Doctor and the Disk Tools programs should be sufficiently powerful to meet the challenges imposed by most disk problems. However, there is one disk problem, file fragmentation, that is better solved with a dedicated stand-alone program. In the next chapter we'll look at the Norton Desktop's answer to file fragmentation and hard-disk optimization in the Speed Disk program.

CHAPTER 14

Optimizing Your
Disk Drives

F iles are written to your disks in a unit of disk space known as a *cluster*. When you write a short file to disk, it occupies the first available cluster. When you write another short file to the same disk, this file occupies the next available cluster. Now if you modify the first file and increase its size to over one cluster, and then save it under the same file name, DOS cannot push the second file forward on the disk to make room for the larger first file. Instead, DOS has to *fragment* this file by splitting it in two pieces, one occupying the first cluster and one occupying the *third* cluster. This is the way DOS was designed to work.

See the Appendix for a complete discussion of disk terminology.

File fragmentation is problematic, however, because the disk heads have to move to different locations on the disk to read or write to a fragmented file. This takes more time than reading the same file from a series of consecutive clusters. By reducing or eliminating fragmentation, you can increase the performance of your disk substantially.

If you need to recover erased files, do so before you unfragment a disk with Speed Disk.

To remove the effects of file fragmentation, all the files on the disk must be rearranged so that they fill consecutive clusters. You can do this yourself by backing up all your files using Norton Backup, reformatting the hard disk, and reloading all the files back onto the hard disk—but that would be a tremendous amount of tedious work. It is much easier to use a program designed for eliminating file fragmentation—the Norton Speed Disk program.

Another benefit of unfragmenting a disk is that DOS is less likely to fragment files that you subsequently add to the disk. If you should delete and then try to unerase any of these added files, your chances of success would be higher because unfragmented files are usually easier to unerase. On the other hand, unfragmenting, or *optimizing,* your disk will probably make it impossible to recover any files that were deleted before the optimization. Speed Disk "moves" files by rewriting them at new locations, so it will probably write over any erased files in the process.

PRECAUTIONS TO TAKE BEFORE RUNNING SPEED DISK ON YOUR HARD DISK

Be sure to use Norton Backup to make the full hard-disk backup.

Before you have Speed Disk actually reorganize the files on your disk, you should take a few precautions:

◆ Back up your hard disk completely in case your system and Speed Disk are incompatible. Problems sometimes occur because of the enormous number of potential combinations of disks and disk controllers.

◆ Do not turn off your computer while Speed Disk is running. The only safe way to interrupt Speed Disk is by pressing the Escape key. Speed Disk will not stop working immediately but will continue to run until it reaches a safe, convenient point at which to do so.

◆ Be sure to disable any memory-resident software that might access the disk while Speed Disk is running. For example, some programs save your work to the hard disk at set time intervals. This type of software must be turned off.

◆ If you are using the DOS FASTOPEN utility or any other disk-buffering program, turn it off before running Speed Disk. Because Speed Disk changes directory and file locations on the disk as it optimizes the disk, FASTOPEN might not find your files where it expects to find them. If DOS displays the message File not found after you run Speed Disk, reboot your computer and try again.

 The Norton Disk Doctor is discussed in Chapter 13.

◆ Run the DOS CHKDSK command to remove any lost clusters and run the Norton Disk Doctor to find and fix any bad sectors on your disk. This gives Speed Disk a clean system to work with.

UNFRAGMENTING YOUR HARD DISK WITH SPEED DISK

NOTE NOTE *Although Speed Disk reports on specific files and directories, you cannot unfragment just selected files or directories—that is, you can only unfragment entire disks.*

Select Speed Disk from the Norton Desktop Tools menu, or start Speed Disk from the DOS prompt by typing:

SPEEDISK

The program starts with the display shown in Figure 14.1.

Select the drive letter of the disk you want to optimize, then click on OK or press Enter. You can also double-click on the drive letter with the mouse. After Speed Disk reads and analyzes the data on the chosen drive, it visually displays disk usage and informs you which level of optimization is required. Figure 14.2 shows this display for a 33MB hard disk.

In Figure 14.2, Speed Disk shows the percentage of fragmentation for the 33MB hard disk and recommends an optimization method based on this percentage. The two boxes on the screen give you the choice of optimizing your disk or configuring Speed Disk. The first time you run Speed Disk, press the Escape key to go to the Configure pull-down menu. After you have examined all the possible options, you can run the optimization.

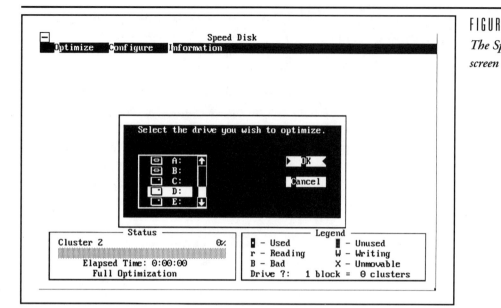

FIGURE 14.1:
The Speed Disk startup screen

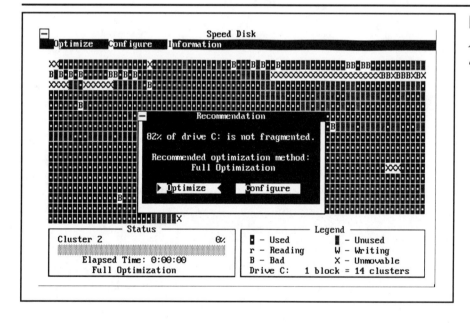

FIGURE 14.2:
A Speed Disk map for drive C

You cannot use Speed Disk on a network drive, or on a disk that has been compressed by either SuperStor, a DR DOS utility from Digital Research, or by Stacker from Stac Electronics. If you use DR DOS, unfragment your files using the DR DOS DISKOPT utility; if you use Stacker, you can unfragment your files with the Stacker utility program SDEFRAG.

Unlike some disk optimizing programs, Speed Disk is smart enough to know when optimzation is not needed and will display the message **No Optimization Needed.**

The Legend box, at the lower-right corner of the screen, defines the graphic characters used to make the disk-usage map. The characters represent the following elements:

◆ Used Block. The "used block" character designates the area of the disk currently occupied by files. It represents all the directories and files in the data area of the disk.

◆ Unused Block. The "unused block" character designates the area of the disk occupied by clusters not allocated to files. Speed Disk can consolidate this space and make it available as part of the unused disk space at the end of the files' area on the disk.

◆ Bad Block. The "bad block" character—an uppercase **B**—represents any bad blocks on the disk. Note that Figure 14.2 shows a disk with several bad blocks.

◆ Unmovable Block. The "unmovable block" character—an uppercase **X**—marks the position of any files or directories that Speed Disk cannot move. The **X** characters at the upper-left corner of the display in Figure 14.2 represent the hidden DOS system files. To avoid the possibility of interfering with copy-protection schemes, Speed Disk does not move hidden files.

Depending on the size of the current disk, each legend character on the screen represents a specific amount of disk space. In Figure 14.2 each character represents 14 clusters.

The Status box at the lower left of the screen displays Speed Disk's progress after you start the optimization. The current cluster number and percentage-complete value are shown as numbers, along with the optimization type and the time that has elapsed so far. The horizontal bar shows an analog display of the percentage of the operation that has been completed.

CHOOSING THE RIGHT OPTIMIZATION METHOD

Speed Disk provides menus that let you configure the program and make the appropriate optimization selection. Selecting the Optimize menu displays the following selections:

Don't start optimizing until you're sure that all options are set correctly.

Begin Optimization (Alt+B). This begins the process of unfragmenting the drive. Don't select this option until you're sure that all the other options are set correctly.

Drive. This option lets you switch to another drive. It opens a window that is similar to the initial drive selection screen you used when Speed Disk first started. Use the arrow keys to highlight a new drive letter, or type in the drive letter and press Enter. With the mouse, just double-click on the new drive letter.

Optimization Method. Choose the type of optimization that Speed Disk will run on your disk. When you select this choice, the Select Optimization Method window opens, as shown in Figure 14.3.

FIGURE 14.3:
You choose Speed Disk's optimization method in this window

Choose the method that is best suited to your disk and the way you work with your system; you don't always have to use the same method every time. Here you can select one of the following options:

◆ **Full Optimization.** This option unfragments all your files, but it does not move directories or move files selected in the Files to Place First list. This option runs very quickly; when it is completed, there will be no unused areas of disk space between your files.

◆ **Full with Directories First.** This selection unfragments your files and moves directories to the front of the disk.

◆ **Full with File Reorder.** This is the most complete option available in Speed Disk; it performs a complete optimization of your hard disk. It takes the longest to run, but also provides the greatest speed increase afterwards.

◆ **Unfragment Files Only.** This option unfragments all the files that it can, but may leave some unused space between files when it is complete. Some large files may remain fragmented even after Speed Disk has finished.

◆ **Unfragment Free Space.** This option moves files to fill the unused space left between them, but does not actually unfragment any files. You can use this selection to create a single large block of free space before you install a new software package.

CONFIGURING SPEED DISK

The Configure menu, shown in Figure 14.4, contains six options to complete the optimization setup:

Directory Order. This selection lets you manipulate the order in which Speed Disk arranges the directories. You do this by working with a graphic display of the disk's directory, as shown in Figure 14.5.

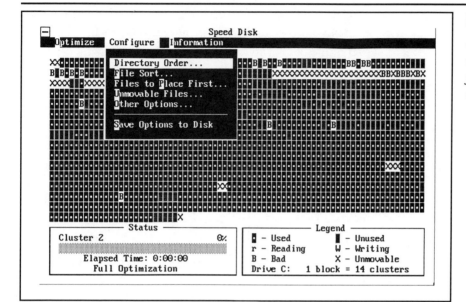

Speed Disk's Configure menu offers six options for completing the optimization setup

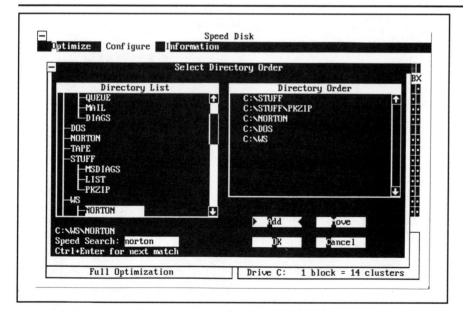

The Select Directory Order window lets you organize your directories

This window is divided into two parts: the Directory List shows all the directories on your disk in a graphical form, and Directory Order shows the sequence in which the directories are arranged. The default directory order is taken from the path you established in your AUTOEXEC.BAT file. To select a directory from the Directory List, use the up and down arrow keys or the mouse to highlight the directory name, and then press Enter or use the Add button. You will see the directory name appear at the top of the list in the Directory Order display. You can also use the Speed Search box to move directly to a specific directory. Just type in enough letters to make the entry unique, and Speed Disk will automatically select the right directory. Press the Ctrl and Enter keys together to move to the next match if you have several directories with very similar names.

Use the left and right arrows to move between the two windows. The Directory Order display provides more options:

Delete. To delete a directory from the Directory Order screen, highlight its name, and click on the Delete button.

Move. To move a directory, highlight the name, and then use the up and down arrow keys to place the directory at its new location. Press Enter to confirm the position of the directory.

OK. When you are satisfied with the placement of directories, select OK to return to the main Speed Disk screen.

File Sort. Use this selection to specify the order in which you want your files arranged. The File Sort window is shown in Figure 14.6. File Sort arranges your files according to one selection from the Sort Criterion list. You can sort by name, extension, date and time, and file size—in ascending or descending order. You can also choose unsorted. Unsorted does not change the order of your files; it leaves them exactly where they are. Select OK after you have made your choice.

Files to Place First. This lets you choose which files to put at the "beginning" or outer edge of the disk. Use this option to position your program files, which do *not* change in size, close to the file allocation table. The first time this window opens it contains two file specifications: *.EXE and *.COM. You can add or remove files, and you can use the DOS wildcard characters in the file specifications.

Putting program files near the outer edge of the disk helps prevent future file fragmentation.

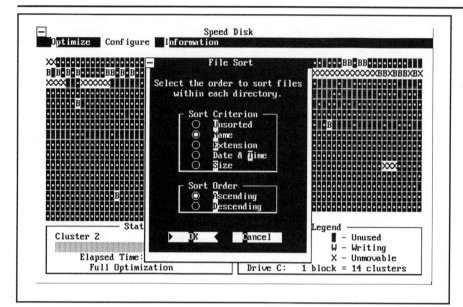

FIGURE 14.6:
The File Sort window lets you choose how your files will be arranged

Position your data files—which *do* change size when you modify them—after your program files. This arrangement avoids future file fragmentation by preventing space from opening up near the outer edge of the disk. The Files to Place First window is shown in Figure 14.7.

You can use wildcards to help relocate files. For example, to relocate all .EXE files, you would type *.**EXE** into the highlighted box. Use the Delete, Insert, and Move buttons to rearrange the entries in the list.

Delete. To remove an entry from the list, highlight the entry, and click on Delete.

Insert. To insert a new entry, highlight the entry immediately below where you want to make the insertion, and click on Insert. A blank space opens for you to add the new file specification.

Move. To move an entry, place the highlight over the entry, and click on Move. Then use the up and down arrow keys or the mouse to move the entry to its new location and press Enter.

After you have completed your entries, select OK to return to the Configure menu on the main Speed Disk screen.

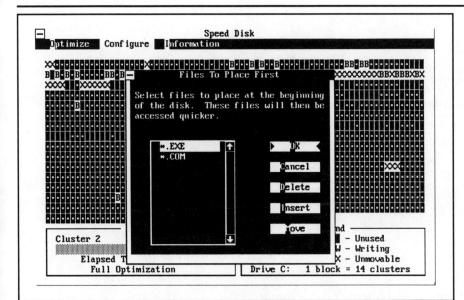

FIGURE 14.7:

The Files to Place First window lets you position files where you want them

Unmovable Files. Use this selection to enter the names of files that you do not want to be moved during optimization. This window holds only ten entries, but you can use the DOS wildcard characters to extend the selection to more than ten files.

Other Options. This selection includes three options. Note that you can choose more than one option from this list:

> **Read-After-Write.** By default, Speed Disk uses this setting as a check for the optimization process.
>
> **Clear Unused Space.** Speed Disk can wipe clean all areas of the disk that are not being used to store files or directories. The Clear Unused Space option writes zeros into all the unused clusters on the disk during the optimization process.
>
> **Beep When Done.** Speed Disk will sound a tone when the optimization is complete.

Save Options to Disk. This selection saves the options you have chosen to a small hidden file (called SD.INI) in the root directory of the disk you are optimizing, and returns you to the main Speed Disk screen. The next time you run Speed Disk, these configuration options are loaded from the SD.INI file and used as the default startup settings.

SPEED DISK INFORMATION

The selections in the Information menu let you look at fragmentation and disk statistics.

Choose Fragmentation Report to check the degree to which a file, directory, or disk is fragmented before you decide whether to start the file reorganization process. Daily and weekly file fragmentation reports show you how fragmentation on your disk is changing over time and tell you how often you should run Speed Disk to get the best results.

The report is shown in Figure 14.8. The left side of the File Fragmentation Report window shows a graphical display of your directory structure, and the right side shows the files in the directory. As you change to a different directory in the left window, the file display changes to show the files in the new directory. You can also use Speed Search to enter a directory name. A "percent unfragmented" figure is given for each file in the directory. A value of 100% means that the file is not fragmented and that all its clusters are consecutive. A value lower than 100% signifies some degree of fragmentation in the file. Fragmented files are bulleted and shown in a different color in the file list.

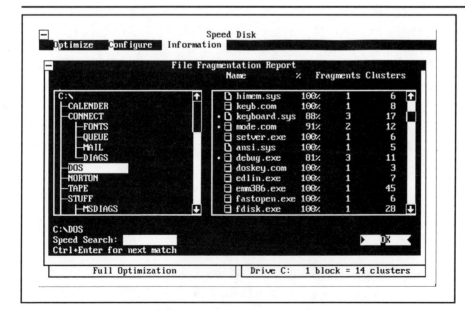

FIGURE 14.8:

Speed Disk reports the percentage of fragmentation for all files in the directory

This window also shows the number of fragments each file or directory is broken into, as well as the total number of clusters the file or directory occupies. File names are shown in lowercase, and directory names are displayed in uppercase. Click on OK to return to the main Speed Disk screen. The other selections in the Information menu provide useful information about files and disks. You can choose from the following selections:

Disk Statistics. Disk Statistics provides detailed information about the drive you selected for optimization. Figure 14.9 shows the statistics for a 33MB hard disk.

The statistics include the disk size, the amount of the disk used, the percentage of unfragmented files, and the number of files and directories. Also shown are details about the clusters allocated to movable and unmovable files, the clusters allocated to directories, the number of bad and unused clusters, and the total number of clusters on the disk.

Map Legend. This selection opens an information window that shows the characters used on the disk map display while the disk is being optimized. This window, shown in Figure 14.10, is more detailed than the Legend box displayed on the main Speed Disk screen.

As the optimization proceeds, you will see different characters on the screen, each one representing a different part of the process. Disk space in use by files or directories is indicated by the block with a dot in the center, and unused disk space is represented by an unfilled block. Clusters occupied by unmovable files are marked with an X; bad blocks are represented by B. An r character shows the area of the disk currently being read, a W shows clusters being written, and a V shows that the data is being verified. If you selected Clear Unused Space in the Other Options from the Configure menu, you will see a C character to indicate clearing.

Show Static Files. This selection opens the Static Files window, which lists all the files that Speed Disk cannot move. Figure 14.11 shows the DOS system files, IO.SYS and MSDOS.SYS, listed in the Static Files window along with several other files. (The PC-DOS names for these two files are IBMBIOS.COM and IBMDOS.COM.)

The Disk Statistics window shows information for drive C

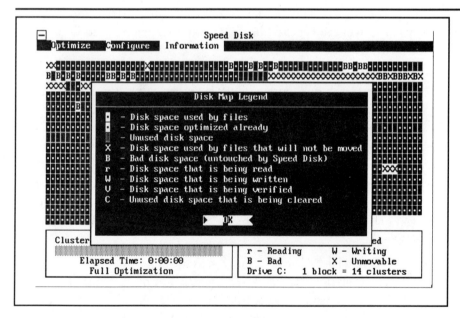

The Disk Map Legend shows the characters used during the optimization process

These files are position-sensitive; they must be at a *specific* location on your disk; therefore, Speed Disk will not move them.

Walk Map. This selection lets you use the arrow keys to move around the disk map and display which files occupy which locations on your disk. The cluster range represented by the block character under the cursor is shown at the lower left of the disk map screen. When you find an area of the disk you want to look at more closely, press Enter or click on the area of the disk you want to examine to open the Contents of Map Block window, as shown in Figure 14.12.

The window includes three columns of information: Cluster, File, and Status. The Cluster column lists the cluster numbers, the File column displays the name of the file that occupies that cluster, and the Status column indicates whether the file is fragmented or optimized. You might also see a cluster labeled as Bad Cluster, Unmovable, or simply Not Used. Use the arrow keys or PgUp and PgDn to move through the display, or click on the scroll bars with the mouse. Press Enter to return to the Walk Map, and press the Escape key to return to the main Speed Disk screen.

Use the Quit menu selection to return you back to DOS, or to the Norton Desktop, depending on the method you used to start Speed Disk.

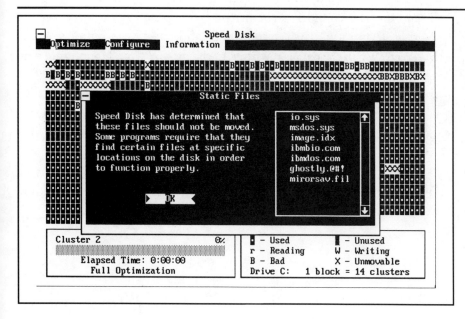

FIGURE 14.11:

The Static Files window lists files that will not be moved during the optimization

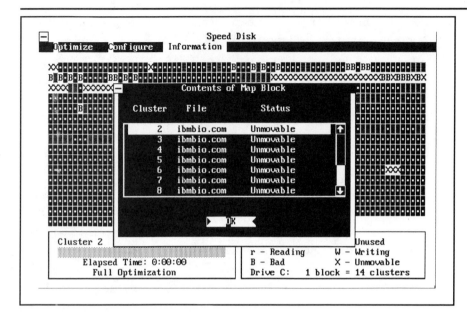

The Contents of Map Block window gives details of the chosen cluster range

RUNNING SPEED DISK

Optimization can take a long time, especially if you are unfragmenting an entire disk. Monitor the Status box to get an idea of how long the entire process will take. Press the Escape key if you need to stop the optimization.

When you are sure that all the options have been set correctly, choose Begin Optimization from the Optimize menu to start the process. Speed Disk unfragments the selected item(s), collecting all the free space and placing it at the end of the used blocks. The disk-usage map shows you this process as Speed Disk works. As data is read from the disk, the r character moves across the screen. When the data is rewritten to the disk, W is used to indicate writing. If you turn the Verify option on, V indicates the progress of the verification process. A C represents unused disk space that is being cleared.

You can press the Escape key if you want to interrupt Speed Disk, but Speed Disk might not stop instantly—it will take a few moments to complete the current operation and tidy up before stopping.

Speed Disk beeps when it is finished. This means you can focus your attention on more important work during the entire process and still know when the optimization is complete.

SPEED DISK AND COPY-PROTECTION SCHEMES

Some copy-protection methods that rely on hidden files insist that the hidden files stay in exactly the same place on the disk. For example, Lotus 1-2-3 Version 2.01 uses this method. If your copy-protection method uses hidden files and you move them to another location on the disk, your application program will often refuse to work—it thinks you are using an illegal copy. Speed Disk recognizes this problem and does not move hidden files in case moving them interferes with the copy-protection system. In fact, Speed Disk goes further than this—it will not move any .EXE file that does not have a standard file header. All such files are left alone. Also, Speed Disk will not move the hidden files—IBMBIOS.COM and IBMDOS.COM or IO.SYS and MSDOS.SYS—that DOS places at the beginning of all bootable disks. Remember, however, that the only way to be absolutely sure that Speed Disk will not interfere with a copy-protection scheme is to completely remove the software package before running Speed Disk, and then to reinstall it again after Speed Disk is finished. You can also contact the vendors of copy-protected software for their recommendations.

RUNNING SPEED DISK FROM THE DOS PROMPT

If you run Speed Disk from the DOS prompt, you can take advantage of the special Speed Disk switches, some of which are extremely powerful. For example, if you want to use the Unfragment Free Space option to collect all the free space on your C drive into one large piece, you can do so by typing:

SPEEDISK C: /Q

from the DOS prompt. Speed Disk runs the optimization automatically, without any prompting. Chapter 19 contains a complete list of the Speed Disk command-line options.

CHAPTER 15

Safeguarding Your System Against Viruses

Norton AntiVirus is a program that can defend your system from attack by over 1,000 strains of over 330 different computer viruses. Before we look at how to use Norton AntiVirus in detail, let's take a moment to look at the different types of viruses and how they might get onto your computer system in the first place.

OF VIRUSES, WORMS, AND TROJAN HORSES

The term *virus* is a general name for any program that alters something about the way your system runs without your knowledge or permission. In the personal computer world there are actually three main kinds of intruders:

◆ A *virus* is a program that attaches itself to your program files and then spreads to your other programs, infecting them all as it goes. Other viruses attach themselves to your partition table or to the boot sector on your hard-disk system. Not all viruses are harmful, some are just plain annoying. The most famous virus of all is probably the Israeli or Jerusalem virus, also known as Friday the 13th, first seen on a computer at the University of Jerusalem in July of 1987. This virus slows down your system and draws black boxes on the lower-left portion of your screen. If the virus is in memory on Friday the 13th of any month, every program executed is erased from your hard disk.

◆ A *worm* is a tiny program that reproduces itself many times over; it is not usually designed to be harmful. Eventually, however, your computer memory or disk system will fill up completely.

◆ A *Trojan horse* is an apparently useful program that suddenly turns malicious. It might, for example, attempt to low-level format your hard disk.

There are several safe-computing precautions you can take to avoid infection, including:

◆ Don't use pirated copies of software. Not only is this illegal, but the program may be infected, allowing a virus to sneak onto your system. Buy legal copies of software and write-protect the original floppy disks as soon as you open the package.

◆ If you download files from a bulletin board, make sure that the system operator (sysop) checks for viruses before the programs are posted on the bulletin board; most sysops run checks on a regular basis.

◆ Back up your important files so that you can reinstall the original uninfected copies of your programs if you do find a virus.

◆ Check your own system for viruses on a routine basis.

◆ Check commercial off-the-shelf purchased software too; there have been several instances of major companies releasing software that inadvertently contained a virus.

The Norton AntiVirus uses two different approaches to protect your system against attack:

Virus Intercept is a small terminate-and-stay-resident program loaded every time you start your computer that alerts you if it detects an infected file or suspects that a virus may be present on your system.

Norton AntiVirus is a tool you can load from the Desktop to scan your computer memory or any hard or floppy disk looking for a virus, and take appropriate action if one is found.

In the next section we'll look at Virus Intercept, then we'll go on to cover Norton AntiVirus later in this chapter.

USING VIRUS INTERCEPT ON YOUR SYSTEM

Virus Intercept is the terminate-and-stay-resident (TSR) portion of Norton AntiVirus; it is loaded using CONFIG.SYS every time you start up your computer. Place the command to load Virus Intercept after any memory-management or disk-compression software on your system, but before any other application.

 If you load both these virus-detecting programs, only the first one loaded into your computer will actually work.

If you selected AntiVirus during the Desktop installation procedure, or with NDConfig, it is already installed in your CONFIG.SYS file. The Virus Intercept TSR program is a special kind of program that loads into memory and stays there, watching for any suspicious virus-like activity on your system as you work.

There are three different ways to install Virus Intercept in your CONFIG.SYS files. They are as follows:

◆ If you have limited memory, or you use a large number of terminate-and-stay-resident programs on your system, add the line **NAV&.SYS** into your CONFIG.SYS file. This program occupies about 1K of memory, and because of its small size, it cannot detect boot sector infections. This configuration scans for viruses *only* when you launch an application.

◆ To add boot-sector protection, use the line **NAV&.SYS /B**. This configuration takes about 4K of memory, scans for viruses when you launch applications, and also detects boot-sector viruses on floppy disks.

◆ For complete protection, use **NAV_.SYS** in your CONFIG.SYS file. This program combines the protection afforded by the smaller programs, and adds the capability to scan files during a DOS copy operation. Also, NAV_.SYS will prevent you from accidentally copying an infected program from a floppy disk onto your hard disk, and can detect boot-sector and partition-table viruses. NAV_.SYS occupies approximately 38K of memory on your system.

As you use your computer, Virus Intercept scans for viruses when you:

◆ launch an application program

◆ copy a file

◆ perform a warm boot by pressing the Alt, Ctrl, and Del keys on the keyboard, or turn your computer off and on using the power switch

Virus Intercept also scans files, looking for and verifying inoculation information to see if it has changed. Any change in this inoculation information could indicate a virus attack on your system.

If Virus Intercept finds evidence of virus activity, a dialog box opens containing the name of the affected file and the name of the virus. *Do not proceed, but use Norton AntiVirus immediately to clear up the infection.*

There are certain limiting circumstances under which Virus Intercept cannot check for viruses:

◆ when the DOS DISKCOPY command is used to make an exact duplicate of a disk

◆ when you download a file from a bulletin board via modem

◆ when you transfer a file from one computer to another using a program such as Desktop Link, pcANYWHERE or Commander Link

◆ when you restore files from a compressed backup media such as tape

◆ when you use an application compressed by a self-extracting compression program. To compress a file, you use a program and a set of (often quite complex and cryptic) command-line switches. To decompress or restore the file so that it can be used again, the same program is run, but with a different set of switches. A *self-extracting* program does not need this second step; the program decompresses automatically when you launch the application.

TIP *If you don't want Virus Intercept loaded, wait until you hear the beep from your computer as it starts running, then hold down both Shift keys at the same time. You will see the message Norton Anti-Virus not loaded.*

Virus Intercept cannot locate viruses inside compressed or archived files created by programs such as PKZIP, or PKARC, or the Compress option from the Desktop File menu, so you must uncompress these files first, then use Norton AntiVirus to check them out before you use them.

Virus Intercept works with DESQview and the DOS 5 task switcher.

It is also a good idea to mark Virus Intercept as a copy-protected file before using Norton Backup. This way Norton Backup will not attempt to access any of the virus-protection files while making the backup. Many backup programs recommend that you do not run programs such as Virus Intercept while the backup is in progress.

To protect itself from an attack by a virus, Virus Intercept does not allow any application to read or write to the NAV_.SYS file. This means that you cannot view or delete the NAV_.SYS file, or modify any of the file's attributes when Virus Intercept is active on your system. Be aware that the smaller program, NAV&.SYS, cannot protect itself in this way, and so it is possible that NAV&.SYS could be attacked.

SCANNING FOR VIRUSES WITH NORTON ANTIVIRUS

Check the original Norton Desktop program disks to see if there is a README.NAV file. This file may contain late information that did not make it into the manual.

If you haven't scanned your system looking for viruses, *do it now.* Launch Norton AntiVirus from the Desktop Tools menu or type

NAV

from the DOS command line to start the program running.

The Norton AntiVirus window opens as Figure 15.1 shows. This main window contains a menu bar, the Scan dialog box, and a long line of command buttons:

You should rescan your disk drives after installing any new software or any software upgrades so that the information Norton AntiVirus uses to check your files is always up to date.

Scan allows you to rescan a selected disk drive, directory, or file.

Cancel aborts the scan.

Repair lets you attempt a repair of the infected file. If you do attempt a repair, always remember to rescan the file immediately, just to be sure all traces of the virus have been eradicated.

Delete allows you to delete an infected file. If several files are infected, use the Delete All option from the Delete File dialog box.

*Use either Repair or Delete **immediately** if you find a virus. This is one of those cases where doing nothing is the worst possible thing you can do.*

Norton AntiVirus will not run on Tandy 1000 series computers.

Reinoc lets you reinoculate the file. Only use this option if you are absolutely sure that no virus has attacked the file.

Print allows you to print the results of the scan.

Exit lets you quit the Norton AntiVirus. You can also use the Exit option from the Scan menu.

The first time you use Norton AntiVirus, make sure that you scan all your hard-disk drives, as well as any CD-ROM drives or Bernoulli boxes on your system. Your network administrator will scan your network drives for you.

Memory is also checked for viruses on this first scan, and if evidence of a virus is found, the scan halts. See the section "Using Norton AntiVirus from a Floppy Disk" later in this chapter for instructions on how to deal with a virus in memory. At the end of a drive scan you will see the Scan Results dialog box as Figure 15.2 shows.

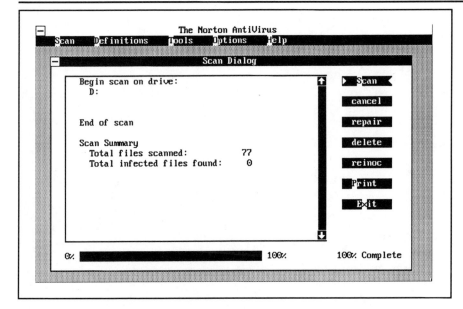

FIGURE 15.1:

The main Norton AntiVirus window contains a menu bar, the Scan dialog box, and a set of command buttons

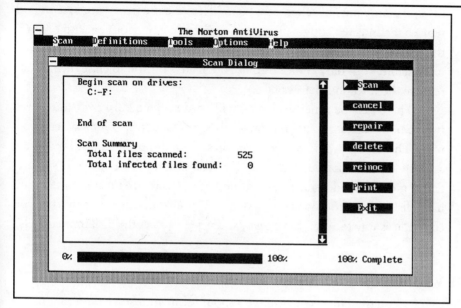

How to Remove Infections

If Norton AntiVirus detected the presence of any viruses during the scan, the infected files are listed in the Scan Results dialog box, along with the name of the infecting virus. If no viruses were detected, summary information is shown in the Scan Results dialog box.

If one or more strains of virus were found on your system, you should get rid of them immediately.

◆ If the virus is in memory, see the section called "Using Norton Anti-Virus from a Floppy Disk" later in this chapter for instructions on how to proceed.

◆ If a file is infected, use the Repair button if it is available, to remove the virus from the file.

◆ If the Repair button is not available, use the Delete button to erase the file, and then replace it with an uninfected copy.

If Norton AntiVirus recognizes the strain of virus, you may be able to use the Repair command button to remove the virus from the file. However, many viruses cause irreparable damage to the files that they infect. In these cases, the only possible alternative is to delete the file from your system and replace the infected copy with a good copy from a previous backup or from the original distribution disks. If the Repair button is dimmed and therefore unavailable, your only choice is to use the Delete button to erase the file and remove the infection that way.

There may be times when you will need a "rescue diskette" to recover from a boot-sector or partition-table virus. See Chapter 13 for a description of the Disk Tools program; one of the options in this program lets you create a rescue diskette. If you don't have a rescue disk available for your system, take a moment and make one right now. You won't need it until after your hard disk refuses to boot your system because of damage, but by then, of course, it is way too late. Do it *now*, and write-protect the disk immediately.

PREVENTING REINFECTION

Once you have removed a virus, you should scan your stock of programs on floppy disk in an attempt to locate and eradicate the source of the infection. On any subsequent scans using Norton AntiVirus, you can make the appropriate selection from the Scan menu to work with just a single file, a single directory, or a whole drive, depending on the circumstances.

When you acquire new software, from whatever source, you should always scan all the disks to check for viruses before you complete the installation on your system. As I mentioned earlier, there have been several instances recently where major software houses have released commercial products that inadvertently contained viruses.

INOCULATING A DRIVE, DIRECTORY, OR FILE

When you run Norton AntiVirus on your system with the Detect Unknown Viruses check box checked in the Global dialog box, certain information about all your files is stored in an *inoculation file*. (The Global dialog box is accessed from the Options menu.) When you next scan your files, they are compared against this information in the inoculation file. Any changes between the two sets of information are suspicious and will be referred to as a possible unknown virus.

Files are inoculated in two ways:

Norton AntiVirus. The fastest way to inoculate all files on a drive is to enable Auto-inoculate in the Global dialog box from the Options menu.

Virus Intercept. When Auto-inoculate is enabled, Virus Intercept automatically creates inoculation data for all files that have not previously been inoculated.

Here's how you can use Norton AntiVirus to scan and inoculate a file, directory, or a whole disk:

1. Choose Norton AntiVirus from the Desktop Tools menu.
2. Select Global from the Options menu.
3. Check Detect Unknown Viruses and Auto-inoculate, and choose OK to save your changes.
4. Choose Drive, Directory, or File from the Scan menu. To scan one or more drives, specify the drive name and type; to scan specific directories, specify complete path information; and to scan an individual file, specify the file name, directory, and drive.
5. Select OK to start the scan running. The progress and results of the scan appear in the Scan Results dialog box.

As the inoculation proceeds, Norton AntiVirus stores the inoculation information in a hidden system file in the root directory. This file is called NAV._NO. On a network drive, this file is not stored in the root directory, but is stored in the directory specified in Global Settings. See the section titled "Global Settings" later in this chapter.

UNINOCULATING A DRIVE

If you are constantly adding to and changing the files on your system, your inoculation file may grow unwieldy and become out of date. Under these circumstances, the best course of action is to remove the old inoculation information, then immediately rescan your drive to establish new inoculation information.

To remove the inoculation file, select Uninoculate from the Tools menu, and select the drive or drives you want to uninoculate from this dialog box. Then rescan the drive or drives to create new inoculation information.

CONFIGURING VIRUS PROTECTION

There are several different configuration options you can use to control both the Norton AntiVirus and the Virus Intercept programs. You can also set global options that control both programs and set or remove password protection if you wish.

CONFIGURING NORTON ANTIVIRUS

To set the options that Norton AntiVirus uses during a scan, select Clinic from the Options menu. This command opens the dialog box shown in Figure 15.3. These check boxes control the command buttons available in the Scan Results, Repair Files, Delete Files, and Reinoculate dialog boxes. If the box is checked, the command will be available when appropriate; if the box is not checked, the command will be dimmed and unavailable.

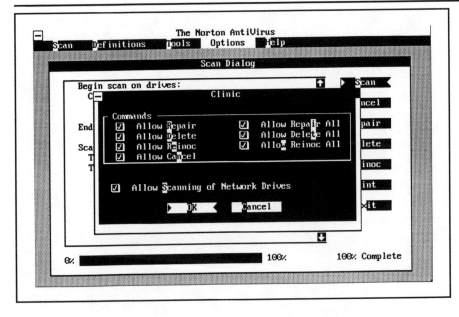

FIGURE 15.3:

Set the scan options you want to use in the Clinic dialog box

If you want to be able to scan all the network drives that you are logged on to, check the Allow Scanning of Network Drives check box. Remember though, some network drives are very large, and a complete scan may take a very long time. This is a task that is better left for your network administrator to perform when network traffic is light.

CONFIGURING VIRUS INTERCEPT

When Virus Intercept locates a virus or any suspicious activity on your system, it opens a pop-up alert box. To control these alert boxes, select Intercept from the Options menu to open the dialog box shown in Figure 15.4.

The Intercept dialog box contains the following check boxes:

◆ **Enable Beep Alert.** Check this box if you want to hear an audible alert when a virus is detected.

◆ **Enable Popup Alert.** Check this box to see the alert box when a virus is detected. This alert box cannot appear while you are running Windows; you will always hear a beep, regardless of the setting used for Enable Beep Alert.

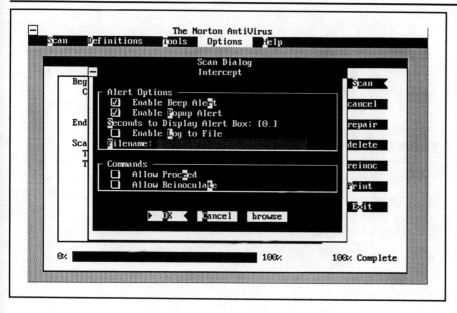

FIGURE 15.4:

Select the options and commands you want to use in Virus Intercept alert boxes

◆ **Seconds to Display Alert Box.** Enter the length of time, in seconds, that you want Virus Intercept to display the alert box. Use zero to make the alert box stay on the screen until you decide to clear it.

◆ **Enable Log to File.** To store a log of all Virus Intercept alert boxes and your responses to them, check this box and enter a file name into the Filename text box below.

◆ **Allow Proceed.** Check this box if you want to continue after a virus has been found. This can be very dangerous, so be careful. The best course of action after a virus has been found is to launch Norton AntiVirus immediately to remove the infection.

 If you reinoculate an infected file, you are telling Norton AntiVirus to protect it, so be careful how you use the Allow Reinoculate check box.

◆ **Allow Reinoculate.** This option allows you to reinoculate a file after Virus Intercept has found an unknown virus. Do not reinoculate a file unless you are *absolutely certain* that it is not infected. I recommend that you leave this box unchecked to avoid any problems. Again, the safest course of action is to launch Norton AntiVirus immediately, and remove the infection.

Make your selections from this dialog box, then use OK to return to the main Norton AntiVirus dialog box.

GLOBAL SETTINGS

You can change several settings that affect both Virus Intercept and Norton AntiVirus if you choose Global from the Options menu. The dialog box shown in Figure 15.5 opens when you choose Global.

This dialog box contains the following settings:

◆ **Detect Unknown Viruses.** Check this box if you want Norton AntiVirus to scan for all possible viruses. If you do not check this box, Norton AntiVirus only checks for known viruses. Known viruses are those that are described in the virus definition file. See the section at the end of this chapter called "Keeping Norton Anti-Virus Up to Date" for more information on this definition file.

◆ **Auto-inoculate.** Check this box if you want Norton AntiVirus to inoculate an uninoculated application program when it is first launched.

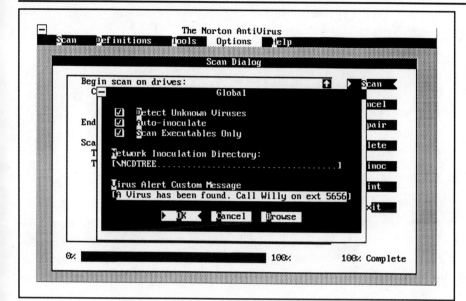

You can specify a virus alert custom message in the Global dialog box

---

◆ **Scan Executables** Only. If you check this box, the scan process is limited to files with file-name extensions such as .EXE, .COM, .SYS, .DRV, and .OVL.

◆ **Network Inoculation Directory**. Enter the name of the directory on your network where you want to store the network inoculation information.

◆ **Virus Alert Custom Message**. If you want to use a custom message with Virus Intercept, enter your message into this text box.

ADDING PASSWORD PROTECTION

If you want to, you can add password protection to certain parts of Norton AntiVirus:

◆ Clinic, Intercept, and Global in the Options menu

◆ Uninoculate in the Tools menu

The dialog boxes used when setting, changing, and removing the password work exactly the same as those used in other places on the Norton Desktop, and so they will not be described here.

USING NORTON ANTIVIRUS FROM A FLOPPY DISK

There may be circumstances where the Norton AntiVirus program on the Desktop can offer only limited assistance:

◆ when Norton AntiVirus detects that a virus is present in memory right now

◆ when your Desktop files are themselves infected

◆ when important DOS files are infected

◆ when the boot sector on your hard disk is infected

◆ when the partition table information on your hard disk is infected

Under these circumstances, you can run the Norton AntiVirus program directly from the first disk of the distribution disks using the DOS command line.

REMOVING A VIRUS FROM MEMORY

A virus present in your computer memory is a serious threat to all your files; indeed, a virus in memory can infect any file that Norton Antivirus scans. The first thing to do is to reboot your computer from a known good disk to bypass the virus, then use the Norton AntiVirus program on Disk #1 to fix the problem. Here are the steps:

1. Turn off your computer, then reboot using a write-protected floppy disk containing the same version of DOS that you normally use from your hard disk.

2. When you see the A:> prompt on your screen, take out the DOS disk and insert Disk #1 of the original Norton Desktop program disks into drive A. Make sure this disk is also write-protected.

3. At the A:> prompt, type:

   NAV

   followed by the Enter key.

4. When Norton AntiVirus starts running, scan the infected disk or disks, and repair or delete files as necessary. If Norton AntiVirus again reports a virus present in memory, then the DOS floppy disk you just booted from is also infected. Find another DOS disk and try again.

5. When all traces of the virus has been obliterated, remove the floppy disk from drive A and reboot your computer. Run Norton Anti-Virus once again just to make sure all is now well with your system.

If the virus was detected in memory while you were installing the Norton Desktop, you can now continue with that installation.

REPAIRING INFECTED DESKTOP FILES

If your Desktop files have been damaged, you will not be able to run Norton AntiVirus from the Desktop. The Norton Desktop is too big to run from a floppy disk, so you must remove the virus using Norton AntiVirus from the DOS command line. The process is very similar to that described in the preceding section.

If your files were very badly damaged by the virus, you may have to reload all the Norton Desktop files from a backup or from the original disks.

REPAIRING INFECTED DOS FILES

If your COMMAND.COM file becomes infected or if one of the DOS hidden system files (IO.SYS and MSDOS.SYS for MS-DOS, or IBMBIOS.COM and IBMDOS.COM for PC-DOS) becomes infected, first try to repair the file after the initial scan. If a repair is impossible (the Repair button is dimmed and un-available), the only possible choice of action is to delete the file and then reinstall the file from an uninfected copy. Here are the steps:

1. Delete the system file or COMMAND.COM using the Delete button in Norton AntiVirus.

2. Choose Exit from the Scan menu. At this point, you may see a message indicating that COMMAND.COM is missing.

3. Reboot your system using a write-protected floppy disk containing the same version of DOS used on your hard disk.

4. Copy COMMAND.COM into the root directory of your hard disk.

5. If you are restoring the DOS hidden system files, type:

C:*pathname* \SYS C:

where *pathname* contains the name of the directory where you keep your DOS files. You should see a System transferred message indicating that you have restored your DOS system files.

RECOVERING FROM BOOT-SECTOR OR PARTITION-TABLE INFECTIONS

The problem with boot-sector and partition-table viruses is that they load themselves onto your system very early on in the boot-up process; well before DOS and Virus Intercept are loaded.

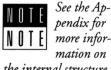

See the Appendix for more information on the internal structure of disks, drives, and directories.

A boot-sector virus replaces a portion of the boot sector on the infected disk, and a partition-table virus infects the tiny program that identifies the bootable partition on your hard disk. A partition-table virus may prevent your computer from starting up at all from the infected hard disk.

There are two main ways that these types of virus can gain access to your system:

◆ Booting (or even attempting to boot) your computer from a floppy disk with an infected boot sector. All disks, both hard disks and floppy disks have a boot sector, even though it may never be used. Floppy disks do not have partition tables.

◆ Using a file that infects boot sectors or partition tables.

Here are the steps to follow to remove one of these viruses:

1. Scan the disk using Norton AntiVirus.

2. Try to repair the infected item using the Repair button.

If the Repair button is dimmed and this function is not available, then the recovery process becomes rather more complex:

1. Turn off your computer, then reboot using a write-protected floppy disk containing the same version of DOS that you normally use from your hard disk.

2. When you see the A:> prompt on your screen, take out the DOS disk and insert Disk #1 of the original Norton Desktop program disks into drive A. Make sure this disk is also write-protected.

3. At the A:> prompt, type:

   NAV

   followed by the Enter key.

4. When Norton AntiVirus starts running, select Cancel to skip the scan.

5. Choose Restore from Rescue Disk from the Tools menu.

6. Follow the prompts on the screen to restore the boot sector or the partition table from the rescue disk.

7. When all traces of the virus have been obliterated, remove the floppy disk from drive A and reboot your computer. Run Norton AntiVirus once again just to make sure all is now well with your system.

> **NOTE**
> **NOTE**
> *You can make a rescue disk using Disk Tools, described in Chapter 13, or by using the Create Rescue Disk selection in the Norton Anti-Virus Tools menu.*

When your system is back running normally again, check all the floppy disks you can find to try to locate the source of the infection.

KEEPING NORTON ANTIVIRUS UP TO DATE

Norton AntiVirus protects your system against over 1,000 virus strains by keeping information on all the known viruses in a virus definitions file. Because the virus-makers keep changing the way viruses work, it is important that you keep the information in this definitions file as up to date as possible. As new viruses are detected, new versions of the definitions file are made available by Symantec.

You can use your communications software to download a copy of this file from the Symantec bulletin board or from the Norton (NORUTL) forum on CompuServe. After you download the file, copy it into the ND directory, then launch Norton AntiVirus and choose Load from File from the Definitions menu. Select the new virus file in the Files list box, and click on OK to load the new definitions.

You can also enter the new definition information by hand using a printed or faxed list of the new virus definitions and the Modify List command in the Definitions menu. Click the Add button, and then enter the name, length, checksum value, and virus definition into the appropriate text boxes. This is a long procedure with plenty of potential for making mistakes, although AntiVirus does check for obvious typing errors. You should only use Modify List as a last resort; downloading the definition files from a bulletin board is a much more efficient way of updating your virus definitions.

NOTE *Call the Symantec bulletin board at (408) 973-9598 if you have a 300- to 2400-baud modem or at (408) 973-9834 if you have a 9600-baud modem. You can download a complete set of virus definitions, or you can download just those definitions published since the last release of the virus definition file.*

PART FIVE

Using the Desktop Utilities

Part V describes how to get the most out of the Desktop utilities including how to use the Scheduler to automate backups, how to send MCI mail, and how to increase system performance using file compression and the Norton disk cache. Chapter 19 contains a complete reference to all the command-line switches you can use with the programs supplied as part of the Norton Desktop for DOS.

CHAPTER 16

Using the Norton Productivity Tools

his chapter describes three Norton Desktop productivity tools: the Scheduler, used for automatically running programs and posting reminder messages; the Calendar, with its notes; and the Desktop Calculator. We'll start with the Scheduler.

MAKING APPOINTMENTS WITH THE SCHEDULER

 Make sure the system time is correct on your computer before you rely on the Scheduler!

You can use the Norton Desktop Scheduler to send yourself reminder messages about important events or to schedule programs to run at a specific time, even when you are away from your computer. You tell the Scheduler what the event is, when the event takes place, and how frequently you want to repeat the event, and it takes care of the rest. If you tell it to launch a program, the Scheduler will start the program as soon as the designated time has come. If some other event prevents the Scheduler from starting the application program—perhaps your printer is busy—the Scheduler will launch the program as soon as possible after the system resource becomes free. You can even use the Scheduler to launch several applications at the same moment, but be careful about the sequence you use in case these programs communicate with each other and the launch sequence is important.

In order for the Scheduler to post reminder messages and run programs unattended, the Scheduler must be active and running on your system. The most convenient way of doing this is to load the NSched program onto your system by your AUTOEXEC.BAT file. If NSched is not loaded, and you choose the Scheduler option from the Desktop Tools menu, you will see the reminder dialog box shown in Figure 16.1.

You can also type:

NSCHED

at the DOS prompt at any time to install the program.

Once NSched is installed on your system, you will see the start-up message Norton Scheduler Installed, followed by an indication of whether extended memory, expanded memory, or your hard disk is being used as NSched swap space, and finally a message giving you the status of any pending Scheduler events.

NSched is also required by Sleeper, the Desktop screen saver.

Chapter 9 describes how to use NDConfig to install the NSched terminate-and-stay-resident program. NSched takes about 12K of memory space.

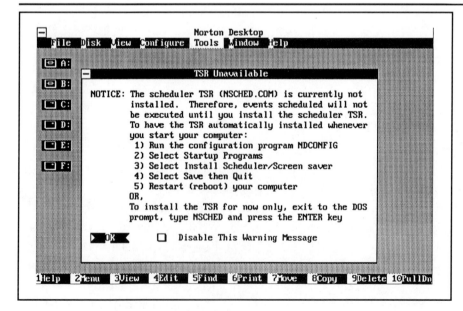

FIGURE 16.1:

You will see this dialog box if the terminate-and-stay-resident program Nsched is not loaded onto your system

To work with the Scheduler, select it from the Tools menu, and the Scheduler window opens on the Desktop, as Figure 16.2 shows.

This main Scheduler window lets you set up, check, and remove events. On the left of the Scheduler window, you will see a calendar for the current month with today's date highlighted, and on the right, a list of your currently scheduled events, along with their times and dates. If there are too many events scheduled, use the scroll bars at the side of this list box to bring the other events into view. You can change the month as you wish:

The Scheduler can display any date between January 1980 and December 2107.

◆ To go straight to the first day of the month, use Home.

◆ To go directly to the last day of the month, use End.

◆ To display a later month, press PgDn or Ctrl+→. With the mouse, click the right arrowhead on the month title bar.

◆ To display an earlier month, press PgUp or Ctrl+←. If you are a mouse user, click the left arrowhead on the month title bar.

◆ To display the same month a year earlier, use Ctrl+PgUp or click the right mouse button on the left arrowhead on the month title bar.

◆ To display the same month a year later, use Ctrl+PgDn or click the right mouse button on the right arrowhead on the month title bar.

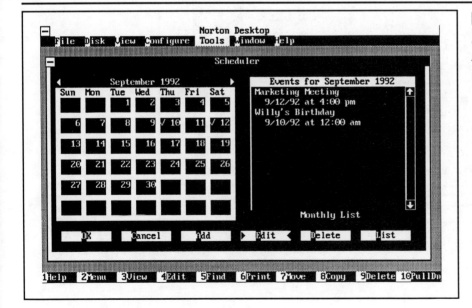

FIGURE 16.2:

Scheduled events are shown in the Scheduler window

ORGANIZING YOUR SCHEDULE

All the events you currently have scheduled are shown in the list box to the right of the window, as either a one- or two-line display. We'll see how to change this in a moment.

There are several command buttons along the bottom of this window, including the usual OK and Cancel buttons, that you use to work with the Scheduler. I'll discuss remaining command buttons next.

Adding Events

When you want to add a new entry to the Scheduler's list of events, click on Add to open the Event Editor dialog box shown in Figure 16.3. This dialog box is the same as the dialog box used for editing events, described later. There are two major group boxes in the Add Event dialog box, When and What. When establishes timing and frequency for your event, and What decides the nature of the event.

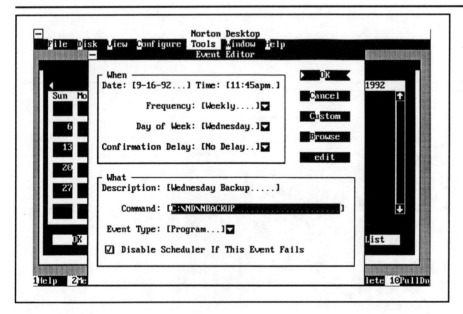

FIGURE 16.3:

Add or Edit Scheduler events using the Event Editor dialog box

There are several important entries in the When group box, as follows:

Date. Shows the current computer date. You can accept this date, or change it to another.

Time. Shows the current computer time. You can accept this time or change it if you wish.

Frequency. Use this drop-down list box to establish the frequency of the event. Choose from:

◆ Once

◆ Hourly

◆ Weekdays

◆ Daily

◆ Weekly

◆ Monthly

◆ Custom

Day of Week. Use this drop-down list box to select the day of the week for your event. This is grayed out until Frequency is set to Weekly.

Confirmation Delay. Check this box if you want to see a confirmation dialog box open on your screen before a scheduled batch file or program starts. If you schedule a program such as Norton Backup, which may take a long time to complete its task, there may be times when you are using your computer when the appointed moment arrives, and it is just not convenient to run the backup.

The confirmation dialog box gives you the option of running the scheduled program right now, postponing it for a period of time that you select, canceling this specific event, or disabling the Scheduler so that all scheduled events are canceled.

Confirmation delay is set to No Delay as the default, but you can select delay periods from 30 seconds to Forever. If you don't see the confirmation dialog box, or you ignore it, the dialog box stays on your screen for the time period you selected, then your scheduled event runs automatically.

Confirmation Delay is dimmed if you select Reminder; it becomes available when you select Program or Batch File.

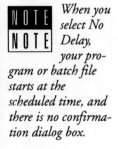

When you select No Delay, your program or batch file starts at the scheduled time, and there is no confirmation dialog box.

If you want to schedule an event more than just once a week, choose the Custom command button, and check the days of the week you want from the list shown in the Custom Scheduling dialog box.

You use the entries in the What group box to establish the kind of event you want to work with:

Description. The description you enter into this text box is shown in the event list in the main Scheduler window.

Command. If you plan to schedule either a program or a batch file, type the name of the program or batch file into this text box. Include complete path information if your event is not in the Norton Desktop directory or in your path statement in your AUTOEXEC.BAT file. You must also include complete path information if you are a network user and your event is not included in a Novell network Map command. Click on the Browse button to help locate the program or batch file name you want to run.

Event Type. Select one of the three options in this drop-down list box: Reminder, to make the Scheduler post a reminder message of up to 160 characters long; Program, to run any DOS application; or Batch File, to run any batch file.

Disable Scheduler If This Event Fails. Use this selection to disable all subsequent scheduled events if this particular program or batch file fails to run.

Click on OK when you have completed the entries in this dialog box, and you will return to the main Scheduler dialog box.

Edit

If you want to modify or edit an existing event, highlight the event in the Scheduler list box, then click on Edit to open the Event Editor dialog box to make the changes. This is the same dialog box we have just looked at under Add. Click on OK when your changes are complete.

Delete

If you want to delete an event, highlight it in the Scheduler list box, then click on the Delete command button. There is no need to delete events that just occur once because the Scheduler will delete these events automatically as soon as they have been processed. A message box opens, indicating that the expired event is about to be dropped from your list of events. When you click on OK, the event is removed from your event list.

List

Use the List command button to open the Event List Options dialog box, shown in Figure 16.4.

You can control how much information is shown in the main Scheduler dialog box for each event using the settings in the Event List Options dialog box:

Event Type. Select an option button to specify which events are displayed. Monthly shows all the scheduled events for the month, Daily displays the events for one day, and All Events displays all currently scheduled events.

Event Display. Select an option button to specify how events are displayed. One Line shows just a brief description of the event, while Two Lines displays the description as well as the frequency, date, and time of the event. Two Lines is the default setting.

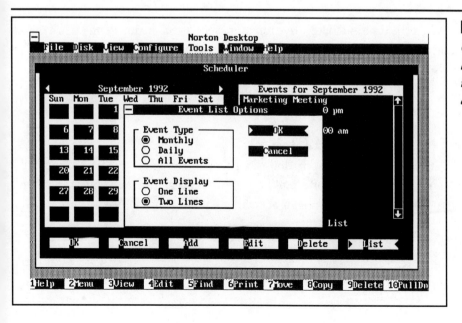

FIGURE 16.4:

Configure the Scheduler list box using settings in the Event List Options dialog box

Select the OK command button to save your settings and return to the main Scheduler dialog box.

CREATING A REMINDER MESSAGE

Now that you are familiar with the components of the Scheduler window, let's look at the steps needed to create a reminder message. Select Scheduler from the Desktop Tools menu to open the main Scheduler window, then:

1. Click on the Add command button to open the Event Editor dialog box.

2. Specify how often you want this event to occur from the choices in the Frequency list box and complete the time, day, and date information.

3. Enter a description of your event, birthday, wedding anniversary, or dinner appointment. This description will appear in the scrollable list in the main Scheduler window, so make it as obvious as you can in the space provided.

4. Choose the Reminder option and enter your message, up to 160 characters in length, into the Command text box.

5. Click on OK to return to the main Scheduler window. You should see your new event displayed in the scrollable list in this window.

When the time and date arrive for your event, the Scheduler will open a message box on the screen, displaying the message text you entered. A beep will also sound to attract your attention. The message box will stay open until you click on OK to indicate that you have received the message.

SCHEDULING A PROGRAM

The steps involved in scheduling a particular program are very similar to those just described for a reminder message. Start the Scheduler from the Tools menu. When the main Scheduler window opens:

1. Click on the Add command button to open the Event Editor dialog box.

2. Specify the frequency and the time that you want the program launched.

3. Enter a brief description of the program you plan to launch. Make this description as obvious as possible so that you won't forget which program you are scheduling.

4. Choose the Program option as the event type, and in the Command text box enter the name of the program you want to run. Your command-line entry can be up to 128 characters in length, so you can also specify any command-line switches you like to use with this application program.

5. Click on OK to return to the main Scheduler window. You should see your new event displayed in the scrollable list in this window.

When the designated time arrives, your application program will start.

SCHEDULING A BACKUP

Combining the power of the Norton Backup program and the Scheduler is an excellent way to back up your hard disk. You can have the Scheduler post a reminder message, indicating it is time to run the Backup program, or—better still—you can make the Scheduler run the program for you at the appointed time. You can use one of the setup files, described in Chapter 11, to make configuring Norton Backup fast and easy, and then use the Scheduler to launch Norton Backup automatically. That way you don't have to remember to configure or launch anything—Scheduler will do it all for you.

Follow the steps outlined above under the heading "Scheduling a Program," but bear in mind the following points if you want the backup to be performed while unattended:

◆ The system time and date on your computer must be correct and must be relatively accurate. Be especially careful if you work with networks, as the network software can sometimes reset the local workstation time to be the same as the network time.

◆ The files you want to back up must fit on a single floppy disk or tape, because you may not be by your computer to change disks. This is less of a problem if you back up to a DOS path using another hard disk.

◆ Make sure you turn off all the settings in Norton Backup that might stop the backup to wait for a response from you, the user, such as overwrite warnings.

◆ Use a Norton Backup setup file in the Command text box in Scheduler. Your entry might look like this:

NBACKUP.EXE ASSIST.SET

or you might add some of the other Norton Backup command-line switches to preconfigure the program. These switches are described in detail at the end of Chapter 11 under the heading "Using Command-Line Switches."

◆ Choose a sensible time to schedule the backup. If you eat lunch every day at 12:00, try scheduling the backup for noon. If you schedule the backup to take place after you have left work, remember to insert the backup floppy disk before you leave, or schedule a message timed to appear just before you leave to remind you to insert the floppy disk.

Of course, you can schedule different kinds of backups to take place on different days, too, perhaps a full backup on Fridays and an incremental backup Monday through Thursday.

CREATING AND EDITING BATCH FILES

You can also use the Event Editor dialog box to create or change a batch file; here are the steps:

1. Choose Batch File from the Event Type drop-down list box.

2. Type the name of the batch file. This can be the name of an existing batch file that you want to edit or the name of a new file.

3. If the file does not exist, you will see a dialog box containing the message Batch file does not exist. Create new file. Click on OK to create this new file.

4. The Batch File Editor window opens, as Figure 16.5 shows, ready for you to type the commands for your batch file.

5. When your batch file is complete, click on Save to save your new batch file and return to the Event Editor dialog box.

6. Select the OK command button to add this batch file as a scheduled event.

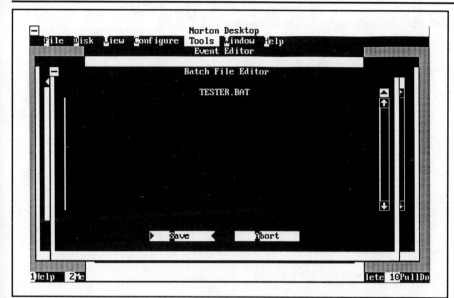

FIGURE 16.5:
Enter and edit the
commands in your batch
file using the Batch File
Editor window

The Batch File Editor is like a cut-down version of the Desktop Editor described in Chapter 7, but with the menu bar and configuration options removed. Table 16.1 summarizes the keyboard commands you can use in the Batch File Editor.

The Batch File Editor may not contain all the power of the Desktop Editor, but you can still edit text with it very easily. You can mark text by dragging the mouse, you can cut and paste marked text to and from a clipboard, and you can delete marked text by pressing the Delete key. Several commands open their own dialog boxes. You can insert another text file into the Batch File Editor with Ctrl+E, find specific text with Ctrl+F, find and replace specific text with Ctrl+R, or print the batch file using Ctrl+P.

From the keyboard, the PgUp, PgDn, Home, End, and the arrow keys all work just as you would expect, and you can use Ctrl+Home to go to the first line in the file, or Ctrl+End to go to the last line in the file. Backspace removes the character to the left of the cursor, and the Delete key removes the character above the cursor.

TABLE 16.1:

Commands available in the Batch File Editor

KEYSTROKE	FUNCTION
Backspace	deletes the character to the left of the cursor
Ctrl+C	copies marked text to the clipboard
Ctrl+E	inserts a file
Ctrl+F	locates specific text
Ctrl+H	same as Backspace
Ctrl+I	same as Tab
Ctrl+J	adds a new line
Ctrl+M	adds a carriage return
Ctrl+P	prints the batch file
Ctrl+R	locates and replaces specific text
Ctrl+V	pastes clipboard text into the batch file at the current cursor location
Ctrl+X	cuts the marked text to the clipboard
Ctrl+End	moves the cursor to the end of the current batch file
Ctrl+Home	moves the cursor to the beginning of the current batch file
Delete	deletes the character above the cursor, or deletes a block of marked text
End	moves the cursor to the end of the current line
End End	moves the cursor to the end of the current window
End End End	moves the cursor to the end of the current batch file
Home	moves the cursor to the beginning of the current line
Home Home	moves the cursor to the beginning of the current window
Home Home Home	moves the cursor to the beginning of the current batch file

Moving around inside the Batch File Editor is a breeze with a mouse. Click on the scroll bars to move up and down through the file, or click on the << or >> symbols to go the the beginning or the end of a particularly long line that cannot be displayed in the window in its entirety.

USING THE DESKTOP TOOLS WITH SCHEDULER

It is critical that the more powerful tools on the Desktop are never interrupted as they work, because this can mean lost data or missing files. To make absolutely sure that this does not happen on the Desktop, several of the advanced utility programs detect the presence of the Scheduler. The following programs can turn the Scheduler off when they start; then they run and turn the Scheduler back on again when they are finished:

◆ Disk Tools

◆ Image

◆ Norton Disk Doctor

◆ Norton Mail

◆ Safe Format

◆ UnErase

◆ UnFormat

If a program or batch file was scheduled to run during the time that Scheduler was turned off, a dialog box opens as soon as the Scheduler starts working again, to display your reminder message or to ask if you would like to run the scheduled program now.

WORKING WITH THE DESKTOP CALENDAR

You can use the Desktop Calendar to keep track of important dates and appointments just like you would on a paper calendar; you can even attach your own notes to particular dates.

Choose Calendar in the Desktop Tools menu, and you will see the Calendar dialog box open as Figure 16.6 shows.

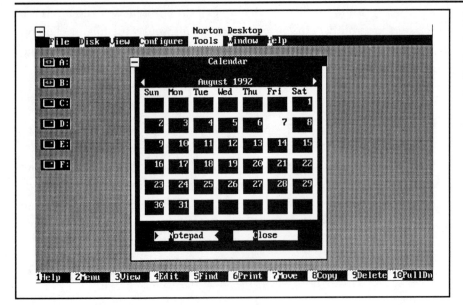

FIGURE 16.6:

Choose Calendar from the Desktop Tools menu to open the Calendar dialog box

CHANGING THE DATE

When the Calendar opens, you will see the current month displayed and today's date highlighted. You can change the month as you wish, just as you can in the Scheduler:

◆ To display a later month, press PgDn or Ctrl+→. With the mouse, click the right arrowhead on the month title bar.

◆ To display an earlier month, press PgUp or Ctrl+←. If you are a mouse user, click the left arrowhead on the month title bar.

◆ To display the same month a year earlier, use Ctrl+PgUp. With the mouse, click the right mouse button on the left arrowhead on the month title bar.

◆ To display the same month a year later, use Ctrl+PgDn, or click the right mouse button on the right arrowhead on the month title bar.

◆ To go straight to the first of the current month, use Home.

◆ To go directly to the last day in the current month, use End.

◆ To go straight to January of the current year, use Ctrl+Home.

◆ To go directly to December of the current year, press Ctrl+End.

ADDING NOTES TO YOUR CALENDAR

One of the main purposes of keeping a calendar is to add notes to it indicating important events including meetings, anniversaries, birthdays, vacations, and so on. You can even keep notes containing to-do lists.

To add a note to a date on the Desktop Calendar, first select the date with the mouse or the arrow keys, then choose the Notepad command button at the bottom of the Calendar dialog box. The Notepad opens as Figure 16.7 shows.

Type in the text you want to associate with the date you selected, and when you are finished, click on OK to save your note. Now, when you return to the main Calendar dialog box, you will see that there is a check mark shown on the date to remind you that a note is attached. Anytime you see this check mark, you know that a note is attached.

NOTE *The top line of the Notepad includes the date, which reminds you which day this note is attached to.*

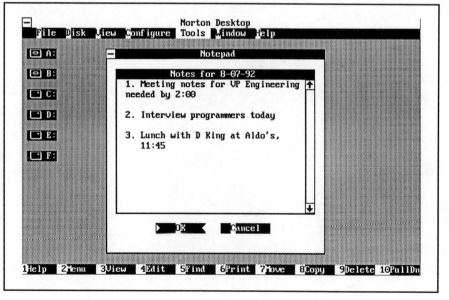

FIGURE 16.7:

Enter a note for the selected date

The Calendar Notepad works in much the same way as the Batch File Editor, described earlier in this chapter; the commands listed in Table 16.1 will also work in a Calendar Notepad. When you are ready to leave the Calendar and return to the Desktop, choose the Close command button in the main Calendar dialog box.

USING THE DESKTOP CALCULATOR

It used to be that you had to search through your desk drawers to find your pocket calculator every time you wanted to add a couple of numbers together—now all that has changed. The Norton Desktop Tools menu includes a convenient, easy-to-use, four-function calculator for your everyday calculations.

Before you use the numbers on your ten-key pad, make sure that the Num Lock key is toggled on.

When you select Calculator from the Tools menu, you will see the Calculator display as Figure 16.8 shows.

With the mouse, just click on the number or function you want to use. If you are a keyboard user, you can use the corresponding keys on the keyboard. If you use the numbers on the keypad, make sure that the Num Lock key is toggled on; otherwise, nothing will happen. Table 16.2 lists the calculator operator keys and shows all their functions.

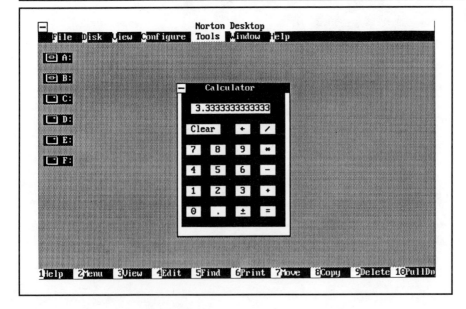

FIGURE 16.8:

The Desktop Calculator

OPERATOR	FUNCTION
+	addition
−	subtraction
/	division
*	multiplication
=	calculate final result
+/−	change the sign
←	backspace
Clear	clear the calculator display

TABLE 16.2:
Desktop Calculator Operators and Functions

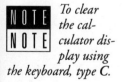

Some calculators don't use infix notation, but use Reverse Polish Notation (RPN) instead. With RPN you enter the numbers for the calculation first, and the operator (plus, minus, multiply, or divide) last.

The Desktop Calculator uses normal infix notation for the entry of numbers, where you enter a number, the operator, then another number. For example, to divide 10 by 3, enter:

10 / 3

You can use the equals key (=) or the Enter key to generate the answer—it doesn't matter because they are equivalent. The Desktop Calculator can display 14 significant digits in the display; the decimal point usually occupies the other digit.

If you make a mistake as you enter a number, use the ← (backspace) key to remove individual numbers one at a time from the right, or use the Clear key to reset the calculator. If you want to enter a negative number, enter the number first, then click on the change sign (+/−) key, or press the backslash (\) key from the keyboard. Each time you use the change sign key, the number toggles from positive to negative.

To clear the calculator display using the keyboard, type C.

The Calculator always checks certain kinds of calculations for validity and posts a message if you try something impossible. For example, if you try to divide a number by zero, you will see the message **Error** in the calculator display. Just press C from the keyboard, or click on Clear to dismiss the message.

When you have finished your calculations, press the Escape key, or double-click on the close box (in the upper-left corner of the Calculator), to close the Calculator and return to the Desktop.

CHAPTER 17

Using the Norton Desktop Communications Tools

This chapter concentrates on three Norton Desktop communications tools. The first part of the chapter describes how you can use Norton Mail to manage all your MCI electronic mail transactions. Next, PC-to-PC and PC-to-network connections are covered in sections that detail Desktop Link and Network Link. Finally we'll see how to use the Network Message command to broadcast a message to all users on your network. We'll start with Norton Mail.

USING NORTON MAIL

Norton Mail is an electronic mail system on the Desktop that you can use to send and receive e-mail using your MCI account. You must configure Norton Mail before you can use it, and there are several pieces of information

You must first have an MCI Mail account before you can use Norton Mail.

you must collect together for this configuration process, including:

◆ Your MCI access telephone number

◆ Information about your telephone—whether it is pulse or touch-tone.

◆ Your MCI account identification number and password

◆ Information about your modem, including the name of the port it is attached to and its baud rate.

With this information close at hand, we can now start and configure Norton Mail.

NORTON MAIL CONFIGURATION

In this section we will look at all the Norton Mail configuration screens, one after another, in the order in which they occur in the program. If you change your mind and decide you want to change one or more of these settings later, use the selections from the Setup menu to access each of these dialog boxes directly.

Start Norton Mail by choosing Mail from the Desktop Tools menu, or by typing the following at the DOS prompt:

NMAIL

If you have Commander Mail or Lotus Express, you can import information from these mail systems into Norton Mail. Norton Mail will also use the Commander Mail IN, OUT, and SENT directories, so these names will not appear in the Directories dialog box.

The New Directories dialog box appears, listing up to six directory names. Norton Mail uses these directories to separate your incoming and outgoing mail, and any mailing lists you create. These directories are created as subdirectories to your Norton Desktop directory. Norton Mail often refers to these directories as *folders:*

In. Contains messages received from MCI Mail.

Out. Stores messages waiting to be sent the next time you use MCI Mail.

Sent. Stores messages already sent via MCI Mail.

Draft. Contains messages that you are working on now. They will be moved to the Out folder when you are ready to send them.

Folders. Contains any additional private folders you create.

Mlists. Contains mailing lists for mass mailings.

Choose the Yes Command button to create these directories, or the Abort command button to cancel Norton Mail and return to the Desktop. If you want to use different names for these directories, click on the Edit command button to open the Directories dialog box so that you can change the names. If you do change any of the directory names, be sure you do not leave any of them blank; each entry must have a valid directory name.

Next, the MCI Accounts dialog box opens so that you can set up from one to six MCI accounts; you must set up at least one to use Norton Mail. Select the New command button in this dialog box to open the Account Information dialog box shown in Figure 17.1.

This dialog box has the following entries:

MCI User Name. Enter your user name as provided by MCI.

MCI Password. Enter your MCI password. You will only see asterisks as you enter your password for security reasons.

MCI ID. Enter your MCI identification number, up to a maximum of 12 characters.

Make Account Active. Check this box to make this account an active account. To send and receive mail, the account must be active.

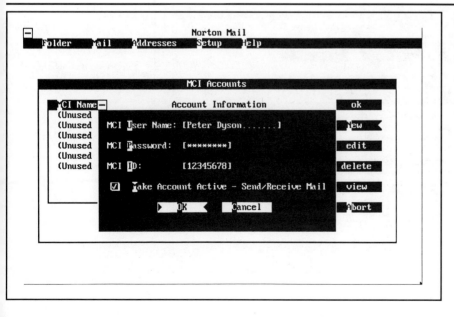

FIGURE 17.1:

Enter your MCI account details into the Account Information dialog box

Select OK to dismiss the Account Information dialog box, and choose OK a second time to leave the MCI Accounts dialog box.

Next, you use the MCI Telephone dialog box, shown in Figure 17.2 to establish the telephone numbers you will use. Select the Primary number, or if you prefer, enter another number, and choose Alternate. Then select the option button that corresponds to the dial-out prefix for your phone. Many office phone systems require that you dial 8 or 9 for an outside line.

Choose Custom if you want to enter a different prefix, or if you always want to cancel call waiting as you start an MCI session.

The next step in setting up Norton Mail is to configure the program for your modem. The Modem Settings dialog box is shown in Figure 17.3, and contains the following selections:

Choose Custom and enter *70 if you want to cancel call waiting.

MCI does not yet support 9600 baud modems.

Baud Rate. Select the correct baud rate for your modem: 300, 1200, 2400, or 9600 baud. The higher the number, the faster the data transmission rate. Many modern modems can operate at several different rates; they detect the speed of the transmission and change their baud rate setting as required to match the other modem. Use the fastest speed you can to keep your line charges as low as possible.

Dial Type. Choose between pulse dial or tone dial.

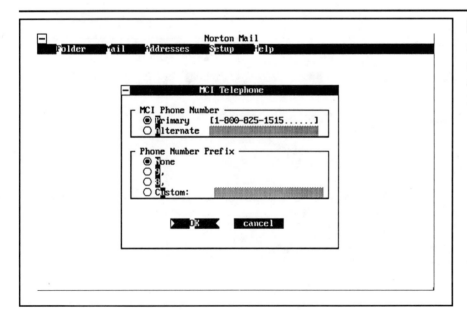

FIGURE 17.2:

Select a telephone number and a dial-out code in the MCI Telephone dialog box

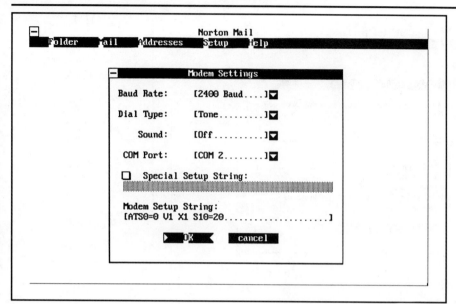

FIGURE 17.3:

Enter the appropriate settings for your modem

Sound. Select On if you want to listen to your modem as it dials out to MCI, or Off if you want your modem to remain silent.

COM Port. Choose the serial port on your computer associated with your modem—COM1, COM2, COM3, or COM4.

Special Setup String. Check this box if you want to enter a setup string for your modem. This is an advanced option you can use to send an initialization string to your modem; see your modem manual for more information on modem initialization. The text box under this entry contains an example setup string for a Hayes or Hayes-compatible modem. Don't change this text box unless you are an experienced and accomplished modem user.

The last part of the configuration process is to set the Norton Mail options, using the dialog box shown in Figure 17.4.

First, choose the folder or directory you want to use for newly created messages. You can select Out or Draft, or if you use the last option button, Prompt User for Folder Name, Norton Mail will ask you for a folder name when you create a new message. There are five check boxes in the lower part of this dialog box:

Full Page Read. Select this option to see messages displayed full-screen, or leave it unchecked to see a message as part of a dialog box.

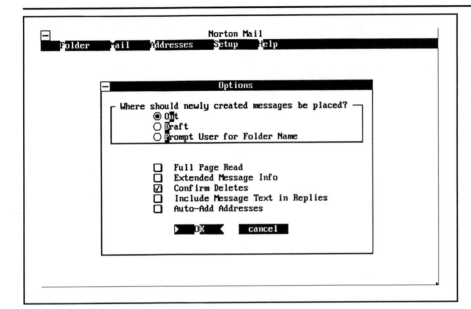

FIGURE 17.4:

Specify additional Norton Mail settings with the Options dialog box

Extended Message Info. Select this option to see complete information about each message, including message time, and the name and size of the file, or leave it blank to see a one-line summary.

Confirm Deletes. Check this box to see a dialog box open every time you try to delete something in Norton Mail. This is the safest setting and is also the default.

Include Message Text in Replies. When this box is checked, the text of the original message will appear in the reply. The default setting is for this box to be unchecked.

Auto-Add Addresses. Check this box if you always want to add any new MCI addresses to your address book automatically. The default setting is for this box to remain unchecked.

Click on OK to dismiss the Options dialog box, and the Configuration of Norton Mail is complete. Now we can use Norton Mail to manage your MCI mail.

MANAGING YOUR MAIL

The next window shown on the screen is the main Norton Mail window. From this window you can perform all the major Norton Mail functions:

◆ Create new messages

◆ Send and receive MCI Mail messages

◆ Read your mail

◆ Forward messages to other MCI subscribers

◆ Reply to your messages

◆ Print messages

◆ Delete messages

Many of these functions can be accessed by command buttons directly from the main Norton Mail window, or you can use the equivalent menu selections if you prefer. All of the Norton Mail menus are available from within the Message From dialog box for your convenience.

Creating a New Message

All messages that you create will be shown in the main window with a ← symbol in the left margin, indicating they can be sent.

Here are the steps you need to follow to enter a new message:

1. Select the New command button or select New Message (Ctrl+N) from the Mail menu, and you will see the Message From dialog box open as Figure 17.5 shows.

2. Choose the message recipient from those available in the To drop-down list box, and choose the people to whom you want to send copies of this message from the list in the cc drop-down list box. You cannot type directly into the To or the cc boxes; you must choose an existing addressee from those available to Norton Mail. For more information on how to add new addressees, see the next section, "Working with Addresses." Every message must be addressed to a recipient; otherwise, it will not be accepted by Norton Mail. A count to the right of these drop-down list boxes shows the number of people selected to receive this message, as well as the number of people who will receive copies.

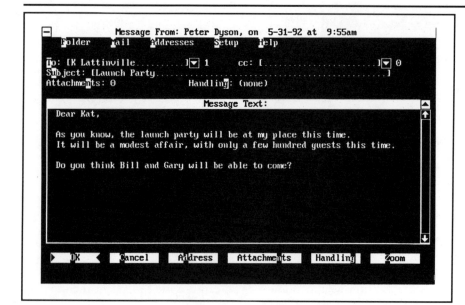

Enter the appropriate routing information as well as the message text using the Message From dialog box

3. Enter a descriptive title for this message into the Subject text box. Your subject can be up to 59 characters long.

4. Type in the text of your message using the large Message Text box. See the description of the Desktop Editor in Chapter 7 for a description of the editing commands you can use in this text box.

5. When the message is complete, select OK to dismiss this dialog box. If you did not select an addressee earlier on, Norton Mail prompts you to choose one now.

To zoom the Message Text window to full screen size, press Ctrl+PgUp or Ctrl+PgDn from the keyboard, or click on the Zoom button at the bottom of the window.

This message is automatically stored in the folder designated to receive new messages until you next log onto MCI and send the message.

There are several command buttons at the bottom of this window in addition to the usual Cancel and OK buttons:

Address. Opens the Selected Addresses dialog box described in the next section.

Attachments. You can mark up to 32 additional files and send them along with your message as attachments. Use the Browse command button to select files for attachment.

Handling. A message may occasionally need special handling; see your MCI documentation for more information.

Zoom. Expands the Message Text box to fill the whole screen; use Ctrl+PgDn or Ctrl+PgUp to return to the normal dialog box.

There are several other important commands in the Mail menu you can use to manipulate your messages. Copy (Ctrl+C) duplicates a message from one folder or directory to another, while Move (Ctrl+V) copies the message but deletes the original copy. You can also edit an existing message. Highlight the message you want to copy, move, or edit from the list in the main Norton Mail window, then choose the appropriate command from the Mail menu. Copy and Move open their respective dialog boxes, while Edit reopens the Message From dialog box I have just described.

You can use one of the Sort options in the Mail menu to specify how your messages are displayed in the main Norton Mail window. The default, and most useful setting, is Sort by Date, but you can also choose Sort by Subject (alphabetical order of subject) or Sort by From (alphabetical order of message originator). All these sort settings are toggles; you can only choose one to be active at a time. The check mark to the left of the menu item indicates which sort setting is active.

Working with Addresses

NOTE NOTE

You can import existing MCI Mail information from existing applications; see the section called "Importing Norton Commander and Lotus Express Information" later in this chapter.

Norton Mail provides an address book that contains addresses for all the people to whom you can send mail. You can add, edit, and delete addresses from this address book as you wish, and you can also collect sets of addresses together to form mail lists. We'll look at all these functions, but first we'll look at how you enter and edit addressees for messages and copies.

From the Norton Mail main window, choose Address Book from the Addresses menu, and you will see the Address Book dialog box shown in Figure 17.6. This dialog box lists all the names in your address book on the left side of the dialog box, an optional note in the center column, and an address type designation in the rightmost column. If you open the Address Book from the Address menu, you will see that the top command button is labeled Close. If you open the Address Book from the Mail Lists or Message From dialog boxes, you will see the more usual OK and Cancel command buttons.

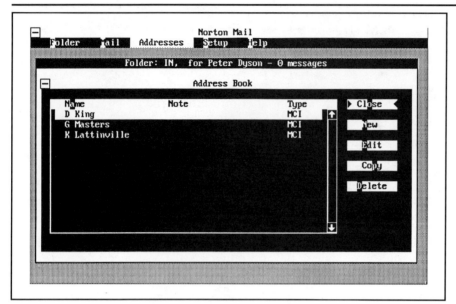

FIGURE 17.6:
*Add, Edit, or Delete
addresses in the Address
Book dialog box*

To add a new address, choose the New command button, and you will see the MCI Address dialog box as Figure 17.7 shows. Select the appropriate address type using the list of option buttons in this dialog box. Choose from:

◆ Paper Mail

◆ Telex

◆ EMS

◆ FAX

◆ MCI Instant

MCI Instant is the default setting. When you select an address type, the text boxes associated with that address type appear in the appropriate dialog boxes. Complete the address entry by entering the usual name, MCI ID, MCI name, and phone number information into the other text boxes in this dialog box. You can also attach a short note to each address if you wish, as a reminder, using the Note text box. You might use these notes to add information about the person's job title or company name to your address book. To enter another address of a different type, just choose the correct Address Type option button and enter the new information. Otherwise click on OK or Close, depending on how you initially entered this dialog box.

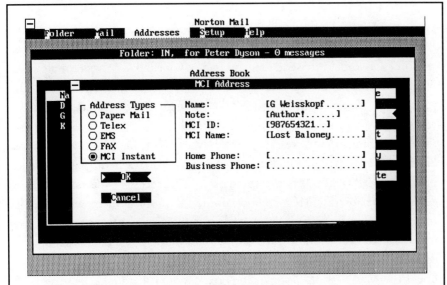

FIGURE 17.7:

Add a new address with the MCI Address dialog box

If address or phone number information changes, highlight the address in the Address Book dialog box, and choose the Edit command button. This command button reopens the MCI Address dialog box so that you can enter the changes. When you have made all the changes, choose OK to return to the Address Book dialog box.

You can use the Copy command button to duplicate an address. In some cases this may be faster than entering all the address information from scratch, particularly if the two addresses are very similar. Highlight the address you want to copy in the Address Book dialog box, then choose the Copy command button. This command button opens the MCI Address dialog box, so you can complete all the address entries.

When an address is not longer needed, you can use the Delete command button to remove it from your Address Book. Highlight the address you want to remove, and choose Delete. The address type in the Address Book dialog box now becomes Deleted. If you highlight a deleted address, the Delete command button changes into the Undelete command button, and you can use Undelete to bring the address back again.

Sending and Receiving Messages

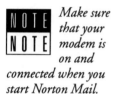

Make sure that your modem is on and connected when you start Norton Mail.

Norton Mail dials the appropriate MCI telephone number, sends and receives your messages, and disconnects your modem at the end of your session. You can both send and receive MCI Mail during a single MCI Mail session. Norton Mail sends all the messages contained in your Out folder, then places copies of these messages into your Sent folder. All newly received messages go straight into your In folder.

To send or receive your mail, start Norton Mail, and choose Send/Receive (Ctrl+S) from the Mail menu to open the Send/Receive dialog box. This dialog box lists the messages being processed, the estimated and elapsed time for this MCI Mail account, the number of messages sent or received, and an indication of the modem status, either transmitting or receiving. If you left the sound turned on, you may hear your modem dial out and connect to the MCI service. When your session is complete, Norton Mail opens the Mail Session Done dialog box; choose OK to end the session.

Reading Your Mail

All incoming messages have an asterisk in front of them to show that they have not been read yet; when you read the message, this symbol disappears. To read a message, highlight the message you are interested in, then select the Read command button, or use Read from the Mail menu. You can also double-click on the message. You cannot make any changes to a message as you read it; you cannot edit the text or change the addressees.

Replying to a Message

When you reply to a message, you can choose to have the original message text included in your reply. Here are the steps:

1. Select the message you want to reply to, and choose the Reply command button. You can also use Reply (Ctrl+R) in the Mail menu.

2. The Message From dialog box opens, showing the sender's name as the addressee. The original subject text is transferred to the new message's Subject text box.

3. Enter the text of your message, just as you would for a new message.

4. Choose OK to save your message, and close the Message From dialog box.

The message is moved into the directory you designated to hold new messages.

Forwarding a Message

You can forward an existing message to a different recipient, rather than reenter that message by hand. Highlight the message you want to forward, and select the Forward command button. You can also use the Forward command (Ctrl+F) from the Mail menu. The Message From dialog box opens again, this time with the To and the cc text boxes empty, and the subject information copied from the original message. You can enter new text and add to the original message if you wish. Select OK when you are done, and the message is moved into the folder you use for new messages.

Printing a Message

At some point you will want to print some or all of your messages. You can print them one at a time, or you can print several messages together. Highlight the message or messages you want to print and choose the Print command button, or open the Mail menu and choose Print. For details on how to set up your printer for the Norton Desktop, see Chapter 9. To access the Configure Printer dialog box directly from within Norton Mail, use Printer from the Setup menu.

Deleting a Message

When you have no further use for a message, you can highlight it, then use the Delete command button or the Delete option (Ctrl+D) from the Mail menu to throw the message away. This will also make more room for messages you may receive in the future.

Working with Folders

Earlier in this chapter, in the section called "Norton Mail Configuration," we looked at the functions performed by the default Norton Mail folders. You don't have to use these default names if you don't want to; indeed there is a Norton Mail menu option available so that you can create, rename, or delete your own folders. You can only rename or delete folders that you created; you cannot rename or delete folders created by Norton Mail.

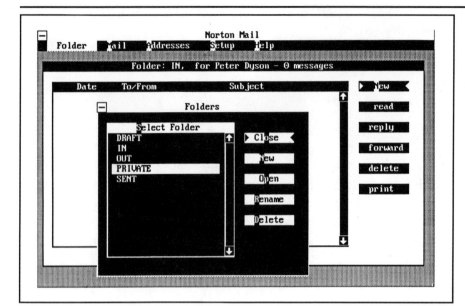

FIGURE 17.8:

*Use the Mail Lists dialog
box to create or view
your mail lists*

Choose Folders from the Folder menu to open the dialog box shown
in Figure 17.8. The command buttons in this dialog box let you create a new
folder, open any folder (the shortcut command to open your In folder is
Ctrl+B), and rename or delete any folder that you created. The In, Out, Sent,
and Draft folders cannot be deleted.

Using a Mail List

A mail list is a convenient way of collecting addresses and cc information
together in a file stored in the Mlists folder on your system. If you send and cc
messages to the same group of people over and over again, then mail lists are the
answer for you. When you select a mail list, your message is sent to all the addressees on the mail list and is copied to all the cc addresses in the list.

Choose the Mail Lists selection from the Addresses menu to open the
dialog box shown in Figure 17.9.

Here are the steps to use to create a new mail list:

1. Choose the New command button in the Mail Lists dialog box.

2. When the New dialog box opens, enter a file name into the text
box for your new mail list.

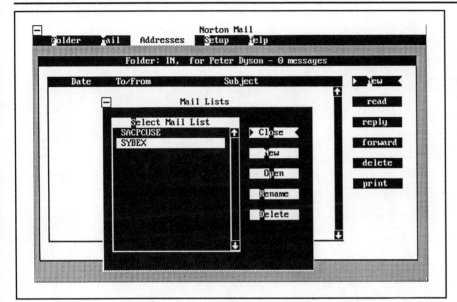

FIGURE 17.9:

Use the Mail Lists dialog box to create or view your mail lists

3. The Selected Addresses dialog box appears. Choose either the To: List or the cc: List option button, depending on the type of addressee. Then select the Add command button.

4. The Address Book dialog box opens. Select the addresses you want to include in this mail list.

5. Select OK to close the Address Book dialog box, then either choose the other option button in the Selected Addresses dialog box to add to the cc:List, or choose OK to close this dialog box as well.

6. The name of this new mail list now appears along with your other mail lists in the Mail List dialog box.

You can now use the other command buttons in this dialog box to open the mail list, or you can rename it or delete it if you find that you no longer use the list.

Importing Norton Commander and Lotus Express Information

The Import command in the Setup menu can save you a great deal of repetitive work if you already have MCI Mail information entered in either Lotus Express or the Norton Commander. Select Import, then choose either Commander

V3.0 Mail or Lotus Express V1.0, depending on the program you use. We'll look at the dialog box used to import Commander information first, then at the Lotus Express dialog box.

When you choose Commander V3.0 Mail, you will see the dialog box shown in Figure 17.10. This dialog box contains one text box and several check boxes:

Directory. Enter complete path information for the directory that contains your Norton Commander files. You can also use the Browse command button in this dialog box to select this path information.

Address Book. Check this box if you want to merge your Norton Commander address book with your Norton Mail address book.

Accounts. If you check this box, you can use MCI Mail accounts set up under the Commander. Norton Mail can handle up to six different accounts.

Configuration. Add a check mark to this box if you want to import configuration information for your modem, including the modem setup string, baud rate, port number, and MCI phone number. Any configuration information imported from the Norton Commander will overwrite that same information in Norton Mail; any other information will be unchanged in Norton Mail.

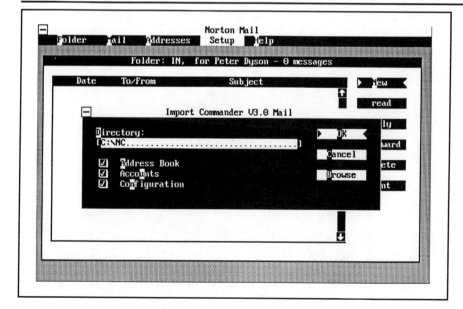

FIGURE 17.10:

You can import MCI Mail information directly from the Norton Commander

To import information from Lotus Express, use the dialog box shown in Figure 17.11.

This dialog box has the following options:

Directory for Mail Lists. Check this box if you want to import your mail lists from Lotus Express. Each mail list imported is given a unique name so that no information is overwritten in Norton Mail. If you check this box, you must also enter path information for the directory that contains your Lotus Express mail lists. The Browse command button is also available in this dialog box.

Directory for Accounts and Configuration. Enter path and configuration information for your Lotus Express MCI account, or use the Browse command button to locate the correct directory.

Directory for Message Folders. Enter path information for the directory that contains your Lotus Express message folders.

Confirmation. Check this box to import modem configuration information from Lotus Express.

Accounts. Check this box to import the MCI Mail accounts used in Lotus Express but not the mail messages for those accounts.

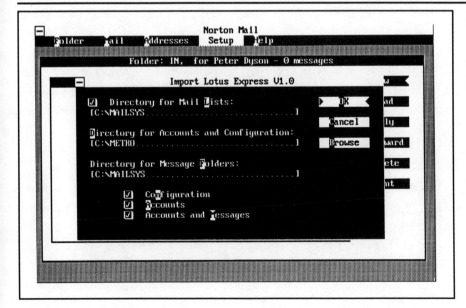

FIGURE 17.11:

You can import MCI Mail information directly from the Norton Commander

Accounts and Messages. Check this box if you want to import account information as well as their associated messages.

Choose the OK command button to start the import process when you are happy with the settings in the Import dialog box.

LINKING TWO COMPUTERS TOGETHER

Norton Desktop lets you transfer files from one computer to another over a serial or parallel cable or over a network connection. Choose Serve Remote Link from the Desktop Disk menu, and you will see two more selections: Desktop Link and Network Link. You use Desktop Link to connect to another PC to transfer files, and you use Network Link to share files with other users over the network.

First, some terminology. For this process to work, one computer acts as the *server* for one or more personal computers, known as *clients*. Clients may be other personal computers connected to the same network, or they may be computers linked to the server by a serial or parallel cable. The server begins and ends each session but cannot be used for any other computing purpose during the session. This is because DOS can only run one program at a time; if DOS is managing the desktop or network link, it cannot do anything else during that time. Once the link is established, clients can access the server's files and transfer files from one computer to the other.

We'll look at how to link two computers together with Desktop Link first, then see how you can make a clone of the Norton Desktop on a remote computer. Finally, in the last part of this section, we'll look at Network Link.

Establishing a Desktop Link

Desktop Link lets you connect two computers together using either a parallel cable or a serial cable. Neither the parallel nor the serial cables are standard cables; they have to be modified or used with special adapters. See the section called "Using Desktop Link with a Null-Modem Cable" later in this chapter for more details on the serial cable.

As their names suggest, a parallel cable transfers data several bits at a time, while a serial cable transfers one data bit at a time in a sequential

Transferring files from one computer to another with Desktop Link is a lot faster and more convenient than copying files onto a set of disks, then reloading all the disks onto the other computer.

fashion. Using a parallel or serial cable usually requires that the two computers be located fairly close together, so that a reasonable amount of cable can be used. The last point about cabling is to remember that you must use the same *type* of port on both computers; you can use parallel ports or you can use serial ports, but you cannot use a parallel port on one computer and a serial port on the other.

Desktop Link can find and configure the ports on your computer automatically, choosing the best settings for the hardware that you have available on your computer. All the ports on your computer are searched in turn. Desktop Link checks the parallel ports first, because parallel ports can transfer data faster than the serial ports, and then it checks the serial ports. If you are using serial ports, Desktop Link optimizes the appropriate communications parameters. If you want to override these automatic settings or establish settings of your own, use Desktop Link from the Desktop Configure menu, as described in Chapter 9.

Making the Connection

To make a desktop link, you should first connect the two computers together using a modified cable, or a standard cable and an adapter, next set up the Desktop on the server, and then link the client to the server. Here are the steps:

1. With Norton Desktop running on the server computer, select Desktop Link from the Disk menu.

2. Choose Serve Remote Link, and then choose Desktop Link. A dialog box opens containing the message Attempting to establish connection. Please wait....

3. Go to the client PC and start the Desktop.

4. Choose the Open Window selection from the Desktop Window menu, as shown in Figure 17.12, and check the Desktop Link option button. As you check this option, the Browse command button changes into the Connect command button. Click on the Connect command button to establish the link. If a link is established, this Connect command button changes function once again—this time it becomes the Disconnect command button.

Select Desktop Link as the window type in the Open Window dialog box

5. If a desktop link is successfully established, the Open Window dialog box reappears, showing the name of the server's current drive and directory in the drive selector box.

6. Select OK to complete the connection, and open a drive window on the server's current drive.

Next, you will see a drive window containing a tree and file pane for the current drive on the server. You will see the word LINK just before the drive and directory information on the title bar of the drive window to remind you that this drive window is open on a Desktop Link drive.

This drive window works just like a regular Norton Desktop drive window with one important exception—you cannot launch any applications; if you try, the communications link will be broken automatically. When the link is established, the server displays the Connection Status dialog box, with the message Acting as server on *portn*, where *portn* is the name of the communications port in use on the server.

Now you can use normal Desktop methods on the client computer to copy, rename, or delete files on any of the server's disk drives. You can only open a single drive window on the server's drives, but you can use it to display information for any drive. Use the drive selector if you want to change to a different disk drive on the server, including the floppy-disk drives. You can open as many drive windows for drives on the client computer as you wish, and you can copy files from one to the other with ease.

Copying Files over a Desktop Link

I think it is time we looked at an example to demonstrate all this flexibility. Imagine you want to copy several files from drive E on one computer to drive C on another computer. The files are large and would fill several floppy disks, so a desktop link is the ideal solution. Here are the steps you would follow:

1. Establish a desktop link between the two computers, as we have just described.

2. If drive E is on the server computer, use the drive selector in the linked drive window to display the appropriate directory on drive E, and select the files you want to copy.

3. If drive C is on the client computer, click on the drive icon on the Desktop to open a normal drive window in the usual way.

4. Choose Copy from the Desktop File menu, and confirm that you want to copy the selected files from drive E on the server to drive C on the client computer. Click on OK to start the copy.

5. When you have finished copying the files, use the Close command from the drive window's control menu, or press Ctrl+F4 to close the drive window.

It takes a lot longer to explain all these steps than it takes to actually copy the files. If you can use Desktop drive windows for normal file copy operations, doing the same thing over a Desktop Link is a breeze. You can even use the mouse to drag and drop files from one drive window to another, just as you can using regular Norton Desktop drive windows.

Breaking the Connection

Before you terminate a Desktop Link session, you should always look at the Connection Status dialog box on the server to make sure that no one is accessing the server. To sever the connection, just choose Cancel from the Connection Status dialog box on the server computer, or close the drive window on the client computer that displays the server's files and directories.

HOW TO CLONE THE DESKTOP

NOTE NOTE *You must use a serial cable if you want to clone the Desktop; you cannot use a parallel cable.*

In the previous section we assumed that the Norton Desktop was installed on both computers, but what do you do if it is only installed on one of them? The designers of the Desktop have solved that problem too, by providing a mechanism that lets you move, or *clone*, the files needed for a desktop link to a remote computer over the desktop link itself. To save time and disk space, only the files needed to support a desktop link and a network link are transferred, rather than all the files that make up the whole Norton Desktop package. The following files are transferred:

Norton Desktop	ND.EXE
Configuration Overlay	NDEDIT.OVL
Initialization File	NORTON.INI
Menu File	LONG.NDM
Desktop Help File	ND.HLP
Norton Commander Help File	NC.HLP
Compressed File Overlay	ZIP.OVL

In the descriptions that follow, the term *local* refers to the computer that already has the Desktop package installed, and the term *remote* refers to the computer that doesn't. In other words, we will clone the Desktop from the local computer to the remote computer.

To clone the Desktop, you need:

♦ A modified serial cable, or a normal serial cable with the appropriate null-modem adapter.

♦ 2MB of free disk space on the remote computer for all the Desktop files, plus another $1/2$ MB of free space if you want to use a disk-based swap file.

♦ COM1 or COM2 must be available on the remote computer.

Follow these steps to clone the Desktop:

1. Connect the two computers using the serial cable.

2. Choose Desktop Link from the Configure menu to open the Configure Desktop Link Dialog box.

3. This dialog box has three command buttons: OK, Cancel, and Clone. Select Clone to open the Clone dialog box shown in Figure 17.13.

4. Select the option button that represents the port you want to use on the remote computer; you must use either COM1 or COM2.

Perform the next two steps on the remote computer:

5. On the remote computer, change to or create and then change to the directory you want to use for the desktop link files.

6. To use COM1 on the remote computer, type the following commands at the DOS prompt:

MODE COM1:2400,N,8,1,P
CTTY COM1:

and you will see the message Resident portion of MODE loaded. If you want to use the second serial port, just substitute COM2 for COM1 in the Mode and Ctty commands. The Mode command sets the baud rate to 2400, the parity to none, the data word length to 8 bits, and the number of stop bits at the end of the data word to 1 stop bit, and the P switch forces part of the Mode command to stay in memory. The Ctty command specifies that command input should be accepted from COM 1 rather than from the standard device of keyboard and screen.

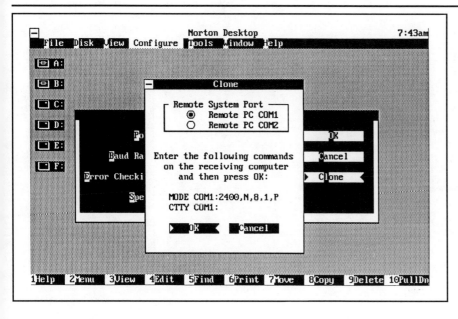

FIGURE 17.13:

Follow the instructions in the Clone dialog box to configure the remote computer's serial port

Now back to the local, or sending, computer for the next two steps:

7. Select OK in the Configure Desktop Link dialog box, and you will see the Cloning Status dialog box open. The seven files needed to support the desktop link and the network link are transferred from the local computer to the remote computer. A horizontal progress bar in this dialog box shows the percentage of the Desktop Link file transfer that has been completed. You will see the message Loading bootstrap on the remote computer as the transfer begins, and you will also see another message for each file transferred across, showing the file name, size, and percentage complete. Figure 17.14 shows a complete clone session from the point of view of the remote, or receiving, computer. The whole file-transfer process is very fast and takes only a few minutes to complete.

8. When the transfer is complete, select the Cancel command button to dismiss the Clone dialog box, and select Cancel again to close the Configure Desktop Link dialog box.

Now back to the remote computer for the last two steps:

9. On the remote computer, type **ND** and press the Enter key to start the Desktop.

10. Use the selections from the Configure menu to set up the cloned copy of the Norton Desktop.

```
D:\>MODE COM2:2400,N,8,1,P

Resident portion of MODE loaded

COM2: 2400,n,8,1,p

D:\>CTTY COM2:
Loading bootstrap
Receiving Norton Desktop (1,084,146 bytes) 100%
Receiving Configuration Overlay (202,345 bytes) 100%
Receiving Initialization File (2,691 bytes) 100%
Receiving Menu File (5,681 bytes) 100%
Receiving Desktop Help File (245,098 bytes) 100%
Receiving Commander Help File (158,689 bytes) 100%
Receiving Compressed File Overlay (253,440 bytes) 100%


D:\>
```

FIGURE 17.14:

The complete dialog for a Desktop Link Clone session shown on the remote computer

Now that you have cloned the Desktop, you can start a normal Desktop Link session, and use the regular methods of copying, renaming, or deleting files as described in an earlier section called "Copying Files with a Desktop Link."

Only the files required to support a desktop link and a network link are transferred to the remote computer, but all the usual menus appear on the cloned copy of the Desktop. Some of these will work as you expect, but others will not. Many of the selections in the Tools menu actually load other external programs, and these program files are not cloned along with the Desktop—this saves time during the transfer and saves space on the receiving computer. For example, if you try to launch UnErase from the Tools menu, you will see a dialog box containing the message Error: Cannot locate UNERASE.EXE; just click on the OK command button to dismiss this dialog box.

USING DESKTOP LINK WITH A NULL-MODEM CABLE

You can use Desktop Link with a direct physical connection, using either a serial port or a parallel port on your computer. If you plan to clone the Desktop to another computer, you must use a serial cable. Serial cables can be up to 30 or 40 feet long, without significant loss of signal quality.

Computers use an industry standard for communications over serial lines known as RS-232. This standard defines the voltages and signal characteristics for serial communication. The cable you use to connect two personal computers together for a desktop link is a special serial cable known as a *null-modem* cable. This cable has sending and receiving wires crossed over, so that the wires used for sending by one computer are used for receiving data by the other computer, and vice versa. You can make your own null-modem cable if you modify a cable as shown in Figure 17.15. Figure 17.15 shows detailed wiring information for both 9- and 25-pin serial connectors; the other wires in this 25-wire standard can be ignored.

Alternatively, you can use a normal, unmodified serial cable with a null-modem adapter. Your local computer store will be able to supply all these items. However, not all null-modem adapters are identical; you need one with the connections shown in Figure 17.15.

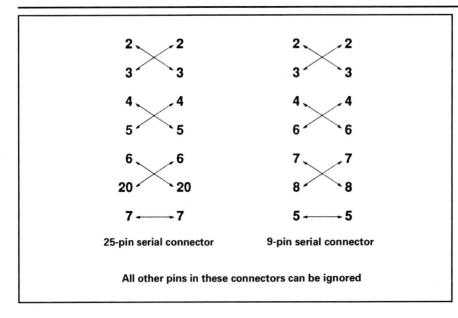

Desktop Link serial cable connections for both 9- and 25-pin connectors

25-pin serial connector

9-pin serial connector

All other pins in these connectors can be ignored

You can also use a modified parallel cable, or a parallel cable with an adapter, to establish a normal desktop link. The parallel cable used for a desktop link should not be any longer that 10 or 15 feet; a longer cable will start to suffer from significant signal loss.

ESTABLISHING A NETWORK LINK

Once you can use the Desktop Link, using the Network Link only requires a couple of additional steps. Your network must support the NetBIOS interface; Banyan Vines, Novell, LAN Manager, Lantastic, and 3COM will all work well.

For a network link, you set up your computer as a server, and then select the network user or group of users, who can access your files. These users can copy, rename, or delete any file or files on your hard disk. Here are the steps to follow to establish your computer as a server:

1. Log on to the network in the usual way.

2. Start the Norton Desktop.

3. Choose Serve Remote Link from the Desktop Disk menu, and choose Network Link. This opens the Network Link dialog box.

4. From the list box in the Network Link dialog box, select the names of the network users who may access your files. To select all logged-on users, click on the All command button; to deselect all users, click on the None command button.

5. When you have chosen the names, click on OK, and you will see the Connection Status dialog box showing the message Attempting to establish connection. Please wait.

Any of the users you selected can access files on your hard disk by following these steps to complete the second part of this process:

1. Log on to the network.

2. Launch Norton Desktop.

3. Choose the Open Window selection from the Desktop Window menu. In the Open Window dialog box, select the Network Link option button, and click on the Connect command button.

4. The Network Link Servers dialog box opens, listing the PCs that have been set up as network link servers. Choose the name of the network link server you want to access, then click on OK to dismiss this dialog box.

5. The name of the drive you wanted to access appears in the drive selector of the Open Window dialog box, just as it did for the desktop link. Click on OK to open a drive window for this drive on your Desktop.

Now you can copy, rename, or delete any file or files from this disk. Just as with the Desktop Link, you cannot start an application; if you try to start a program, the communications link will be severed immediately.

To terminate your Network session, select the Open Window option from the Window menu, and click on the Disconnect command button.

SENDING NETWORK MESSAGES

If your computer is attached to a network, you can use Network Message from the Tools menu to broadcast a message to all users logged on the network. For example, if you are the network administrator, you can use this command to tell all logged-on users that you are about to back up the file

NOTE NOTE *If your computer is not attached to a network, the Network Message command in the Tools menu is dimmed out and unavailable.*

server, so they should close their files and log off the network. Messages will be received unless:

◆ A network user has invoked a special network command to turn off the display of messages.

◆ The Trap Network Messages option in the Configure Network dialog box has been checked, and the network user is in a DOS session or has started a Norton Desktop application. In this case, the user will see your message upon returning to the Desktop.

SENDING A MESSAGE

Here are the steps to send a message:

1. Select Network Message from the Desktop Tools menu. The Network Message dialog box opens on the screen, showing your user name in the Message From line.

2. Click on the Recipients command button to open the Connected Network Users dialog box.

3. Select the appropriate file server by name from the list in the File Server drop-down list box.

4. Select the network users to whom you want to send a messsage from the list of names in the list box at the bottom of the dialog box. Either double-click on the name, or highlight the name, then press the spacebar. You can also use the All command button to select all users or the None command button to deselect all user names. If the list of user names is too long to fit into this box, use the scroll bars to move through the names. Alternatively, you can use Speed Search; just start typing a user name, and as soon as a match is found, the highlight moves to that name so you can select it.

5. Select the OK command button to close the Connected Network Users dialog box, then choose OK in the Network Message dialog box to send your message.

The network users don't even have to be using the Desktop to see your message; however, if they log off the network before receiving your message, the Desktop posts a message telling you that the message could not be delivered.

REPLYING TO A MESSAGE

When you receive a message from another network user, the text of the message appears on your screen in the Network Message dialog box. This dialog box also shows the user name of the person who sent the message, and the time and date of the message.

To reply to this message:

1. Choose the Reply command button in the Network Message dialog box. Your user name is shown on the From line, and the name of the person who sent you the message is shown on the To line.

2. To send your reply to additional users, choose the Recipients command button to select these users. As before, the All command button selects all network users as recipients, and the None command button deselects any selected users.

3. Select OK to leave the Connected Network Users dialog box, and then select OK again to send your reply.

Messages can come from two sources: other network users or the file server itself. You can reply to messages from other users, but you cannot reply to the file server.

CHAPTER 18

Working with the System Tools

This chapter concentrates on the system tools available as part of the Norton Desktop: System Information, Norton Cache, Batch Enhancer, and the Compress option from the Desktop File menu.

System Information lets you inspect a great deal of internal computer information that you normally do not see; it also compares the performance of your computer with three industry-standard computers. Norton Cache is a disk-caching program you can use to improve the performance of your disk systems, and the Batch Enhancer contains a set of useful features for improving your DOS batch-file programming. Finally, Compress, from the Desktop File menu, helps you compress your files so that they take less disk space. Let's begin with System Information.

USING SYSTEM INFORMATION

The System Information program provides a wealth of information about your computer's hardware, including disk specifications, and memory layout and usage. It calculates performance indices and can even print a detailed report of its findings. If your job entails installing, demonstrating, or troubleshooting hardware or software products on unfamiliar computers, this is the program for you. System Information can also save the average computer user a lot of time and frustration. Many application programs require users to supply hardware information during installation; however, most people do not know the details of their computer's hardware, particularly if they did not actually install it themselves. Also, some hardware can be used in different modes, which can further confuse the issue. Running System Information is a quick, efficient way to gather this information. You can run System Information from the DOS prompt or by selecting System Info from the Tools menu in the Norton Desktop. To run System Information from the DOS prompt, type:

SYSINFO

Across the top of the opening screen you will see several menu selections. You can specify one of these options directly by selecting it from the menu or by clicking on it with your mouse; you can also use the Next and Previous buttons at the bottom of the screen to cycle through all of the menu options in System Information in sequence. Use the Print button to print a particular screen or store the information in a file. Use the Cancel button to return to the main System Information screen. I will describe all of the options in System Information in the sequence you will see them if you select the Next button, starting with the System Summary screen.

SYSTEM SUMMARY

The System Summary screen, shown in Figure 18.1, details the basic configuration of your computer, listing information about your disks, memory, and other hardware systems.

Several of the other dialog boxes in System Information expand on the basic information shown in the System Summary screen. This screen contains important information that is useful to all computer users; therefore, I will describe each of the elements in detail:

◆ Computer Name: System Information retrieves the name of the computer from the system's read-only memory (ROM). For many IBM compatibles, System Information displays only a copyright notice or a general computer type rather than the actual computer name.

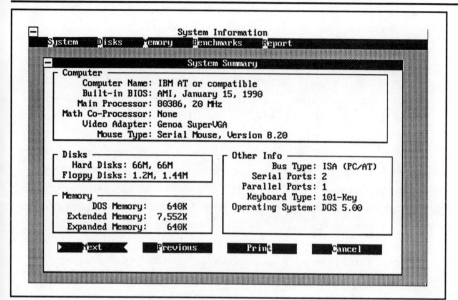

FIGURE 18.1:

The System Summary screen

◆ Built-in BIOS: This is the name of the read-only memory basic input/output system (ROM BIOS) and the date it was made. The BIOS is a layer of software that loads from ROM and lets DOS communicate with the computer's hardware. The BIOS handles the basic input and output functions in the computer.

◆ Main Processor: This is the name of the microprocessor used in your computer. The microprocessor is the computer's engine: It translates information from RAM, ROM, or the files on a disk into instructions that it can execute, and it executes them very quickly. The IBM PC, IBM PC/XT, and most compatibles use the Intel 8086 or 8088 microprocessor. The PC/AT computer and compatibles use the Intel 80286 chip. More recent machines use the Intel or AMD 80386 or the 80486 chip. The clock speed in MHz is also shown on the same line.

◆ Math Coprocessor: The Intel microprocessors used in PCs are designed so that other chips can be linked to them, thus increasing their power. One such additional chip is a math, or floating point, coprocessor. The IBM PC and most compatibles include a socket on the main motherboard for this coprocessor. Each Intel chip has a matching math coprocessor. For example, the 8087 is used with the 8086, the 80287 is used with the 80286, and the 80387 is used with the 80386. These '87s perform some of the number-crunching operations that the main microprocessors normally execute; in doing so, the coprocessors greatly increase the speed and accuracy of numeric calculations. In addition to simple add/subtract/multiply/divide operations, math coprocessors can do trigonometric calculations such as sine, cosine, and tangent. CAD applications and scientific or statistical programs usually benefit from the use of a coprocessor, whereas word processors generally do not. The speed gained by using a math coprocessor varies widely from application to application, but generally a math coprocessor performs calculations five to fifty times faster than a regular processor.

◆ Video Adapter: This is the name of the current video display adapter. Five types of video adapter boards are available: the monochrome display adapter (MDA); the color graphics adapter (CGA); the Hercules graphics adapter, which is also known as the monochrome graphics display adapter (MGDA); the enhanced graphics adapter (EGA); and the video graphics array (VGA), which was introduced with the IBM PS/2 computer in April 1987.

◆ Mouse Type: This is the name of the mouse (if one is in use) that is connected to your computer. In Figure 18.1, the example system includes a serial mouse.

◆ Hard disks: This field lists the size of your hard disks in megabytes.

◆ Floppy disks: This entry provides details about your floppy disks.

◆ DOS Memory: This is the amount of main memory present in your computer.

◆ Extended Memory and Expanded Memory: These fields show the amount of additional memory you have installed in your computer.

◆ Bus Type: This describes the type of data bus your computer uses. ISA (Industry Standard Architecture) is found in PC/XT and

PC/AT computers; EISA (Extended Industry Standard Architecture) is a new type of bus that supports 32-bit operations but retains compatibility with the original ISA; and MCA (Micro Channel Architecture) is IBM's proprietary bus for PS/2 computers.

◆ Serial Ports and Parallel Ports: These entries report the number of installed parallel and serial interface ports. DOS 3.2 and earlier supported only two serial ports, but beginning with DOS 3.3, the number increased to four. The parallel port is normally used to connect the system printer; the serial ports can connect a variety of serial devices, including a modem, a mouse, a serial printer, or a digitizer. As their names imply, the serial port can handle data one bit at a time, and the parallel port handles eight data bits at once; consequently, the data transfer rate of a parallel port is usually higher than that of a serial port. The serial port, however, is more flexible and can be configured to work with a variety of devices.

◆ Keyboard Type: This lists either a standard 84-key or an extended 101-key keyboard.

◆ Operating System: This is the version of DOS being run on the computer.

Video Summary

Choose Video Summary from the System menu, or click on the Next button to display the Video Summary screen, as shown in Figure 18.2.

All video systems except the MDA can be programmed with different parameters. This enables you to select from several different video modes. Each video mode is characterized by the resolution (the number of pixels displayed horizontally and vertically) and by the number of different colors that can be displayed at the same time. CGA video modes include 80-column-by-25-line mode and 40-column-by-25-line mode. The EGA can support as many as 43 lines of text; the VGA can support as many as 50 lines of text. The amount of video memory needed to support these different display adapters varies in each case.

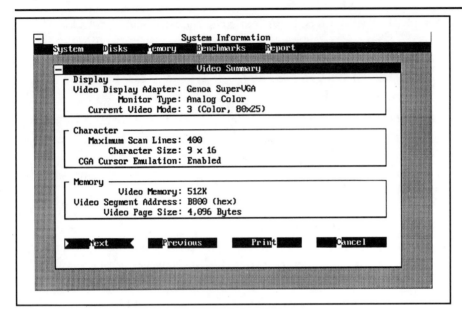

HARDWARE INTERRUPTS

Before I discuss the information in the next two screens, Hardware Interrupts and Software Interrupts, let's briefly examine what interrupts are and how they work.

Often, after you have given the computer a task to perform, you will need it to respond quickly to a new request; for example, to begin a new task at the press of a key or the click of a mouse. The mechanism that accomplishes this is known as an *interrupt*. An interrupt is an "event" that causes the processor to suspend its current activity, save its place, and look up an *interrupt vector* in the *interrupt vector table*. The interrupt vector tells the processor the address of the *interrupt handler*, or service routine, that it should branch to. After the service routine performs its task, control is returned to the suspended process. DOS interrupts are often divided into three types: internal hardware, external hardware, and software interrupts. The Intel 80x 86 family of processors supports 256 prioritized interrupts, of which the first 64 are reserved for use by the system hardware or by DOS itself.

In the PC, the main processor does not accept interrupts from hardware devices directly; instead interrupts are routed to an Intel 8259A Programmable Interrupt Controller (PIC) chip. This chip responds to each hardware interrupt, assigns a priority, and forwards it to the main processor. Each hardware device is hard-wired, or "jumpered," into inputs known as IRQs or *interrupt requests,* and this is why you see an IRQ assigned to an interrupt.

A hardware interrupt is generated by a device such as the keyboard, the computer clock, or one of the parallel or serial ports on the computer. To see a list of the IRQs on your computer, select Hardware Interrupts from the System menu. Your display will look similar to Figure 18.3.

At the left of the screen is the list of IRQs, followed by their hex addresses. The hardware devices that need the most attention have lower IRQs, so the system timer has IRQ 00, the keyboard has IRQ 01, and so on up the list. The name of the owner of the interrupt is displayed at the right.

If you have a PC or a PC/XT (or clone) computer, you have one 8259A chip, and you will see eight IRQs in the display, numbered from zero to seven.

If you have a PC/AT (or clone) or a Micro Channel PS/2 computer, you have two programmable interrupt controllers tied together. That is, interrupt two on one of the interrupt controllers accepts its input from the other 8259A chip. This generates a total of 15 interrupts, with interrupt two usually described as the *cascade.*

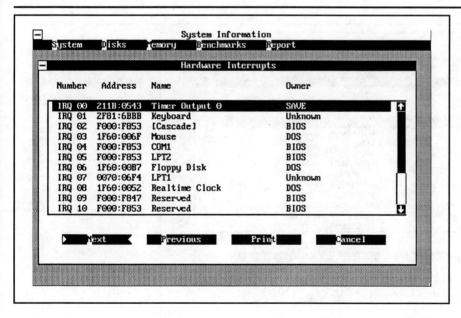

FIGURE 18.3:

The Hardware Interrupts screen

The Model 25 and 30, like the PC and the PC/XT have a total of eight interrupts, but they are shared. Interrupt one, assigned to the keyboard in PC-type computers, is shared by the keyboard, the mouse, and the time-of-day clock on the Model 25 and 30.

SOFTWARE INTERRUPTS

All interrupts on the PC are channeled through a common internal vector table called the *interrupt vector table,* regardless of whether the interrupt is generated as an external or an internal hardware interrupt, or as a software interrupt. The entry into this table for hardware devices is directly related to the IRQ number. To find the address of the interrupt handling routine for a hardware interrupt in the interrupt vector table, add eight to the IRQ number.

Select Software Interrupts from the System menu to see a list of all the entries in the interrupt vector table on your computer. Figure 18.4 shows a sample display for an 80386 computer.

Many of the software interrupts perform more than one single service. For example, interrupt 21H is the main entry point for DOS services and offers the programmer more than 100 different *function calls,* including character input and output, file creation, file reading and writing, and file deletion.

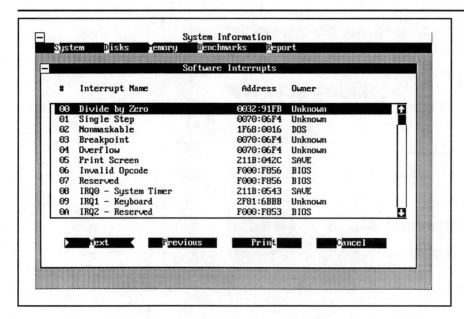

FIGURE 18.4:

The Software Interrupts screen lists the entries in the interrupt vector table

CMOS VALUES

Computers that were made after the PC/AT use a portion of Complementary Metal Oxide Semiconductor memory (usually abbreviated as CMOS) to hold basic configuration information for the computer. This CMOS memory requires such low power levels that it can be maintained by a small battery; therefore, this information is not lost when you turn off the power at the end of your session. To examine the information held in CMOS, select CMOS Status from the System menu in System Information. Figure 18.5 shows a typical example from an 80386 computer.

One of the most crucial pieces of information on this screen is the hard-disk type number shown in the Hard Disks box at the upper left of the screen. In Figure 18.5 the disk type number for the first, or primary, hard-disk drive is 1. The BIOS in your computer can read many types of hard disk from different manufacturers; this hard-disk type number is the code that tells the BIOS how many heads and cylinders your specific disk drive has. If your computer's battery loses power, the contents of CMOS memory will be lost, and you will not be able to boot up your computer from the hard disk until you replace the battery and reset this number. With some computers

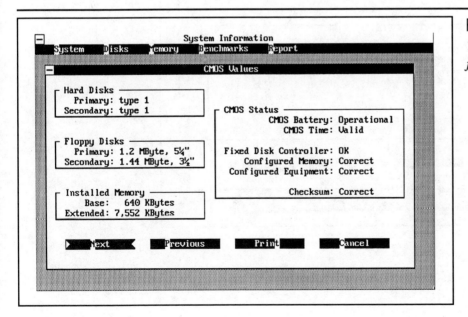

FIGURE 18.5:

Typical CMOS values from an 80386 computer

you must use the "setup" disk that came with your computer to reset the number; other computers have the setup routines built into the ROM BIOS itself.

Use Disk Tools, described in Chapter 13, to store your CMOS information in a disk file.

The rest of this screen displays details about your floppy-disk types and installed memory, and includes additional information that is contained in CMOS. Click on the Print button to make a hard copy of the CMOS Status screen. Keep the report in a safe place so that you can reenter these values if your computer battery fails.

DISK SUMMARY

Select Disk Summary from the Disks menu to see a single-screen listing of all the disks on your computer, as shown in Figure 18.6.

In Figure 18.6, drive A is a 5¼-inch floppy disk and drive B is a 3½-inch floppy disk. Drives C, D, E, and F are four partitions on two 65MB drives. The remaining drive letters are shown to be available.

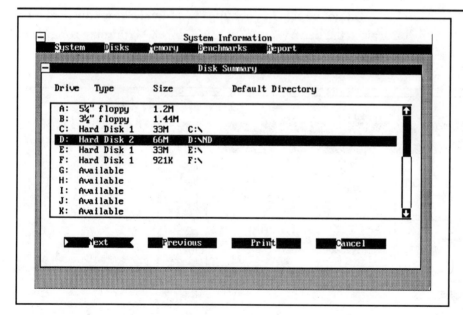

FIGURE 18.6:

The Disk Summary screen lists the disks on your computer system

DISK CHARACTERISTICS

Choose Disk Characteristics from the Disks menu to see more detailed information about the disk drives on your computer. Figure 18.7 shows the Disk Characteristics screen for the same system depicted in the previous figure.

Use the selection bar at the right side of the screen to choose the drive you want to examine. Figure 18.7 shows information for drive C, a 33MB partition on a 65MB disk. The display is divided into two main sections: Logical Characteristics and Physical Characteristics.

The Logical Characteristics box contains information about the layout of the disk from the DOS viewpoint, including the number of bytes per sector, the number of sectors per cluster, the total number of clusters, the number and type of the file allocation table (FAT), and the media descriptor byte. It also includes details of the starting location and size of the FAT, root directory, and the data area. If you are using a RAM disk, notice that it contains only one copy of the FAT.

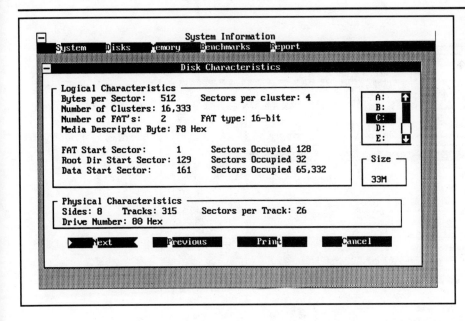

FIGURE 18.7:

Disk Characteristics screen gives more detailed disk information

The Physical Characteristics box provides details about the actual disk hardware, including the number of disk sides and tracks, and the number of sectors per track. If you examine a RAM disk with this option, the Physical Characteristics box contains the message No physical information.

PARTITION TABLES

Select Partition Tables from the Disks menu to display the partition table information for your computer, as shown in Figure 18.8.

Figure 18.8 provides details about all three partitions on the example 65MB hard disk, including starting and ending side, track, and sector numbers. Note that partition number 1 is the partition from which the disk boots up. Individual partition details are given at the bottom of the screen. In this example, the first partition is located on hard disk number 1, which has 8 sides, or heads, and 639 tracks configured with 26 sectors per track.

If you reconfigure your system after a hard-disk repair or replacement, you can use the values from this screen to rebuild your disk system.

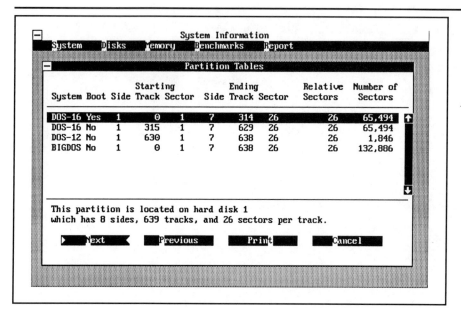

FIGURE 18.8:

The Partition Tables display screen gives details of all three partitions on this 65MB hard disk

MEMORY SUMMARY

To see a one-screen synopsis of the memory available in your computer, select Memory Usage Summary from the Memory menu. Your display will be similar to the one shown in Figure 18.9.

DOS reports how much memory it can access, the amount of memory being used by DOS and any terminate-and-stay-resident (TSR) programs you have loaded, and the remaining memory available for use by your application program(s). System Information doesn't merely take DOS's word for the amount of memory present in the computer; it goes out and checks for itself. The second part of the screen, titled Overall, lists the memory that System Information actually found in your computer. Some computers might lock up and report a memory parity error when System Information makes its memory check. This does not harm your computer, although you must reboot to recover. You can bypass this memory test if you start System Information from the DOS command line by typing:

SYSINFO /N

Finally, any ROM BIOS extensions that System Information finds are listed separately. The ROM chips that contain these extensions do not have

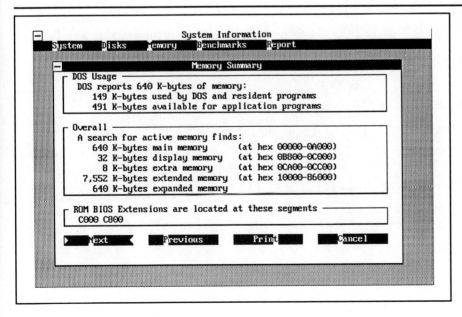

FIGURE 18.9:

The Memory Summary screen for an 80386 computer with 8MB of memory

to be on the motherboard; they also can be on expansion boards plugged into the bus. The ROM BIOS extensions needed to run these accessories are loaded automatically when you boot up the computer. The only constraint is that no two extensions can occupy the same memory area. That is why most add-on boards include jumpers or switches that let you alter their configurations—so you can reassign the addresses used by their BIOS extensions.

EXPANDED MEMORY

Expanded memory is system memory above 1MB based on the Expanded Memory Specification developed by Lotus, Intel, and Microsoft (LIM EMS). There are two major versions of the specification, 3.2 and 4.0, and they determine how programs interact with this memory. An installable device driver called the Expanded Memory Manager organizes this memory.

The Expanded Memory window (see Figure 18.10) displays memory usage, and shows the version number of the Expanded Memory Manager (EMM) in use on your system. The EMM maps 16K pages or blocks of memory (standard pages are 16K, raw pages can be multiples of 16K) from expanded memory into reserved areas called *page frames* in an accessible memory area that the application program can reach. When a block of memory is allocated, the application program receives a handle to (or the address of) the block. System Information can find these handles and display information associated with them, including the number of pages associated with the handle and the owner of the block. System Information also lists the number of total and free handles, raw pages, and standard pages.

EXTENDED MEMORY

Extended memory is system memory above 1MB, available in 286 or later computers, based on the Extended Memory Specification (XMS) developed by Lotus, Microsoft, Intel, and AST Research. This memory is not managed by DOS, but by an installable device driver called HIMEM.SYS when provided by Microsoft, QEMM386.SYS when provided by Quarterdeck Office Systems, or 386MAX.SYS when supplied by Qualitas. You must have this memory and one of these device drivers loaded onto your system to use the Extended Memory entry in the Memory menu, otherwise the entry is grayed out.

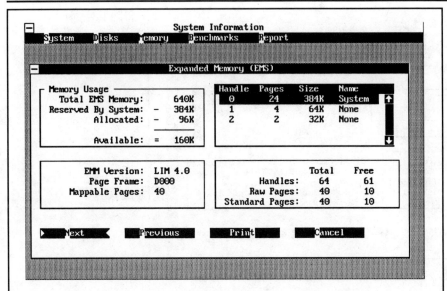

FIGURE 18.10:

The Expanded Memory window

The Extended Memory window in Figure 18.11 shows memory usage on your computer and gives details of the device driver, including version number and revision level. The A20 line is an address line in your computer that gives it access to the high memory area. As with expanded memory, the application receives a handle to the block of extended memory, and System Information can display information associated with that handle.

System Information can also display information on Upper Memory Blocks (UMBs) if you are using DOS 5 on a 386 or 486 computer. Most computers have 384K of memory space immediately adjacent to the 640K of conventional memory. This area is not usually available to programs, because it is used for system and video information. Parts of this area, however, are not used, and these gaps are known as the Upper Memory Blocks. DOS 5 on a 386 or 486 computer with extended memory can map device drivers and certain memory-resident programs into these UMBs where they can run successfully. This leaves more conventional memory available for running your application programs.

The latest versions of extended memory managers such as QEMM386 can support both extended and expanded memory, providing whatever kind

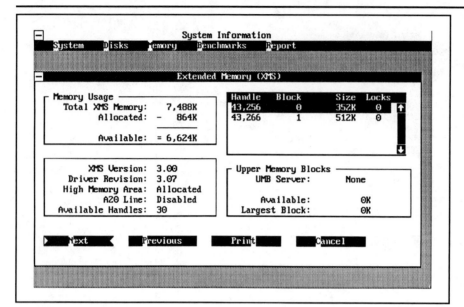

FIGURE 18.11:

The Extended Memory screen

of memory your application program requests; this obviously represents the best of both worlds.

DOS MEMORY BLOCKS

Select Memory Block List to examine how the memory in your computer is being used. The DOS Memory Blocks screen is shown in Figure 18.12.

At the left of the screen is a list of hex addresses used by your programs. The size in bytes is given next and is followed by the name of the owner, which could be, for example, the DOS system area or COMMAND.COM. Finally, the right column specifies the type of the memory block—either data, program, free memory, or environment. The *environment* is a section of memory used primarily to store the settings of the variables for the DOS PATH, SET, and PROMPT commands. When DOS loads a program, it gives the program a copy of the environment. The program may modify its copy of the environment, but this will not affect the original settings maintained by the command processor. Any program that remains resident in memory retains its copy of the environment; however, this copy is not updated by any subsequent commands that alter DOS's copy of the environment.

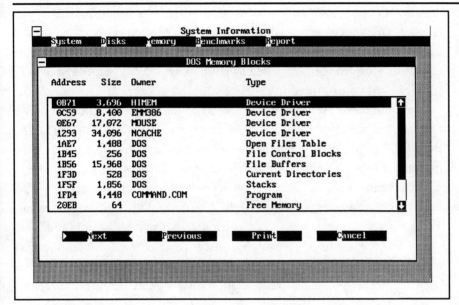

FIGURE 18.12:
Memory Block List
shows you how the
memory in your
computer is being used

TSR PROGRAMS

One of the main limitations of DOS is that it cannot support more than one program running at one time. DOS is a single-user, single-tasking operating system. The *terminate-and-stay-resident* (TSR) program is an ingenious method that partially overcomes this limitation.

After you load a TSR program into memory, it returns control to DOS but waits in the background. When you press a certain key combination (the *hotkey*), the TSR interrupts the application program you were running and executes its own services. When you finish using the TSR program and exit, control returns to your application program again.

Other memory-resident programs work in a slightly different way: they attach themselves to the operating system and remain in memory, working constantly in the background. The DOS PRINT utility is an example of this; indeed, PRINT is often called the first real memory-resident program.

Because DOS interrupts are always channeled through the same interrupt vector table, it is relatively easy for a TSR program to alter these vectors to change the way the interrupts work. For example, virtually all programs read the keyboard through interrupt 16H, which normally points to a service routine in the BIOS. It is a simple matter for a program to change the response of the system to keyboard-read requests by rerouting this vector through an alternative procedure. These replaced vectors are called *hooked* vectors. If you choose TSR Programs from the Memory menu, you can list all of the TSR programs installed in your computer. You can see several of these hooked vectors listed in Figure 18.13.

As you move the highlight up and down the list of TSR programs, System Information displays additional information if it is available, including the path, the command-line arguments used to load the program, and the number of Memory Allocation Blocks the program uses.

You can switch between the Memory Summary display and the TSR Programs display to evaluate the effects of loading additional TSR programs. The amount of memory in your computer is fixed, so as you add TSR programs, the amount of memory space available for your application programs decreases. At some point you may find that you cannot open a large spreadsheet or use a large application program because there is no longer sufficient room. You must then decide if the utility of your TSRs is worth the memory space that they occupy; try to strike the right balance for the way you work.

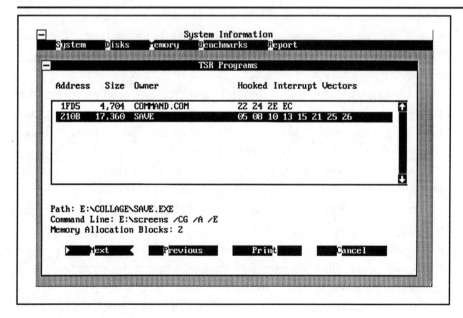

FIGURE 18.13:

System Information's TSR Programs screen lists program names and hooked vectors

DEVICE DRIVERS

A *device driver* is a special program that manipulates one specific piece of hardware. DOS uses device drivers as extensions to the operating system. Some device drivers are actually part of DOS; these are called *built-in device drivers*. Others exist as separate files and are called *loadable device drivers*. These drivers free DOS from having to include code for every single piece of hardware that can be attached to a computer. As long as there is a device driver supplied with hardware, you can use it on your computer. When you want to use a new piece of hardware, just connect it to your system, copy the device driver into a directory on your boot disk, and add a statement to your CONFIG.SYS or AUTOEXEC.BAT file to load the device driver at boot-up time. Loadable device drivers also reduce memory requirements; you only have to load the device drivers that you need for your specific hardware configuration.

For example, if you want to use the Norton Batch Enhancer to full advantage, you must add a line to your CONFIG.SYS file to load the ANSI.SYS device driver. This device driver alters the way that DOS handles the keyboard and screen, often called the *console*. Also, even if you plug a mouse into a serial port, DOS does not know about the device until you add the device driver, often called MOUSE.SYS, into your configuration file.

Select Device Drivers from the Memory menu to display a list of the device drivers in use on your system. Your screen will look similar to the one shown in Figure 18.14.

In Figure 18.14, you can see the loadable device driver called MS$MOUSE. Notice also the built-in drivers for the keyboard, screen, and serial and parallel ports.

CPU SPEED

Select CPU Speed from the Benchmarks menu to display a CPU Speed screen similar to the one in Figure 18.15.

The Computing Index is a measure of your computer's CPU or disk-independent computing power. A basic IBM PC/XT running an 8088 at 4.77MHz has a computing index equal to 1, an IBM PC/AT running an 80286 at 8MHz has a computing index of 4.4, and a Compaq 386 running an 80386 at 33MHz has a computing index of 34.7. In other words, the

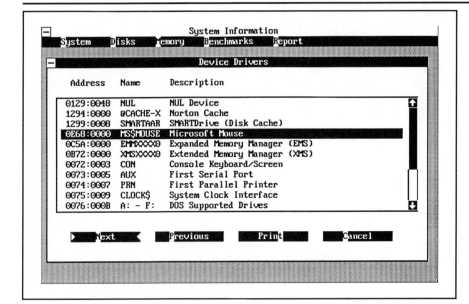

Loadable device drivers,
such as MOUSE.SYS,
are shown in this display

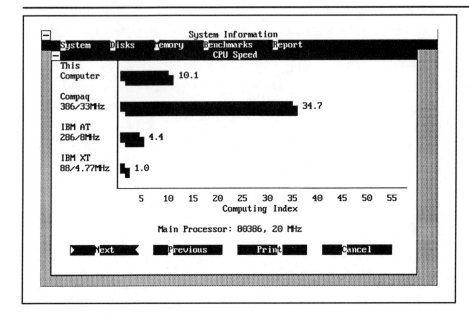

The CPU Speed
screen compares the
performance of your
computer with that of
three industry-standard
computers

Compaq 386 runs the System Information computing index tests 34.7 times faster than the original IBM PC/XT.

The computing index is calculated constantly, so you can immediately see the effect that something as simple as moving the mouse has on the computing index. The type of processor in your computer and its speed in MHz is shown directly under the graph. If your computer has a "turbo" button, press it to see what effect changing the speed has on your computing index.

DISK SPEED

To evaluate the speed of your hard disk against other industry standards, select Hard Disk Speed from the Benchmarks menu. The Disk Index is the second System Information calculated index, intended this time to let you rate your hard disk's performance against the same three industry-standard computers used in the previous test. Figure 18.16 shows the screen that reports the results of the Disk Index tests. A disk cache program such as Norton Cache, described later in this chapter, will increase your disk's speed. For this benchmark calculation, however, if Norton Cache is loaded on your system, System Information turns it off to give a truer evaluation of the performance

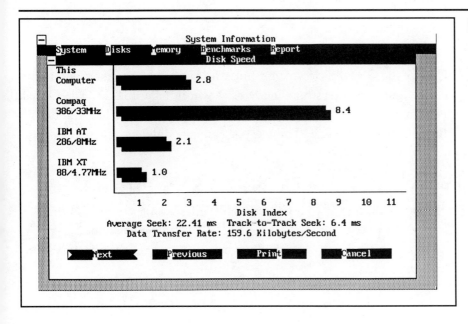

FIGURE 18.16:

The Hard Disk Speed Benchmark calculates the Disk Index

of your hardware. As soon as the test is complete, Norton Cache is turned on again.

Under the bar graph, the program displays several statistics for your hard disk, including the Average Seek time and the Track-to-Track seek or access time (both in milliseconds), and the Data Transfer Rate (in kilobytes per second).

The *average seek time* is the average length of time the disk takes to access a random piece of data, based on a large number of disk accesses. Actual access times range from less than 15 milliseconds to as long as 150 milliseconds. *Track-to-track access time* is the length of time the disk takes to move from one track to the adjacent track. Both these measurements are determined by hard-disk design and construction, specifically in the type of head used and the number of platters in the disk. This is not the complete story of disk speed, however. The disk does not work in isolation; it also must work with the disk controller and the software controlling the drive.

A more complete measurement of system performance is the *data transfer rate* —the rate at which data is read from the disk and passes through the disk controller card to the computer itself. This measurement encompasses raw disk speed, the effectiveness of the disk interface, and the computer data bus speed. After all, the performance of a fast disk might be bogged down by a slow controller or data bus.

OVERALL PERFORMANCE INDEX

Choose the Overall Performance Index from the Benchmarks menu to calculate your computer's final index, as shown in Figure 18.17. The Overall Performance Index is the integration of the Computing Index and Disk Index into a single value. This lets you compare different systems easily.

DISPLAYING YOUR CONFIG.SYS FILE

To display a listing of your CONFIG.SYS file, choose View CONFIG.SYS from the Report menu. The contents of the file are shown on the screen. Use the cursor control keys to scroll through the listing, or click on the scroll bars with the mouse.

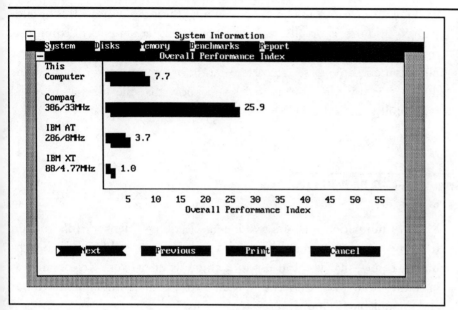

FIGURE 18.17:

*The Overall
Performance Index
benchmark display*

DISPLAYING YOUR AUTOEXEC.BAT FILE

To display a listing of your AUTOEXEC.BAT, choose file View AUTOEXEC.BAT from the Report menu. Again, the contents of the file are displayed on the screen. Use the cursor control keys to scroll the listing, or click on the scroll bars with the mouse.

PRINT REPORT

The last selection in the Report menu is Print Report. Choosing this selection displays the dialog box shown in Figure 18.18. This screen lets you configure the System Information report to your requirements. Use the Tab key or the arrow keys to move through the items on the display. To turn an option on or off, press the X key or the spacebar, or click on the option with the mouse. After you have completed your choice of the report options, click on the Printer button to send the report to your printer, or choose File to send the report to a file. The default file name is SIREPORT.TXT, but the program lets you change this name. This file is created in the directory where you started System Information. You can also enter a line of text into the Report Header screen for inclusion at the top of the report file. If you are working on a customer's computer, you might want to indicate this by adding text into the report file. Similarly, you can enter ten lines of comments that will be printed at the end of the report. For example, you could use these notes as the record of a service visit. After the program saves the report to the disk, a small window opens to let you know that the file was recorded successfully.

USING SYSTEM INFORMATION ON A NETWORK

System Information includes two menu selections—Network Information from the System menu and Network Performance Speed from the Benchmarks menu—that you can use to examine your network. If you are not operating from a Novell network, these two selections will be dimmed out and unavailable from their respective menus.

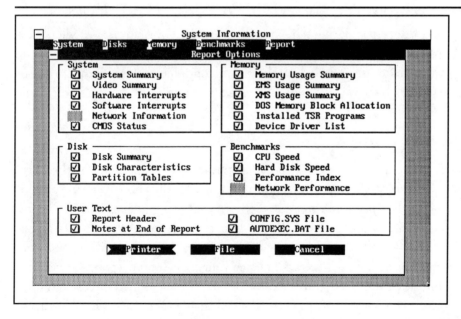

FIGURE 18.18:

The Report Options dialog box lets you select the System Information elements you want to be included in your printed report

NETWORK INFORMATION

The Network Information selection from the System menu summarizes network information. The user name and network identification number are displayed with the login date and time. The file server name and details about the version and date of the Novell network software are also shown.

NETWORK PERFORMANCE SPEED

The Network Performance Speed selection from the Benchmarks menu, tests the speed of the network in terms of disk reads and disk writes. The Network Drive Benchmark screen depicts the relative speed of reads and writes for the system as a bar graph that indicates the average throughput in kilobytes per second.

IMPROVING COMPUTER PERFORMANCE WITH NORTON CACHE

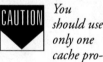

You should use only one cache program at a time.

When your application program needs data from the disk, it asks DOS to find it. DOS reads the data and passes it to the application program. If you are updating your database, for example, this can mean that the same data is requested and read many times during the update. A *disk cache* program mediates between the application and the hard-disk controller. Now, when the application program requests data that is on the disk, the cache program first checks to see if the data is already in the cache memory. If it is, the disk cache program loads the data from the cache memory rather than from the hard disk. If the data is not in memory, the cache program reads the data from the disk, copies it into the cache memory for future reference, and then passes the data to the application program. Figure 18.19 shows how a disk cache program works.

If you primarily work with programs such as word processors that do not read data from the hard disk often, you will see a modest speed increase from the disk cache; however, if you use a database or a language compiler that continually reads the disk, you will see a startling increase in speed. Because a database program often needs to read the same file (such as an index) many times during an update, chances are good that the data is already in

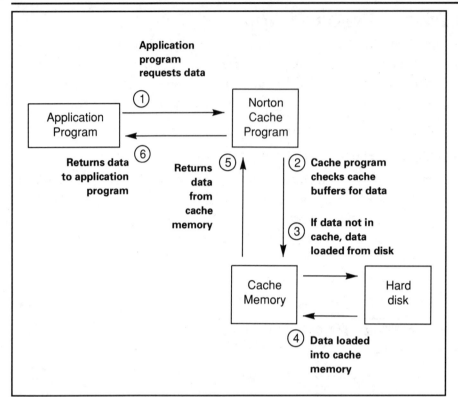

FIGURE 18.19:

The disk cache program mediates between your application program and the hard-disk controller

the cache. If your system includes extended or expanded memory, the cache program can locate its cache buffer in extended or expanded memory, thus using only a small amount of conventional memory for the program that controls the cache. A disk cache program can let DOS read and write to a floppy disk 50 times faster and can make hard-disk access 10 times faster.

Because computer users constantly face choices between increasing speed and using more memory, the Norton Desktop provides a very flexible disk-caching program. You can install the Norton Cache using the default settings or you can tailor the cache to your exact requirements. To decide how to do this, you must first examine both your computer hardware and the way in which you use your computer.

LOADING NORTON CACHE

If you use Stacker's SSWAP, or any other program that lets you swap drive letters, make sure all swapping is complete before installing Norton Cache. If you swap drive letters after installing Norton Cache, data may be written to the wrong disk and overwrite existing information.

You can load the Norton Cache program during your initial installation of the Norton Desktop, or you can make the installation yourself. Start NDConfig, select the Select Startup Programs command button, choose the Norton Cache option, and you will see the configuration screen shown in Figure 18.20.

Your configuration options in this window are as follows:

◆ **Loading.** You can load Norton Cache using either CONFIG.SYS or AUTOEXEC.BAT (but not both), or you can choose not to load it at all. Using CONFIG.SYS makes the most sense, because a disk cache program is usually a permanent addition to your system. The only advantage to loading Norton Cache with AUTO-EXEC.BAT is that you can remove it from memory without rebooting your computer. To achieve this, Norton Cache must be loaded as the last terminate-and-stay-resident program.

◆ **High Memory.** Choose whether the cache is loaded into conventional memory below 640K or into high memory. If you have extended or expanded memory available on your system, you should use it for the cache rather than conventional, or low, memory.

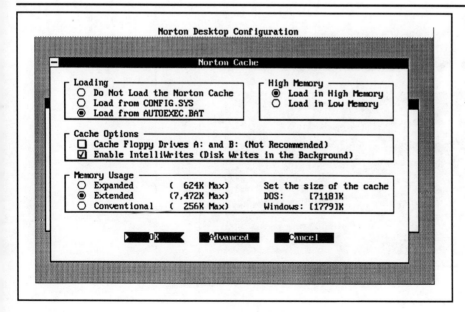

FIGURE 18.20:

The Norton Cache window in the Norton Desktop Configuration program

◆ **Cache Options.** You can use the Norton Cache program to cache drives A and B if you have them, but since floppy-disk drives are so slow, there is little advantage in caching them. Check the Enable IntelliWrites box if you want Norton Cache to delay writes to your disk until the write-back buffer is full. Using IntelliWrites usually minimizes disk-head movement and increases the amount of data written to the disk at any given time.

◆ **Memory Usage.** Choose the amount of memory as well as the type of memory you want to use for the cache from this part of the screen. You can also make adjustments if you run Windows. The maximum values for your system are shown at the right side of this window.

Make your selections in this window, then click on Advanced to open the window shown in Figure 18.21.

This screen controls some of the more advanced Norton Cache configuration options, as follows:

◆ **Buffering.** The Buffering options allow you to configure the Norton Cache to your own requirements. The read-ahead buffer determines the maximum amount of data that may be read ahead

Caching floppy disks is not recommended, but if you do cache them and use IntelliWrites, remember to wait for the delayed write operation to finish before you remove the disk from the drive, otherwise you may lose data.

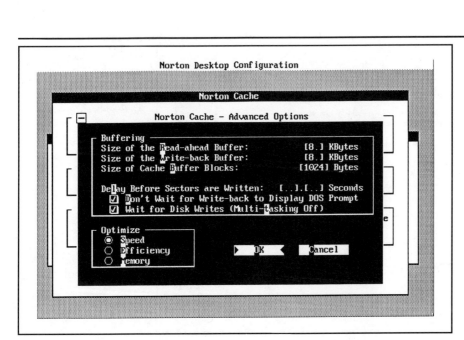

FIGURE 18.21:

The Norton Cache Advanced Options window

TIP ▼ *Install Norton Cache before you start Windows. If you run Windows in 386 enhanced mode with IntelliWrites turned on, you may need to edit the following line in the [386Enh] section of SYSTEM.INI: VirtualHDirq=OFF. The Windows default is On for AT-compatible computers and Off for other computers.*

on a cached drive. Set the size of the read-ahead buffer to a value between 8K and 64K; the default is 8K. A value of zero disables the read-ahead buffer. Next set the size of the write-back buffer. This is the amount of data that will be written to your hard disk at a time. Again, specify a value between 8K and 64K; a value of zero disables write-back IntelliWrites. Set the size of the cache buffer blocks to either 512, 1,024, 2,048, 4,096, or 8,192 bytes. Larger blocks allow the cache table to be smaller, and smaller blocks mean that the cache buffer is used more efficiently. The Delay setting tells Norton Cache to defer disk writes for this period of time, in seconds and decimal seconds, for each disk cached with IntelliWrites. The last setting tells Norton Cache whether or not to wait for the write-back to finish before displaying the DOS prompt again.

◆ **Optimize.** Choose whether you want to optimize your cache for speed, efficiency, or memory usage. This selection is discussed in detail in the section called "Optimizing Your Cache" later in this chapter.

TIP ▼ *If your AUTOEXE C.BAT file contains a BUFFERS statement, set BUFFERS to a number between 3 and 10. If the file does not contain a BUFFERS statement, now is a good time to add one.*

When you have finished with this window, select OK to return to the Norton Cache window, and OK again to move on to a display of either CONFIG.SYS or AUTOEXEC.BAT, depending on how you chose to load the Norton Cache program. Use the Move command button to move the line that loads Norton Cache to the optimum location in the file, then click on Save to store the changes. Finally, you return to the Norton Configuration main window, where you can select Quit and return to DOS. If you made changes to CONFIG.SYS or to AUTOEXEC.BAT, remember to reboot your computer to have those changes take effect.

UNDERSTANDING THE CACHE REPORT

After you have been using the Norton Cache for some time on your system, use the /REPORT switch to see the screen shown in Figure 18.22. The top portion of the screen shows how the memory in your computer is being used by the cache and the cache management program. The next line, Total Cache Size, shows you the size of your cache and how much of it is being used. If you have only recently started to use the cache, it may be less than full.

Next comes a listing of all the configurable cache program options and their current settings; below this is a list of all the drives on your system, showing how each is configured as far as the cache is concerned. A plus sign in this part of the display indicates that an option is on for that drive, while a minus sign shows that it is off. In Figure 18.22, neither drive A nor drive B is being cached, as the minus signs in the column headed A indicate. The columns in this part of the display are as follows:

A   caching is enabled for this drive

C   cache additional sectors for this drive

I   IntelliWrites are enabled for this drive

W   write-through caching is enabled for this drive

P   write protection is applied to this drive

R   size of the read-ahead buffer, in kilobytes. The D character indicates that the read-ahead is dynamic and will take place when contiguous sectors are being read but will not take place when more random reads are taking place

FIGURE 18.22:

The Norton Cache Report screen

```
Norton Cache, Norton Utilities 6 with Norton Desktop 1.00
Copyright 1992 by Symantec Corporation

    Conventional memory:        0K cache    33K management    491K free
    High DOS memory:            0K cache     0K management      0K free
    Expanded (EMS) memory:      0K cache     0K management    160K free
    Extended (XMS) memory:    512K cache      8K management   6624K free

      Total cache size is 512.0K - Currently using 330.0K  (64.4%)

DOS = 0K                BLOCK = 8192    USEHIGH  = ON     DELAY = 1.00
EXP = 0K, 0K            READ  = 8K      USEHMA   = ON     QUICK = ON
EXT = 512K, 0K          WRITE = 13K     OPTIMIZE = SPEED  MULTI = OFF

        A   C   I   W   P     R      G     Cache Hits / Disk Reads
   A:   -   +   -   +   -     D8    128          0 / 0          (0.0%)
   B:   -   +   -   +   -     D8    128          0 / 0          (0.0%)
   C:   +   +   +   +   -     D8    128         44 / 286       (15.3%)
   D:   +   +   +   +   -     D8    128         66 / 884        (7.4%)
   E:   +   +   +   +   -     D8    128         82 / 318       (25.7%)
   F:   +   +   +   +   -     D8    128          0 / 1          (0.0%)

C:\>
```

G   indicates that Norton Cache will not allow sector group reads of larger than this value to take place. The default is 128 sectors

The Cache Hits/Disk Reads part of this display shows how many sectors (not files) have been read from the cache rather than from the disk, and how many have been read directly from the disk. The higher these percentage numbers, the more efficiently the cache is performing. Remember that because all the data must originally be read from the disk, it is unlikely that you will ever see a value of 100%.

OPTIMIZING YOUR CACHE

One of the options for Norton Cache is the Optimize setting I described in the previous section; you must choose to optimize for either speed, efficiency, or memory usage. Optimize attempts to balance the different needs of performance against memory use by changing the cache configuration, depending on the selection you make. You can also use the /OPTIMIZE switch from inside CONFIG.SYS or AUTOEXEC.BAT and achieve the same effect. The default configurations for each of the cache options are as follows.

Speed

CAUTION

Do not use the DOS FASTOPEN command with the Norton Cache program. Norton Cache is faster and more efficient than FASTOPEN.

If you choose to optimize the Norton Cache for speed, add the command-line switch

/OPTIMIZE = S

to your installation file, and the following default cache settings will be used:

Read-ahead buffer	8K
IntelliWrite write-back buffer	the size of the largest track, in K, of all cached disks
Delay	1 second
Block	8,192 bytes

Efficiency

If you want to optimize your cache for efficiency, use

/OPTIMIZE = E

and the following default cache settings will be used:

Read-ahead buffer	8K
IntelliWrite write-back buffer	8K
Delay	1 second
Block	the smallest block size for the specified cache size, usually 512 to 1,024 bytes

Memory

If you want to optimize your cache for memory, use:

/OPTIMIZE = M

and the following default cache settings will be used:

Read-ahead buffer	0, to disable read-ahead
IntelliWrite write-back buffer	0, to disable IntelliWrites
Delay	0, to disable deferred writes
Block	8,192 bytes

You can, of course, change any of these settings if you wish by using the other command-line switches. These switches are listed in Chapter 19.

RECONFIGURING YOUR CACHE

Once you have installed the Norton Cache program, there are several reconfigure switches you can use to change the cache configuration without having to reboot your computer.

If you loaded Norton Cache as the last memory-resident program using AUTOEXEC.BAT, you can remove it from memory cache if you type

NCACHE2 /UNINSTALL

from the DOS prompt.

To reset the cache, use /RESET. This command completely resets the cache, flushing all data for all drives and completing any pending Intelli-Writes. This command is the best method of resetting the cache. However, if you do not want a global reset but just want to reset one drive, use the /F or flush command with the appropriate drive letter.

If you want to change the delay setting for IntelliWrites, use /DELAY=*ss.hh,* where *ss* represents seconds and *hh* represents hundredths of seconds.

You can also use the drive switches as part of your initial configuration on startup or as command-line switches after the cache program is running. Add a plus sign just before the switch letter to turn the option on or a minus sign to turn the option off. For example, use /+I to turn IntelliWrites on for a drive, and use /−I to turn them off. You can use the following drive switches:

A	enable caching for this drive
C	cache additional sectors for this drive
I	enable IntelliWrites for this drive
W	enable write-through caching for this drive
P	write protect this drive
R	set the size of the read-ahead buffer, in kilobytes
G	prevents Norton Cache from allowing sector group reads of larger than a specified value to take place

When you have made all your changes, use the command-line /SAVE option to save the current settings into the NCACHE.INI file, so that the same settings will be used next time you start your computer.

AUTOMATING OPERATIONS WITH BATCH FILES

Batch-file programming, which can automate many of your daily computer tasks, is a powerful tool that you may find indispensable after you know how to use it. *Batch,* a term that originated with mainframe computers, signifies a series of commands contained in a file that are invoked by running the file. In a DOS batch file, you can include any of the DOS internal and external commands, exactly as you would if you were using them at the command prompt. Batch files can also accomplish more complex tasks if they include elements of the DOS batch-programming language. This limited language allows for looping, conditional branching, prompting the user for input, and pausing.

The main advantages of batch files are:

◆ Batch files can speed up your work by automating complex or repetitive tasks. With a batch file, you only have to remember one command, instead of many.

◆ Batch files help customize DOS to your needs. You can create a batch file that performs exactly the task you need.

The Norton Desktop provide several extensions to the DOS batch-programming language. These extensions are grouped together into the BE (Batch Enhancer) program; they let you control the screen, open and close windows, position text anywhere on the screen, and add capabilities to make truly interactive batch files.

All DOS batch files are ASCII text files, with a carriage return and a line feed at the end of every line. You cannot include any word processor formatting commands in them. Every batch file must have a unique name and .BAT as its file-name extension, so that DOS knows to invoke the batch-file processor. However, you do not have to type the .BAT extension when you run the file.

When you run a batch file, the DOS batch-file processor executes each of the file's commands in order. After DOS has run all of the batch file's commands, you are returned to the DOS prompt. Batch files are useful for automating lengthy processes. For example, a batch file can set up your system automatically when you boot the computer, or it can simplify the procedure for backing up your hard disk.

How Do I Make a Batch File?

There are several different ways to make a batch file. You can use DOS's EDLIN program to make a batch file, or, if you are using DOS 5, you can use EDIT. However, by far the easiest way to create a batch file is to use the Desktop Editor, described in detail in Chapter 7.

Starting and Stopping a Batch File

To run a batch file, just type the file name at the DOS prompt and press Enter, or use the Run command from the Desktop File menu. There is no need to specify its .BAT extension. Each command line in the batch file is executed exactly as if you had typed it at the DOS prompt. At the end of the batch file, execution stops, and the DOS prompt reappears.

To abort, or interrupt, a batch file while it is running, type Ctrl+C or Ctrl+Break. This sends a break character to DOS and usually results in the message:

Terminate batch job (Y/N)?

Typing **Y** stops the batch file completely and returns you to the DOS prompt. If you want to stop the current command's execution but continue with the next command in the batch file, type **N**. Some programs do not recognize the break character and will not stop when you press Break. Other programs may not be able to stop immediately.

Using a Batch File to Run a Program

One common use of a batch file is to start a program quickly. For example, if you have the word processor AmiPro installed on your hard disk in a directory called AMI, you must enter several commands to start the program. You can place these commands in a batch file and give the file a meaningful, easy-to-remember name. Running the batch file will then execute the commands automatically. In this example, you could create a batch file called AMIS-TART.BAT and include the following commands in it:

```
CD \ AMI
AMIPRO
```

When you run the batch file, the command CD \AMI makes the AMI directory current, and the command AMIPRO starts the word processor. You can even name the batch file after yourself, the primary user of the word processor; then all you have to do is type your name after booting the computer.

Using a Batch File to Automate a Common Process

Another common use of a batch file is to automate a complex procedure, simplifying it to an easy-to-remember name. For example, if you have an Epson- or IBM-compatible printer, you can create a batch file that puts the printer into 132-column (compressed) mode. Just include the following line:

MODE LPT1: 132

in a batch file called COMPRESS.BAT. If you make another batch file called NORMAL.BAT that includes the line:

MODE LPT1: 80

you now have an easy way of setting and resetting your printer width. To choose compressed mode, type:

COMPRESS

Any output you then send to the printer will be printed in 132 columns across the page. To return the printer to the normal mode, type:

NORMAL

The printer will now print in the more usual 80-column width.

THE BATCH PROGRAMMING LANGUAGE

In this section I introduce the DOS batch-programming language and describe some of the more important commands and concepts. Keep in mind that you can only use these commands in batch files; you cannot use them from the DOS prompt. However, you can add regular DOS commands into your batch files whenever you need to.

Table 18.1 lists all the commands available in the batch programming language, and in the next part of this chapter, we'll review how to use some of the more common commands.

Using ECHO

Normally, DOS displays batch-file commands as the batch file executes them. If you don't want the commands to be displayed, place the line:

ECHO OFF

at the beginning of the batch file. To turn the display of commands on again, include the following line:

ECHO ON

You can also use ECHO to display short text messages on the screen to help you or other users follow the batch file's processing. To send a message to the

COMMAND	FUNCTION
CALL	Runs a second batch file, and then returns control to the original batch file
ECHO	Displays messages on the screen
FOR	Repeats a command for a group of files or directories, or for a specific number of times
GOTO	Controls program flow in a batch file
IF	Carries out a command based on a specific condition
PAUSE	Temporarily stops your batch program running until you press a key
REM	Indicates that the text is an annotation and not for execution
SHIFT	Changes the position of replaceable parameters

TABLE 18.1:
DOS Batch Programming Commands

screen with ECHO, use the form:

ECHO *message*

The message will be displayed on the screen even if you included the ECHO OFF statement at the beginning of the batch file—the displayed message is the *result* of the command, not the command itself. For example, if ECHO is off and you run a batch file that contains the line:

ECHO This is a short message.

DOS will display:

This is a short message.

However, if ECHO is on, the resulting display is:

ECHO This is a short message.
This is a short message.

You see both the command and its output.

After you understand how ECHO works, it isn't so confusing; just be careful to turn ECHO on and off again in the appropriate places in the batch file.

In DOS 3.3 and later versions, there is another way to stop commands from being displayed. Simply add the @ character to the beginning of the batch-file command that you do not want displayed. Thus the statement:

@ECHO OFF

instructs DOS to execute this command without displaying it on the screen. (ECHO OFF, in turn, tells DOS to do the same for subsequent commands in the batch file.)

Another command that is often used in this way is the CLS (clear screen) command. If you use ECHO OFF followed by CLS, you will not see the ECHO OFF command because the screen will be cleared quickly by CLS. You can start your batch files with the sequence:

ECHO OFF
CLS

so that they start at the top of a clear screen.

Including Remarks in Your Batch Files

You can add comments or remarks to a batch file with the REM command. A REM statement is simply the word REM followed by any text. If ECHO is on, the REM statements are displayed, including the word REM. If you want to add comments to your batch file that are never displayed, regardless of whether ECHO is on or off, add a colon to the beginning of the comment line. Such comments help explain what the batch file is doing. Although this may be obvious to you when you write the batch file, you may forget some or all of the details in a year's time, particularly if the batch file executes complicated procedures.

Pausing Your Batch Files

You can use the PAUSE command to halt a batch file's execution and give instructions to the user. For example, you can include the command:

PAUSE Position Paper!

in a batch file that sends output to the printer. However, you must also use ECHO ON in the batch file to display the instruction, but this displays the whole command. The following lines demonstrate a cleaner way of doing the same thing:

@ECHO OFF
ECHO Position Paper!
PAUSE

When the batch file pauses, DOS displays the message:

Strike a key when ready

After following the displayed instruction, the user just presses any key to continue executing the batch file.

Running Batch Files from within Other Batch Files Using CALL

By using the CALL command, introduced in DOS 3.3, you can have a batch file execute another batch file as part of its process; the second batch file is treated as a subroutine. After the subroutine has been called and executed, the original batch file continues executing the rest of its commands. For example, if you want to write your name and your company address at the top of a page, you can call a batch file called ADDRESS.BAT from inside another batch file by including the following line:

CALL ADDRESS

in the batch file. When ADDRESS.BAT has written out your name and the company address, control returns to the original batch file, which then executes the command following the CALL command. Having ADDRESS-.BAT as a separate file enables you to use it in different batch files, without having to retype it for each file. This way, if you change your address, you only have to modify ADDRESS.BAT, not all the other batch files.

Starting One Batch File from Another Batch File

You can also run a batch file from another batch file by invoking the second file in the last line of the first one. However, if you invoke the second file before the last line of the first file, any remaining commands in the first file will not be executed because control passes to the second file and does not return to the first batch file.

Testing Results with ERRORLEVEL

ERRORLEVEL is a variable within DOS that can be set by a DOS command, an application program, or a batch file. Several DOS commands, including BACKUP, FORMAT, and RESTORE, return an ERRORLEVEL code when they finish running, indicating whether they completed successfully or encountered an error. ERRORLEVEL can contain a number between 0 and 255. When used with IF and GOTO, ERRORLEVEL can help your batch files make complex decisions.

Creating Alternative Procedures with IF and GOTO

IF allows conditional branching in a batch file. A *conditional branch* simply means: "If a certain thing is true, do this; otherwise, do that."

With this capability you can create batch files to run increasingly complicated procedures. For example, you can use IF and GOTO with ERROR-LEVEL codes to test your program or batch-file commands. When ERRORLEVEL reports a code, the file's execution would continue as intended. However, if there is an ERRORLEVEL code, the GOTO statement would send control to lines that would deal with it in some way. GOTO passes control to a point in the program indicated by a label, in effect bypassing a section of the batch file. A *label* is merely a name of up to eight characters, usually preceded by a colon (although the colon is optional in the GOTO statement), which identifies a section of code. The label indicates where execution should continue; it is not executable code. For example, when DOS encounters the line:

GOTO :END

in a batch file, it jumps to the line:

:END

(usually the last line in the file) and returns you to the DOS prompt.

Using Replaceable Parameters in a Batch File

You can set up placeholding variables in a batch file so that you can specify different parameters when you invoke the file. By doing so, you can run the batch file with different files, for example. You can specify as many as ten variables in a batch file, each identified by a percent sign followed by a number. Suppose you make a batch file called R.BAT that contains the statement:

RENAME %1 %2

To run it, you would type:

R FILE1 FILE2

DOS will replace the %1 with the first name, FILE1, and it will replace the %2 with the second name, FILE2. In other words, the DOS batch-file processor translates the sequence you typed to:

RENAME FILE1 FILE2

The SHIFT command moves all the variables down one number; for example, %2 become %1, %3 becomes %2, and so on. The %1 variable is lost each time you use SHIFT. This lets you create batch files that can handle more than ten replaceable parameters at a time.

The CONFIG.SYS File

The CONFIG.SYS file resembles a batch file in that you create it and it executes commands; however, it can only contain special DOS configuration commands. CONFIG.SYS is loaded only when you boot the computer, and its commands are restricted to those that set up your system for DOS; other commands cannot be included in the file. If DOS doesn't find this file in the root directory of the disk used to boot the system, it provides default values for the system's setup.

The commands in your CONFIG.SYS file configure your computer's hardware, allowing you to set certain internal DOS variables and load special device drivers. These commands each have the general form:

COMMAND = *value*

The AUTOEXEC.BAT File

AUTOEXEC.BAT is similar in concept to the CONFIG.SYS file, but there is an important difference between the two files. AUTOEXEC.BAT can contain *any* DOS command you want to use every time you start up your computer, unlike CONFIG.SYS, which can use only configuration commands. For example, it can load terminate-and-stay-resident (TSR) programs, such as the Norton Cache, or start an application program.

After DOS boots itself, it looks for AUTOEXEC.BAT in the root directory of the boot disk. If the file is present, DOS executes its contents line by line until they have all been processed, exactly like any other batch file.

USING THE BATCH ENHANCER IN YOUR BATCH FILES

The Norton Desktop Batch Enhancer (BE) program includes several commands that you can use to extend the scope of your batch programming. BE provides more control over the screen colors and attributes than the DOS ANSI.SYS driver does. You can also use its subprograms' routines to clear the screen, draw a box on the screen, open exploding windows, position the cursor at a particular location on the screen, and write a character on the screen.

Script Files

You can use Batch Enhancer commands in your DOS batch files, but if you find that you are using a lot of Batch Enhancer commands, particularly screen-drawing commands, you can collect these commands together into what Norton calls a *script file*. This will speed up the execution of the screen drawing commands many times over. A script file is an ASCII text file, just like a batch file, and you can use the Desktop Editor to create one.

You can use any BE command in a script file, but if you include any DOS commands, they will be ignored. I will show you how to make a script file later in this chapter.

BE SA (Screen Attributes)

BE SA lets you set the screen colors and attributes either from the DOS prompt or from inside a batch file. You can specify the color names as BE SA's parameters, although when you become more familiar with them, you can abbreviate them to their first three letters. Table 18.2 shows the list of settings you can use with BE SA.

Application programs often set their own colors and attributes when they start running, and some programs are so well behaved that they reset the screen when they finish running. Because other programs do not do this, however, you can make a batch file called RESET.BAT that contains the following BE SA command:

BE SA BRIGHT WHITE ON BLUE

To reset the screen quickly, all you have to do is invoke this file.

You can also include BE SA in a batch file to change the screen and draw attention to whatever the batch file next executes. For example, the following BE SA command will get your attention no matter what you are doing:

BE SA REVERSE

BE SA settings will produce different results on different systems. Some monochrome screens can produce gradations of their color to correspond to the colors set by BE SA, while others cannot. You will have to experiment with BE SA to discover which settings you find the most appealing.

SCREEN SETTING	COLOR
Color (background and foreground)	Black
	Red
	Green
	Yellow
	Blue
	Magenta
	Cyan
	White
Intensity	Bright (Bold)
	Blinking
Text on screen	Normal
	Reverse
	Underline

TABLE 18.1:
BE SA's Attributes

BE BOX

BE BOX draws a box on the screen of a specified size at a specified location. The command uses the following general format:

BE BOX *top left bottom right* [SINGLE or DOUBLE] *color*

in which *top* and *left* are the pair of screen coordinates defining the row and column position of the top-left corner of the box, and *bottom* and *right* similarly define the position of the bottom-right corner of the box on the screen. SINGLE or DOUBLE makes the box outline either a single line or a double line, and *color* specifies the color of the box's outline. In fact, you can even specify two colors for it. For example, if you enter:

BE BOX *top left bottom right* GREEN ON BLUE

your box will have an attractive two-toned frame. See Table 18.2 for the list of colors you can use.

BE BOX draws a box anywhere on the screen. The following example:

BE BOX 10 10 20 20 DOUBLE RED

draws a red double-lined box from row 10, column 10 to row 20, column 20.

BE CLS

BE CLS clears the screen and positions the cursor at the top-left corner, which is called the *home* position.

Using BE CLS is simple. To include it in a batch file, just add the line:

BE CLS

Place this command in batch files that draw windows or boxes; preceding the drawing command with BE CLS ensures that you start with a fresh screen.

BE GOTO

BE GOTO transfers the flow of the batch file to another place in the file by referencing a label. A label is a string of up to eight characters preceded by a colon. For example, to skip a section of code in a batch file, you might add the following lines to your batch file:

```
BE GOTO LAST
more code here
:LAST
```

BE WINDOW

BE WINDOW is similar to BE BOX, except that two more parameters can be defined. SHADOW draws a drop shadow below and to the right of the window, and EXPLODE makes the window zoom to its full size. When you omit SHADOW, the window does not have a drop shadow; when you omit EXPLODE, the full-sized window appears immediately, and you will not see it enlarge on the screen.

Although BE WINDOW's *color* parameter uses the same format as *color* in BE BOX, it operates differently. When you specify two colors, the first color becomes the window's outline and the second fills in as the background color.

BE WINDOW uses the following general format:

BE WINDOW *top left bottom right color* SHADOW EXPLODE

For example, try the following WINDOW sequence directly from the DOS command line:

BE WINDOW 5 20 20 60 RED ON CYAN SHADOW EXPLODE

just to see what happens. If you specify coordinates that position one window on top of another, the second window will overlay the first one, displaying the uncovered portion of the first window.

BE PRINTCHAR

BE PRINTCHAR can display a character a specified number of times at the cursor's current location. This command uses the following general format:

BE PRINTCHAR *character repetitions* [*color*]

in which *character* is any character that you type, and *repetitions* specifies how many times the character is to be repeated. The optional *color* parameter lets you specify the character's color.

Try this PRINTCHAR sequence just to see what happens:

BE PRINTCHAR 1 20 RED

BE ROWCOL

BE ROWCOL positions the cursor at a particular row and column location on the screen, displaying the specified text in the requested color. It uses the following general format:

BE ROWCOL *row column* ["*text*"] [*color*]

If you use ROWCOL with WINDOW, you can place text in windows. For example, the following batch file creates three windows, labeling them WINDOW 1, WINDOW 2, and WINDOW 3.

```
@ECHO OFF
BE CLS
BE SA BRIGHT WHITE ON BLUE
BE WINDOW 4 4 14 64 SHADOW
BE ROWCOL 9 25 "WINDOW 1" YELLOW ON BLUE
BE WINDOW 8 8 18 68 SHADOW
BE ROWCOL 13 29 "WINDOW 2" YELLOW ON BLUE
BE WINDOW 12 12 22 72 SHADOW
BE ROWCOL 17 33 "WINDOW 3" YELLOW ON BLUE
```

Each window overlays part of the previous window.

Now that you have set up overlapping windows, you can reverse the order by having window 2 cover part of window 3 and window 1 cover part of window 2. To do this, add the following commands to the end of the batch file:

```
BE WINDOW 8 8 18 68 SHADOW
BE ROWCOL 13 29 "WINDOW 2" YELLOW ON BLUE
BE WINDOW 4 4 14 64 SHADOW
BE ROWCOL 9 25 "WINDOW 1" YELLOW ON BLUE
BE ROWCOL 24 0
:EXIT
```

This redraws the second and first windows in that order. The last ROWCOL command sends the cursor to the last position on the screen and returns you to DOS.

BE ASK

BE ASK provides an easy way to add conditional branching to a DOS batch file. It pauses the batch file during its execution and prompts the user to choose the branch that the batch file should then take. When you include a BE ASK command in a batch file, you need to specify which keystrokes are associated with the possible branches. You can also instruct BE ASK how long it should await a keystroke before returning a default value that you specify.

The general format of BE ASK is as follows:

```
BE ASK "prompt" key-list DEFAULT=key TIMEOUT=n ADJUST=m color /DEBUG
```

in which

◆ *"prompt"* is a text string, often a question, that gives two or more choices.

◆ *key-list* lists the valid keystrokes as responses to *"prompt."* If no *key-list* is given, any key from the keyboard is accepted.

◆ DEFAULT=*key* specifies the key BE ASK will use if no key is pressed within the TIMEOUT period.

◆ TIMEOUT=*n* specifies a wait period in seconds. If you set TIMEOUT to zero or don't specify any value, BE ASK waits forever.

◆ ADJUST=*m* adjusts the return value by the value of *m*.

◆ *color* sets the color of the prompt text.

◆ /DEBUG is optional. It displays the returned ERRORLEVEL value, which can be useful if you are troubleshooting a batch file that is misbehaving.

After you type a key at the prompt, BE ASK transfers control back to the batch file, passing along the ERRORLEVEL value that corresponds to the key you pressed. This is ASK's method of setting the value for the keystroke. For example, if you type the first key in the list, ASK generates an ERROR-LEVEL value of 1. The IF statement then evaluates the value returned in ER-RORLEVEL, and the GOTO command passes control to the branch of the batch file that is indicated by that value.

Let's examine a branching batch file that contains two IF statements as an example. This file could be used to make a simple yes/no decision because it offers two branching choices. So that the batch file can evaluate these choices correctly, you need to list them in reverse order in the file; that is, the statement IF ERRORLEVEL 2 must precede IF ERRORLEVEL 1. The entire batch file might resemble this sequence:

```
@ECHO OFF
BE CLS
BE ASK "Yes or No ? ( Press Y or N ) ", YN TIMEOUT=30 DEFAULT=2
IF ERRORLEVEL 2 GOTO NO
IF ERRORLEVEL 1 GOTO YES

:YES
ECHO YES
GOTO END
```

```
:NO
ECHO NO
GOTO END
:END
```

When you run this batch file, it turns ECHO off, clears the screen, and prompts:

Yes or No ? (Press Y or N)

If you answer **Y** for yes, BE ASK sets ERRORLEVEL to 1, which is then tested by the IF statement. Control passes to the subroutine labeled :YES, which echoes the word YES to the screen. The GOTO END statement ends the batch file.

If you answer **N** for no, BE ASK sets ERRORLEVEL to 2, which is then tested by the IF statement. Control passes to the subroutine called :NO, which echoes the word NO to the screen. Control is passed to the label :END and the batch file terminates.

If you do not press a key in thirty seconds, BE ASK returns the default ERRORLEVEL value, which is 2 in this example.

BE BEEP

You can use BE BEEP to play a single note from the DOS prompt or play a series of notes loaded from an ASCII text file. You can specify the frequency and the duration of a note, the number of times a note is repeated, and the length of the wait period between notes.

BEEP uses the ticks of your system clock as its timer. Because the system clock ticks about 18.2 times a second, BEEP requires that you enter values in eighteenths of a second for notes' durations and wait periods.

The general format of BE BEEP is:

BE BEEP *switches*

or

BE BEEP *filename* / E

To specify durations and wait periods, you can include the following switches in your BEEP command:

◆ /D*n* specifies the duration of the note in $\frac{1}{18}$ of a second.

◆ /F*n* specifies the frequency of the note in hertz, or cycles per second.

◆ /R*n* tells BEEP how many times a note is to be repeated.

◆ /W*n* establishes the length of the wait period between notes in $\frac{1}{18}$ of a second.

◆ /E echoes any text in quotation marks following the notes.

Remember that you replace *n* with the number you want.

To practice working with BEEP, enter:

BE BEEP

at the DOS prompt. This produces a single short tone. Entering the following:

BE BEEP /F50/D18/R5/W18

plays five low notes a second apart. Each note is one second long. The following example:

BE BEEP /F3000/D1/R5/W9

plays five short-duration high notes at half-second intervals.

When you specify a file name as input for BE BEEP, you can specify its path; however, you cannot include wildcards in the file name.

Let's assume you want to create a file called BEEPTEST. Remember to include a comment line prefaced with a colon to describe what the file does. For example, BEEPTEST might contain the following:

```
:This generates three low, medium, and high notes
/F100/D9/R3/W18
/F500/D18/R3/W18
/F1000/D36/R3/W18
```

This file plays three low notes that are each half a second long, three middle notes that are one second long, and three high notes that are two seconds long. To invoke this file from the DOS prompt, type:

BE BEEP BEEPTEST

By providing a file as input, you enabled BE BEEP to play a simple tune. Although you can use BE BEEP in a variety of ways, it is most convenient for signaling the completion of a process in a batch file.

BE DELAY

BE DELAY lets you specify the delay period in a batch file that must elapse before the batch file can continue executing. To include BE DELAY in your batch file, use the general format:

BE DELAY *time*

in which *time* is specified in $\frac{1}{18}$ of a second, as in BE BEEP. For example, when the batch-file processor encounters a delay of $\frac{9}{18}$ of a second, which is the command:

BE DELAY 9

it waits half a second before continuing with the next command in the file.

BE EXIT

The BE EXIT command ends execution of a Batch Enhancer script file; it has no function if executed directly from DOS. Normally, script files start running at the beginning of the file and run all the way to the last line. Now you can use EXIT to stop at a point other than the end of the file.

BE JUMP

BE JUMP lets you make conditional branches inside a Batch Enhancer script file. When JUMP is combined with EXIT, you can execute selective parts of your script file, rather than process the file in a start-to-finish fashion.

JUMP performs a branch based on the exit code provided by the previous command, so if you were using ASK in a script file, you could perform a JUMP based on the number returned by ASK. Similarly, you can use JUMP with WEEKDAY, MONTHDAY, or SHIFTSTATE. You specify the locations you want to branch to by a series of labels after the JUMP, as follows:

JUMP label1, label*n*, /DEFAULT:label

There must be at least one label after the JUMP statement; it is selected when the return code of the previous command equals 1. Execution of the script file continues at this label. The second label is used if the return code equals 2, the third if the return code equals 3, and so on. Each of these labels must exist inside the script file. Use the /DEFAULT switch to add a catch-all label that JUMP will use if the return code is zero, or if the return code is larger than the number of labels—for example, if the return code equals 7 but there are only six labels after the JUMP.

BE MONTHDAY

BE MONTHDAY returns the day of the month, from 1 to 31. You can then look at this return code using ERRORLEVEL or JUMP and branch to a new location in the batch or script file.

BE REBOOT

The BE REBOOT command adds the ability to reboot the computer from a batch file. Use the /VERIFY switch to make BE REBOOT ask Reboot the computer now? and wait for the user to type a character as confirmation before rebooting.

BE SHIFTSTATE

BE SHIFTSTATE returns an exit code that shows which of the Alt, Ctrl, or left and right Shift keys were pressed when BE SHIFTSTATE was run. Because each of the keys can be detected individually, you can determine whether two keys were pressed at the same time. Then you can use ERROR-LEVEL or JUMP to branch to a different part of the batch file. SHIFTSTATE returns the following values:

right Shift key	1
left Shift key	2
Ctrl key	4
Alt key	8

BE TRIGGER

BE TRIGGER halts execution of a batch file until the time you specify in the batch file. You can enter the time in 24-hour format, or in 12-hour format if you use the meridian indicators AM or PM. The general form of the command is as follows:

BE TRIGGER *hh:mm*

If you are using a 12-hour format, add AM or PM after the time.

BE WEEKDAY

BE WEEKDAY returns a code equal to the day of the week, where Sunday is 1 and Saturday is 7. BE WEEKDAY is similar to BE MONTHDAY, except that WEEKDAY returns the day of the week and MONTHDAY returns the day of the month.

Use the ERRORLEVEL or JUMP commands to evaluate the return code and to decide which part of the batch file to execute next.

COMBINING NORTON AND DOS COMMANDS IN A BATCH FILE

Using batch files can make tedious, repetitive, or complex DOS operations much more straightforward. BE's subprograms are an important addition to the batch-programming language: they let you create interactive conditional branching in a batch file and make complex screen handling and windowing easy to do.

If you find that your batch file runs too slowly, remember that you can speed it up considerably by using two files instead of just one. You can collect many of the screen-drawing commands together into a Batch Enhancer script file. A script file can contain BE commands but will ignore any DOS commands. To do this, place all the commands for drawing the windows and dialog boxes in a separate script file called MYFILE.TXT. This file will then be loaded by your main batch program at the appropriate point.

If you plan to use the BE utility extensively, copy the BE.EXE program to a RAM disk. All the BE programs will run more quickly because they will be executing from memory rather than from your hard disk.

SAVING DISK SPACE WITH COMPRESS

Many bulletin boards use PKZIP to compress files because compressed files take less time to transmit over a modem.

File compression programs have been around in the personal computer world for a long time. Famous examples include programs like PKARC, LHARC, and PKZIP. These programs have always been popular with programmers who use them to compress program source code after a project is complete. By using PKZIP, they can squash their source code files down so that they occupy very little disk space. Some software packages (like the Norton Desktop, for example) are distributed in a compressed form on the original program disks to save space. The Install program not only copies the files, but also decompresses them at the same time.

PKZIP uses one set of complex command-line arguments to compress your files, and another set to decompress them.

The only problem with some of these compression programs is that the command-line syntax can sometimes be complex and rather daunting. Well, the Norton Desktop provides an easy answer to this—it completely does away with complex command-line arguments, and makes the Desktop do all the work for you.

COMPRESSING FILES

Choose Compress from the Desktop File menu to open the dialog box shown in Figure 18.23. You can select single files, groups of related files, or even complete directories, and compress them all into one single file. This is a good way to make sure that all the files associated with a particular project are collected together and compressed, or archived, into the same compressed file.

Files compressed on the Desktop are completely compatible with PKZIP; indeed they share the same default file-name extension, .ZIP.

The amount of disk space you will save as a result of the compression depends on the kind of file you are working with. You will see the smallest saving when you compress .EXE files, the greatest saving when you compress text files. Other common file types like word processing or spreadsheet files will fall somewhere in between.

There is no point in compressing files that have already been compressed. In fact, if you try this, you may find that the resulting file is larger rather than smaller. This has to do with the amount of overhead inherent in managing the compression.

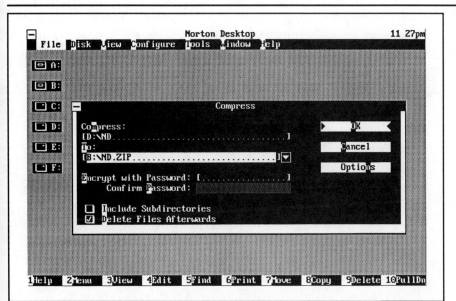

Select file compression options from the Compress dialog box

As always on the Desktop, there are several different methods you can use to select the files you want to compress:

◆ Select a file in a drive window, then select Compress. The file name will automatically appear in the Compress text box. If you select several files, a count of the number of files will be shown instead of file names.

◆ Type the name of the file directly into the Compress text box.

◆ Type the names of several files into the Compress text box, separating them with a comma, a space, a plus sign (+), or a semicolon (;).

◆ Specify groups of files using the DOS ? or * wildcard characters.

◆ Select a directory from a drive window. All files in the directory will be compressed.

◆ Type the name of the directory directly into the Compress text box.

Now that you have selected the file or files to compress, you must tell the Desktop where to store the result. Enter the file name and path information using the To text box, or select an entry from the drop-down list box. This drop-down list box contains information for the last ten compressed files you created. You can enter a file-name extension for the compressed file, but if you don't, the Desktop will use the default, .ZIP.

If you want to encrypt this file, enter a password. This means that you will have to remember and enter this same password before you can decompress and therefore use the files contained inside this compressed file. Verify your password by entering it for a second time into the Confirm Password text box.

There are two more check boxes in this dialog box:

Include Subdirectories lets you compress files contained in subdirectories of the directory you entered in the Compress text box. If you clear this check box, files in subdirectories are not included.

Delete Files Afterwards deletes all the original files you selected for compression, once the compression process is complete. This is how you save disk space; the compressed files will occupy much less space than the original files. There is no point in keeping both sets of files on the same disk at the same time, because this occupies even more disk space than the original files. If you need a file back in its original form, you can decompress the whole compressed file, or just extract the individual file you need. We'll see how to do this in the next section in this chapter.

When you are happy with the settings in this dialog box, choose the OK button to start the compression process. Another dialog box opens, reminding you which of your original files are being compressed to what compressed-file name. A horizontal bar graph shows you progress made on each file.

Configuring Compress

Select the Options button in the Compress dialog box if you want to change any of the compression parameters. This command button opens the same dialog box described in Chapter 9 under the heading "Selecting File Compression Options" and shown in Figure 9.20, so the description here will be just a brief reminder.

First, choose the file compression method you want to use from Implode, Shrink, or Automatically Select Best Method. Implode produces the greatest degree of compression, but runs slower than Shrink. Shrink, on the other hand, is faster, but does not compress the file quite so much. You can specify which method you want to use, or as a convenient alternative, you can let the Desktop decide by choosing the Automatically Select Best Method option button. To store the full path as well as the file name in the compressed file, check the Store Full Pathnames check box.

As a file is compressed, a temporary storage area is used to contain interim information as the process proceeds, and when the compression is complete, this temporary information is deleted. This means that you have to have more free disk space available than that used by the original and the compressed versions of your file—you need additional space for this interim information. To create the compressed file on a different drive, check the Use Temporary Work Directory check box, and enter the name of the drive and directory. When the compression is complete, you can copy the compressed file back to the original drive if you wish.

Finally, you must decide how you want to handle the timestamp on your compressed file. There are three choices:

> **Set to Current Time and Date** assigns the current system time and date to the compressed file. This is the default setting, and is the one you will use most often.

> **Set to Timestamp of Most Recent File** uses the time and date from the most recent file as the time and date for the compressed file, and ignores all earlier files.

> **Do Not Change Timestamp** keeps the original timestamp, and does not change it when the compressed file is updated.

Click on OK to return to the Compress dialog box.

MANAGING COMPRESSED FILES

It can be easy to forget which original files are inside a compressed file. The Desktop offers two solutions to this problem; you can use the Norton Viewer to look into the file, or you can open a compressed-file window on the file. Once you know which files are contained in a compressed file, you may well want to add or delete files as time goes by.

Viewing Compressed Files

The Norton Viewer was described in detail in Chapter 6, so this will serve as a quick reminder. Select the compressed file you want to look at in a drive window file pane, then use F3, the View function key, to open the Norton

Viewer, as Figure 18.24 shows.

Figure 18.24 shows the files contained inside a compressed file on one of the original Norton Desktop distribution disks. From left to right, the columns in this window show the original file name and size, the compressed size and compression percentage (this is, how much it shrank by), the time and date from the original file, the compression method used, and the compression checksum.

If you don't want to use the Viewer, the Desktop makes looking inside a compressed file even easier; you can open a compressed file window instead. This window acts very much like a drive window except that it shows the contents of a single compressed file. First select the compressed file you want to work with in a normal drive window file pane. Then select the Desktop Window menu, and choose Open Window. In the dialog box that opens next, choose Compressed File. A compressed file window, like the one shown in Figure 18.25 will open on the Desktop.

Opening this window is even easier with the mouse—just double-click on the compressed file in the file pane, and the compressed file window will open on the Desktop. The columns in this window are, from left to right, file-type icon, original name, size, and timestamp. Instead of seeing a drive letter and directory path information in the window title bar, you will see just

NOTE *You can look at the contents of a .ZIP file with a compressed file window, but you cannot look at the actual contents of these compressed files.*

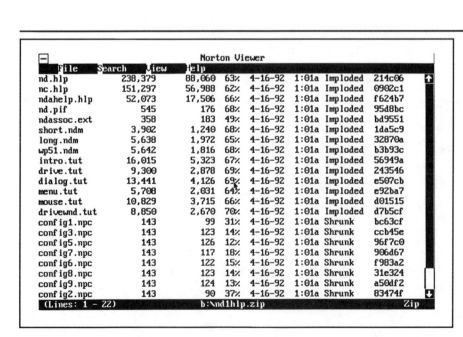

Norton Viewer

```
 File   Search   View   Help
nd.hlp         238,379    88,060  63%  4-16-92  1:01a  Imploded  214c06
nc.hlp         151,297    56,988  62%  4-16-92  1:01a  Imploded  0902c1
ndahelp.hlp     52,073    17,506  66%  4-16-92  1:01a  Imploded  f624b7
nd.pif             545       176  68%  4-16-92  1:01a  Imploded  95d8bc
ndassoc.ext        358       183  49%  4-16-92  1:01a  Imploded  bd9551
short.ndm        3,902     1,240  68%  4-16-92  1:01a  Imploded  1da5c9
long.ndm         5,638     1,972  65%  4-16-92  1:01a  Imploded  32870a
wp51.ndm         5,642     1,816  68%  4-16-92  1:01a  Imploded  b3b93c
intro.tut       16,015     5,323  67%  4-16-92  1:01a  Imploded  56949a
drive.tut        9,300     2,878  69%  4-16-92  1:01a  Imploded  243546
dialog.tut      13,441     4,126  69%  4-16-92  1:01a  Imploded  e507cb
menu.tut         5,708     2,031  64%  4-16-92  1:01a  Imploded  e92ba7
mouse.tut       10,829     3,715  66%  4-16-92  1:01a  Imploded  d01515
drivewnd.tut     8,850     2,670  70%  4-16-92  1:01a  Imploded  d7b5cf
config1.npc        143        99  31%  4-16-92  1:01a  Shrunk    bc63cf
config3.npc        143       123  14%  4-16-92  1:01a  Shrunk    ccb45e
config5.npc        143       126  12%  4-16-92  1:01a  Shrunk    96f7c0
config7.npc        143       117  18%  4-16-92  1:01a  Shrunk    906d67
config6.npc        143       122  15%  4-16-92  1:01a  Shrunk    f983a2
config8.npc        143       123  14%  4-16-92  1:01a  Shrunk    31e324
config9.npc        143       124  13%  4-16-92  1:01a  Shrunk    a50df2
config2.npc        143        90  37%  4-16-92  1:01a  Shrunk    83474f
 (Lines: 1 - 22)              b:\nd1hlp.zip                      Zip
```

FIGURE 18.24:

Open the Norton Viewer on a compressed file to see details of the files it contains

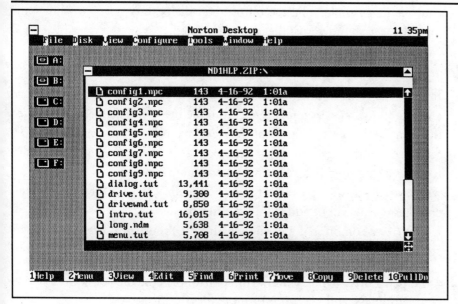

FIGURE 18.25:

Open a compressed file drive window to see the contents of a compressed file

the name and extension of the compressed file in a compressed file window. You can think of the compressed file window in the same way that you might think about a normal directory—you can compress new files, and decompress files one at a time or in groups, as you wish. We'll look at all these operations in the next few sections.

Decompressing Files

Decompressing a file could hardly be easier, just follow these steps:

1. Open a compressed file window on the compressed file that contains the files you want to decompress.

2. Open a normal drive window on the disk you want to receive the decompressed files.

3. Select the file or files for decompression in the compressed file window. You use normal Desktop file-selection techniques to select one or more files or directories for decompression.

4. Drag these files or directories to the destination drive.

And it's that simple. The Decompression dialog box opens to show you progress as each individual file is decompressed.

Adding Another File to a Compressed File

If you forgot to include a file when you created the compressed file, you can always add it later. Open Compress from the Desktop File menu, and enter the name of the file into the Compress text box. Now use the prompt button at the end of the To drop-down list box to select the same compressed file name that you used before. If the correct name is not in this list, then you will have to type the name into the To box again. Click on OK, and the uncompressed file will be added into the compressed file you specified.

With a compressed file window and the mouse, it is even easier; here are the steps:

1. Open a drive window on the drive that holds the file you want to compress, and select one or more files or directories.

2. Open a compressed file window on the compressed file to which you want to add this file.

3. Drag the file you want to compress to the compressed file window, and when the file icon is over the compressed file, release the mouse button.

4. The new file takes its place in the compressed file.

Deleting a File from within a Compressed File Window

You can also delete a single file or a group of files from inside a compressed file without decompressing the whole compressed file. Open a compressed file window, select your victims, and use the normal Delete command from the Desktop File menu. The usual "Are you sure" dialog boxes open, and when you confirm your intentions, the files are removed from the compressed file.

The Compress option from the Desktop File menu takes all the hard work out of managing your compressed files; it is difficult to imagine how the process could be made any easier. If you have ever puzzled over which command-line switches to use with PKZIP, then Compress is the answer for you.

CHAPTER 19

The Reference Guide to the Norton Desktop

This chapter lists all of the programs that make up the Norton Desktop package, and gives a short description of each program. The syntax and use of all command-line switches are also presented. Table 19.1 lists file and program names.

To make the syntax easier to read, I have substituted categorical names for the parameters that you can use for a particular command. The possible choices are then listed and described individually. The most common parameters are as follows:

◆ *drive,* which should be replaced by the appropriate drive letter, followed by a colon.

◆ *filename,* which should be replaced by a specific file name (and path when necessary). This denotes one particular file, so you cannot use the DOS wildcard characters with this specification.

◆ *filespec,* which should be replaced by a file name (and path when necessary). This is a more general specification, so you can use the DOS wildcard characters to include more than one file.

PROGRAM NAME	EXECUTABLE FILE NAME
Batch Enhancer	BE
Calculator	NDCALC
Disk Tools	DISKTOOL
Image	IMAGE
Norton AntiVirus	NAV
Norton Backup	NBACKUP
Norton Cache	NCACHE2
Norton Desktop	ND
Norton Desktop Configuration	NDCONFIG
Norton Disk Doctor	NDD
Norton Mail	NMAIL
Norton Menu	NMENU
Norton Scheduler	NSCHED
Norton Viewer	VIEW
Safe Format	SFORMAT
SmartCan	SMARTCAN
Speed Disk	SPEEDISK
System Info	SYSINFO
UnErase	UNERASE
UnFormat	UNFORMAT

TABLE 19.1:
Norton Desktop Program Names and Executable File Names

◆ *directoryspec*, which should be replaced by a directory name (and path when necessary).

◆ *n*, which should be replaced by a number. The size of the number varies according to the utility you are using.

VIDEO MODES AND GLOBAL SWITCHES

Because several Norton Desktop programs let you specify video switches from the DOS command line, these switches are listed here rather than repeated under each program:

/BW

forces a color display to monochrome.

/G0

disables font redefinition, changing the option buttons and check boxes from graphics characters to text characters.

/G1

disables graphical mouse cursor.

/LCD

forces the use of the LCD color set.

/M0

enables a nongraphical mouse cursor.

/M1

enables a graphical mouse cursor.

/MULTITASK

turns off the check for a multitasking environment.

/NOZOOM

turns off dialog box zooming.

If you do not use one of these switches, the default settings will be loaded from NORTON.INI and used instead.

Finally, remember that, unless noted otherwise, all parameters are optional.

BATCH ENHANCER

BE (Batch Enhancer) adds several important mechanisms for improved screen handling to the DOS batch-programming language. BE also enables you to create interactive decision-making in a batch file with its ASK subcommand.

Syntax To run BE from the DOS prompt, type:

BE *subcommand*

or

BE *filename*

Description You can use BE followed by one of the subcommands listed here, or you can use BE with a file that contains all the subcommands and their parameters. When you group the subcommands together in a file and specify the file with BE, the commands will be executed much faster because BE is only invoked once instead of individually for every command. Those BE commands that return a value via ERRORLEVEL have a /DEBUG parameter as the last switch. The commands are BE ASK, BE MONTHDAY, BE WEEKDAY, and BE SHIFTSTATE. You can use the /DEBUG parameter to display the value returned in ERRORLEVEL on the screen to make sure your batch file is receiving the expected input.

SUBCOMMANDS

Following is a list of the possible subcommands that you can include in a batch file.

BE ASK

This provides a way to perform conditional branching from a batch file. The prompt you include in the command will be displayed on the screen when the batch file executes the command, and the answer given by the user tells the batch file which commands to execute next.

Syntax To use BE ASK in a batch file, follow this syntax:

BE ASK "*prompt* " *list* DEFAULT=*key* TIMEOUT=*n* ADJUST=*n color*

Description The following list explains each parameter:

"*prompt* "

is any text string, usually a question, that offers the user two or more choices. You should also include a list of valid responses, so that the user knows which key to press.

list

specifies the valid keystrokes for BE ASK. If you don't specify anything for *list*, ASK accepts any keystrokes.

DEFAULT=*key*

indicates the response to use if no key is pressed before the allotted time has expired or if Enter is pressed.

TIMEOUT=*n*

specifies the number of seconds BE ASK will wait for a keystroke after the *prompt* test has been displayed. If TIMEOUT equals zero or if you do not include TIMEOUT in the command statement, BE ASK waits forever for a keystroke.

ADJUST=*n*

adjusts the return value by the amount *n*.

color

specifies the color of the prompt text. See BE SA for a description of the available colors.

BE BEEP

This plays a tone on the computer's speaker. A single tone can be specified at the DOS prompt, or a series of tones can be played by loading a file.

Syntax To use BE BEEP, add the following to your batch file:

BE BEEP *switches*

plays a single tone.

BE BEEP *filename*

plays all the tones specified by the switches in the file. You can include a path name to specify a file in another directory, but you cannot use wildcard characters.

Description To create a single tone, you need to include the /D*n* and /F*n* switches in the command statement. You can also repeat the tone by adding the /R*n* and /W*n* switches to the same statement. Here is what each switch does:

/D*n*

gives the duration of the tone in 18ths of a second.

/E

echoes the text in the file specified by *filename.*

/F*n*

specifies the frequency of the tone in Hertz (cycles per second). Setting /F equal to 1 sounds a moderately low note; setting it to 10,000 sounds a high-pitched squeak.

/R*n*

tells BE BEEP how many times to repeat the tone.

/W*n*

specifies the duration of the wait period between tones, in 18ths of a second.

BE BOX

This program draws a box on the screen, according to your specifications.

Syntax To run BE BOX, use:

BOX *top left bottom right outline color*

in your batch file.

Description To draw a box, you must include the *top, left, bottom,* and *right* parameters. The two remaining parameters are optional. Here is what all of these parameters represent:

top

specifies the row of the top-left corner of the box.

left

specifies the column of the top-left corner of the box.

bottom

specifies the row of the bottom-right corner of the box.

right

specifies the column of the bottom-right corner of the box.

outline

specifying SINGLE draws a single-line outline for the box; specifying DOUBLE draws a double-line outline for the box.

color

specifies the color of the box. (See BE SA for a description of the color selections.)

BE CLS

This program clears the screen and positions the cursor at the home position, which is the top-left corner of the screen.

Syntax To use BE CLS, type:

BE CLS

BE CLS does not take any parameters.

BE DELAY

This program sets a specified time delay before executing the next command in the batch file.

Syntax To use BE DELAY:

BE DELAY *counts*

Description You must specify the *counts* parameter when you invoke BE DELAY. You can use this program to display text for a set period of time, such as in a message in a window or in a prompt that gives instructions.

counts

determines how long (in 18ths of a second) the batch-file processor will wait before continuing to execute the batch file.

BE GOTO

This command causes a batch file to branch to a label line somewhere else in the batch file.

Syntax To perform a branch in a batch file, add the following line:

BE GOTO *label*

Description BE GOTO requires a destination label.

label

specifies the destination which execution branches in the batch file

BE PRINTCHAR

This program displays the specified character at the current cursor location.

Syntax Use BE PRINTCHAR as follows:

BE PRINTCHAR *character repetitions color*

Description The definitions for PRINTCHAR's parameters are as follows:

character

specifies the character to be displayed.

repetitions

specifies the number of times the character will be displayed, to a maximum of 80 repetitions.

color

determines the color to be used for the character.

BE ROWCOL

This function moves the cursor to the specified location on the screen and can display text.

Syntax To use BE ROWCOL in your batch files, use this syntax:

BE ROWCOL *row column text color*

Description You don't have to specify *text* or *color* when you invoke BE ROWCOL. The program accepts the following parameters:

row

specifies a new row for the cursor.

column

specifies a new column for the cursor.

text

provides optional text to be displayed at the new cursor location. If the text contains space characters, enclose the entire string in quotation marks.

color

specifies the color to be used for the text. (See the description of BE SA for the colors available.)

BE SA

This function enables you to set the screen foreground and background colors, and vary the intensity of the characters. BE SA works only if the ANSI.SYS driver is installed in your CONFIG.SYS file. If ANSI.SYS is not installed, BE displays an error message telling you that ANSI.SYS is required.

BE SA can be used in two ways.

Syntax 1 The first syntax:

BE SA *main-setting switches*

lets you set up your screen's display of text.

Description 1 The *main-setting* parameter can be one of the following:

NORMAL
REVERSE
UNDERLINE

The *switches* you can include are:

/N

does not set the border color. The EGA is a borderless display so using this switch with an EGA will have no effect; however, you can set the border for a VGA by omitting this switch.

/CLS

clears the screen after setting the color and screen attributes.

Syntax 2 The second syntax:

BE SA *intensity foreground* ON *background switches*

lets you set the screen colors' attributes.

Description 2 The *switches* are the same ones you can use with BE SA's first syntax. The remaining parameters are:

intensity	BRIGHT
	BLINKING
	BOLD
foreground	WHITE
	BLACK
	RED
	MAGENTA
	BLUE
	GREEN
	CYAN
	YELLOW
background	same color as *foreground*

You can abbreviate the color in the command statement by listing only the first three letters of their name. Therefore,

BE SA BRIGHT WHITE ON BLUE

can be specified as:

BE SA BRI WHI ON BLU

BE WINDOW

This function creates a window to your specifications on the screen.

Syntax To use BE WINDOW in your batch files, follow this syntax:

BE WINDOW *top left bottom right color switches*

Description BE WINDOW accepts the following parameters:

top

specifies the row of the top-left corner of the window.

left

specifies the column of the top-left corner of the window.

bottom

specifies the row of the bottom-right corner of the window.

right

specifies the column of the bottom-right corner of the window.

SHADOW

adds an optional drop shadow to the window.

EXPLODE

makes the window zoom, or expand, as it opens.

BE EXIT

Use this command to terminate a batch file before the end of the file is reached.

Syntax To use BE EXIT, add this line to your batch file:

BE EXIT

Description BE EXIT lets you exit from a batch file at a place other than the end of the file, then return to DOS.

BE JUMP

This function provides a mechanism for conditional branching inside a BE script file.

Syntax BE JUMP can only be used inside a batch file:

BE JUMP

Description BE JUMP lets you specify a series of labels, and the exit code of the previous command determines which label to jump to in the file. Execution continues at the appropriate label. Using JUMP avoids having to use a series of IF ERRORLEVEL statements to evaluate the previous command's return code.

BE MONTHDAY

This function returns the day of the month to the batch file.

Syntax You can use BE MONTHDAY if you add the following line to your batch file:

BE MONTHDAY

Description BE MONTHDAY determines the day of the month, from 1 to 31, depending on the month, and returns this value to the batch file. You can use IF ERRORLEVEL statements in a batch file, or the BE JUMP statement in a BE script file to evaluate this returned value.

BE REBOOT

This function performs a warm boot of the computer.

Syntax To use BE REBOOT, add this line to your batch file:

BE REBOOT /VERIFY

Description BE REBOOT lets you decide to reboot your computer from inside a batch file:

/VERIFY

asks **Reboot the computer now?** so that you can confirm that you want to reboot.

BE SHIFTSTATE

This function returns the state of the Shift, Alt, and Ctrl keys.

Syntax To use BE SHIFTSTATE in your batch file, add this line:

BE SHIFTSTATE

Description BE SHIFTSTATE returns a code depending on which of the Shift, Alt, or Ctrl keys were pressed at the time that the command ran. SHIFTSTATE returns the following codes, so that you can use it to separate the Right and Left Shift keys, and to tell whether two keys were pressed at the same time:

1	Right Shift
2	Left Shift
4	Ctrl key
8	Alt key

BE TRIGGER

This halts the execution of the batch file until the time specified.

Syntax Here is the syntax for BE TRIGGER:

BE TRIGGER *hh:mm* (*am/pm*)

Description BE TRIGGER delays execution of your batch file until the time specified by *hh:mm*. Time can be entered using the 24-hour clock (no indicator needed), or in 12-hour form with am or pm to indicate meridian.

BE WEEKDAY

This function returns a value corresponding to the day of the week.

Syntax To use BE WEEKDAY in your batch file, add this line:

BE WEEKDAY

Description BE WEEKDAY returns a code to the batch file indicating the day of the week, where Sunday is 1 and Saturday is 7. You can test this return code using IF ERRORLEVEL and GOTO or JUMP statements.

CALCULATOR

Norton Desktop includes an easy-to-use four-function calculator.

Syntax To start the calculator from the DOS command line, type:

NDCALC

Description NDCALC does not accept command-line switches.

DISK TOOLS

Disk Tools always operates in full-screen mode, but you can use command-line switches to start the program for a preselected operation. Disk Tools includes functions that let you make a disk into a bootable disk, recover from the DOS RECOVER command, revive a hard-to-read diskette, and make or restore a rescue disk containing a copy of the system area of your hard disk.

Syntax To run Disk Tools from the DOS command line, type:

DISKTOOL

Description You can use the following switches to start the program:

/DOSRECOVER

recovers from the DOS RECOVER command.

/MAKEBOOT

makes a disk bootable.

/RESTORE

reloads the information from a Rescue Disk.

/REVIVE

revives a defective disk.

/SAVERESCUE

creates a Rescue Disk.

/SKIPHIGH

does not load into high memory.

IMAGE

Image takes an instant picture of the system area (boot record, file allocation tables, and root directory information) and stores the information in a file in the root directory of your hard disk. UnFormat and UnErase will both use the Image file if it is present.

Syntax To use Image from the DOS prompt, type:

IMAGE *drive switch*

If you have several logical drives, you can protect all of them if you include an Image drive statement for your drives in your AUTOEXEC.BAT file. For example, to protect drives C, D, and E, add:

IMAGE C: D: E:

to your AUTOEXEC.BAT file.

Description There is only one switch you can use with Image:

/NOBACKUP

prevents the creation of a backup copy of the Image data file, IMAGE.BAK.

NORTON ANTIVIRUS

The Norton AntiVirus finds and removes over 1,000 strains of computer virus.

Syntax Start Norton AntiVirus from the DOS prompt by typing:

NAV *drive switches*

Description There are many switches you can use to configure Norton AntiVirus:

/A

scans all drives.

/B

scans just the boot sectors of the specified drives.

/BOX[+!–]

enables or disables the virus intercept visible alert.

/FIL:*pathname*

scans all the items in the *pathname.*

/M[+!–]

performs or skips the memory scan.

/NS

continues the scan without waiting for a keystroke after a virus is found.

/PRESENCE

determines whether a compatible intercept is present in memory.

/REFRESH

inoculates or reinoculates all files scanned.

/S

includes subdirectories in the scan.

/SO[+!–]

enables or disables the virus intercept audible alarm.

/STOP

cancels a scan when a virus is found, and halts the system until Ctrl+C is pressed from the keyboard.

The two Norton AntiVirus device driver files do not accept any command-line arguments. Choose one or the other, and load them onto your system using a **DEVICE** = statement in your CONFIG.SYS file.

Norton AntiVirus sets the DOS ERRORLEVEL variable when the program exits, as follows:

ERRORLEVEL

Value	Description
1	virus was found in memory
2	Virus Clinic may be infected
3	viruses were detected during the scan
4	no viruses were detected during the scan
5	the device driver is not active in memory
6	the device driver is active in memory
255	the virus scan was not completed

NORTON BACKUP

Norton Backup lets you back up important files and directories from your hard disk to floppy disks or to a QIC-40 or QIC-80 tape drive.

Syntax You can make a backup from the DOS prompt by typing:

NBACKUP [@] [*setup file*][*switches*]

but if you want to restore files, use this syntax:

NBACKUP /R [*catalog name*][*filespec*][*switches*]

Description The following parameters are available when making a backup:

@

starts the macro associated with the setup file.

setup file

name of the setup file you want to use with Norton Backup. This setup file must have a file-name extension of .SET.

/A

runs AUTOBACK and performs an unattended automatic backup.

/TF

performs a full backup.

/TI

performs an incremental backup.

/TD

performs a differential backup.

/TC

performs a full-copy backup.

/TO

performs an incremental copy backup.

The following switches are available when restoring files from a backup:

/R

indicates you are restoring files.

catalog name

restores files from *catalog name* that match the following *filespec*.

filespec

restores all files that match *filespec*. Note that *filespec* must also include Path information.

/S

restores files in subdirectories.

NORTON CACHE

The Norton Cache program creates a memory buffer to speed up hard-disk reads and writes.

Syntax When you install Ncache2, you include the following line in either your CONFIG.SYS or your AUTOEXEC.BAT file:

NCACHE2 *install-switches drive drive-switches*

but if you are reconfiguring Ncache2 after it is loaded, you use the following:

NCACHE2 *reconfigure-switches drive drive-switches*

Description There are many different options you can use to configure the cache program to your own individual working environment. Because there are potentially hundreds of different combinations of computer hardware and applications software, it is very difficult to suggest values for the following parameters. You should follow the general guidelines given here and then experiment with different settings until you find the combination that works best for you.

You can use the following installation switches:

/INSTALL

installs Ncache2 using the default values stored in the initialization file, NCACHE.INI.

/OPTIMIZE=

optimizes the cache for speed (S), efficiency (E), or memory use (M).

/DOS=*n*

specifies the amount of conventional memory for the cache. If *n* is unspecified, the default is 128K. If you use a negative value, that amount of memory will be reserved for applications and the remaining memory will be used for the cache. /DOS connot be used in combination with /EXT or /EXP.

/EXT=*n,m*

specifies the amount of extended memory to use for the cache. If *n* is unspecified, all extended memory (less 16K) is used. If you use a negative value, that amount of memory will be reserved for applications and the remaining memory will be used for the cache. The variable *m* is the minimum amount of extended memory to reserve for the cache when running Microsoft Windows in enhanced mode. The default value of *m* is 25% of *n*.

/EXP=*n,m*

specifies the amount of expanded memory to use for the cache. If *n* is unspecified, all expanded memory is used. If you use a negative value, that amount of memory will be reserved for applications and the remaining memory will be used for the cache. *m* is the minimum amount of expanded memory to reserve for the cache when running Microsoft Windows in enhanced mode. The default value of *m* is 25% of *n*.

/BLOCK=*n*

specifies the size of the cache blocks as either 512, 1,024, 2,048, 4,096, or 8,192 bytes.

/DELAY=*ss.hh*

specifies the time delay to use with IntelliWrites, where *ss* represents seconds and *hh* represents hundredths of seconds. Seconds must be in the range of 0 to 59, and hundredths in the range of 0 to 99.

/INI=*filespec*

specifies the Ncache2 initialization file to use. This file is created with the /SAVE switch.

/MULTI=

enables the multitasking features of IntelliWrites when set to ON; disables them when set to off. If you experience compatibility problems, try running Ncache2 with /MULTI=OFF.

/QUICK=

configures Ncache2 to return the DOS prompt before all deferred writes are complete when set to ON (the default). When set to OFF, Ncache2 waits until all writes are complete before returning the DOS prompt.

/READ=*n*

specifies the size of the read-ahead buffer. Must be in the range of 8K to 64K in increments of 1K; a value of 0 disables the read-ahead. The default is 8K.

/REPORT=

displays complete Ncache2 information when set to ON. Set this switch to OFF to suppress the report.

/STATUS=

displays abbreviated Ncache2 information when set to ON.

/USEHIGH=

enables use of high memory when set to ON, and disables this usage when set to OFF. The default setting is ON, unless a memory manager is used to load high.

/USEHMA=

enables use of XMS high memory area when set to ON, disabling it when set to OFF.

/WRITE=*n*

specifies the buffer size for IntelliWrites. Must be in the range of 8K to 64K, in 1K increments; a value of 0 disables IntelliWrites. The default is 8K.

After Ncache2 is installed, you can use the /DELAY, /OPTIMIZE, /QUICK, /MULTI, /REPORT, and /STATUS switches, as well as the following reconfigure switches:

/RESET

resets the entire cache.

/DUMP

forces all the data waiting in the cache buffers to be written to disk.

/UNINSTALL

removes Ncache2 from memory if it was the last TSR program loaded by AUTOEXEC.BAT. You cannot remove Ncache2 from memory if other TSR programs were loaded afterwards, or if Ncache2 was loaded using CONFIG.SYS.

/SAVE

stores the current cache configuration in the specified file.

The following drive switches are available during installation or reconfiguration. To turn one of these options on, add a + sign, as in /+A; to turn one of them off, add a minus sign, as in /−A:

/A

activates the cache for the specified drive.

/C

enables or disables reading of extra sectors for the specified drive.

/DISKRESET=ON|OFF

dumps all the information currently held in the cache when a program issues a reset drive command using the DOS interrupt 21 function call 0DH. Most programs never issue a drive reset and are not affected by this switch; other programs may issue a reset as they exit. These resets will appear to slow down the cache performance. If you use programs that perform many drive resets, set DISKRESET=OFF. When DISKRESET is set to OFF, Ncache2 ignores all reset drive calls.

/F

flushes the cache for the specifies drive.

/G=*n*

limits caching of group-sector reads; the default is 128.

/I

enables or disables IntelliWrites for the drive.

/P

enables or disables write protection for the specified drive.

/R=D*n*

limits read-ahead for the specified drive. The D option enables read-ahead for sequential but not random reads. The variable *n* specifies the amount of data to read in increments of 1K; the default is 8K.

/W

enables or disables the write-through for the specified drives.

NORTON DESKTOP

The Norton Desktop is the heart of the whole Desktop package. It combines an easy-to-use interface with a set of nontechnical tools that make file and directory maintenance quick and easy.

Syntax To start the Norton Desktop from the DOS command line, type:

ND *switches*

Description The following switches are available:

/FORGET

resets all history, and returns to the default drive window position, size, and pane settings.

/SKIPHIGH

does not load into high memory.

/SWAP=

enables swapping to extended memory when set to X, expanded memory when set to E, or to disk when set to D.

NORTON DESKTOP CONFIGURATION

The Norton Configuration program sets up passwords, video and mouse parameters, and the Norton Cache program, and it helps you make the appropriate changes to your AUTOEXEC.BAT and CONFIG.SYS files.

Syntax To use the Configuration program, type:

NDCONFIG

Description NDCONFIG does not accept command-line switches.

NORTON DISK DOCTOR

Norton Disk Doctor automatically finds and corrects logical and physical errors on hard and floppy disks. You can run Norton Disk Doctor from the Desktop Tools menu or from the DOS command line. Both modes enable you to test the disk completely or partially.

Syntax To run the Norton Disk Doctor directly from the DOS prompt, type:

NDD *drive drive switches*

Description The following switches modify the NDD command:

> *drive*
>
> selects the drive to be tested. You can select more than one drive for testing at the same time if you separate each drive letter from the next with a space.
>
> /C
>
> includes all tests for both the system area and the data area.
>
> /DT
>
> performs just the surface test.
>
> /Q
>
> includes all tests except the surface test.
>
> /R:*filename*
>
> sends the NDD report to the file specified by *filename*.
>
> /RA:*filename*
>
> appends the NDD report to the file specified by *filename*.

/X:*drive*

excludes the drives specified by *drive* from physical testing.

/REBUILD

rebuilds an entire disk after it has been damaged.

/SKIPHIGH

does not load into high memory.

/UNDELETE

restores a DOS partition that you previously skipped undeleting.

NORTON MAIL

Norton Mail simplifies all your MCI Mail chores.

Syntax To run Norton Mail from the command line, type:

NMAIL *switches*

Description Use the following switches with Norton Mail:

/PURGE

removes all the marked addresses, and saves space in the address book.

/SEND

sends and receives MCI Mail.

/UNERASE

reads addresses, even if they were marked as deleted.

NORTON MENU

Norton Menu is an automatic menu-building program that searches your hard disk looking for applications to install into the menu.

Syntax To start Norton Menu from the DOS command line, type:

NMENU [*file name*][/EDIT ¦ /RUN]

Description NMENU switches are as follows:

file name

name of the menu file you want to load. This file will have the file-name extension .NMF.

/EDIT

allows for both running the menus and also editing them too.

/RUN

allows for running the menus only, with no editing capabilities.

NORTON SCHEDULER

You can use the Norton Scheduler to post reminder messages to yourself or to run programs at specific times.

Syntax Load Norton Scheduler with AUTOEXEC.BAT using the following syntax:

NSCHED *switches*

Description The following switches are available with NSCHED:

/S=

enables swapping to extended memory when set to X, to expanded memory when set to E, or to disk when set to D.

/D

disables the Scheduler. The Scheduler remains in memory and can be reactivated with /E.

/E

enables the Scheduler after it has been disabled with /D.

/NOSAVER

disables the screen saver.

/SKIPHIGH

does not load into high memory.

/ T=n

if no key is pressed within n minutes of the reminder appearing, start the scheduled process. The default is 1 minute. Set /T=WAIT if you always want to wait for confirmation to start the event.

/TSR

allows other terminate-and-stay-resident programs to be loaded after the Scheduler. This is not recommended.

/U

uninstalls or removes the Scheduler from memory.

To see a report on the current status of the Scheduler, type:

NSCHED

at the DOS prompt. Press the Ctrl, Alt, and Z keys together if you want to activate the screen saver manually.

NORTON VIEWER

Norton Viewer lets you look at the contents of data files without loading the application program that created the files in the first place. Files are displayed in a format matched to the data that they contain.

Syntax To start the Norton Viewer from the DOS prompt, type:

VIEW [*file name*]

Description View does not accept command-line switches, but you can add a *file name* if you wish.

SAFE FORMAT

Safe Format is a fast and safe alternative to the DOS FORMAT command; it lets you easily recover from an accidentally reformatted disk because it does not overwrite the existing data when you format a disk.

Syntax To run Safe Format in full-screen mode, type:

SFORMAT

To run it from the command line, type:

SFORMAT *drive switches*

Description You can use any of the following switches to specify a particular format for a disk:

/A

puts Safe Format into automatic mode, which is useful in batch files.

/S

copies the DOS system files to the disk.

/B

leaves space on the disk for the DOS system files so you can add them later.

/V:*label*

adds a volume name, specified by *label*, of 11 characters or less.

/1

selects single-sided formatting.

/4

formats a 360K floppy disk in a 1.2MB drive.

/8

formats 8 sectors per track.

/N:*n*

selects the number of sectors per track (*n* can be 8, 9, 15, 18, or 36 sectors per track).

/T:*n*

selects the number of tracks (*n* can be either 40 or 80 tracks).

/*size*

selects the size of the floppy disk. For example, use /720 for a 720K floppy disk or /2.88 for a 2.88MB floppy disk.

/Q

selects the quick format. This places a new system area on the disk, leaving everything else intact.

/D

selects the DOS format in which everything on the disk is erased.

SMARTCAN

SmartCan is a memory-resident program that moves erased or deleted files into a hidden directory called SMARTCAN, so that they can be easily recovered by UnErase if necessary.

Syntax Here is the syntax for SmartCan:

SMARTCAN *switches*

Description You can use the following switches with SmartCan:

/CONVERT

searches for and converts TRASHCAN directories created by the Norton Utilities Erase Protect program into SMARTCAN directories that SmartCan is able to use.

/ON

turns SmartCan on.

/OFF

turns SmartCan off.

/SKIPHIGH

does not load into high memory.

/STATUS

displays the current status of SmartCan.

/UNINSTALL

removes SmartCan from memory.

SPEED DISK

Speed Disk optimizes your hard disk performance by eliminating file fragmentation and by reorganizing the layout of files and directories on your disk.

Syntax To run Speed Disk, type:

SPEEDISK *drive switches*

Description You can use the following switches with Speed Disk:

/B

reboots the computer when the optimization is complete.

/F

performs a full optimization.

/FD

performs a full optimization, placing directories first.

/FF

performs a full optimization, reordering files.

/Q

consolidates the free space on the disk.

/U

unfragments files only.

/V

turns on the read-after-write verification. Each sector is read and verified after it is written to the disk.

/SKIPHIGH

does not load into high memory.

If you are sorting files, you can reverse the sort order (making it descending) by adding a minus sign after the sort-key letter:

/SN[−]

sorts files by name.

/SE[−]

sorts files by extension.

/SD[−]

sorts files by date.

/SS[−]

sorts files by size.

SYSTEM INFO

System Info displays information about your computer's configuration and calculates three performance indicators.

Syntax To run System Info, enter:

SYSINFO *switches*

Description You can use the following switches with System Info:

/AUTO:*n*

selects the automatic mode. System Info cycles through all information screens, displaying each one for *n* seconds before moving on to the next screen.

/DEMO

cycles through the benchmark tests and summary screen only.

/DI

prints a single screen of information on the current or specified drive.

/TSR

prints a list of all your terminate-and-stay-resident (TSR) programs to the screen or to a file (if you use the DOS redirection capabilities).

/N

skips the live memory test, which will require you to reboot your computer should it fail.

/SOUND

beeps between the CPU tests.

/SUMMARY

prints the System Info summary screen.

UNERASE

UnErase finds and recovers accidentally erased files in automatic or in manual mode.

Syntax To run UnErase, type:

UNERASE *filespec switches*

Description You can use a file specification with UnErase. If you know the original file name, including the first letter, you can use UnErase from the DOS prompt. For example, typing

UNERASE MYFILE.TXT

recovers the file without UnErase going into full-screen mode.

If you have forgotten the first letter, specify the ? DOS wildcard character instead, and UnErase opens into full-screen mode. For example, type:

UNERASE ?YFILE.TXT

and use the normal UnErase techniques to recover the file.

You can use the following UnErase switches:

/IMAGE

uses information contained in the Image data file for file recovery and excludes the use of Mirror information.

/MIRROR

uses information contained in the Mirror data file for file recovery and excludes the use of Image information.

/NOTRACK

excludes the use of Delete Tracking information provided by DOS 5.

/SMARTCAN

only recovers files saved by SmartCan.

/NOSMARTCAN

excludes files saved by SmartCan.

/SKIPHIGH

does not load into high memory.

UNFORMAT

UnFormat recovers data and program files from a hard disk after it has been reformatted by the DOS FORMAT command.

Syntax To run UnFormat, type:

UNFORMAT *drive switches*

Description You can use the following switches:

/IMAGE

uses information contained in the Image data file for file recovery and excludes the use of Mirror information.

/MIRROR

uses information contained in the Mirror data file for file recovery and excludes the use of Image information.

APPENDIX

An Introduction to Disk and Directory Structure

here are many basic aspects of disk organization that, when explained, help to make sense of the technical details of file recovery and hard-disk management. In this Appendix I describe floppy- and hard-disk characteristics, and give a complete picture of the physical and logical framework of floppy and hard disks under DOS.

DISK STRUCTURE

The better you understand how the underlying hardware works, the easier it will be to understand what happens when you add or delete a file in DOS, and the procedures you must follow if you have to recover a deleted file.

SIDES

In early versions of DOS, single-sided disks were common; that is, only one side of the disk was used.

The most fundamental characteristic of a floppy disk is that it has two sides. Data can be written to or read from either side. The system considers the first side as side 0 and the second side as side 1.

Hard disks, by contrast, have several recording surfaces, which are called *platters*. Platters are mounted on the same spindle inside the hard disk's sealed enclosure, and each platter has two sides. The numbering scheme is as follows: the first side is 0, the next is 1, the first side of the second platter is 2, and so on. Each side of a floppy disk and each side of a hard disk's platter has its own read/write head. Figure A.1 shows a cut-away view of a hard disk. Most hard disks have between two and eight platters.

TRACKS

Each disk or platter side is divided into concentric circles known as *tracks*. The outermost track on the top of the disk is numbered track 0, side 0, and the outermost track on the other side of the disk is numbered track 0, side 1. Track numbering increases inwards toward the center of the disk (or platter).

The number of tracks on a disk varies with the media type: 360K floppy disks have 40 tracks per side, while 1.2MB floppy disks have 80 tracks per

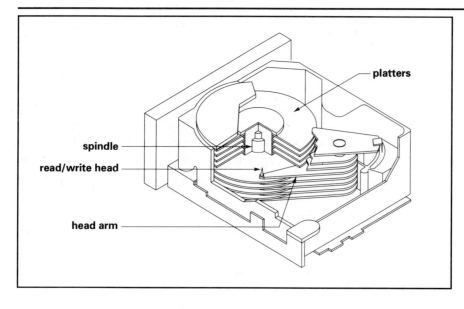

FIGURE A.1:

Cut-away illustration of a hard disk

side, as do 720K and 1.44MB floppies. Hard disks can have from 300 to 600 tracks per platter side. On a floppy disk, the tracks cover only a small area of the disk, about three-quarters of an inch. A 360K floppy disk is recorded with 48 tracks per inch and a 1.2MB floppy disk is recorded with 96 tracks per inch.

CYLINDERS

Tracks that are at the same concentric position on a disk (or on a set of platters) are referred to collectively as a *cylinder.* On a floppy disk, a cylinder contains two tracks (for example, track 0, side 0 and track 0, side 1); on a hard disk with four platters, a cylinder comprises eight tracks. Figure A.2 shows cylinders on such a hard disk.

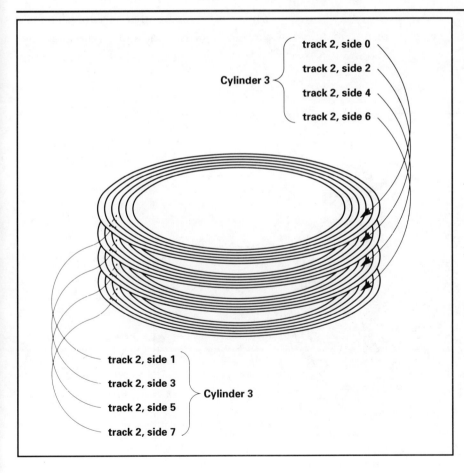

FIGURE A.2:

Cylinders on a hard disk with four platters

track 2, side 0
track 2, side 2
Cylinder 3
track 2, side 4
track 2, side 6

track 2, side 1
track 2, side 3
Cylinder 3
track 2, side 5
track 2, side 7

Sectors and Absolute Sectors

When DOS reads or writes data to a disk, it must read or write at least one complete sector.

Each track on a disk is divided into *sectors*. Each track on the disk contains the same number of sectors. In all versions of DOS, a sector consists of 512 bytes and is the smallest single area of disk space that DOS can read or write. Each sector has a unique sector address contained in the sector header and is separated from the next sector by an intersector gap. The number of sectors contained in each track on the disk varies according to the media type. A 360K floppy disk has 9 sectors per track, a 1.2MB floppy disk has 15, a 720K floppy has 9, a 1.44MB floppy has 18, and most hard disks have 17 or 26. Figure A.3 shows the relationship between tracks and sectors on a 360K floppy disk, which has 40 tracks numbered from 0 to 39, and 9 sectors per track.

DOS identifies the sectors on a disk by numbering them sequentially. On a 360K floppy, for example, the sectors are numbered 0–719; a specific sector might be identified as, say, sector 317. Another way to reference a given sector is to identify it according to its disk side and cylinder and then specify its position in that cylinder. In this case, you might give a sector's

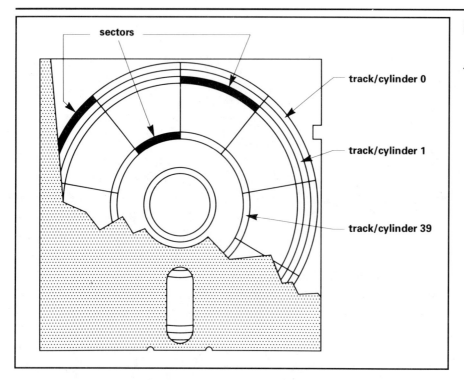

FIGURE A.3:

Tracks and sectors on a 360K floppy disk

location as side 0, cylinder 25, sector 7. When you use this method, you are referring to *absolute sectors*.

THE INTERLEAVE FACTOR

For several reasons, the sectors on a disk are not always numbered sequentially. The main reason is that a floppy disk rotates at about 200 rpm inside the disk drive and a hard disk rotates at about 3,600 rpm; DOS reads and writes data in single sectors, but by the time a sector's worth of data is read and stored in memory, and the PC is ready to read the next sector, this sector may already have passed under the head. The PC must now wait through a complete disk rotation before it can read the next sector. To minimize this delay, an *interleave factor* is introduced. Interleaving requires that logically sequential sectors are not physically adjacent to each other on the disk but are separated by some number of sectors. In this way, the performance of the disk and the layout of the sectors on the disk can be optimized.

CLUSTERS

The number of sectors per cluster depends on the disk media and the DOS version: 360K and 720K floppy disks have two sectors per cluster, while 1.2MB and 1.44MB disks have clusters of a single 512-byte sector. Hard disks have clusters of 4, 8, or 16 sectors.

Although DOS can read and write a single sector, it allocates disk space for files in *clusters,* which consist of one or more sectors. No matter how small a file is, it always occupies at least one cluster on the disk: a one-byte file occupies one cluster, while a 511-byte file on a 1.2MB disk also occupies one cluster. Figure A.4 shows a file of 1,025 bytes and a cluster size of 1,024 bytes, or two sectors. The file data occupies all of the first cluster and only one byte of the second cluster, yet the area of the second cluster not filled with data is not available for another file. This unused area is called *slack.* The next file must start at the next available cluster. If the first file increases in length, it will occupy more of the second cluster. If the cluster is filled up and more space is needed, the file will continue in the next available cluster.

DOS identifies clusters by numbering them sequentially, with the first cluster labeled cluster 2. Cluster numbering begins in the data area of the disk, so the first cluster on a disk (cluster 2) is actually the *first* cluster in the data area. This is less confusing when you understand that, unlike tracks and sectors, clusters are not physically demarcated on the disk. DOS merely views groups of sectors as clusters for its own convenience.

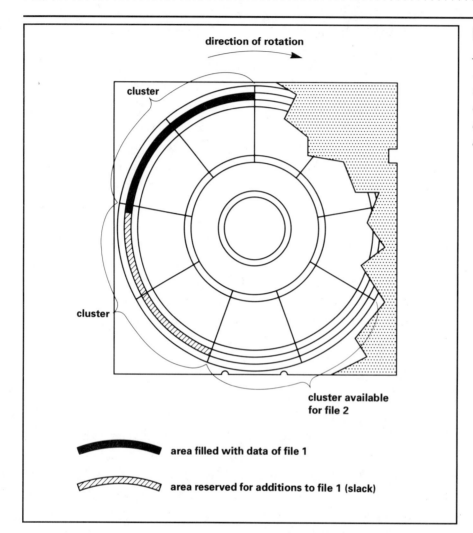

direction of rotation

cluster

cluster

cluster available for file 2

▬ **area filled with data of file 1**

▨ **area reserved for additions to file 1 (slack)**

FIGURE A.4:

A file that takes up 1,025 bytes of disk space is one byte bigger than one cluster and so must occupy two complete clusters

Clusters are called logical units. Tracks and sectors are physical units.

Remember that the absolute-sector method of locating sectors locates them according to their physical position on the disk. Because clusters have no physical manifestation, however, there is no absolute method of referencing them.

The efficiency of your hard-disk storage depends in part on the relationship between the cluster size and the most common size of your files. Disk performance becomes a consideration when, to access even the smallest file, DOS has to load a cluster that may contain many empty sectors.

EXAMINING THE SYSTEM AREA

You can reference sectors in the system area with the DOS numbering system or the absolute-sector method. You cannot reference clusters in the system area because cluster numbering starts in the data area.

When you format a disk, DOS always reserves the outermost track on side 0 for its own use. This area is called the *system area* and is subdivided into three parts: the *boot record,* the *file allocation table* or FAT (of which there are usually two identical copies), and the *root directory.* The remaining space on the disk after the system area is called the *data area.* This is the part of the disk where application programs and data are located. The data area is far larger than the system area. On a 360K floppy disk, the system area occupies 1.6% of the whole disk; on a 65MB hard disk the system area occupies less than 0.1% of the total disk space.

THE BOOT RECORD

The disk space occupied by the boot record is one sector, which includes the BPB, boot program, and slack.

The boot record, which is on all formatted disks, contains the BIOS parameter block (BPB). This block holds information about the disk's physical characteristics, which is needed by device drivers. The information contained in the BPB is shown in Table A.1.

The boot record also contains the boot program that is used to start the computer after a system reset or after power is turned on. When you turn on your computer, it runs a set of diagnostic routines to ensure that the hardware is in good order. The ROM bootstrap program next loads the boot record from disk into the computer's memory.

The bootstrap program checks the disk for the DOS system files (IO.SYS or MSDOS.SYS, and IBMBIOS.DOM or IBMDOS.COM). If the files are there, it loads them into the computer and passes complete system control to COMMAND.COM. During this process, the CONFIG.SYS and AUTOEXEC.BAT files are loaded, as are any installable device drivers that a mouse or a RAM disk may need (for example, the device drivers MOUSE.SYS or VDISK.SYS). Once everything has been loaded and you see the DOS prompt, your computer is ready for use.

INFORMATION STORED	BYTES USED	ADDITIONAL INFORMATION
Version of DOS used to format the disk	8	
Number of bytes per sector	2	
Number of sectors per cluster, per track, and per disk (or hard-disk partition)	1	
Number of reserved sectors used by the system area	2	
Number of FAT copies and sectors used	1	
Number of root directory entries	2	112 entries on 360K floppy or 1024 entries on hard disk
Number of sectors on disk	2	720 sectors for 360K floppy, thousands for hard disk
Media descriptor	1	Indicates the type of disk
Number of sectors per FAT	2	Sectors per FAT vary depending to disk's capacity (FAT references every cluster)
Number of sectors per track	2	360K floppy has 9 sectors per track, 1.2MB floppy has 15, hard disk usually has 17
Number of heads	2, 4	Floppy-disk drive has 2 bytes; hard disk has 4 bytes
Number of hidden sectors	2	Hidden sectors are the system area

TABLE A.1:

Information contained in the BIOS parameter block (in the boot record)

However, when the computer can't find the DOS system files, it displays the error message

Non-System disk or disk error
Replace and strike any key when ready

and waits for you either to remove the nonsystem disk from the floppy-disk drive so it can use the hard disk, or to place a system disk in your drive.

THE PARTITION TABLE

The DOS command FDISK establishes the partition table after low-level formatting of the disk is complete. You can use it to create or delete a DOS partition, to change the active partition, or to display the current active partition data.

Floppy disks do not have partition tables and cannot be shared between different operating systems.

The partition table, present on all hard disks, allows you to divide a hard disk into areas (called *partitions*) that appear to DOS as separate disks. The partition table also allows you to reserve space for other operating systems (which you can then install and use to create their own partitions). For example, you can run both DOS and XENIX on the same computer, at different times, of course. A DOS disk can contain as many as four partitions, but only one of these may be active at any one time.

The partition table begins with a code called the *master boot record.* This code contains a record of which partition was the *active* partition, that is, the one used to boot the system. The master boot record also contains the locations of the boot records for the operating system of the active partition (and any other operating system installed on the disk). When the computer is started, it uses this information to boot the active partition's operating system. If you are running DOS and no other operating system, you should make the DOS partition occupy the whole hard disk.

THE FILE ALLOCATION TABLE

The next part of a disk's system area is occupied by the file allocation table (FAT), which is also created by the DOS FORMAT command. The FAT is part of the system that DOS uses to keep track of where files are stored on a disk. The FAT is so important that DOS actually creates two copies of it. If the first copy becomes corrupted, DOS uses the second copy. Think of the FAT as a two-column table. One column is a sequential list of the clusters in the disk's data area. The other column is another list of numbers that gives specific information about each cluster. If a cluster is being used to store file data, the second column in that row contains the number of the next cluster in that file. (Remember that data in a file is not necessarily stored in consecutive clusters.) Otherwise, the second column contains a code that indicates one of the following:

(0)000H	The cluster is available for storing data.
(F)FF7H	The cluster is bad and cannot be used for storing data.
(F)FF0–(F)FF6H	The cluster is reserved and cannot be used for storing data.
(F)FF8–(F)FFFH	The cluster is the last cluster in a file.

Figure A.5 illustrates how FAT entries are chained together. File A starts in cluster 2, then jumps to cluster 8. The next cluster used by the file is cluster 11. Cluster 11 is followed by cluster 12, where according to the FAT, the file ends. Thus file A is split among four clusters, two of which are not in sequence. This process of dividing the file into separate pieces is called *fragmentation* and was discussed in some detail in Chapter 14 during the description of the Speed Disk program. In Figure A.5, file B occupies clusters 3, 4, 6, 7, 9, and 10. The sequence skips cluster 5 because it is bad, and skips cluster 8 because it is already being used by file A.

THE ROOT DIRECTORY

NOTE
NOTE
On a 720K floppy disk, the root directory takes up seven sectors of disk space.

Every disk contains at least one directory—the root directory. The root directory follows the FAT sectors, and forms the third part of the system area found on a formatted disk. The root directory's size is fixed and cannot be changed, but it is proportional to the media type. For example, 360K and 720K floppy disks have space for 112 entries in the root, 1.2MB and 1.44MB floppy disks have space for 224 entries, while a hard disk has space for 512 entries.

If the disk is a system disk, the first two files in the root directory are always the files containing the DOS BIOS interface and the DOS kernel. The disk bootstrap program uses these entries when it loads the operating system into memory and starts executing DOS.

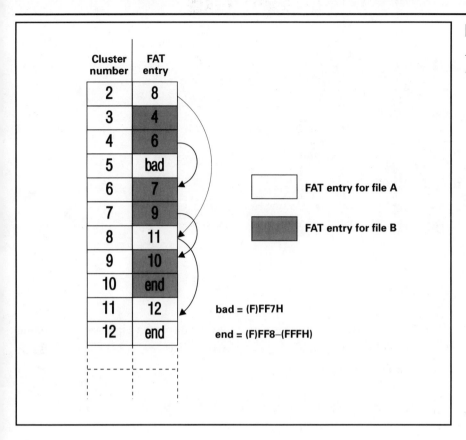

FIGURE A.5:

FAT entries chained together

Each directory entry is 32 bytes long and may contain information about a file or a subdirectory. The format of a file entry in the root directory is as follows:

File name	8 bytes, ASCII
File-name Extension	3 bytes, ASCII
Attribute	1 byte, each bit represents an attribute
	bit 0, file is read-only
	bit 1, file is hidden

	bit 2, file is a system file
	bit 3, entry is a volume label
	bit 4, entry is a subdirectory
	bit 5, archive bit
	bit 6, unused
	bit 7, unused
Reserved	10 bytes, reserved for future use
Time	2 bytes
Date	2 bytes
Starting FAT entry	2 bytes
File size	4 bytes

> **NOTE**
>
> *You can use letters, numbers, and any other characters except . " / \ [ ] | < > + : * ? , = ; and a space in your file names and extensions.*

The file name is an eleven-byte entry, divided into an eight-byte file name and a three-byte file-name extension, separated by a period. The period is not stored as a byte but you must type it between the eighth and ninth characters to use a file extension.

If the first byte of a file name has a value of 0, the directory entry is unused; this indicates the end of the active directory entries.

If the first byte of a file name is a lowercase Greek sigma (σ ASCII 229 decimal, E5 hexadecimal), the file has been erased. When erasing a file using DEL or ERASE, DOS marks the first character of the file name with the E5H character to show that it has been erased and then clears the file's entries from the FAT. As DOS leaves the starting cluster number and the file length in the directory, and leaves the actual data on the disk, the first cluster of a file can be found and recovered quite easily, as long as the clusters have not been overwritten by another file.

The attribute byte can have one or more of the attribute bits set at the same time. For example, a system file can also be hidden. An attribute is said to be *set* if the appropriate attribute bit is set to 1. If the attribute byte has no bits set or has a value of 0, the file is a normal data or program file that can be written to or erased. This probably applies to the majority of your files. Attributes are defined as follows:

◆ *Read-only files* can be used, but you can't make changes to their contents.

◆ *Hidden files* do not appear in directory listings made by DIR. You can't duplicate them with the COPY command or delete them with ERASE or DEL. However, you can copy them with the DOS DISKCOPY command.

◆ *System files* are read-only files.

◆ The *volume label* is a short piece of text used to identify the disk. You can specify up to eleven characters for it when you label your disk. The label's directory entry looks like a file that has no length.

◆ *Subdirectory* names have the same format as file names.

◆ The *archive bit* is used when backing up. If a new file is written to disk or an existing file is modified, this bit is set (changed to 1). After the backup program has copied the file, it resets the bit to 0. This way, the backup program knows which files need to be copied.

The root directory is represented by a backslash (\) symbol. You can use this symbol if you want to change from the current directory to the root directory with a single command if you type:

CD \

at the DOS prompt.

SUBDIRECTORIES

All directories (except the root directory) have names. The current directory can be referred to by its name or by a period (.). The parent directory of the current directory can be referred to by its name or by a double period (..). When you use the DOS DIR command to review files and directories, you will see these shorthand symbols shown at the top of the list. You can use the double period symbol if you want to change to the parent of the current directory; in other words, you can use it when you want to move up one layer in your directory structure. Just type:

CD ..

And if you type this command often enough, you will end up back at the root directory.

 *Subdirectories are usually just called "directories."*

Two subdirectories in the same directory cannot have the same name; however, subdirectories of different directories can have the same name. For example, you cannot have two subdirectories both called WORK in your WP51 directory, but you can have a subdirectory called WORK in the WP51 directory, and another subdirectory also called WORK in your 123 directory.

As we have seen, the root directory has a fixed size and location on the disk. In contrast, *subdirectories* can be of any size and can be located anywhere they are needed on the disk. You cannot delete the root directory, but you can create, delete, rename, expand, or contract a subdirectory as needed.

EXAMINING THE DATA AREA

The rest of the DOS partition (or unpartitioned hard disk or floppy disk) is the data area, used for storing files and subdirectories. This is the largest part of the disk and is where all your programs are found, including spreadsheets, word processors, program-language compilers, and data files.

Figures A.6 and A.7 illustrate disk structure in different ways and draw together many of the concepts presented so far in this chapter. Both figures assume a 720K floppy disk.

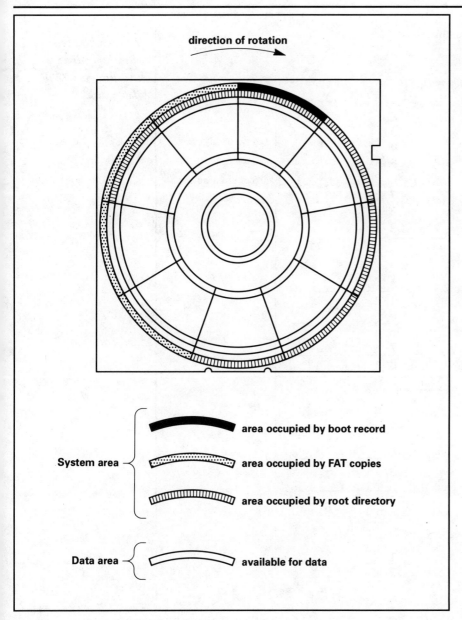

Locations of the systems and data areas on a 720K floppy disk

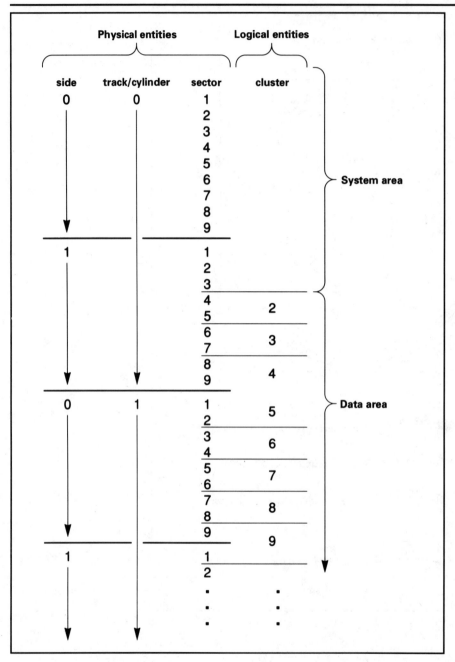

INDEX

Z

SYBEX ®

FREE CATALOG!

Mail us this form today, and we'll send you a full-color catalog of Sybex books.

Name _____

Street _____

City/State/Zip _____

Phone _____

Please supply the name of the Sybex book purchased.

_____

How would you rate it?

_____ Excellent   _____ Very Good   _____ Average   _____ Poor

Why did you select this particular book?

_____ Recommended to me by a friend

_____ Recommended to me by store personnel

_____ Saw an advertisement in _____

_____ Author's reputation

_____ Saw in Sybex catalog

_____ Required textbook

_____ Sybex reputation

_____ Read book review in _____

_____ In-store display

_____ Other _____

Where did you buy it?

_____ Bookstore

_____ Computer Store or Software Store

_____ Catalog (name: _____)

_____ Direct from Sybex

_____ Other: _____

Did you buy this book with your personal funds?

_____ Yes   _____ No

About how many computer books do you buy each year?

_____ 1-3   _____ 3-5   _____ 5-7   _____ 7-9   _____ 10+

About how many Sybex books do you own?

_____ 1-3   _____ 3-5   _____ 5-7   _____ 7-9   _____ 10+

Please indicate your level of experience with the software covered in this book:

_____ Beginner   _____ Intermediate   _____ Advanced

Which types of software packages do you use regularly?

_____ Accounting	_____ Databases	_____ Networks
_____ Amiga	_____ Desktop Publishing	_____ Operating Systems
_____ Apple/Mac	_____ File Utilities	_____ Spreadsheets
_____ CAD	_____ Money Management	_____ Word Processing
_____ Communications	_____ Languages	_____ Other _____
		(please specify)

Which of the following best describes your job title?

_____ Administrative/Secretarial	_____ President/CEO
_____ Director	_____ Manager/Supervisor
_____ Engineer/Technician	_____ Other _____
	(please specify)

Comments on the weaknesses/strengths of this book: _____

_____

_____

_____

_____

PLEASE FOLD, SEAL, AND MAIL TO SYBEX

- - - - - - - - - - - - - - - - - - - -

SYBEX, INC.

Department M
2021 CHALLENGER DR.
ALAMEDA, CALIFORNIA USA
94501

SYBEX ®

SEAL

TASK	PROGRAM	CHAPTER
Arrange disk-drive icons	Desktop	9
Back up a hard disk	Norton Backup	11
Cache a hard disk	Ncache2	14
Calculate performance benchmarks	System Information	18
Cascade windows	Desktop	3
Change file attributes	Desktop	5
Change a volume label	Desktop	5
Clear the screen	Sleeper	18
Communicate between two computers	Desktop Link	17
Compare backed-up files	Norton Desktop	11
Compress a file or files	Compress	18
Configure Norton Desktop	Desktop	9
Copy disk	Desktop	5
Copy files	Desktop	5
Create custom menus	Norton Menu	10
Create a directory	Desktop	5
Create a Rescue disk	Disk Tools	13
Decompress a file or files	Compress	18
Delete a directory	Desktop	5
Delete a file	Desktop	5
Detect a virus	Norton AntiVirus	15
Edit a text file	Desktop Editor	7
Find disk problems	Norton Disk Doctor	13
Fix a bad boot track	Norton Disk Doctor	13
Fix a bad file allocation table	Norton Disk Doctor	13
Fix a bad partition table	Norton Disk Doctor	13
Format a floppy disk	Desktop	5
Label a disk	Desktop	5
List disk information	System Information	18